Lockdown Leisure

This book examines the concept of 'lockdown leisure' as closely related to the Covid-19 pandemic. Through a range of inter-disciplinary chapters, the volume unpacks leisure life in lockdown contexts through a range of empirical, conceptual and theoretical contributions.

In many countries, a key response to the global Covid-19 pandemic was the implementation of national, regional or local lockdowns. Focusing on the diverse medium and long-term socio-cultural impacts of the Covid-19 pandemic, this book examining how various forms of lockdowns impacted leisure activities, industries, cultures and spaces across a variety of transnational contexts. It contains original chapters on topics including but not limited to physical activity, cultural participation, recreation and green spaces, technology, and social exclusion. And so, it shows how Covid-19 lockdowns transformed existing, and produced new, leisure activities.

This book is a fascinating reading for students and researchers of leisure studies, sociology, media and cultural studies, youth studies, and educational studies. The chapters in this book were originally published in the journal, *Leisure Studies*.

Jan Andre Lee Ludvigsen is Senior Lecturer in International Relations and Politics with Sociology at Liverpool John Moores University. His research interests are, broadly, situated within the political sociology of sport. His recent books include *Sport Mega-Events, Security and Covid-19* (Routledge, 2022) and *Sport and Crime: Towards a Critical Criminology of Sport* (Routledge, 2022, with Peter Millward and Jonathan Sly).

Katherine Harrison is Senior Lecturer in Media and Culture at Leeds Beckett University, UK. She has published research on women's domestic craft practices, knitting circles, representations of place and space and weight stigma in 'poverty porn' television, and older people's participation in online Pilates classes during Covid-19. Katherine's current research focuses on the visual culture of the commercial 'NewSpace' age and the emergence of luxury space tourism.

Peter Millward is Professor of Contemporary Sociology at Liverpool John Moores University, UK. He has published widely including recent books *Sport and Crime: Towards a Critical Criminology of Sport* (2022, with Jan Andre Lee Ludvigsen and Jonathan Sly, Routledge) and *Football Fandom, Sexualities and Activism: A Cultural Relational Sociology* (2023, Routledge).

Cassandra A. Ogden is Senior Lecturer in Sociology at Liverpool John Moores University. Her recent work explores the effect on lockdown amongst people living in the UK during 2020–2022 on their personal, social and working lives as well as the impact upon their physical and mental health.

She has explored the relationship between women, knitting and feminism which she examines using a range of creative methods. She has further utilised the narrative inquiry technique to explore issues of social exclusion and illness. Cassandra has published and co-published on social disgust and stigma of particular bodies, disability hate crime, representations of 'obesity' and disability in 'povertyporn' documentaries and childhood illness experiences.

Lockdown Leisure

Edited by
Jan Andre Lee Ludvigsen, Katherine Harrison, Peter Millward and Cassandra A. Ogden

LONDON AND NEW YORK

First published 2024
by Routledge
4 Park Square, Milton Park, Abingdon, Oxon OX14 4RN

and by Routledge
605 Third Avenue, New York, NY 10158

Routledge is an imprint of the Taylor & Francis Group, an informa business

Introduction, Chapters 4–10 and 12 © 2024 Taylor & Francis

Chapter 1 © 2022 Nicola McCullogh, Francisca Trigo Pereira, Andrea Scott-Bell, Rosa Stalenberg and John Hayton. Originally published as Open Access.

Chapter 2 © 2022 Georgia Allen and Philippa Velija. Originally published as Open Access.

Chapter 3 © 2022 Tal Feder, Siobhan McAndrew, Dave O'Brien and Mark Taylor. Originally published as Open Access.

Chapter 11 © 2022 Ellie Gennings, Hazel J Brown, Denise Hewlett and John Batten. Originally published as Open Access.

With the exception of Chapters 1, 2, 3 and 11, no part of this book may be reprinted or reproduced or utilised in any form or by any electronic, mechanical, or other means, now known or hereafter invented, including photocopying and recording, or in any information storage or retrieval system, without permission in writing from the publishers. For details on the rights for Chapters 1, 2, 3 and 11, please see the chapters' Open Access footnotes.

Trademark notice: Product or corporate names may be trademarks or registered trademarks, and are used only for identification and explanation without intent to infringe.

British Library Cataloguing in Publication Data
A catalogue record for this book is available from the British Library

ISBN13: 978-1-032-63092-2 (hbk)
ISBN13: 978-1-032-63093-9 (pbk)
ISBN13: 978-1-032-63095-3 (ebk)

DOI: 10.4324/9781032630953

Typeset in Minion Pro
by Newgen Publishing UK

Publisher's Note
The publisher accepts responsibility for any inconsistencies that may have arisen during the conversion of this book from journal articles to book chapters, namely the inclusion of journal terminology.

Disclaimer
Every effort has been made to contact copyright holders for their permission to reprint material in this book. The publishers would be grateful to hear from any copyright holder who is not here acknowledged and will undertake to rectify any errors or omissions in future editions of this book.

Contents

Citation Information vii
Notes on Contributors ix

Introduction: Lockdown leisure 1
Jan Andre Lee Ludvigsen, Katherine Harrison, Peter Millward and Cassandra A. Ogden

1 Exploring how a disability sport charity utilises exchange relationships with external organisations to sustain operations in times of lockdown 8
Nicola McCullogh, Francisca Trigo Pereira, Andrea Scott-Bell, Rosa Stalenberg and John Hayton

2 Parents perceptions of online physical activity and leisure with early years children during Covid-19 and beyond 23
Georgia Allen and Philippa Velija

3 Cultural consumption and Covid-19: evidence from the *Taking Part* and *COVID-19 Cultural Participation Monitor* surveys 38
Tal Feder, Siobhan McAndrew, Dave O'Brien and Mark Taylor

4 Time use, work and leisure in the UK before, during, between and following the Covid-19 lockdowns 56
Ken Roberts

5 CrossFit during lockdown. The promises and pitfalls of digitally mediated training for leisure-time physical activity 69
Verena Lenneis, Jeppe Klarskov Hansen and Sine Agergaard

6 COVID-19 and outdoor recreation in the post-anthropause 85
Jacob J. Bustad, Samuel M. Clevenger and Oliver J.C. Rick

7 Sports participation during a lockdown. How COVID-19 changed the sports frequency and motivation of participants in club, event, and online sports 100
Erik Thibaut, Bram Constandt, Veerle De Bosscher, Annick Willem, Margot Ricour and Jeroen Scheerder

8 Nearby nature in lockdown: Practices and affordances for leisure in urban green spaces 114
Katherine King and Janet Dickinson

9 "I felt there was a big chunk taken out of my life": COVID-19 and older adults' library-based magazine leisure reading 132
Nicole K. Dalmer, Dana Sawchuk and Mina Ly

10 Armchair travel through video games: stories from elsewheres and elsewhens 147
Serkan Uzunogullari

11 Children and young people's perspectives from UK lockdown: leisure-less experiences 161
Ellie Gennings, Hazel J Brown, Denise Hewlett and John Batten

12 A ramp that leads to nothing: outdoor recreation experiences of children with physical disabilities during the COVID-19 pandemic 170
Annika L. Vogt, Chris A. B. Zajchowski and Eddie L. Hill

Index 181

Citation Information

The following chapters were originally published in various volumes and issues of the journal *Leisure Studies*. When citing this material, please use the original page numbering for each article, as follows:

Chapter 1
Exploring how a disability sport charity utilises exchange relationships with external organisations to sustain operations in times of lockdown
Nicola McCullogh, Francisca Trigo Pereira, Andrea Scott-Bell, Rosa Stalenberg and John Hayton
Leisure Studies, volume 42, issue 1 (2023), pp. 8–22

Chapter 2
Parents perceptions of online physical activity and leisure with early years children during Covid-19 and beyond
Georgia Allen and Philippa Velija
Leisure Studies, volume 42, issue 1 (2023), pp. 23–37

Chapter 3
Cultural consumption and Covid-19: evidence from the Taking Part *and* COVID-19 Cultural Participation Monitor *surveys*
Tal Feder, Siobhan McAndrew, Dave O'Brien and Mark Taylor
Leisure Studies, volume 42, issue 1 (2023), pp. 38–55

Chapter 4
Time use, work and leisure in the UK before, during, between and following the Covid-19 lockdowns
Ken Roberts
Leisure Studies, volume 42, issue 1 (2023), pp. 56–68

Chapter 5
CrossFit during lockdown. The promises and pitfalls of digitally mediated training for leisure-time physical activity
Verena Lenneis, Jeppe Klarskov Hansen and Sine Agergaard
Leisure Studies, volume 42, issue 1 (2023), pp. 69–84

Chapter 6
COVID-19 and outdoor recreation in the post-anthropause
Jacob J. Bustad, Samuel M. Clevenger and Oliver J.C. Rick
Leisure Studies, volume 42, issue 1 (2023), pp. 85–99

Chapter 7
Sports participation during a lockdown. How COVID-19 changed the sports frequency and motivation of participants in club, event, and online sports
Erik Thibaut, Bram Constandt, Veerle De Bosscher, Annick Willem, Margot Ricour and Jeroen Scheerder
Leisure Studies, volume 41, issue 4 (2022), pp. 457–470

Chapter 8
Nearby nature in lockdown: Practices and affordances for leisure in urban green spaces
Katherine King and Janet Dickinson
Leisure Studies, volume 42, issue 1 (2023), pp. 100–117

Chapter 9
"I felt there was a big chunk taken out of my life": COVID-19 and older adults' library-based magazine leisure reading
Nicole K. Dalmer, Dana Sawchuk and Mina Ly
Leisure Studies, volume 42, issue 1 (2023), pp. 118–132

Chapter 10
Armchair travel through video games: stories from elsewheres and elsewhens
Serkan Uzunogullari
Leisure Studies, volume 42, issue 1 (2023), pp. 133–146

Chapter 11
Children and young people's perspectives from UK lockdown: leisure-less experiences
Ellie Gennings, Hazel J Brown, Denise Hewlett and John Batten
Leisure Studies, volume 42, issue 1 (2023), pp. 147–155

Chapter 12
A ramp that leads to nothing: outdoor recreation experiences of children with physical disabilities during the COVID-19 pandemic
Annika L. Vogt, Chris A. B. Zajchowski and Eddie L. Hill
Leisure Studies, volume 41, issue 5 (2022), pp. 742–752

For any permission-related enquiries please visit:
www.tandfonline.com/page/help/permissions

Notes on Contributors

Sine Agergaard, Sports and Social Issues, Department of Health Science and Technology, Aalborg University, Aalborg, Denmark.

Georgia Allen, Faculty of Health and Life Sciences, Northumbria University, Newcastle upon Tyne, UK.

John Batten, School of Sport, Health and Community, University of Winchester, Winchester, UK.

Hazel J Brown, School of Sport, Health and Community, University of Winchester, Winchester, UK.

Jacob J. Bustad, Department of Kinesiology, Towson University, Towson, MD, USA.

Samuel M. Clevenger, Department of Kinesiology, Towson University, Towson, MD, USA.

Bram Constandt, Department of Movement and Sports Sciences, Ghent University, Ghent, Belgium.

Nicole K. Dalmer, Department of Health, Aging and Society; Gilbrea Centre for Studies in Aging, McMaster University, Hamilton, Ontario, Canada.

Veerle De Bosscher, Department of Sport Policy and Management, Vrije Universiteit Brussel, Brussels, Belgium.

Janet Dickinson, Department of Sport and Event Management, Bournemouth University Business School, Bournemouth University, Poole, UK.

Tal Feder, Faculty of Architecture and Town Planning, Technion – Israel Institute of Technology, Haifa, Israel.

Ellie Gennings, Department of Sport and Event Management, Bournemouth University, Poole, UK.

Jeppe Klarskov Hansen, Sports and Social Issues, Department of Health Science and Technology, Aalborg University, Aalborg, Denmark.

Katherine Harrison, School of Humanities and Social Sciences, Leeds Beckett University, UK.

John Hayton, Department of Sport, Exercise and Rehabilitation, Northumbria University, Newcastle upon Tyne, UK.

Denise Hewlett, School of Sport, Health and Community, University of Winchester, Winchester, UK.

Eddie L. Hill, Park, Recreation and Tourism Studies, Old Dominion University, Norfolk, VA, USA.

Katherine King, Department of Sport and Event Management, Bournemouth University Business School, Bournemouth University, Poole, UK.

Jan Andre Lee Ludvigsen, Faculty of Arts Professional and Social Studies, Liverpool John Moores University, England.

Verena Lenneis, Sports and Social Issues, Department of Health Science and Technology, Aalborg University, Aalborg, Denmark.

Mina Ly, Department of Sociology, Wilfrid Laurier University Waterloo, Ontario, Canada.

Siobhan McAndrew, Sheffield Methods Institute, University of Sheffield, Sheffield, UK.

Nicola McCullogh, Department of Sport, Exercise and Rehabilitation, Northumbria University, Newcastle upon Tyne, UK.

Peter Millward, Department of Sociology, Liverpool John Moores University, UK.

Dave O'Brien, Sheffield University Management School, Sheffield, UK.

Cassandra A. Ogden, Department of Sociology, Liverpool John Moores University, UK.

Oliver J.C. Rick, Department of Sport Management and Recreation, Springfield College, Springfield, MA, USA.

Margot Ricour, Policy Research Center on Sport, Flanders, Belgium; Department of Sport Policy and Management, Vrije Universiteit Brussel, Brussels, Belgium.

Ken Roberts, School of Law and Social Justice, University of Liverpool, Liverpool, England.

Dana Sawchuk, Department of Sociology, Wilfrid Laurier University Waterloo, Ontario, Canada.

Jeroen Scheerder, Policy in Sports & Physical Activity Research Group, KU Leuven, Leuven, Belgium.

Andrea Scott-Bell, Department of Sport, Exercise and Rehabilitation, Northumbria University, Newcastle upon Tyne, UK.

Rosa Stalenberg, Department of Health Sciences, Vrije Universiteit Amsterdam, Netherlands.

Mark Taylor, Sheffield Methods Institute, University of Sheffield, Sheffield, UK.

Erik Thibaut, Policy in Sports & Physical Activity Research Group, KU Leuven, Leuven, Belgium; Unit Sport, University College Thomas More, Turnhout, Belgium; Policy Research Center on Sport, Flanders, Belgium; Department of Movement and Sports Sciences, Ghent University, Ghent, Belgium.

Francisca Trigo Pereira, Department of Sport, Exercise and Rehabilitation, Northumbria University, Newcastle upon Tyne, UK.

Serkan Uzunogullari, Department of Tourism, University of Sunderland, Sunderland, UK.

Philippa Velija, School of Sport, Health and Social Sciences, Solent University, Southampton, UK.

Annika L. Vogt, Special Education, University of Hawai'i at Mānoa.

Annick Willem, Department of Movement and Sports Sciences, Ghent University, Ghent, Belgium.

Chris A. B. Zajchowski, Park, Recreation and Tourism Studies, Old Dominion University, Norfolk, VA, USA.

Introduction: Lockdown leisure

Jan Andre Lee Ludvigsen [ID], Katherine Harrison [ID], Peter Millward [ID] and Cassandra A. Ogden [ID]

ABSTRACT
This editorial sets the scene for this special issue by unpacking the concept of 'lockdown leisure' as closely linked with the Coronavirus disease 2019 (COVID-19) pandemic which spread globally in early 2020 and throughout 2021 and 2022. It provides a snapshot of the parameters of lockdown leisure, outlines the separate articles in this special issue, and considers the medium-to-long term implications of the pandemic for leisure studies. By incorporating perspectives from a plethora of academic disciplines, the special issue advances our understanding of the social, spatial and cultural impacts of the various lockdowns on leisure and our lives more broadly.

Introduction: lockdown leisure

This special issue explores the complex relationship between lockdown and leisure. As the Guest Editors, our two overarching and inter-related aims were tied, first, to extending our knowledge on the medium-and long-term impacts of lockdown on leisure lives. Second, the issue seeks to provide a critical, transnational and leisure-oriented understanding of the diverse meanings, compositions and performances of leisure across what we may understand as the '(post-)lockdown' worlds. This is achieved by incorporating the various perspectives represented in the 10 articles that, individually and collectively, advance our theoretical and empirical understanding of the pandemic's social and cultural impacts.

From early 2020 and onwards, across many countries, one of the key responses to the Coronavirus disease 2019 (COVID-19) pandemic was the implementation of various forms of national and local lockdowns. At their most basic level, COVID-19 related lockdowns tended to involve (and still do, in some cases) social and disease control restrictions, curfews and quarantines. In this sense, lockdown and other 'stay-at-home' policies became largely synonymous with countries' or regions' attempts to reduce social contact and simultaneously prevent the spread of COVID-19 and reduce its impact on public health services. Lockdowns – where and when implemented – thus represented a significant departure from 'normality'. A temporal period – preceding a so-called '*new* normal' – emerged and instantly impacted the daily lives of populations across the world by altering their ability to work, travel, and maintain social or family relations and, as we explore in this issue, their *leisure lives*.

In explaining the emergence of what he conceptualised as 'locked down' leisure in Britain, Ken Roberts (2020), in the summer of 2020, explored a myriad of relevant questions for the study of leisure in a time of lockdown. These spoke to, *inter alia*, the impact of social distancing measures on leisure, the sanitation of leisure lives, the lockdown's different impacts on different demographic groups, and the new practices of leisure providers. Roberts also drew attention to the importance of time. This temporal aspect, we argue, remains imperative in this context for, as Roberts noted, the medium- and long-term legacies of lockdown on leisure cultures and activities were still likely to play out at the time of writing his paper. Indeed, Roberts concluded that:

> There will be more lessons for leisure scholars on the 'other side' of the 2020 pandemic. We will gain new, more penetrating insights into for whom, why and which leisure really matters. This paper's timeline finishes in June 2020 but the narrative is ongoing. It will run for years to come. *(Roberts, 2020, p. 626).*

Crucially, in many countries, several shorter and longer lockdowns were implemented after the publication of Roberts' paper (and this special issue's call for papers), due to the emergence of new COVID-19 variants, increases in transmission, and the absence of a vaccine until late 2020 (which, in many cases, took several months to get rolled out for many populations). That being said, this special issue represents a concentrated and collective effort to gauge and accumulate the lessons for leisure scholars and leisure studies nearly three years after the global lockdowns began. It does this by providing a collection of original research articles focused on various national and cultural contexts and on the multifaceted impacts of lockdown(s) on leisure activities, cultures and industries.

The importance and parameters of leisure in lockdown

As a critical juncture in modern societies, the pandemic warrants critical, social scientific engagement. As Connell (2020) reminds us, the COVID-19 pandemic, as much as it is a medical disaster, must also be considered a social disaster that has impacted global societies and local communities alike. Similarly, Matthewman and Huppatz (2020) argue that disasters such as COVID-19 must also be approached as social phenomena. Resultantly, the social sciences have been responsive, and numerous books, edited collections, journal articles and conferences quickly emerged, which reflect on and assess COVID-19's social impacts following its global spread in early 2020. Indeed, a significant bulk of this work has considered the concept of 'leisure' or leisure activities (e.g. Mowatt, 2021; Roberts, 2020; Sharp et al., 2022). As the pandemic unfolded, leisure life was not solely a domain that was deemed crucial from individuals' points of view, but it was also highly politicised and actively encouraged through public discourses highlighting the social and physical advantages of an active leisure life (Nugent, 2020). And so, within the social study of COVID-19 which Connell (2020) called for, and which still remains under construction, we argue that *leisure* must be positioned centrally in any social analysis of COVID-19. Of course, one of the primary reasons for this is because national lockdowns have ignited a series of critical questions about the elements of rupture, transformation and continuity in people's (leisure) lives and behaviours. Indeed, as Joe Moran (2020) reminds us, '[l]ockdown has laid bare the strangeness of the everyday. It has severed us from many of our routines'. And so, if leisure time broadly refers to 'that portion of the day not used for meeting the exigencies of existence' (Weiss, 1965, p. 1), then, for millions of people, lockdown may have brought about *more* time for leisure although, for others, it may have merely served to blur the work-leisure boundaries.

However, despite the potential quantitative increase in leisure *time*, COVID-19 restrictions also led to the closure of leisure spaces – particularly those taking place indoors or visited by large crowds. Examples of this, as captured by the separate articles in this special issue, include the shutdowns of gyms, galleries, theatres, museums, libraries, leisure centres and the restrictions on team sport trainings and group practices (e.g. Agostino et al., 2020). Sport mega-events (like the 2020 Olympics and Euro 2020), cultural events and festivals, meanwhile, were largely cancelled or took place behind closed doors – without spectators – in 2020 and early 2021 (Lee Ludvigsen, 2022). In terms of the leisure economies, lockdowns also directly influenced the businesses and employees of the sport, exercise and leisure sectors (Bratland-Sanda et al., 2021; McCullogh et al., 2022), and those scheduled to volunteer or work at sports events (Lee Ludvigsen, 2022). In other words, lockdowns thus dramatically impacted when, how and with whom individuals could interact during their leisure times (Gammon & Ramshaw, 2021). In that sense, we would argue that lockdowns, for many people and societies, became largely synonymous with the *re-definition, re-negotiation* and *re-conceptualisation* of leisure, especially in terms of altering or adapting the practices of an already existing leisure activity or provisions (see Lenneis et al., 2022), or simply by finding new or rediscovering old leisure activities. During times of lockdown, we also observe the importance of leisure's 'digital turn', or the digital leisure cultures which depend largely on technologies (Silk et al., 2016), as many 'offline' (e.g. physical spaces) leisure services or domains were shut down temporarily or for good.

Throughout the COVID-19 lockdowns, the proliferation of home fitness videos (Allen and Velija, 2022), social media-based challenges such as the 'stay-at-home challenge' or #ToiletRollChallenge (Bond et al., 2021), and the migration of professional sport events such as darts and chess (Davis, 2022) and quizzes (Ng, 2021) to home-based online platforms, were among the many adaptions of *physical* practices which emerged across the world. It is thus important to emphasise that the implementation of lockdowns did not automatically translate into the *absence* of leisure activities. Rather, the meanings assigned to leisure by individuals, groups and other stakeholders significantly transformed. Essentially, the study of lockdown leisure is strongly linked to the study of 'digital leisure'.

Lockdowns have also impacted various populations differently in different places. For example, as Bratland-Sanda et al. (2021) note, COVID-19 meant that in some cases older people with underlying health conditions, or people from ethnic minority backgrounds, had fewer opportunities to participate in outdoor physical activities. Moreover, leisure's increasingly digital turn, described above, relied and continues to rely heavily on access to and understandings of technologies, wi-fi and specific devices (e.g. tablets, computers, smartphones). Hence, the trends that emerged within the realm of lockdown leisure also say something about and reflect wider structural issues of social inequality and exclusion that the pandemic, in many ways, amplified and exacerbated. In this regard, one of the key premises upon which our special issue was originally motivated by was the idea that COVID-19 and lockdowns represented one of – if not *the* – biggest social transformations scholars of leisure in the post-War era would come to analyse, especially in relation to '(lockdown) leisure'. As the emerging and often responsive scholarship in the area implies, we are not the first ones to acknowledge the nexus between lockdown and leisure. Nevertheless, the timing of the publication of this special issue means that the medium- and- long-term impacts of lockdown have played out to a greater extent than they had in 2020 and 2021, and therefore could be uniquely captured in the various articles included here.

This special issue: a summary

This special issue consists of 10 articles written by scholars from across various disciplines including, but not limited to, leisure studies, sociology, sport management, education and early childhood studies, and cultural studies. Indeed, whilst this reflects the multi-disciplinary interest in lockdowns across the world, it simultaneously indicates something about the sheer importance of public health measures for individuals and societies. It is also necessary to mention the variety of methodological approaches taken by the authors which were designed with social distancing measures and pandemic restrictions in mind.

Contributions to the special issue are divided into two broad inter-connecting themes: *changing leisure practices* and *reconfigured leisure spaces*. First, with regards to *changing leisure practices*, we get an insight into how leisure practices were modified by individuals and leisure providers to adapt to lockdown restrictions in diverse national contexts. This, however, opens up larger questions regarding inequality, access, digital leisure and inclusion. On local, national and international levels, the periods of lockdown have amplified (or made visible) pre-existing inequalities and socially exclusionary practices. In this context, McCullogh et al. (2022) empirically explore how the services provided by disability sport charities were impacted by lockdowns in the UK. The organisation they call '*Admit*' (a pseudonym) was able to extend its organisational mission in relation to social inclusion and physical activity for children and adults by adapting their working practices through online working practices, delivery packages and physical activity programmes. The theme of (online) physical activity is also explored by Allen and Velija (2022) who draw upon survey and interview data to explore how physical activity was managed by pre-school children's parents during the UK lockdown. Whilst their study highlights the importance of alternative digital technologies to maintain levels of physical activity in home environments, they also document how the pandemic led to a reduction in physical activity for many toddlers and pre-school aged children and the challenges associated with some of the physical activity videos.

Despite the potential of diversifying audiences through new online platforms (e.g. the 'National Theatre at Home'), however, Feder et al.'s (2022) quantitative analysis of two cultural participation monitor surveys (measuring the frequency and ways in which people consumed culture during the global pandemic in England) demonstrate that cultural consumption remained the same as pre-pandemic trends. They found people who had never previously participated in cultural forms did not increase their participation and any reduction in cultural consumption was amongst those who already faced barriers to their participation (e.g. due to health or geographical barriers). The only increase in cultural consumption was amongst those who were already highly engaged in consuming forms of culture pre-pandemic. Ultimately, inequalities in the cultural sector were reproduced during the pandemic and if more diverse audiences of culture are to be reached, further creative vision and motivation for change is required. This article is followed by Roberts' (2022) examination of time use in the UK before, during, between and following the COVID-19 lockdowns in 2020 and 2021. As Roberts finds, the results revealed no rush back to the 'old normal' post-lockdown – whereas extra leisure time was primarily filled by the use of media.

The altered meanings of leisure are also located at the core of Lenneis et al.'s (2022) empirical study into CrossFit in the Danish context. In the context of closed CrossFit gyms, the authors seek to give a voice to the users of these gyms – the CrossFitters – to understand how these individuals perceived the transformations to their leisure lives. The migration towards online-based workouts emerges as one key theme – specifically, the article constructs an understanding of how digitally mediated communities can work to complement physical training. Whilst clearly highlighting the social aspects of CrossFit, Lenneis et al.'s study will also prove useful for future (post-lockdown) work in the area, as they present a series of important questions for other researchers to engage with regards to 'traditional' gym goers as well as CrossFitters. Then, Thibaut et al. (2022) examine changed leisure and sport practices in Flanders. Drawing on questionnaire data, they show, for example, how the closure of sport clubs and cancelled events had negative impact on the motivation of some sports participants.

In relation to the second theme of the special issue – *reconfigured leisure spaces* - three articles pay specific attention to the socio-spatial implications of lockdown and how – as some public spaces were closed down - 'new' spaces emerged or were given new meanings or negotiated by its users. The importance of spaces has been highlighted in the pandemic's context and COVID-19 'has provoked our understandings of fixed spatial scales' (Jensen, 2021, p. 78). For example, the slow-down of human mobility and activity in the months of lockdown caused what Bustad et al. (2022) call the 'anthropause' which captures the enormous interruption on contemporary patterns of human interaction and action. This time limited period was, *inter alia*, characterised by empty streets, little traffic, and the return of animals to human-centred spaces which are explored in relation to the prospects of a post-anthropause period; that is to say, when mobility and activity gradually resumed. By highlighting the ecological impacts of the resumed human activity and consumption in the post-anthropause, Bustad et al. break new conceptual ground as they point out that the post-anthropause – as a diagnostic and conceptual relation – helps us understand the intersection between human activity, environments, and the future.

Urban green spaces are also central to King and Dickinson's (2022) investigation into how exactly green spaces were valued by individuals in lockdown. Drawing from participants' Mobile

Instant Messaging Diaries through the smartphone app WhatsApp, their paper aids our understanding of how social practices are built into leisure lives in green spaces. The public nature of urban green spaces provided participants with a feeling of shared spaces and an escape from lockdown's boredom and, to that end, King and Dickinson provide new evidence of how green spaces became purposeful spaces during 'post-lockdown'. Dalmer et al.'s (2022) study of older adults' is concerned with the closure of another leisure space, namely, public libraries in Canada. More specifically, the authors investigate how the library closures impacted older adults' magazine leisure reading practices. As they argue, the pandemic became a catalyst for adapted practices where the library as a *place of leisure* became transformed as it became a virtual space where online portals and magazines could be accessed and read. As Dalmer et al. maintain, however, the reading of digital magazines was also disliked by many participants, indicating the barriers to adaption and older adults' reading preferences. Then, Uzunogullari's (2022) article analyses lockdown leisure through the exemplar of single-player sandbox videogames. With relevance to reconfigured spaces, Uzunogullari discusses how videogames became a tool for 'armchair travel' and how domestic spaces could be 'escaped from' through the sensory and emotional experiences generated from videogames. Furthermore, children and young people's perspectives of lockdown in the UK are explored by Gennings et al. (2022) in their research note. Their study documents how the lockdown disrupted children's and young people's usual leisure lives and milestones and provided an isolated 'leisure-experience' despite finding some positive impacts of lockdown (e.g. a better appreciation of what was once considered normal or mundane). In terms of outdoor spaces, Vogt et al. (2022) examine the outdoor recreation experiences of children with physical disabilities and discuss some barriers that children experienced during the pandemic.

Future directions

To end this editorial, we re-emphasise that the collection of articles in this special issue, when taken together, provide a clear indication of the social importance of leisure lives in lockdown. As Jensen (2021, p. 78) writes, 'dramatic events like COVID-19 not only require instant reaction but also opens up for reflections and analysis of existing conditions'. This is a contention we agree with, and it is hoped that the articles included here represent a collective effort to do exactly this: to reflect and analyse. We also concede that many questions remain unanswered and that it might take decades to understand and measure the full impacts of COVID-19, especially the impact of lockdowns on leisure practices and the discipline of leisure studies. In this regard, the papers included in this special issue act as a stepping stone for future studies of the leisure-related impacts of COVID-19. Indeed, as Roberts (2020, p. 625) has noted, the 'worldwide debate about a new normal' remains ongoing. Moreover, uncertainty persists given the current invasion of Ukraine, global financial crisis, and the long-term impacts of COVID-19. Hence, as Guest Editors, we remain both hopeful and positive that this special issue will ignite continued and sustained work and research initiatives on leisure in what is often characterised as 'post-pandemic' societies, and especially in relation to 'for whom, why and which leisure really matters' (Roberts, 2020, p. 626) in times of crisis and recovery.

Disclosure statement

No potential conflict of interest was reported by the authors.

References

Agostino, D., Arnaboldi, M., & Lampis, A. (2020). Italian state museums during the COVID-19 crisis: From onsite closure to online openness. *Museum Management and Curatorship*, 35(4), 362–372. https://doi.org/10.1080/09647775.2020.1790029

Allen, G., & Velija, P. (2022). Parents perceptions of online physical activity and leisure with early years children during Covid-19 and beyond. *Leisure Studies*, 1–15.

Bond, A. J., Widdop, P., Cockayne, D., & Parnell, D. (2021). Prosumption, networks and value during a global pandemic: Lockdown leisure and COVID-19. *Leisure Sciences*, 43(1–2), 70–77. https://doi.org/10.1080/01490400.2020.1773985

Bratland-Sanda, S., Giulianotti, R., Støa, E. M., Langseth, T., & Rosenbaum, S. (2021). Sports and active living during the Covid-19 pandemic. *Frontiers in Sports and Active Living*, 3, 1–3. https://doi.org/10.3389/fspor.2021.714986

Bustad, J. J., Clevenger, S. M., & Rick, O. J. (2022). COVID-19 and outdoor recreation in the post-anthropause. *Leisure Studies*, 1–15.

Connell, R. (2020). COVID-19/sociology. *Journal of Sociology*, 56(4), 745–751. https://doi.org/10.1177/1440783320943262

Dalmer, N. K., Sawchuk, D., & Ly, M. 2022 "I felt there was a big chunk taken out of my life": COVID-19 and older adults' library-based magazine leisure reading. Leisure Studies, 1–15.

Davis, L. (2022). The adaptation of the live PDC darts event during the COVID-19 lockdown. *Managing Sport and Leisure*, 27(3), 247–253. https://doi.org/10.1080/23750472.2020.1782251

Feder, T., McAndrew, S., O'Brien, D., & Taylor, M. (2022). Cultural consumption and Covid-19: Evidence from the Taking Part and COVID-19 Cultural Participation Monitor surveys. *Leisure Studies*, 1–18.

Gammon, S., & Ramshaw, G. (2021). Distancing from the present: Nostalgia and leisure in lockdown. *Leisure Sciences*, 43(1–2), 131–137. https://doi.org/10.1080/01490400.2020.1773993

Gennings, E., Brown, H. J., Hewlett, D., & Batten, J. (2022). Children and young people's perspectives from UK lockdown: Leisure-less experiences. *Leisure Studies*, 1–9.

Jensen, O. B. (2021). Pandemic disruption, extended bodies, and elastic situations - reflections on COVID-19 and mobilities. *Mobilities*, 16(1), 66–80. https://doi.org/10.1080/17450101.2021.1867296

King, K., & Dickinson, J. (2022). Nearby nature in lockdown: Practices and affordances for leisure in urban green spaces. *Leisure Studies*, 1–15.

Lee Ludvigsen, J. A. (2022). *Sport mega-events, security and covid-19: Securing the football world*. Routledge.

Lee Ludvigsen, J. A., & Hayton, J. W. (2022). Toward COVID-19 secure events: Considerations for organizing the safe resumption of major sporting events. *Managing Sport and Leisure*, 27(1–2), 135–145. https://doi.org/10.1080/23750472.2020.1782252

Lenneis, V., Klarskov Hansen, J., & Agergaard, S. (2022). CrossFit during lockdown. The promises and pitfalls of digitally mediated training for leisure-time physical activity. *Leisure Studies*, 1–16.

Matthewman, S., & Huppatz, K. (2020). A sociology of Covid-19. *Journal of Sociology*, 56(4), 675–683.

McCullogh, N., Trigo Pereira, F., Scott-Bell, A., Stalenberg, R., & Hayton, J. (2022). Exploring how a disability sport charity utilises exchange relationships with external organisations to sustain operations in times of lockdown. *Leisure Studies*, 1–15.

Moran, J. (2020). All cities are the same at dawn: Everyday life in lockdown. *The TLS*. https://www.the-tls.co.uk/articles/everyday-life-in-lockdown-essay-joe-moran/ (Accessed November 2022).

Mowatt, R. A. (2021). A people's future of leisure studies: Leisure with the enemy under COVID-19. *Leisure Sciences*, 43(1–2), 43–49. https://doi.org/10.1080/01490400.2020.1773981

Ng, K. (2021). Meet the people still doing Zoom pub quizzes a year into lockdown. *The Independent*. https://www.independent.co.uk/news/uk/home-news/coronavirus-lockdown-zoom-pub-quiz-b1823230.html (Accessed November 2022).

Nugent, C. (2020). "I was too fat." Prime Minister Boris Johnson says Brits must lose weight to fight coronavirus. *Time*. https://time.com/5872175/boris-johnson-weight-loss-coronavirus/ (Accessed November 2022).

Roberts, K. (2020). Locked down leisure in Britain. *Leisure Studies*, *39*(5), 617–628. https://doi.org/10.1080/02614367.2020.1791937

Roberts, K. (2022). Time use, work and leisure in the UK before, during, between and following the Covid-19 lockdowns. *Leisure Studies*, 1–13.

Sharp, B., Finkel, R., & Dashper, K. (Eds.). (2022). *Transforming leisure in the pandemic: Re-imagining interaction and activity during crisis*. Routledge.

Silk, M., Millington, B., Rich, E., & Bush, A. (2016). (Re-) thinking digital leisure. *Leisure Studies*, *35*(6), 712–723. https://doi.org/10.1080/02614367.2016.1240223

Uzunogullari, S. (2022). Armchair travel through video games: Stories from elsewheres and elsewhens. *Leisure Studies*, 1–14.

Weiss, P. (1965). A philosophical definition of leisure. *Quest*, *5*(1), 1–7. https://doi.org/10.1080/00336297.1965.10519593

Jan Andre Lee Ludvigsen
http://orcid.org/0000-0002-0085-2321

Katherine Harrison
http://orcid.org/0000-0002-2866-4189

Peter Millward and Cassie Ogden
http://orcid.org/0000-0001-8003-1840
http://orcid.org/0000-0002-3721-805X

Exploring how a disability sport charity utilises exchange relationships with external organisations to sustain operations in times of lockdown

Nicola McCullogh, Francisca Trigo Pereira, Andrea Scott-Bell, Rosa Stalenberg and John Hayton

ABSTRACT
National lockdowns exacerbated the inequalities that many disabled people faced in accessing and engaging in sport and physical activity. Like many organisations, disability sport and physical recreation-focused charities were constrained in their ability to deliver and sustain their services during such periods. This study explored the exchange relationships between a disability sport charity and its existing and prospective business clients as the former rolled key elements of its provision online. Resource mobilisation theory was employed as a framework by which to identify key resource types and mechanisms underpinning the exchanges between the businesses and the charity. Semi-structured interviews with participants from eight businesses were conducted to understand the dynamics of such resource exchange. Moral resources featured prominently in participants' accounts, particularly in relation to the legitimacy of the charity and authenticity of its delivery, with human resources also receiving much attention due to facilitators' engaging delivery styles. Overall, the charity was able to extend its organisational mission of increasing inclusion in physical activity beyond its own programmes via businesses through which it shares exchange relationships, emphasising the importance of such relationships both during and beyond lockdown periods.

Introduction

In their research examining the effects of the Covid-19 global pandemic on Business-to-Business (B2B) companies' operations, Cortez and Johnston (2020) compared such implications with those of traditional financial crises, such as the 2008–2009 global economic recession. Financial-based crises are typically triggered by endogenous mechanisms within markets, whereas, and unprecipitated by financial factors, the exogenous shock and socio-biological and transmissive nature of Covid-19 exposed a lack of organisational preparedness and protocols of businesses and enterprises for navigating a global public health pandemic – bringing about operational uncertainty in ways that financial crises alone do not (Cortez & Johnston, 2020).

In the UK, government-imposed national, regional, and residential lockdowns were legally enforced to prevent person-to-person transmission of the virus by restricting people's movement, confining millions of people to their own homes at intervals during the pandemic (Roberts, 2020).

Non-essential services and business were not exempt from lockdown, and instead forced to close their work premises. As Ken Roberts wrote, 'the industries catering for out-of-home leisure were the first to be hit and the hardest hit by the lockdown' (2020, p. 626). Consequently, the sustainability of smaller enterprises which are non-profit in nature (and often without cash reserves) and that are essential to the provision of active leisure, sport, and physical recreation were placed in an especially precarious financial position (European Non-Governmental Sports Organization, 2020; Hayton, 2022;). Non-profit organisations – such as disability sport charities (DSCs) – present vital sources of physical recreation for marginalised groups, groups which such opportunities seemingly became limited for disabled people[1] during periods of lockdown (Activity Alliance, 2021; Hayton, 2022; Kamyuka et al., 2020).

Many businesses had to alter their operating procedures in response to Covid-19 restrictions, which, during lockdowns, resulted in the full or partial shutting down of their facilities as well as reductions to staffing (Cortez & Johnston, 2020). For those staff still working in times of lockdown, society witnessed a large scale shift to socially distanced and online working practices, yet, according to Cortez and Johnston (2020), virtual platforms were deemed to diminish operational effectiveness and business impact. From their findings with B2B employees, Cortez and Johnston (2020) indicated that the pre-existing relationships with current partners and customers grew ever more salient to navigating the crisis and organisational survival.

The purpose of this article therefore is to examine the exchange relationships between a DSC and their business clients during lockdown(s) and the resources that are exchanged via such relationships, in order to demonstrate how the DSC: a) generates revenue in times of resource scarcity, and b) is able to deliver to and extend its organisational mission of increasing accessibility and inclusion in sport and active leisure beyond its own sport programmes and via those business clients through which it shares such exchange relationships. To do this, we apply the framework of resource mobilisation theory to illustrate key resource types and mechanisms underpinning their exchange. The research on which this article is based concerns a DSC operating in the North East of England. Established in 2013, this DSC provides disability sport and physical activity programmes and delivers disability awareness training to businesses and organisations operating in and across the field of sport, physical recreation, and active leisure. Rather than centre our analysis on data yielded directly from the DSC, we utilise interviews with key management personnel that represent eight client organisations of the DSC that have either bought services from the DSC in the past, have availed themselves of their digital services during lockdown, or would consider obtaining such services in the future.

The overarching argument that we present in the article is twofold: first, that the relationships shared between the charity and businesses are crucial to the sustenance of the charity and its operations both within and beyond times of lockdown; and second, that the nature of the DSC's dual service nature in combination with such exchange relationships enables it to extend its organisational mission via recipient organisations, thus continuing to contribute to a much broader movement for social inclusion whilst society was held in the grip of a global health pandemic. The article contributes to the leisure studies and sport literature in several ways. We apply RMT to the study of disability-focused sport, recreation, and leisure provision in a way that, to the best of our knowledge, has not been done previously. We utilise RMT to dissect how a DSC 'leans in' to lockdown to draw in resources, sustain its operations, and continue to pursue and extend its mission objectives. By virtue of points one and two, we highlight the salience of those organisations that sit somewhat outside of mainstream sport structures in the provision of accessible and inclusive sport and physical recreation services.

Inclusive sport, physical recreation, and active leisure and the role of the third sector

Emphasising the rhetoric around the centrality of sport and physical activity to the health and wellbeing of all members of society, Sport England's (2021) recent strategy commits to redoubling its efforts to tackle inequalities that detract from people's access to and quality of experience in sport and physical recreation. The strategy highlights the necessity of working with and learning from 'partners' within the sport industry to harness best practice from across the sector to understand, inform, and deliver inclusive and enjoyable experiences for everyone, and especially those that have traditionally been marginalised from such opportunities. Specific mention is given to disabled persons as is the emergence of care homes as a priority area for ensuring that the salience of physical activity resonates, and that quality provision becomes an integrated feature of residents' lives[2] (Sport England, 2021). The third sector plays an important role in contributing to this agenda.

However, the operational hiatus imposed upon third sector organisations (TSOs) by the Covid-19 pandemic and resulting state response has deepened the financial 'crisis' in the sector, undermining the ability of charities to support vulnerable beneficiaries and calling into question the long-term sustainability of such organisations (Butler, 2020). In combination with the UK's exit from the European Union (EU) and the economic austerity policies adopted by successive governments, the impact of Covid-19 completes a triple 'whammy' of financial challenges faced by the third sector (Hill, 2020; Third Sector, 2020; Walker & Hayton, 2018). Indeed, the rolling back of the public sector in the UK since 2010 has ever increasingly beckoned TSOs to fill gaps in 'frontline' social service provision, thus transferring significant risk onto TSOs and away from the state (Dagdeviren et al., 2019).

As local authority sport provision has retrenched further and further, TSOs are becoming the key delivery agents for sport, recreation, and leisure, and this is particularly so for vulnerable groups (Walker & Hayton, 2018). Faced with an increasing demand for services, TSOs have been impacted by diminishing sources, sums, and durations of grant funding from within both the public and private sectors, and this has substantially increased the level of competition within the sector for the ever scarcer financial resources available (Hastings et al., 2015). In response, and in line with the sector more broadly, third sector sport organisations (TSSOs) have become more business-orientated, typically pursuing a pluralisation of revenue streams beyond traditional grant dependencies (Walker & Hayton, 2017, 2018).

One outlet for some TSSOs had been to scope funding beyond domestic bodies by targeting EU social funding (Walker and Hayton, 2017). As a consequence of the UK's exit from the European Union, however, Hill (2020) states that charities and social enterprises will have less access to EU funding or opportunities to lead on EU funded projects. To put this into further perspective, Cooney and Ferrell-Schweppenstedde (2017) reported that, in 2015, UK charities benefitted from £210.9 million awarded directly by the European Commission, and a further £47.5 million via European Structural and Investment Funds. Thus, the funding landscape available to organisations such as TSSOs grows narrower. In the context of Covid-19, according to Third Sector (2020), charity funding streams during the pandemic have been heavily constrained with many having to fall back on their reserves. Yet, at the onset of the pandemic in the UK, only a quarter of UK charities were estimated to have reserves large enough to sustain them for three months (National Council of Voluntary Organisations, 2020) whilst others have no financial reserves at all (Walker & Hayton, 2017), with many forced to rely on committed donors (Third Sector, 2020).

What is more, the Covid-19 pandemic has brought into sharp relief (and exacerbated) the inequalities that disabled people face in accessing and engaging in sport and physical activity (Hayton, 2022; Kamyuka et al., 2020). In illustration of this, figures released by the Activity Alliance (2021) reported that 59% of disabled people felt that their ability to undertake sport and physical activity has reduced during the pandemic, with the proportion of disabled people who felt that they had the opportunity to be as active as they wanted to be decreasing from 58% to 39% following the onset of Covid-19 in the UK.

Theoretical framework

The focus of this article centres around the work of a TSO to which we have given the pseudonym, *Admit*. The *Admit* organisation is a disability sport charity based in the North East of England. The charity exists to increase awareness and opportunity in disability sport and physical recreation. Its mission is threefold: to promote the health of disabled people; to create opportunities for disabled people to participate in sport and physical activity, and to support all providers of sport and physical activity to include disabled people. To deliver against its mission aims, *Admit* provides disability sport and physical activity events and programmes, as well as disability awareness training courses for individuals and organisations either situated within the sport industry, or who are seeking to incorporate more sport and physical activity into their day-to-day operations.

This article has resonance within two contemporary and related bodies of literature: first, the burgeoning work focused on the increasing significance and operations of TSOs in the delivery of sport and recreation (as contextualised above) and second, literature on the *mainstreaming* of disability sport policy and organisational practice (e.g. Kitchin & Crossin, 2018; Kitchin & Howe, 2014; Kitchin et al., 2019). Implemented across many European countries, mainstreaming presents a structural solution to increasing accessibility to and inclusion in sport for disabled people (Kitchin & Crossin, 2018). Mainstreaming represents the policy of integrating responsibility for formalised disability sport provision into non-disabled sporting organisations, and in England, for example, the responsibility for such disability sport provision is placed within sport-specific NGBs (Kitchin & Howe, 2014). However, research indicates that a gap tends to exist between inclusive 'policy and the operations at the implementation level' within mainstream sport settings which render processes of integration largely structural and superficial (Kitchin & Howe, 2014; Kitchin et al., 2019, p. 433). One underlying reason for this is suggested to be because community sport programming is dominated by a competitive pathway logic geared towards high-performance and elite sport, thus reinforcing outcomes and practices which marginalise those with complex disabilities and/or multiple impairments (Kitchin & Crossin, 2018; Kitchin & Howe, 2014). In conjunction, insufficient planning, organisational capacity, and capacity building characterised by a paucity of actionable strategies, a lack of specialist personnel, limited range activities, and paternalistic provision overseen by largely nondisabled practitioners and decision-makers further serves to marginalise inclusivity (Kitchin & Crossin, 2018; Kitchin et al., 2019).

The work of *Admit* converges with both national and international movements to reduce discrimination and promote inclusive opportunities for disabled adults and children to engage in sport and physical recreation, and to do so with regularity. As aforementioned, in England the most recent national sport (and physical activity) strategy places emphasis on the inequalities of access to and experience of sport and physical activity that marginalised groups such as disabled people have long faced. Entitled *Uniting the Movement*, the strategy document speaks of the radical change required to tackle the underpinning and intersectional dimensions of such inequalities and the importance of organisations (or 'partners') like *Admit* in contributing to this agenda.

Beyond the national level, the work that *Admit* undertakes connects with a much broader human rights movement occurring on an international scale which, in alignment with the 2030 Agenda of the United Nations, seeks to coalesce organisations spanning multiple fields and industries – including sport – 'to end discrimination and transform the lives of the world's 1.2 billion persons with disabilities so they can be visible and active members of an inclusive society' (#WeThe15, 2022). This movement aims to, for example: increase the awareness, visibility, and representation of disabled people; work on governments, businesses, and the public to be more inclusive of disabled people, and to empower disabled people to be active members of society (#WeThe15, 2022). In the context of the current study, such objectives very much chime with Article 30 of the *United Nations Convention on the Rights of People with Disabilities* which was introduced to recognise that disabled people have a right to access services from all areas of citizenship including recreational, leisure, and sporting opportunities, and should experience such services with full and effective participation (United Nations General Assembly, 2006). Indeed, as *Admit* endeavour to work with and develop a network of external businesses to deliver services and, ultimately, extend their organisational mission, by virtue of this they also contribute to the overarching movements outlined here.

The mobilisation of necessary resources is vital to the strength and successes of a social movement (Edwards et al., 2019; McCarthy & Zald, 2002; Millward, in press). Indeed, Millward highlights that resource mobilisation theory (RMT) has proven an influential framework in the study of social movements. Prior to RMT, and according to the classical model, social movements were conceived as irrational, emotionally driven and disorganised behaviour expressed by unconnected and alienated individuals (Hayton et al., 2019; Millward, in press). RMT scholars, on the other hand, contend that social movements are extensions of institutionalised actions and whereby the proliferation of organised collective action, and the impetus it is able to galvanise, is dependent upon the availability of and access to specific resources and the knowledge to use them effectively (Edwards et al., 2019; Jenkins, 1983; Millward, in press).

According to resource mobilisation theory therefore, social movements are driven by rational and organised groups or entities (McCarthy & Zald, 2002). To this McCarthy and Zald (1973, 1977) conceptualised the RMT to explain movement formation and implementation as led by emergent professional organisations, and thus referred to these entrepreneurial organisations as social movement organisations (SMOs). SMOs, then, can be understood as those 'organizations that seek to bring about social change by altering elements of social provision or the distribution of opportunities within a society' (Hayton et al., 2019, p. 24; McCarthy & Zald, 1973, 1977). As formal organisations, SMOs employ professional staff, have permanent leadership, and can take such forms as charities or non-profit organisations (Jenkins, 1983; Hayton et al., 2019; McCarthy & Zald, 1977). What is more, exchange relationships and the ability of SMOs to broker access with external actors and entities are therefore critical to their mission goals and organisational sustainability (Edwards et al., 2019). As Edwards et al. suggest, SMOs 'typically cultivate, maintain, and preserve numerous exchange relationships through which they gain access to the specific mix of resources supporting their endeavours' (Edwards et al., 2019, p. 88).

Edwards et al. (2019) and Millward (in press) outline five distinct resource types: material, human, social-organisational, cultural, and moral. Material resources can refer to financial (money) and physical capital (e.g. property, office space, and equipment; Edwards et al., 2019). Human resources relate to labour, expertise, and leadership (Hayton et al., 2019). Social-organisational resources include networks and social ties and non-proprietary infrastructure such as public parks, cycle ways, and the worldwide web (Hayton et al., 2019). Edwards and Gillham (2013) describe cultural resources as tacit knowledge about how to accomplish specific tasks like designing and delivering inclusive activity sessions or disability awareness workshops or utilising new social media, thus requiring tactical repertoires and technical or strategic know-how required to produce events and services, and to mobilise necessary resources. Whilst specific cultural resources are widely occurring in a society, access to them can be socially or spatially restricted and contingent. Edwards et al. (2019) add that unlike human resources whereby individuals have control of who benefits from their skills and knowledge, cultural resources can diffuse into the public domain, and at which point become more difficult to control by their creators. Cultural products such as workshops, web content or digital tools and packages can facilitate the recruitment and socialisation of new 'adherents' who actively support the goals of the SMO and support it buy contributing resources to it (Edwards & Gillham, 2013). Lastly, moral resources are typically bestowed upon SMOs by external sources who – publicly respected themselves – keenly recognise the work of the organisation and draw positive attention to it (Edwards et al., 2019). Moral resources therefore include legitimacy, integrity, solidarity support, sympathetic support, and celebrity (Edwards et al., 2019). Critical to the leveraging of essential resources, is the ability of SMOs to accord with and satisfy institutionally legitimated expectations of potential sponsors of what is appropriate, proper, and desirable, at least in comparison to other entities also vying for resources (Cohen & Arato, 1997; Edwards & Gillham, 2013; Suchman, 1995). Where such endorsement(s) can be garnered, exists the potential to not only mobilise resources over the long-term, but also via networked reputational propagation.

These resource types provide one part of our organising frame in this study. The second part of this organising frame refers to the mechanisms of access and mobilisation of resources through which an exchange relationship occurs, of which there are four: self-production; aggregation; co-optation, and patronage (Edwards & Gillham, 2013; Edwards et al., 2019). An SMO can produce certain resources itself, and examples of resources that can be self-produced include the training of human resources, running events, cultivating networks, and developing web content (Edwards & Gillham, 2013). The aggregation of resources describes the ways in which an SMO collates and harnesses resources offered by dispersed individuals or organisations to allocate to their own ends (such as the aggregation of monetary donations or human resources in the form of volunteer recruitment; (Edwards & Gillham, 2013; Edwards et al., 2019). Co-optation refers to the ability of, for example, an SMO to utilise its relationships with other organisations to access or borrow resources that they already control or produce (Hayton et al., 2019). Any borrowing of resources is transparent and permitted, and often implies a reciprocal arrangement (Edwards et al., 2019). Edwards and Gillham (2013) suggest that buildings, members, and staff, social networks, or moral authority, for example, can all be co-opted by and between organisations. Finally, resources mobilised through patronage typically, but not always, refer to monetary transfers awarded to, for example, SMOs, by traditional donors or funders such as government departments or national governing bodies who are external to the organisation (Edwards & Gillham, 2013; Hayton et al., 2019). Edwards et al. (2019) highlight that patronage can therefore take the form of service contracts which cedes a degree of proprietary control over what that money is used for and how. Human resources can also be provided as part of a patronage relationship, and whereby, for example, a sympathetic or endorsing organisation can temporarily loan some of their staff to an SMO.

We therefore apply resource mobilisation theory within this study as a framework to explore what is shared in the relationships between the *Admit* charity, as a social movement organisation, and its business clients during a move to online provision. The specific focus on a disability-oriented organisation was twofold. First, disabled people have experienced new barriers to being active during the pandemic compared to non-disabled people, and 'are less likely to take part in activities that have become more common during lockdown restrictions' (like outdoor exercise; Activity Alliance, 2021, p. 100), and so the availability of appropriate–and likely online–provision/ providers offers a social and physical activity lifeline for those who experiencing such impediments. A second and not entirely unconnected reason relates to the issues associated with mainstreaming. To elaborate on this latter point, *Admit* aspire to support all providers of sport and physical activity to include disabled people, whilst Kitchin et al. (2019) emphasise the necessity for mainstream organisations to access partners with competencies in disability rights and awareness to facilitate their inclusion practices – and RMT helps us to illustrate how such networks and relationships have the potential to be cultivated.

Methodology

This article emerges from a broader project whereby the research team worked with the *Admit* organisation to gather information from its business clients to inform, and then subsequently evaluate a range of digital packages developed, piloted, and launched as it sought to roll out its face-to-face provision in online form during the lockdown periods. A major part of this study was to also understand prospective clients' needs and requirements of such packages. Data collection spanned April and June 2021. For context, at the point of writing, England has experienced three full national lockdowns with varying degrees of social restrictions enforced in between until 'all legal limits on social contact were removed' on June 21st, 2021 (Institute for Government, 2021). The three lockdown periods were: March 26th to May 10th, 2020; November 5th to December 2nd, 2020, and from January 6th to March 8th, 2021 (Institute for Government, 2021).

To recruit participants to the study, the Managing Director of *Admit* provided the research team with the email addresses of 13 business clients, with 8 organisations responding to an invitation to participate in the research. As two participants took part in an interview together, a total of nine participants (eight females, one male) representing those eight organisations took part in the study. Table 1 presents the pseudonyms by which participants are referred in this article, along with a brief description of the organisations for which the participants worked and the activities via which they engaged with *Admit*.

The interview schedule was developed together by the research team. Two members of the research team (FP and RS) conducted the interviews (6 and 2, respectively) to ensure that they could be arranged to fit participants' work schedules. The interviewees discussed and rehearsed the content of the interviews prior to commencing the data collection. Interviews were conducted online via Microsoft Teams, and subsequently transcribed before the transcripts were reviewed by the research team. The interviews followed a semi-structured format, with the interviewer asking a set of core questions such as, 'What are the most important things you look for in an organization that offers disability awareness training/sport and physical activity sessions?', 'How do you locate the training?', 'what have your experiences been of any online provision of such packages, so far?', and 'what are your access needs and requirements?'. Where appropriate, participants were prompted for further details and examples to encourage greater depth of responses. The average duration of the interviews was 32 minutes. The project received ethical approval from the Faculty of Health and Life Sciences Research Ethics Committee at Northumbria University (ref. 28,331), and participants provided written consent for their participation.

Table 1. Participant pseudonyms and nature of the work of their organisations with *Admit*.

Participant pseudonym and organisation/role	Nature of work	Services the participant/their organisation has accessed with *Admit* disability sport charity
1. Mandy, local council	Management role in a local council sport and leisure department, including responsibilities for local facilities, sports development and a public health funded programme	• Face-to-face workshops • Online workshops • Point of contact for advice when working on projects
2. Lisa, learning disabilities self-advocacy group	Group worker for a group of adults with learning disabilities to support them with self-advocacy	• Face-to-face physical activity sessions • Online physical activity sessions
3. Vicky, charity for young people with additional needs	Management role in a charity providing leisure activities for 6- to 30-year-olds with additional needs	• Face-to-face physical activity sessions • Online physical activity sessions • Equipment hire
4. Alice, care home activity coordinator	Activity coordinator in a care home for adults with neurological conditions	• Face-to-face physical activity sessions • Online physical activity sessions • Face-to-face boccia training
5. Zach, coordinator for student-athlete practitioner development	National role supporting the development of practitioners at an organisation designed to assist athletes studying at universities in England	• Face-to-face workshops • Online workshops • Creation of bespoke education leaflets
6. Jenna and Donna, National Governing Body	Management roles in a National Governing Body for disability sport, responsible for development (e.g. club, competition) and workforce (primarily volunteers such as officials and coaches, also some paid tutors who deliver training development)	• Face-to-face workshops • Online workshops • Face-to-face physical activity sessions • Working with *Admit* to build disability awareness content into their own products
7. Yvonne, adult weight management programmes	Facilitator on a weight management programme for overweight/ obese adults which has recently been adapted for people with learning disabilities	• Online workshops
8. Lorraine, support officer for a series of daycare centres	Support officer responsible for a series of daycare centres across the county, providing learning experiences (e.g. cookery, crafting) for adults with multiple and complex needs	• Face-to-face physical activity sessions • Online physical activity sessions

A phronetic iterative approach to the data analysis was adopted whereby emic (primary) and etic (secondary) cycles of analyses were undertaken recursively by JH and NM (Tracy, 2019). In undertaking the primary cycle of coding, JH and NM first immersed themselves in the data before inductively analysing the transcripts, making notes and discussing their readings of the data. From this emic analysis, both a manifest and latent sense of relationships emerged prominently from the data – to which key questions unfolded concerning what was exchanged via such relationships and what did this mean in relation to Admit's goals and sustainability. Following this the emic cycle of analysis we then turned to an etic cycle of analysis to which we turned external theories to deductively draw theoretical explanations to frame meaning derived from the data. Etic analysis led us to resource mobilisation theory. RMT was deemed of most theoretical significance as it allowed us to explain what was shared between Admit and its client organisations and to position and contextualise the charity as an SMO. Once this was fed back and agreed amongst the research team, JH and NM subsequently developed a codebook based on the key types of resource (human, cultural, material, moral, and social organisational) and means of resource mobilisation – to which they later imposed on the data. During this second-cycle coding, JH and NM first independently coded the data according to this codebook, before co-coding the transcripts together until consensus was reached across the entirety of the transcripts.

Findings and discussion

The findings from the interviews are discussed below in relation to resource mobilisation theory, with the resource types and mechanisms of resource mobilisation grouped by topics reflecting how these concepts were linked in the participants' accounts. Participants' perspectives on the benefits and drawbacks of online delivery are also presented as these highlight important considerations for future work in this area of practice.

Mutual benefits

Lockdown opened up a new dimension of leisure for client organisations and their residents in the form of 'virtual entertainment' that may have not materialised (or as quickly) otherwise:

> We've been using YouTube a lot ... we've been on virtual trips to Orlando, we did giant rollercoasters yesterday. We've been to the opera, the ballet, we've been to concerts ... We were able to bring *Admit* in digitally, and the technology is a great way of delivering extra things to people, because we can't do things face-to-face, if we couldn't do it virtually, we couldn't do it. (Alice)

As McCarthy and Zald (1977) stated, a supply and demand relationship underpins the sustainability of an SMO, and in this example, Alice indicates both a demand for and a receptivity to innovative entertainment solutions – which *Admit* was able to provide. Following on, Lorraine illustrates the creativity and expertise of the human resources supplied by *Admit* as they delivered a virtual exercise programme in story form. This programme generated ancillary activities that served to further involve the service users (adults with multiple and complex needs) as well as the staff at Lorraine's daycare centres:

> We had to launch everything digitally through the Teams or Zoom platform ... Then along came *Admit* and changed our lives and the staff embraced the opportunity on behalf of the service users, and we had themed events. [Service users] had a choice: would you like to have an interactive session around pirates, astronauts, food, Disney characters? The entire programme, the creative arts, the crafts, the needlecraft, would be building towards the interactive *Admit* sessions. They would sew costumes; they would make masks. In the music class, they would upload songs to go with the themes ... It was lovely ... It was so interactive, and the clients responded so beautifully ... But because our staff were shadowing, were in the sessions to support the learners to get the most out of the opportunity ... the beauty for us was when they exited, when the funding streams ran out, our staff had picked up the skills to be able to roll out that programme in their absence. It had a dual purpose for us, and it was very valuable.

Lorraine's comments demonstrate two points. The first being that *Admit* possesses the expertise to offer tailored virtual physical activities in a way that other online/social media platforms cannot offer. Second, whilst some clients (such as Alice) hired *Admit* to purely deliver services, others had a cost-saving 'dual purpose' in mind: although the funding to hire *Admit* ran out, the service that had been provided had been structured in such a way as to upskill the client's staff, allowing self-production of such programmes of activity in-house (Edwards & Gillham, 2013). Drawing on Edwards et al. (2019), this presents an example wherein the skills and knowledge of *Admit* staff subsequently translate into cultural resources that have diffused into the client organisation's workforce. The upshot of this for *Admit* is threefold. First, this transfer of practice aligns with *Admit*'s organisational mission of widening access to inclusive physical activity and recreation. Second, cultural products – for example, virtual exercise programmes – can generate advocates and supporters for the SMO, from which it has the potential to derive future resources. Third, by having the daycare staff involved as part of this resource exchange, *Admit* was able to co-opt further human resources who were physically in situ to ensure that the exercise programmes 'have really, really engaged and motivated our service users and staff' (Lorraine).

Quality pays dividends

This topic encompasses a number of resource types and mechanisms in relation to both the physical activity sessions and disability awareness workshops, moving from a simple account regarding patronage and material resources to a discussion of how moral resources can be distributed through social-organisational networks.

Lorraine, satisfied by and grateful for the physical activity sessions delivered by *Admit*, explained that she wanted to secure additional funding to procure further services from them, thus representing a form of patronage to the organisation:

> Now that I know I have access to a budget, I want to be able to sustain the *Admit* initiative as well... When the free access to the provision ended through the charitable funding, I liaised with our senior management in the County Council. They've actually paid for some additional sessions.

Lorraine is not alone in this as Mandy also expressed how much she valued *Admit* for their disability awareness workshops, wishing to confer material resources in the form of money in reciprocation for their services:

> Further down the line, we are hoping to get some kind of commissioned work to them, where they come in and deliver some of our disability services on behalf of the Council, because they have that area of specialism which we do not.

Longer-term patronage and partner endorsement is of great importance to the success and sustainability of an organisation (Brinkerhoff, 2005), and as well as wanting to repay *Admit*'s good work with more work, client organisations are willing to promote and recommend the work they do via their networks, therefore adding further reach to their reputation:

> The package has been quite magical so... I did say... "Is there any platform I can go on to highlight or speak my passion to help you get funding?"... We've decided, as a countywide care home, we're going to put some favorable marketing information on Facebook and things to support *Admit*. In the hope that other practitioners will pick up and utilize them as well... I've sent my testimony to [my network]. When we have great practice, I showcase it and send it to all external partners. (Lorraine)

The above represents *Admit*'s ability to access wider social-organisational resources: when good practice is recognised, the service provider is endorsed throughout the client's networks. Propagated via these networks, therefore, are moral resources – such as legitimacy and integrity – which client organisations confer upon the SMO and the quality of their services (Edwards et al., 2019). Thus, two relevant mechanisms of resource mobilisation are implicated here: one facet being that client organisations demonstrate their patronage by drawing positive attention to the services provided by an SMO, and the second pertaining to co-optation – whereby the gaining of access to key networks presents greater opportunities for the SMO to subsequently convert into necessary resources (Edwards et al., 2019).

Legitimate selection

Leading on from the previous topic in relation to legitimacy (moral resources), it was clear that (prospective) client organisations desired providers with good standing and a track record of delivering services satisfying their institutionally legitimated expectations (Cohen & Arato, 1997; Edwards & Gillham, 2013; Suchman, 1995). As Yvonne explained in relation to the workshops:

> We always look for really bespoke training, and to be honest with you, we probably look for a company that's got legitimate experience in delivery themselves. I think that's where it was very nice to understand that they actually have done it themselves ... I look for a company that's got good quality trademark as well, that they're recognized for that sort of service.

It appeared from the interviews that organisations working with disabled people desired providers that not only had experience of working with specific target audiences, but also that employed practitioners able to identify, relate and speak to the intersection between that audience and the subject matter: 'The most important thing would be if they were delivering training about people's learning disabilities, to have somebody with a learning disability involved in delivering the training ... like lived experience' (Lisa).

Emphasising further the importance of legitimacy, Yvonne highlighted that the marketing of some services/products by certain organisations may be somewhat misleading and subsequently not meet expectations: 'The other [non-*Admit*] one that I did, I didn't get from it what I needed. It was sold to me differently than what it actually was'. In such cases, if the experience of a service is incongruent with the user's prior expectations and they deem it to not meet their needs, the provider stands to lose organisational legitimacy, weakening its ability to vie for resources in a competitive marketplace (Cohen & Arato, 1997; Edwards & Gillham, 2013; Suchman, 1995). To guard against this, several of the participants intimated that they would undertake audits across their networks to ensure that they fill gaps in their provision or procure training by hiring organisations that they can have confidence in, and which can signal – or have signalled for them – a particular cachet:

> What we have to ensure is that there is an audit trail, that these people are suitable for working with adults with complex needs ... we've got to be sure that the company is of good status ... we would make sure that their sports coaches were qualified ... [Their training and development] would have to be absolutely top-notch. So as not to cause harm or the potential for harm physically to our students (Lorraine)

Zach similarly brings together social-organisational and moral resources (legitimacy); by profiling their network, his organisation aims to find 'leaders' to deliver workshops in their areas of specialism, and this process helps to reveal and verify legitimate providers such as *Admit*, thereby facilitating the mobilisation of material resources (money) to engage them:

> We conduct audits across the network. We either go directly to the education providers ... or someone who has an area of expertise ... We conduct a needs analysis of our practitioners and their educational needs and try to work out who would be best suited to fill that gap. That's why we work with *Admit* in the disability sport area as one of our providers.

For organisations like *Admit*, such positive endorsements of the service they deliver help them to penetrate key organisational networks related to their field of work and help to ensure that (prospective) clients procure their services in times of lockdown. Moreover, client organisations favoured 'word of mouth' recommendations when sourcing external service provision: 'You hear about different things and once you hear a good review then you go and try it out yourself' (Vicky). Yvonne also highlighted that the volume of providers means that recommendations are often the most efficient way to select one:

> Because I've been in this job for such a long time, I really rate word of mouth really highly, definitely because you do get to trust in your own colleagues' experience ... [and] other health professionals that you've worked with over the years ... Because I think time is really precious, isn't it? ... There are so many different companies and organizations offering you training, you really want it to come first-hand from somebody who has been there and done it and rates the training and rates the experience so you're not wasting your time

The social-organisational resources of social ties, and opportunities for *Admit* to patch itself into relevant networks, are crucially important to gaining work, including repeat custom, enabling revenue generation and delivery on their organisational mandate during lockdown. Whilst Vicky's organisation had 'a little catalogue which has different organizations that you can go to', Donna explained that her organisation was likely to contact providers already known to them:

> We haven't really recruited anybody new. We've perhaps reached out to people that we knew of before in partner organizations as well who have delivered for us. No new formal recruitment but certainly looking at what's out there and finding the best people to fit our need.

The upshots of online provision

The lockdown-driven move to online provision has instigated many organisations to connect with a greater number and wider range of providers when seeking to access online awareness training activities or to procure physical activity sessions/programmes. Many of the interviewees stated that they are likely to continue to both operate and participate in online activities due to, inter alia, their accessibility:

> I don't think there will be a push to travel for a day event especially if we can do it online. So, we'll probably look to do the sessions online, especially if it's information heavy and there isn't a technical aspect to it, which I think *Admit* probably delivers, for the [disability awareness] packages they deliver for us. (Zach)

This trend is likely to benefit *Admit* in several ways. As an organisation based in the North East of England, it is not always logistically practical or affordable for prospective clients to travel long distances from the South/Midlands of the country to attend, for example, a 2-hour workshop. Furthermore, delivering services digitally expands the organisation's reach, as colleagues Donna and Jenna highlighted:

> Donna: Everybody has moved online. I think we're all a bit guilty of that when the stuff was face-to-face ... we didn't go along to it whereas now it's so easy to dial in. I think I've seen more courses now than ever before.
>
> Jenna: We're planning to keep some elements of the virtual things going because actually, from an accessibility point of view, much more people can attend things down the line. We're not just banking on people travelling two hours or whatever to come to an event if we can also host things online or live stream things that we're attending

That online delivery will continue in some sort of permanence will further open up the market for organisations like *Admit* to increase their client-base and the revenue they can generate from it. By possessing and utilising material resources in the form of digital technologies, it can in turn make better use of social-organisational resources (networks and social ties), thus being able to aggregate more income (Edwards & Gillham, 2013; Edwards et al., 2019). Moving further forward, the wider body of clients that *Admit* has been able to amass via digital means during lockdowns may translate into more demand for its face-to-face services upon the denouement of lockdown(s). Several participants spoke to this potentiality; for example, Vicky's organisation was 'actually booking them to come and do some face-to-face which will be so much nicer'. Somewhat connectedly, amongst certain clients prior to the pandemic *Admit* had been better known for, for example, delivering sport and physical activity programmes, yet the shift to digital working practices and information gathering undertaken by businesses during periods of lockdown had facilitated a wider understanding of their services, potentially boosting demand:

> I was just recently browsing their website and noticed that *Admit* provide awareness training as well as the physical activity sessions... I didn't know they did it beforehand. But it's something I would like to know a bit more about. (Vicky)

In sum, resource mobilisation theory draws close attention the exchange relationships between an SMO and the organisations and enterprises that it engages with or hopes to engage with. Our application of RMT here has revealed how the lockdown scenario and a shift to online provision has shaped the form of resources exchanged between the SMO and its clients. It becomes clear that moral resources in the form of legitimacy and authenticity hold prominence for the DSC because, when seeking to identify and select a provider, businesses in this field pay keen attention to recommendations made through their networks as to organisations that will truly understand their clients and how to work with them – and it is in the DSC's human resources where such expertise exists. This, in turn, translates into the material resource of income for the DSC. By illustratively drawing these facets of RMT together we gain a picture of how such exchange relationships drive the sustainability of the charity.

Conclusion

In this article, we have framed the *Admit* organisation as an SMO – given that its organisational mission, practice, and service activities are congruent with national and international movements to promote inclusive opportunities for disabled adults and children to engage in sport and physical recreation. In line with the SMO concept, we have applied the framework of RMT to illustrate types and mechanisms of resource mobilisation underpinning *Admit's* exchange relationships with business clients in times of lockdown. A key argument that we make here is that DSCs such as *Admit* should be seen as more than simply 'on the ground' deliverers of sport and physical activity, but as playing a much wider role in the disability sport movement more broadly. The application of RMT to the disability sport field has allowed us to illustrate how *Admit*–as an SMO–contributes to this broader movement and continues to do so in times of lockdown. Key to its success is the dual services that *Admit* provides: the delivery of sport and physical activity programmes, and disability training and awareness packages. The use of RMT has allowed us to unpack the way that these two services work in tandem to develop the DSC's ability to broker access with external organisations to elicit exchange relationships which are critical to both their mission goals and organisational sustainability, as the former service enables *Admit's* staff to hone and shape good practice which they can share with others via the disability awareness training that they provide (Edwards et al., 2019).

A central finding here, evinced through an RMT lens, is that the quality of service provided – often related to the skill and expertise of the delivering practitioners, coupled with the experience and judgment of these services by the client – is of critical importance to the success, growth, and sustainability of the SMO. The human resources that the SMO are able to deploy are therefore crucial because clients can and will subsequently vouch for the quality and propriety of the services that they provide, conferring upon the SMO moral resources such as legitimacy as they promulgate endorsements of that SMO through their organisational networks – which will potentially lead to more work and further promotion. This is opportune for both the SMO and potential clients because lockdowns have instigated organisations such as care homes and day centres to explore virtual entertainment and they will often seek to procure engaging service providers that understand or can adapt to the needs of their service users. The receptivity of client organisations to virtual and online platforms has opened up new possibilities for sport, leisure, and entertainment provision which *Admit* has been able to adapt to and capitalise on due to the specialist nature and versatility of its human resources – a key facet of the demand-supply relationship that we contend has underpinned the DSC's organisational resilience during a precarious period for businesses and sport and leisure providers alike.

In contrast then to Cortez and Johnston's (2020) claims that the shift to virtual platforms undertaken by many organisations during lockdown had served to diminish operational effectiveness and business impact, a further key finding was that *Admit* was actually able to extend its organisational mission of increasing inclusion in physical activity beyond the direct provision of sport programmes and services due to the knowledge, skills, and training imparted upon business clients via exchange relationships. The data demonstrated that delivering such services as exercise programmes and disability awareness training can be engaging via online formats, and moreover that online delivery now has a permanence. The capacity of organisations to run online services to either supplement or substitute face-to-face provision has the potential to widen accessibility to disability sport and physical recreation as well for greater promotion of disability awareness than might have been the case prior to the pandemic – not to mention their service reach in terms of revenue generation.

Moreover, because organisations like *Admit* sit outside of mainstream sport structures they are consequently reliant on developing diverse networks outwith sport-specific NGBs to draw in business-critical resources. A further consideration here is that, by its nature, *Admit* exists to support all providers of sport and physical activity to include disabled people, possessing the competence in disability rights and awareness training that Kitchin et al. (2019) highlight that mainstream sport clubs likely require in order to more effectively enact inclusive policies. It would appear then that the work of DSCs like *Admit* confer them legitimacy as niche operators who can complement the integrative goals of mainstream sport organisations (McCarthy & Zald, 2002).

In the call for papers to this special issue, Millward et al. (2021) raised the question: 'How have new leisure providers developed and what does this mean for older providers?'. In the case of the current study however, we might switch the places of the new and old providers and ask instead: 'Has lockdown proven challenging for new entrants to the market?' in the context of inclusive online provision. The business clients in this research stressed not only their desire to source authentic and well-reputed providers, but that they go to great lengths to screen potential candidates that they have knowledge of within their networks. Perhaps the advantage here is with the more established organisations and SMOs with recognised specialisms, as opposed to new companies, or TSOs which ever more often decide to 'chase the funding' to survive (and thus deviate from what they were set up to and are skilled to deliver) – a trend which Hastings et al. (2015) suggest will likely stifle the long-term impact of that organisation. Future research, therefore, could look to plot success, sustainability, and 'mission drift' of diverse types and history of provider operating in sport and leisure spaces. Whilst recognising that SMOs exist within an environment wherein they often compete for resources (Hayton et al., 2019), our novel application and illustration of RMT in the context of the disability sport charity may offer likeminded TSOs a framework by which to assess the strengths of their organisation's footing in a turbulent sector and offer a practical basis by which to identify and pursue purposeful exchange relationships.

Notes

1. In this article we follow the UK social model and exercise 'disability first' language, as opposed to 'people first' language, to emphasise 'disability as an affirmative identity and an underpinning facet of the lived experience of a person with an impairment' (Hayton, 2022, p. 6). In practice, therefore, we refer to 'disabled people' rather than 'people with disabilities'.
2. The authors' conceptualisation of disability aligns with that of the *Admit* organisation that sits at the centre of the article. *Admit* aims to work with participants of any level or type of impairment, including those with high and very high support needs, as well as residents of care homes and daycare centres. Eschewing pervasive norms of able-bodiedness, *Admit* would follow Maika and Danylchuk's (2016) position 'that human ability exists on a spectrum, regardless of impairment' (Maika & Danylchuk, 2016, p. 413), thereby embracing

individual difference and empowering persons that Silva and Howe (2018) consider to be 'differently abled' in and through sport and physical recreation.

Disclosure statement

No potential conflict of interest was reported by the author(s).

ORCID

Nicola McCullogh http://orcid.org/0000-0001-5000-1923
Andrea Scott-Bell http://orcid.org/0000-0002-1022-9023
John Hayton http://orcid.org/0000-0003-2437-1028

References

Activity Alliance. (2021). *Annual disability and activity survey 2020-21*. Activity Alliance.
Brinkerhoff, D. W. (2005). *Organizational legitimacy, capacity and capacity development*. European Centre for Development Policy Management.
Butler, P. (2020, March 16). Charities face cash crisis as virus fears hit fundraising. *The Guardian*. https://www.theguardian.com/society/2020/mar/16/charities-face-cash-crisis-as-virus-fears-hit-fundraising
Cohen, J. L., & Arato, A. (1997). *Civil society and political theory*. MIT Press.
Cooney, C., & Ferrell-Schweppenstedde, D. (2017). *What does brexit mean for UK charities' European Union funding?* Directory of Social Change.
Cortez, R. M., & Johnston, W. (2020). The Coronavirus crisis in B2B settings: Crisis uniqueness and managerial implications based on social exchange theory. *Industrial Marketing Management*, 88, 125–135. https://doi.org/10.1016/j.indmarman.2020.05.004
Dagdeviren, H., Donoghue, M., & Wearmouth, A. (2019). When rhetoric does not translate to reality: Hardship, empowerment and the third sector in austerity localism. *The Sociological Review*, 67(1), 143–160. https://doi.org/10.1177/0038026118807631
Edwards, R., & Gillham, P. (2013). Resource Mobilization Theory. In D. A. Snow, D. Della, B. K. Porta, & D. McAdam (Eds.), *The Wiley-Blackwell encyclopaedia of social and political movements*. Blackwell Publishing. https://doi.org/10.1002/9780470674871.wbespm447
Edwards, B., McCarthy, J. D., & Mataic, D. (2019). The Resource Context of Social Movements. In D. A. Snow, S. A. Soule, H. Kriesi, & H. J. McCammon (Eds.), *The Wiley Blackwell companion to social movements* (2nd ed., pp. 79–97). Wiley Blackwell.

European Non-Governmental Sports Organization. (2020). *Position paper on the impact of the COVID-19 crisis on the sport sector*. https://8ade9a85-fc3c-4023-b164-5a2d96d2060d.usrfiles.com/ugd/8ade9a_d582274187eb433b93cda100dc4382eb.pdf

Hastings, A., Bailey, N., Bramley, G., Gannon, M., & Watkins, D. (2015). *The Cost Of The Cuts: The Impact On Local Government And Poorer Communities*. Joseph Rowntree Foundation.

Hayton, J. W., Blundell, M., Cullinane, D., & Walker, C. M. (2019). Building an inclusive cycling "movement": Exploring the charity-led mobilisation of recreational cycling in communities across Merseyside, England. *Sport Management Review*, 22(1), 21–37. https://doi.org/10.1016/j.smr.2018.09.002

Hayton J. W. (2022). Facilitating Disability Sport and Physical Recreation during the Initial Months of COVID-19: Examining Organizational Innovation in Third Sector Organizations. *Leisure Sciences*, 1–23. https://doi.org/10.1080/01490400.2021.2023373

Hill, I. (2020). *Third Sector*. Birmingham City University: Centre for Brexit Studies. https://www.bcu.ac.uk/centre-for-brexit-studies/projects/third-sector

Institute for Government. (2021). Timeline of UK government coronavirus lockdowns. https://www.instituteforgovernment.org.uk/charts/uk-government-coronavirus-lockdowns

Jenkins, J. C. (1983). Resource mobilization theory and the study of social movements. *Annual Review of Sociology*, 9(1), 527–553. https://doi.org/10.1146/annurev.so.09.080183.002523

Kamyuka, D., Carlin, L., McPherson, G., & Misener, L. (2020). Access to Physical Activity and Sport and the Effects of Isolation and Cordon Sanitaire During COVID-19 for People With Disabilities in Scotland and Canada. *Frontiers in Sports and Active Living*, 2. https://doi.org/10.3389/fspor.2020.594501

Kitchin, P. J., & Howe, D. (2014). The mainstreaming of disability cricket in England and Wales: Integration 'One Game' at a time. *Sport Management Review*, 17(1), 65–77. https://doi.org/10.1016/j.smr.2013.05.003

Kitchin, P. J., & Crossin, A. (2018). Understanding which dimensions of organisational capacity support the vertical integration of disability football clubs. *Managing Sport and Leisure*, 23(1–2), 28–47. https://doi.org/10.1080/23750472.2018.1481764

Kitchin, P. J., Peile, C., & Lowther, J. (2019). Mobilizing capacity to achieve the mainstreaming of disability sport. *Managing Sport and Leisure*, 24(6), 424–444. https://doi.org/10.1080/23750472.2019.1684839

Maika, M., & Danylchuk, K. (2016). Representing Paralympians: the 'other' athletes in Canadian print media coverage of London 2012. *The International Journal of the History of Sport*, 33(4), 401–417. https://doi.org/10.1080/09523367.2016.1160061

McCarthy, J. D., & Zald, M. N. (1973). *The trend of social movements in America: professionalization and resource mobilization*. General Learning Press.

McCarthy, J. D., & Zald, M. N. (1977). Resource mobilization and social movements: A partial theory. *American Journal of Sociology*, 82(6), 1212–1241. https://doi.org/10.1086/226464

McCarthy, J. D., & Zald, M. N. (2002). The Enduring Vitality of the Resource Mobilization Theory of Social Movements. In J. H. Turner (Ed.), *Handbook of sociological theory* (pp. 553–565). Springer.

Millward, P., Harrison, K., Ludvigsen, J. A. L., & Ogden, C. (2021). Lockdown Leisure. *Leisure Studies*. https://think.taylorandfrancis.com/special_issues/leisure-studies-lockdown-leisure/

Millward, P. (2022 - in press). *Football With Pride: Sexualities, Activisms and Cultural Relational Sociology*. Abingdon: Routledge.

National Council for Voluntary Organizations. (2020). *The impact of COVID-19 on the voluntary sector*. https://blogs.ncvo.org.uk/wp-content/uploads/2020/04/NCVO-briefing-Lords-debate-COVID-and-charities.pdf

Roberts, K. (2020). Locked down leisure in Britain. *Leisure Studies*, 39(5), 617–628. https://doi.org/10.1080/02614367.2020.1791937

Silva, C. F., & Howe, P. D. (2018). The social empowerment of difference: the potential influence of para sport. *Physical Medicine and Rehabilitation Clinics*, 29(2), 397–408. https://doi.org/10.1016/j.pmr.2018.01.009

Suchman, M. C. (1995). Managing legitimacy: strategic and institutional approaches. *Academy of Management Review*, 20(3), 571–610. https://doi.org/10.5465/amr.1995.9508080331

Third Sector (2020, April 8). *Analysis: how charities with low reserves are coping with the COVID-19 pandemic. Third Sector*. https://www.thirdsector.co.uk/analysis-charities-low-reserves-coping-COVID-19-pandemic/finance/article/1679646

Tracy, S. J. (2019). *Qualitative research methods: collecting evidence, crafting analysis, communicating impact* (2nd ed.). Wiley Blackwell.

United Nations General Assembly. (2006). Convention on the rights of persons with disabilities. UN Doc A/61/611. https://www.un.org/esa/socdev/enable/rights/convtexte.htm

Walker, C. M., & Hayton, J. W. (2017). Navigating austerity: balancing 'desirability with viability' in a third sector disability sports organisation. *European Sport Management Quarterly*, 17(1), 98–116. https://doi.org/10.1080/16184742.2016.1210190

Walker, C. M., & Hayton, J. W. (2018). An analysis of third sector sport organisations in an era of 'super-austerity'. *International Journal of Sport Policy and Politics*, 10(1), 43–61. https://doi.org/10.1080/19406940.2017.1374296

#WeThe15 (2022). *About*. https://www.wethe15.org/

𝜕 OPEN ACCESS

Parents perceptions of online physical activity and leisure with early years children during Covid-19 and beyond

Georgia Allen and Philippa Velija

ABSTRACT
Prior to Covid-19, businesses offering enrichment activities for pre-school aged children were saturating the early years (0–5 years) market. However, the pandemic caused sudden changes to family routines with regular leisure activities cancelled. Using Lareau's theory of concerted cultivation as a framework, we explored how physical activity (PA) was managed by parents of pre-school children and how routines changed during the pandemic. A UK national online survey was completed by 925 parents. Sixteen tailored, follow-up semi-structured interviews were undertaken with parents. Due to the nature of the pandemic and the age range of the young children, it was the parents who ultimately made decisions about PA, and it was parents who had to adapt, often to a challenging set of circumstances. Our data suggests many parents sought to utilise informal play and online PA during the lockdown periods with mixed levels of success. For those that attended baby, toddler, and pre-school sport sessions provided by commercial businesses prior to lockdown, the vast majority were eager to resume their in-person classes as opposed to continuing online. Parents perceived a wider range of benefits and cultivation for their child if they attended such classes in person (e.g. expert delivery, socialisation, and routine).

Introduction

In this article we discuss parents experience of online physical activities targeted at early years children during various forms of 'lockdown', where normal family leisure opportunities and external structured physical activities were disrupted. In doing so, we provide an understanding of how parents utilised online activities for their pre-school children and why. This is significant as prior to Covid-19, commercial businesses offering enrichment activities for early years children (0–5 years) were saturating the pre-school market. However, during the pandemic there were unprecedented restrictions placed on all aspects of life – family routines suddenly changed and regular leisure activities were cancelled. With this is mind, we draw on the theoretical concepts of concerted cultivation to discuss the changes families experienced during various UK lockdowns as well as locating these in debates about screen use and technology for under 5's. We also explored the decisions made in relation to baby, toddler, and pre-school enrichment routines. Covid-19 was an unparalleled 'lockdown', both in terms of its magnitude and scale but also in the social isolation many governments enforced on their citizens to stop the spread of Coronavirus (SARS-CoV-2). During this time, many people moved to online technology to maintain certain aspects of their life

This is an Open Access article distributed under the terms of the Creative Commons Attribution License (http://creativecommons.org/licenses/by/4. 0/), which permits unrestricted use, distribution, and reproduction in any medium, provided the original work is properly cited.

(e.g. social interactions and leisure) that had been restricted, but little is known about this usage in early childhood during the pandemic.

'Good' parenting and concerted cultivation

Parents, particularly middle-class parents, are increasingly motivated to help their children to develop the skills needed for a successful childhood, so they can get ahead in education and other social situations, providing a competitive advantage (Lareau, 2003; Stirrup et al., 2014Wheeler & Green, 2014). Lareau (2003) uses the term *concerted cultivation* to describe a parenting practice which prepares children for adulthood by fostering talents, skills and abilities and intervening to ensure their children get the best opportunities in a competitive environment. Doing the 'right' thing as a parent and providing numerous opportunities across a range of activities has become an expected contemporary child rearing practice (Gabriel, 2017). In the UK, Vincent and Ball (2007) highlight how class divisions impact on child rearing and how middle-class parents invest in their children by enrolling them on to various enrichment activities. For parents that can afford to, providing numerous opportunities in a range of activities has become an expected contemporary component of parenting practice (Gabriel, 2017).

Facilitating opportunities for children to get ahead in education and other social situations is a growing trend (Lareau, 2003; Stirrup et al., 2014; Wheeler & Green, 2014) as Ball (2003) highlights how parents are concerned about their children attending the 'right' school. The number and variety of activities that young children are involved in is increasingly seen as a way of expressing 'good' parenting and to alleviate (mainly) middle-class anxieties about providing children with rounded and structured activities (Allen et al., 2021; Wheeler, 2018) although there appears to be considerable intra-class diversity in how much parents concertedly cultivate (Wheeler, 2018). Commercialised sporting activities are marketed (Smyth, 2016) at parents in ways that play into contemporary concerns about good parenting and cultivation. For parents who can afford it, they can select activities that are marketed as important for their child's development (Stirrup et al., 2014). We utilise the concept of concerted cultivation as a sensitising concept to understanding parents' approach and the pressures on parents to provide meaningful and cultivating activities for their children pre, during, and post Covid-19.

Growth of early years commercialised sport and leisure spaces

The growth of franchises and commercial businesses offering enrichment activities for the pre-school market (under 5 years old), has been substantial in the last two decades and in line with broader social processes around 'good parenting' (Allen et al., 2021). Parents who can afford to are able to take advantage of a relatively new privatised education system that provides their child(ren) with skills that distinctively set them apart from their peers (Evans & Davies, 2015). Broader social changes such as the rise in dual-income families and shifts in work-life balance have potentially changed attitudes in relation to children's PA and experiences available for early years children.

Furthermore, the reduction in public leisure services such as leisure centres and play parks mainly due to austerity over the last decade (Stenning, 2019) has created a need for safe sport and leisure spaces for young children. Before Covid-19 changed familiar routines, businesses offering sport classes were attractive to a significant number of families (e.g. based on franchise website information, UK membership numbers for popular franchises such as those offering ballet, rugby and swimming ranged from 11,000–42,000 children per week). In the UK, Wheeler and Green (2014, 2019) found that economic status influenced leisure opportunities and the ways in which parents cultivated their children's physical and social capital, especially highlighting the role of external clubs in middle- and upper-class families who value these activities

In addition to the increase in privatised and commercialised provision in baby, toddler, and preschool we have seen in sport and leisure domains, youth sport provision has become subject to global privatisation. This includes formal provision in educational settings as well as out-of-school activities including coaching in sport, leisure and play opportunities (Evans & Davies, 2015, p. 2; Stirrup et al., 2014). Stirrup et al. (2014) argue that under an agenda of private and/or commercial interests (Evans & Davies, 2015; Powell, 2015), parents are consumers buying the best learning opportunities for their children from a very young age and some instances, even before the child is born. For example, one popular, nationwide swimming provider argues on their website that the antenatal classes they provide allows the baby to become familiar with the swimming environment whilst in the womb. With this in mind, Evans and Davies explore what the implications of neoliberalism will be (Evans & Davies, 2014) and what the future impact on the educational market might be when 'social justice is *not* a primary concern' (2015:3). The enrichment activities that parents discuss in this study are an example of this as they are provided by commercial businesses who are not masking as social responsibility. They sell an enrichment opportunity that is perceived by parents to be beneficial during early childhood (but only if parents have the economic capital to access such classes).

Parenting, digital technology and screen time

Once the global pandemic hit, enrichment sessions that had become a regular feature in many preschool children's lives were cancelled. Unsurprisingly, sporting activities declined more than other forms of exercise across all groups (Sport England, 2021). However, our knowledge of the preschool age range and the impact of parental influence on formal and informal PA remains less understood (Harlow et al., 2020). Our initial focus was to examine the impact of Covid-19 on preschool activity and family life, and we sought to understand how parents adapted their routines during the various UK lockdowns. While research on the impact of lockdowns is still emerging, the pandemic did change and restrict people's PA, and as a result, many people turned to online resources.

In line with the growing demand for mobile technology generally, children's access to digital devices has rapidly increased over recent years (Laidlaw et al., 2021). Pre-school children are now engaging with technology at increasingly younger ages and can move seamlessly across online and offline spaces (Laidlaw et al., 2021; Marsh et al., 2016), demonstrating digital fluency from a very young age. Byrne et al. (2021) note that both the amount of time young children spend on screen-based devices is increasingly and the age of first exposure is decreasing. Whilst screen-based devices can offer interaction, cognitive engagement and educational opportunities that may have some benefits, the potential negative consequences of excessive screen time (e.g. poor sleep, cognitive delays, lack of PA and obesity) are often a source of concern for parents (Byrne et al., 2021).

Online technology has transformed the way people access and share information, with digital media now a central part of modern family life (Sandberg et al., 2021). However, parenting in the digital age is challenging (Livingstone & Blum-Ross, 2020; Mollborn et al., 2022). On the one hand, parents have a responsibility to keep their child(ren) safe online (Barnes & Potter, 2021) and are concerned about potential risks (Sandberg et al., 2021). On the other hand, parents are also responsible for creating digitally literate citizens (Sandberg et al., 2021) that will thrive in a digital marketplace. Parents are now having to navigate the complex intersection between societal attitudes and expectations (e.g. appropriate online content and amount of screen time) and the reality of everyday life when it comes to digital technology.

Technology devices are now used for a range of purposes which can cause further complexities and challenges for parents and early care and education providers (ECE) such as nurseries and preschools. Joseph et al. (2019) found that both parents and ECE providers were unaware of specific policies and guidance in relation to screen time. Whilst watching TV remains the most frequent way children use technology (Mollborn et al., 2022; Sandberg et al., 2021), technology is also used for educational purposes, learning, communication, and recreation. This multi-use aspect can cause complications for parents who are negotiating perceptions of good versus bad technology use (Ito, 2019; Mollborn et al., 2022). Activities such as reading, learning/educational tasks, information gathering and developing digital literacy are often perceived to be *good* use of technology, whereas watching TV, gaming, or engaging with non-educational content are often perceived to have 'no human capital advantages' (Mollborn et al., 2022). Ito (2019) argue that parents seek to manage their children's online and technology behaviour in the *right* way even when parents are not sure what that is. Parental concerns reflect the pressure parents are under to cultivate in particular ways that will benefit and not harm their children.

The increased use of online technology during the early phases of the pandemic for purposes such as education, work, and PA saw the usage of some internet services rising 100% compared to pre-lockdown levels (De' et al., 2020). This increased usage also highlighted many inequalities with digital devices and access to online technology, with an estimated 5 million people in the UK not connected to the internet (Allmann, 2020) with low-income families (Beaunoyer et al., 2020), the elderly and disabled (Allmann, 2020) most at risk of digital and/or online exclusion. Many of the companies that provide sport and leisure activities aimed at the pre-school market moved to an online platform when restrictions were put in place, allowing them to stay engaged and connected with their customers (who had online access). Some businesses found the transition easier than others. Those needing specialist equipment, such as swimming pools, found the online transition almost impossible. However, those providing online PA sessions prior to lockdown were able to expand their reach and customer-base further. In this article, we consider how technology and online PA was utilised in an age group often forgotten when discussing leisure and pre-school sport (Harlow et al., 2020). We focus on the decisions parents made in relation to online PA, how they found their pre-schoolers responded to the online environment and whether online PA would endure beyond lockdown.

Materials and methods

The UK Covid-19 context

In March 2020, Coronavirus caused the UK Government (along with many others across the world) to enforce an unprecedented 'lockdown'. Unless you were a key worker, the acute 'stay at home' period resulted in restrictions on daily movement and freedoms that were unparalleled in peace time. Exercising outside – once a day, for one hour, either *'on your own or with members of your household'* - was cited by the Conservative Government as a valid but exceptional reason for leaving home. The only other valid reasons were to buy essential items (food or medication), care for others, and attend work (although employers were encouraged to facilitate home working where possible) (Malcolm & Velija, 2020).

No indoor sports or leisure facilities were open, and playgrounds were closed. Some schools and nurseries remained open for children whose parents were identified as key or essential workers. In some instances, the furlough scheme (also known as the Coronavirus Job Retention Scheme provided financial support for adults who could not undertake their employment duties) provided many families with a slower pace of life and more time to spend together. Whilst those who continued to work (i.e. essential and/or key workers) often found the pressures of balancing work, family life and childcare extremely challenging and found this had an impact on family wellbeing (Chung et al., 2020).

Then England moved to a 'stay alert' phase. From May 2020, you could meet one other person from outside your household and outdoor activities expanded. In June 2020, schools began a phased reopening in England. Groups of six were allowed to meet outdoors. In July, playgrounds reopened, and organised sport restarted, followed by gyms and pools reopening. Soft-play centres were allowed to reopen in August. September saw the restriction to indoor team sport reintroduced, but schools reopened for all pupils. Tiered (1–3) restrictions were implemented at a regional/level throughout England on the 14th October. England then went into its second national lockdown on the 5th November until 2nd December. Rules were relaxed for five days over the Christmas period but England entered its third national lockdown on the 6th January 2021, with restrictions applied to all organised and outdoor activity and closure of indoor leisure spaces such as gyms and pools. Our research captured the initial UK lockdown and then further lockdowns over the winter period.

During this time, ECE providers (e.g. nurseries and pre-schools) and schools were navigating a complexity of local and national restrictions to remain open for pupils. During the initial lockdown ECE providers and schools were closed on Wednesday 18th March 2020, and national examinations due to take place that year were cancelled. Covid-19 caused the biggest disruption to children's education since the start of the Second World War (Timmons, 2021). Home schooling began and lessons moved online for most UK children. Schools did their best to provide devices such as tablets or laptops to families who needed them the most although this scheme was not without its issues and delays. Schools were then allowed to open to key/critical worker children. Yet, despite their best efforts, some ECE providers found staying open for smaller numbers of children unworkable and many private nurseries and pre-schools were forced to shut (with some still charging parents full fees whilst closed). Key/critical worker children who stayed in ECE settings had a more familiar routine, and overall, a different lockdown experience.

Procedures

An online survey was developed through Jisc's Online Survey platform and institutional ethical approval was granted from the second author's institution (approval number: 19177). The survey was devised by the authors, reviewed, and piloted with parents who had pre-school aged children prior to dissemination. The pilot allowed us to determine how long it would likely take for people to complete the survey and to make some very minor changes for clarity and conciseness. The survey opened in October 2020 and closed at the end of January 2021 to capture data across various lockdowns. The survey included a combination of open and closed questions as well Likert scale-based questions and sought to gather information on family demographics and PA pre-and-during the various stages of lockdown in the UK. We also sought to indentify any potential enduring trends developed because of the pandemic.

The survey link was shared by organisations who work with or have an interest in early years children and their families such as group providers and nurseries and social media sites (i.e. Facebook™ and Twitter™). Finally, we asked participants to leave contact information (e.g. an email address) if they were happy to be contacted about participating in a follow up interview at the end of the survey. Procedures were clearly communicated to participants before consent was given and participants were made aware that survey responses were only stored once they pressed the submit button at the end of the survey.

Eighty participants who had left contact details were randomly selected and invited to participate in a follow-up semi-structured interview. Sixteen individuals agreed to take part and were interviewed over Microsoft Teams due to the national focus and restrictions in place at the time of interviewing. All interviews were recorded in Teams but interviewees were not required to switch on their camera. All ethical procedures (e.g. cooling off period, information sheets, informed consent, and debrief) were followed. Interviews ranged from 32 minutes to 60 minutes and were transcribed verbatim.

The survey was compromised of 5 sections: i) demographics (including household income, gender, number and age of children, access to indoor and/or outdoor space, and internet access) ii) physical activity routines prior to Covid-19, iii) physical activity during the stay-at-home phase, iv) physical activity during the stay alert phase, and v) physical activity during ongoing restrictions and lockdowns. The follow-up interviews were designed around the same format and were tailored to each participant based on their survey responses. Questions asked in the interviews were designed to understand survey responses in more depth. For example, we asked parents if they had used online PA resources during lockdown and to provide a list of the apps/resources they had used. If parents had indicated that they had used online PA resources, we explored how the apps/resources were used, how often they were used, how families had found the apps, why online PA was used and for what purposes during the follow-up interviews.

Data analysis

The interview transcripts were analysed using a thematic analysis approach. The survey and the follow-up interviews resulted in a large data set. Therefore, for the purposes of this paper, the analysis focused on aspects of the interview data that related to PA routines prior, during and after various lockdowns including the use of online activities. Familiarisation with the data was an important and necessary first phase. Transcripts were read several times and the appropriate sections of data were then coded (phase 2). Phases three, four and five included generating themes, developing and reviewing themes and then the reordering, reorganising, and renaming those initial themes. This process was undertaken with multiple highlighters and printed out transcripts before moving the relevant quotes back into word documents. The sixth phase involved 'writing matters for analysis' (i.e. writing up the analysis for dissemination) (Braun & Clarke, 2022).

To ensure participant confidentiality and anonymity, pseudonyms were used during the transcription and analysis phases (e.g. P1, P2 and so on). The authors acted as critical friends regularly discussing the analysis of data. This critical dialogue allowed us to challenge the interpretations each had made throughout the analysis process to enhance the rigour of our findings (Smith & McGannon, 2018). As middle-class mothers, we were mindful of our positioning and potential biases when designing the study, we are both women who have children under the age of 11 and whose pandemic experiences were also shaped by working full time at home with small children at home, balancing work, home-schooling and changes to family routines and family life. Having experienced these issues ourselves, we were acutely aware of the parental pressures from media, schools, social groups to ensure children were not falling behind.

Results and discussion

To provide some context to the data, 96% of our survey sample identified as White, 86% had a household income of over £30,000 and 87% perceived PA to be an important or very important part of their under 5's daily routine. The survey results indicate that 348 families (38% of our sample) tried online PA classes/sessions during the pandemic with mixed success. Demographics for the 16 participants who engaged with the follow-up interviews can be seen in Table 1.

Early years and technology use

Parenting, digital technology and screen time

Online technologies have transformed the way people access and share information and parents now also have a responsibility to keep their child(ren) safe online (Barnes & Potter, 2021). Parents are regularly provided with a narrative to protect and monitor their children's screen time and online use which Barnes and Potter (2021) argue is framed within a control paradigm. When we discussed online PA, screen time was a common theme and it seems many of the parents in our survey and subsequent interviews were keen to reduce their child(ren)'s exposure to screens during the pandemic. One parent told us:

> My daughter had quite a bit of screen time, as we used FaceTime so much. I felt like she gets more screen time already with just the video calls and I didn't really want to add too much more screen time. I'm hoping to start taking my daughters to some outside activities where she can be a bit more active (P12)

Table 1. Participant demographic data (for tailored, follow-up interviews).

I.D	Gender	Ethnicity	Household income	Work status during Covid-19	Main care giver during Covid-19	Private outdoor space	Perceived importance of PA	PA activities before Covid-19	PA cost - £ per month
P1	F	White British	More than £100,000	Mother on maternity leave	Both parents	Back garden	Essential	Swimming, football, gymnastics	£120
P2	F	White British	£56,000 - £99,000	Employed part time	Both parents	Front and back garden	Essential	Dancing, swimming, gymnastics	£25
P3	F	White British	£31,000- £55,000	Employed part time	Both parents	Yard (no grass)	Essential	Swimming, football, dance, gymnastics	£80
P4	F	White British	£31,000- £55,000	Employed part time	Both parents	Front and back garden	Essential	Football, gymnastics	£90
P5	F	White British	Less than £15,000	Lost job during lockdown/student	Grandparents	Front and back garden	Essential	Dance	£20
P6	F	White British	£31,000- £55,000	Employed full time	Grandparents	Front and back garden	Important	Football, swimming	£60
P7	M	White British	£56,000 - £99,000	Employed part time	Both parents	Front and back garden	Important	Swimming, dance, football	£250
P8	F	White British	£56,000 - £99,000	Employed full time	Nursery/Pre-school (+15 hours per week)	Back garden	Somewhat important	Gymnastics	£50
P9	F	Multiple races	£56,000 - £99,000	Employed full time	Both parents	Front and back garden other	Somewhat important	Swimming	£45+
P10	M	White British	£31,000- £55,000	Employed full time	Mother	None	Somewhat important	Swimming	£60
P11	F	White British	£16,000 - £30,000	Employed full time	Nursery/Pre-school (+15 hours per week)	Yard (no grass)	Somewhat important	Swimming, ballet, acrobatics, gymnastics	£174
P12	F	White British	£56,000 - £99,000	Employed full time	Nursery/Pre-school (+15 hours per week)	Yard (no grass)	Somewhat important	Trips to the park with our dog	£0
P13	F	White British	More than £100,000	Employed full time	Mother	Back garden, balcony	Somewhat important	Informal PA	£0
P14	F	White British	£31,000- £55,000	Employed full time	Both parents	Front and back garden	Important	Soft play	£14
P15	F	White British	£31,000- £55,000	Employed full time	Mother	Yard (no grass)	Important	Informal PA	£0
P16	F	White British	£16,000 - £30,000	Employed part time	Both parents	None	Important	No information	£0

Another parent explained why their daughter's screen time was minimised:

> I tried to continue with the baby classes that had moved online. But they were they were not very physical activity based. Ava was just obsessed with the screen ... I didn't feel right doing these things with the screen. We really wanted to limit her screen activities. I was brought up with the TV on constantly, so I wanted something a little bit different for Ava. It's the pull of the screen, it's like hypnotising ... I felt a little bit of guilt every time I put on a screen. I just wanted to take the time to go outside instead (P16)

The pressure on parents and contemporary parenting styles have meant that parents internalise concerns about screen time and feel that their children should be involved in activities which benefit them. During the pandemic parents were also adjusting to a new way of living, working, and parenting. The guilt associated with not overusing technology was something else for parents to worry about. Such worries reflect current trends in concerted cultivation where parents are under pressure to ensure that children are involved in meaningful activities which will enhance their skills (Lareau, 2003).

Covid-19 lockdowns provided many challenges for families but for those who were required to work from home and juggle childcare, digital technologies provided the opportunity to keep children entertained whilst parents worked:

> He'd [participants husband] would have an important meeting or I'd have a meeting and you just stick them on an iPad, or you stick them in front of the TV and that was the reality. I know that was the reality for a lot of children and a lot of parents, and you don't feel good about it, but you have meetings at a certain time and as much as your job might be flexible around your working hours, you have to do some of it (P2)

The pressures of reducing screen time for young children were felt by many parents, and as the parent above mentions, many did not like using screen time as an entertainment tool but thought that they had no other option when looking after children so young and needing to work. Nursery had closed for this child, leaving the parents to juggle work and childcare which proved to be exhausting. Concerns about screen time and poor parenting can be seen in the work of Vincent and Maxwell (2016) who found that giving children computer games was positioned in the Paired Peers project as passive parenting that lacked imagination and effort. The social interaction between everyday life and societal expectations is complex (Sandberg et al., 2021), and while parents and families may respond differently, all parents are aware of *how* you parent is judged by others, particularly in relation to perceived good versus bad technology use.

Suitability of online physical activity for early years children

The survey asked parents if their young children had used online physical activities during lockdown (yes/no) and asked parents to tell us which apps/online activities they had used in an open text box. Joe Wicks (marketed as an online PE lesson replacement/high intensity interval training) and Cosmic Kids (a yoga programme which uses storytelling to deliver yoga and mindfulness sessions) were the most popular online activities that our sample engaged with. We then asked parents more about their use of online PA during the follow-up interviews to explore their experiences in more depth.

Despite the debates regarding the relevance of Joe Wicks for younger children and the obvious criticism that he is not a PE teacher, Joe Wick's PE sessions were the most popular choice for our families. As mentioned above, Cosmic Kids along with other types of kids' yoga, dancing videos and general fitness sessions were also very popular, however the suitability of these sessions was raised by many parents. The age of the child(ren) was also a common discussion point. It seems that many of the pre-school children were *'too young'* to engage with online activities, even though children are becoming technology literate at an increasingly younger age (Byrne et al., 2021):

> We did give Joe Wicks a go, but I think I enjoyed it more than she [daughter] did. I think she might have been a bit too young for it. I think it was more to do with her doing exercise and having fun. I think at this age it's important that they're ... having fun. I think it was hard for Faye in the first lockdown because she was two, she was too young to understand any of the stuff that was going on the TV or YouTube. We played hide and seek a lot. We played tag a lot, all the little simple games which she seemed to enjoy (P5)

Pressures on parents, alongside the media focus on the importance of activities, such as Joe Wicks, were too much for some parents and families. However, parents were still trying to plan and facilitate activities that were deemed to be meaningful and cultivating in order to be 'good' parents.

Online activities versus live classes

Children's engagement and interest with online activities

Parents pointed out the differences in engagement between live classes (delivered before Covid-19 lockdowns) and classes delivered via online platforms during lockdown.

> It's very different seeing how she engages in the swimming classes or if we're outside. When it comes to screens, I think it's a different reaction. I'm not sure if that's to do with the technology or to do with the screen. I don't think she's old enough to stay engaged. Whereas if she's in the pool and she's with my wife then that's kind of like a controlled environment... She doesn't have the distraction of her toys or wanting to run off and do something else (P10)

Parents often made the comparison between the behaviour and concentrations levels of their child during online classes versus the in-person classes. When talking to the parents there seemed to complexities between the different PA approaches and were often pitted against each other as an either-or dichotomy, with screens depicted as problematic for early years children. For example, other parents told us that online activities did not engage their children despite efforts to get them to do the activities:

> They couldn't maintain their concentration and all three of us got really frustrated, because I'm trying to keep them interested in the classes and they're really not. I was getting frustrated with them for just messing around. They were getting frustrated with me for being so pushy about these classes. They're not going to continue it later in life, even when they're a little bit older. I don't think online classes is something that we'll be able to do properly (P11)

Parents acknowledged the importance of physical activity and often viewed it as a meaningful part of their daily routine. Many parents felt the need to pursue such activities despite a lack of interest which often led to frustration.

Some of the franchises/businesses providing baby, toddler and pre-school enrichment activities found the transition from live classes to online delivery easier than some, but for those who could deliver sessions online, it provided an opportunity to stay engaged with customers during the lockdown periods. One parent whose child was able to maintain their gymnastics activities found the move online helpful as it maintained a familiar routine:

> We did the little gym which is like a gymnastics class. They were really good actually. He liked doing the activities, but he did just like looking at the people and saying hello to them. I think more than anything for me it was the routine, for him it was more just seeing the people's faces. Obviously, it's not as good as being there in person but it's something to do (P1)

As the parent above highlights, engagement with online PA was a way for parents to maintain familiar routines by engaging with the enrichment activities undertaken prior to Covid-19 that have become a key feature of (largely but not exclusively) middle-class parenting. Many parents sought activities that they could do with their young child(ren) whilst allowing them to interact with people outside of their household.

For families that did use online activities and found them useful, many of the parents would go on to say that whilst their young child enjoyed the activities, they were not as good as going to live classes. One parent told us: *'Initially it went quite well, but she got bored much quicker than she would have done in person'* (P2).

Some of our participants mentioned the value of routine and structure these activities gave, whilst others acknowledged that they may have found the activities more beneficial than their children. Parents often found online classes beneficial initially, but their toddlers and/or preschoolers lost interest and/or did not find them as valuable or useful as face-to-face activity. The extent to which online activities can engage early years children sustainably warrants further consideration. It appears for this age group and the reasons why parents value these activities, in-person classes prevail. In-person classes are valued because they are considered to enrich children in ways that online PA cannot and therefore these opportunities cannot provide the same experiences to early years children and their parents.

Importance of specialist and social spaces for early years children
When asked why they thought that their young child(ren) engaged better in face-to-face sessions than online, many of the parents acknowledged the space in which the activities were undertaken in was an important aspect for early years children. One parent told us:

> They've gone [before lockdown] to dance and there is a specific environment, the dance floor with all the mirrors, the mats, and the equipment that they seem to recognise as dancing. I think whatever they learned to associate with the dancing, or with the dance teachers, it's not the same at home, generally. They miss the friends, the mission, the social aspect of it as well. I think they missed the routine of going to certain classes (P11)

Not only were specialist spaces acknowledged as important but so was the social element such classes provided before lockdown. The impact the pandemic would have on the development of social/emotional skills in early years children was regularly raised and discussed throughout the various lockdowns. Fox and colleagues state that socioemotional development was of the greatest concern to families and practitioners with much of the harm 'attributed to the lack of social interaction' (2021: 3). One parent explained why she was looking forward to activities resuming:

> I think what I'm looking forward to the most once things open is her socialising with other children. I think she's been so cooped up with adults. I mean there's been some benefits to that. I've noticed her speech and language come on really well because she's just been locked in with us adults. So, there's been a bit of development with her communication skills but I'd be happier seeing her spend more time with other children (P5)

She then went on to emphasise the importance of peer learning and engagement to her child:

> When she's in a group with other children she first observes, until she feels comfortable and then she joins in. I think she's very much peer led even though she has her own little ways of doing stuff . . . . I think if it's me doing it she gets bored and messes around. But if she's in a group with children of a similar age she'll join in more because she wants to be doing what the other kids are doing (P5).

For parents, they articulate the ways they consider these activities to have wider benefits for early years children to engage with others and follow their peers. Another parent stressed how socialising with other children was the main priority and a key reason for attending classes:

> I think before lockdown it was getting ready, going out, seeing other children, that was the main sort of priority. And online doesn't really do that for children. Probably better for adults I would think (P8)

Parents recognised the importance of, and associations young children make when in, specialised physical spaces, but parents also told us that their children were more likely to engage and listen to another adult (i.e. the teacher or coach as opposed to the parent). This has been a common finding across our research (Allen et al., 2021). For example, one parent highlighted:

> You can't really do gymnastics online. You haven't got the same equipment; you haven't got the same social side that you're playing in a team or playing with a partner. Yeah, it's very different . . . the Joe Wick becomes samey, like you're in your house, you're doing something online and it kind of feels very samey. Whereas when you go to a class it might be a different activity and it just feels different, and you've got more reason to engage with the person and the activities. As we all know, your own children do not listen to you as much as they listen to someone else. I think that's one of the big differences is having that teacher/coach physical person there because they absolutely listen to those more than they would listen to you trying to do a class at home (P4)

Parents often told us the important of the *expert* (e.g. the class teacher or sports coach) in getting their children to listen and follow instructions but also the reassurance that the expert has specific knowledge to develop their child in a way that parents feel they cannot. However, parents felt the expert did not work as well online and children needed to be in the same physical space to get the most out of the expert. One parent noted:

> It was completely different online. When there's a teacher in the room, she will sit, she will listen, she will follow instructions, she'll still be a bit of a loony tune, but she will engage with the teacher. With a teacher online she wasn't engaged (P3)

We have previously acknowledged that the commercial early years sport and leisure market is popular for multiple reasons but one important consideration for parents is that a professional qualified person (e.g. the teacher or coach) is perceived to be listened to more by their young child(ren), and in these settings is able to negotiate and encourage their children more effectively (Allen et al., 2021). Moreover, the baby, toddler, and pre-school market, with specialist coaches has created a space where parents are willing to pay for an activity to have a specialist lead on delivering specific PA skills.

Access and use of technology

Challenges with digital technology and devices

De' et al. (2020) argue that Covid-19 brought a necessary need for internet access and those who did not have access faced total social isolation. During lockdown digital inequality became far more apparent with those in low-income households most likely to be affected both in terms of the number and type of devices but also the amount of data available (Beaunoyer et al., 2020). One parent told us:

> With regards to the online classes, they just couldn't do them. We didn't have the technology for it ... I think maybe if I'd had better technology at home, they might have been more interested. But because it was only on my phone, they couldn't see the teacher properly ... Maybe if there was potentially a bigger screen or something like that, they would have been more engaged. If I'd had the money, I would have bought a smart TV or used Facebook rooms or do the classes with YouTube on my TV (P11)

As with access to digital technology, not all families had access to appropriate indoor and/or outdoor space. Access the families had to outdoor spaces is highlighted in Table 1 but many of families felt that online PA was in fact an indoor pursuit:

> To me it felt like we needed to be doing it outside but then the [football] videos needed to be inside ... it could have been on a tablet or phone, but we didn't actually use them even though they were provided (P4)

The fact that families conducted online activities indoors appeared to cause some issues – replicating sport classes in an indoor home setting appeared to be challenging as one Father pointed out:

> We set up little activities for Oscar like training drills that he does in football to replicate them indoors with some training discs and some cones and that kind of stuff and just got him to go around the living room, that was quite fun, interactive, but we don't live in a mansion, so it's not possible to replicate what they have in the sports hall (P7)

It was also apparent that for some families, PA was enjoyed more in outdoor spaces. This was a common finding in our survey data, where parents told us that during the first lockdown their early years children were active in outdoor spaces (in line the restrictions and exercise guidelines), largely in part to the nice weather the UK was experiencing at the time (Allen & Velija, in press):

> [We preferred] doing the stuff properly outside rather than being inside watching somebody else exercise inside. It's just depressing. If you're gonna do something, do it outside (P14)

Sustainability of online physical activity beyond the pandemic

The pandemic caused many families to adapt and change their usual routines with 38% of the families in our study trying online PA. As we have discussed throughout the paper, there were mixed responses to this new way of being active and we sought to understand how sustainable online PA would be once pandemic restrictions were lifted. When parents were asked if they would use online PA classes beyond the pandemic one parent said:

> I'm gonna carry on with the yoga and meditation because we've been quite enjoying that, and I'm trying to teach her about mindfulness. We'll definitely carry on with some of the things we've discovered on YouTube that she seems to enjoy. But I am really excited for things opening for her. You know, being out there and playing with other kids (P4)

Whilst some of the families we spoke to enjoyed online PA classes, in-person classes prevailed for many parents. For this parent, the dichotomy was not online versus in-person but rather that online PA filled a gap during the pandemic and the online classes that were enjoyed and valued would be included in future routines. However, the overwhelming response was that online activity was unlikely to be part of family routines once restrictions were lifted and pre-lockdown routines could be restarted. One parent said:

> I hope not. I know that there's some baby classes that we did that are still running. Although they are back in person this week, they are still running them online because they've noticed that there's a market for people that can't get out or might be feeling anxious or just having a bad day or whatever that they're still running their sessions online. But I think a lot of it for me is getting out the house. I think she's much more focused if we're actually in the place and she gets a lot more out of it if she's actually in person with the actual prop, seeing other children do the same things that she's doing (P2)

Another parent acknowledged that online PA would remain part of her own routine but was unlikely that her children would continue to engage with online classes, suggesting that online PA provide meaningful experiences for adults but are not perceived to be as valuable for young children:

> I use them for myself. But in terms of my children – probably not. Now we can get out when we can, we can ride our bikes and we can go outside and things like that. I might consider it over winter.... but I probably wouldn't (P15).

Finally, when asked the same question another parent told us:

> If something happened and then they offered an online one because of how things went, we might try it again, but it's not something I would openly pay for. On the flip side, I do see if you are someone with limited transport, if you or someone with limited funds, it may be more beneficial and something that they would be interested in, but just for us it wouldn't be something I would be willing to pay for if it was just online. We are lucky we have cars; we can travel. We have the financial ability to pay for these sessions that are £7, £8, £9 a session for each of them. But if you're in a flat with no car then maybe online would be good. No garden, then something online may be very positive. We're lucky, I guess it's a bit selfish (P4)

It is middle-class parents who are most able to invest in numerous enrichment activities for their young children, and in the case of P4, are aware of this. This parent highlights that online activities might have their place for those without the access to space and travel but those with available funds are able to secure more opportunities for their child(ren).

Conclusion and future considerations

This article highlights the dominance and popularity of commercialised franchises and businesses providing sport-based classes for early years children, as well as presenting what parents did to adapt when these in-person, commercial classes were suddenly removed from family routine. Our data emphasises the reasons why parents value structured and external PA and the perceived benefits they bring. We argue that there are aspects of concerted cultivation in the decisions they make. Concerns that parents have about increased screen time is not only focused on developmental issues but also concerns about what constitutes good parenting. Sourcing opportunities for children to experience a range of enrichment activities is now part of contemporary (middle-class) parenting. This reflects wider trends in parenting identified by Lareau (2003) whereby parents which the capital to do so choose activities that they perceive can enrich their children's skills in ways that may benefit them in school and other settings. While Lareau (2003) and others (e.g., Vincent and Maxwell, 2016; Wheeler and Green, 2018; 2019) have identified patterns relating to concerted cultivation in older children, our research alongside Vincent, Smyth and Harlow et al. suggests a downtrend in which parents of pre-school children are also encouraged to seek opportunities from increasingly earlier ages.

Our data shows that the pandemic resulted in a reduction in PA for many toddlers and pre-school aged children – a trend that appears to be consistent across age groups and countries that experienced similar restrictions to the UK. Digital platforms provided an alternative way for people to maintain their activity in their home environment and were used by over a third of our survey sample. While some found online exercise and PA videos useful, most found them to be a different experience. Online PA classes aimed at toddlers and pre-schoolers did not provide the types of cultivation that parents valued such as expert led engagement with the child, socialisation through group interaction, and routine out of the house that middle-class parents seemed to value and were willing to pay for. Whilst this is not the case for all parents, we certainly identified patterns of behaviour around a desire and pressure experienced by parents for cultivation within our study.

The innovation of digital technology appears to be relentless. Parents and ECE providers have a responsibility to teach young children how to navigate the digital world. Therefore, further research on the suitability of online PA is warranted to understand the use of online PA across the home and ECE settings. Whilst online PA was not appealing for the majority of parents we spoke to, it is possible that online PA has real potential moving forward. As privatisation is here stay (Evans & Davies, 2015), online PA may be of use to families who do not have the economical capital to access the enrichment activities offered by commercialised businesses. Online PA could provide an alternative provision but it could equally be another space that some families are excluded from such as those living in poverty who cannot afford the technology devices and internet access to engage online. There is also a need to understand the use of online PA in ECE and school settings (Joseph et al., 2019). Therefore, we recommend further research is conducted to understand the suitability and sustainability for children and their families to understand who online PA works for and in what situations.

While this paper focused on parents, and their decision making and views, the nature of the pandemic and the age range of the early years children, it was (and continues to be) the parents who ultimately made decisions about the physical activities undertaken by their child(ren). Our article therefore has provided a unique insight into their views of online PA with early years children during UK lockdowns and moving beyond pandemic restrictions. However, further work is warranted as we learn to live with Covid-19 and move beyond the pandemic.

Disclosure statement

No potential conflict of interest was reported by the author(s).

ORCID

Georgia Allen http://orcid.org/0000-0003-0778-7558
Philippa Velija http://orcid.org/0000-0001-7689-4803

References

Allen, G., & Velija, P. (in press). Toddler and pre-school children's physical activity during a pandemic. In Sharp, B., Finkel, R., & Dashper, K. (Eds.), *Leisure in the pandemic: Re-imagining interaction and activity during crisis*. Routledge.

Allen, G., Velija, P., & Dodds, J. (2021). 'We just thought everyone else is going so we might as well': Middle-class parenting and franchised baby/toddler swimming. *Leisure Studies*, *40*(2), 169–182. https://doi.org/10.1080/02614367.2020.1820555

Allmann, K. (2020, April 14). *Covid-19 is increasing digital inequality: We need human connectivity to close the digital divide*. The Oxfordshire Digital Inclusion Project. https://www.law.ox.ac.uk/research-and-subject-groups/oxfordshire-digital-inclusion-project/blog/2020/04/covid-19-increasing

Ball, S. J. (2003). *Class strategies and the education market: The middle classes and social advantage*. Routledge.

Barnes, R., & Potter, A. (2021). Sharenting and parents' digital literacy: An agenda for future research. *Communication Research and Practice*, *7*(1), 6–20. https://doi.org/10.1080/22041451.2020.1847819

Beaunoyer, E., Dupéré, S., & Guitton, M. J. (2020). COVID-19 and digital inequalities: Reciprocal impacts and mitigation strategies. *Computers in Human Behavior*, *111*(6), 106424. https://doi.org/10.1016/j.chb.2020.106424

Braun, V., & Clarke, V. (2022). *Thematic analysis: A practical guide*. Sage.

Byrne, R., Terranova, C. O., & Trost, S. G. (2021). Measurement of screen time among young children aged 0–6 years: A systematic review. *Obesity Reviews : An Official Journal of the International Association for the Study of Obesity*, *22*(8), e13260. https://doi.org/10.1111/obr.13260

Chung, H., Seo, H., Forbes, S., & Birkett, H. (2020). *Working from home during the COVID-19 lockdown: Changing preferences and the future of work*. https://drive.google.com/file/d/1OoyxkO__fCKzMCnG2Ld14fVI8Hl7xRGe/view

De', R., Pandey, N., & Pal, A. (2020). Impact of digital surge during Covid-19 pandemic: A viewpoint on research and practice. *International Journal of Information Management*, *55*(1), 102171. https://doi.org/10.1016/j.ijinfomgt.2020.102171

Evans, J., & Davies, B. (2014). Physical education PLC: Neoliberalism, curriculum, and governance. New directions for PESP research. *Sport, Education and Society*, *19*(7), 869–884. https://doi.org/10.1080/13573322.2013.850072

Evans, J., & Davies, B. (2015). Physical education, privatisation, and social justice. *Sport, Education and Society*, *20*(1), 1–9. https://doi.org/10.1080/13573322.2014.942624

Gabriel, N. (2017). *The sociology of early childhood: Critical perspectives*. Sage.

Harlow, M., Wolman, L., & Fraser-Thomas, J. (2020). Should toddlers and pre-schoolers participate in organized sport? A scoping review of developmental outcomes associated with young children's sport participation. *International Review of Sport and Exercise Psychology*, *13*(1), 40–64. https://doi.org/10.1080/1750984X.2018.1550796

Ito, M. (2019). *Hanging out, messing around, and geeking out: Kids living and learning with new media* (10th ed.). MIT Press.

Joseph, E. D., Kracht, C. L., St Romain, J., Allen, A. T., Barbaree, C., Martin, C. K., & Staiano, A. E. (2019). Young children's screen time and physical activity: Perspectives of parents and early care and education center providers. *Global Paediatric Health*, *6*(1), 2333794X19865856. https://doi.org/10.1177/2333794X19865856

Laidlaw, L., O'Mara, J., & Wong, S. S. H. (2021). 'This is your brain on devices': Media accounts of young children's use of digital technologies and implications for parents and teachers. *Contemporary Issues in Early Childhood*, *22*(3), 268–281. https://doi.org/10.1177/1463949119867400

Lareau, A. (2003). *Unequal childhoods. Class, race, and family life*. University of California Press.

Livingstone, S., & Blum-Ross, A. (2020). *Parenting for a digital future: How hopes and fears about technology shape children's lives*. Oxford University Press.

Malcolm, D., & Velija, P. (2020). COVID-19, exercise, and bodily self-control. *Sociología Del Deporte*, *1*(1), 29–34. https://doi.org/10.46661/socioldeporte.5011

Marsh, J., Plowman, L., & Yamada-Rice, D. (2016). Digital play: A new classification. *Early Years*, *36*(3), 242–253. https://doi.org/10.1080/09575146.2016.1167675

Mollborn, S., Limburg, A., Pace, J., & Fomby, P. (2022). Family socioeconomic status and children's screen time. *Journal of Marriage and Family*, *84*(4), 1129–1151. https://doi.org/10.1111/jomf.12834

Powell, D. (2015). Assembling the privatisation of physical education and the 'inexpert' teacher. *Sport, Education and Society*, *20*(1), 73–88. https://doi.org/10.1080/13573322.2014.941796

Sandberg, H., Sjöberg, U., & Sundin, E. (2021). Toddlers' digital media practices and everyday parental struggles: Interactions and meaning making as digital media are domesticated. *Nordicom Review*, *42*(s4), 59–78. https://doi.org/10.2478/nor-2021-0041

Smith, B., & McGannon, K. R. (2018). Developing rigor in qualitative research: Problems and opportunities within sport and exercise psychology. *International Review of Sport and Exercise Psychology*, *11*(1), 101–121.

Smyth, C. (2016). Getting ahead in the preschool years: An analysis of a preschool enrichment and entertainment market. *Sociology, 50*(4), 731–747. https://doi.org/10.1177/0038038515577916

Sport England. (2021) *Children's activity levels down but many embrace new opportunities.* https://www.sportengland.org/news/childrens-activity-levels-down-many-embrace-new-opportunities

Stenning, A. (2019). *Space to play? Austerity and the loss of play.* The future of the Civic Culture in the UK. https://blogs.ncl.ac.uk/civicculture/2019/10/03/space-to-play-austerity-and-the-loss-of-play/

Stirrup, J., Duncombe, R., & Sandford, R. (2014). Intensive mothering' in the early years: The cultivation and consolidation of (physical) capital. *Sport, Education and Society, 20*(1), 89–106. https://doi.org/10.1080/13573322.2014.941797

Timmons, N. (2021). *Schools and coronavirus: The government's handling of education during the pandemic.* Institute for Government. Retrieved October 6, 2022, from https://www.instituteforgovernment.org.uk/sites/default/files/publications/schools-and-coronavirus.pdf

Vincent, C., & Ball, S. J. (2007). Making up the middle-class child: Families, activities, and class dispositions. *Sociology, 41*(6), 1061–1077. https://doi.org/10.1177/0038038507082315

Vincent, C., & Maxwell, C. (2016). Parenting priorities and pressures: Furthering understanding of 'concerted cultivation'. *Discourse: Studies in the Cultural Politics of Education, 37*(2), 269–281. https://doi.org/10.1080/01596306.2015.1014880

Wheeler, S. (2018). 'Essential assistance' versus 'concerted cultivation': Theorising class-based patterns of parenting in Britain. *Pedagogy, Culture & Society, 26*(3), 327–344. https://doi.org/10.1080/14681366.2017.1401551

Wheeler, S., & Green, K. (2014). Parenting in relation to children's sports participation: Generational changes and potential implications. *Leisure Studies, 33*(3), 267–284. https://doi.org/10.1080/02614367.2012.707227

Wheeler, S., & Green, K. (2019). 'The helping, the fixtures, the kits, the gear, the gum shields, the food, the snacks, the waiting, the rain, the car rides...': Social class, parenting, and children's organised activities. *Sport, Education and Society, 24*(8), 788–800. https://doi.org/10.1080/13573322.2018.1470087

ⓐ OPEN ACCESS

Cultural consumption and Covid-19: evidence from the *Taking Part* and *COVID-19 Cultural Participation Monitor* surveys

Tal Feder, Siobhan McAndrew, Dave O'Brien and Mark Taylor

ABSTRACT
How did cultural consumption change during the Covid-19 pandemic? Whilst the impact of the pandemic on cultural production has been given significant attention, work on consumption has seen less attention. This paper addresses this gap in the literature by presenting a comparative analysis of two, nationally representative, surveys of cultural activity in England. The analysis demonstrates that, when cultural consumption moved online and to digital modes of delivery and engagement as a result of the pandemic, there was no discernible transformation in the stratification of cultural participation in England. The majority of the population, characterised by the absence of participation in formal, and often state-funded, cultural forms, saw no change to their patterns of engagement. Where cultural consumption did increase, this was among the small minority of people who were already highly engaged. This minority maps closely onto pre-existing inequalities identified by existing research on cultural consumption, in England and beyond. For cultural consumption and the stratification of taste, it seems that the 'new normal' of pandemic life was much like the 'old normal' of an art and cultural audience characterised by significant inequality.

The global pandemic that began in 2020 saw terrible damage to societies across the world. The medical crisis brought by Covid-19 went hand in hand with efforts by states and communities to slow viral transmission. For many nations, these efforts were some form of lockdown, shelter in place, or stay at home orders. For many cultural organisations, this meant an immediate stop in both production and consumption. TV and film production was stopped, and galleries, concert venues, and theatres were closed.

Consumers faced a restricted choice of options on how to spend their time, with some experiencing a sharp increase in leisure time although others, due to caring responsibilities, experienced a sharp decline (Roberts, 2020). During the first weeks of 'life under lockdown' many popular accounts emerged of people taking up new cultural interests or enhancing proficiency in cultural practices at home, for example, cooking, drawing, or playing a musical instrument.

In the UK, the initial lockdown of March 2020 demonstrated the agility of much of the cultural and creative sector. The sector saw a proliferation of new modes of engagement with culture, including theatre productions delivered online, virtual museum tours, and livestreamed gigs from musicians' homes. Arts Council England's first emergency response package of £160 million, released on 24 March 2020, was primarily designed to ensure the financial survival of subsidised

---

ⓑ Supplemental data for this article can be accessed online at https://doi.org/10.1080/02614367.2022.2088831

This is an Open Access article distributed under the terms of the Creative Commons Attribution License (http://creativecommons.org/licenses/by/4.0/), which permits unrestricted use, distribution, and reproduction in any medium, provided the original work is properly cited.

organisations and self-employed practitioners facing a catastrophic loss of income and mothballing costs (ACE 2020). The package was also intended to 'buoy the public' during lockdown (Brown, 2020), with the 'National Theatre at Home' Thursday night broadcasts of previously-recorded productions via YouTube a significant early example (Brown, 2020a). At the same time as many people working in the cultural and creative sectors lost projects, employment, and income with the closure of venues, rehearsal,recording spaces and studios, the digital response opened up new consumption opportunities and the promise of new income sources, along with a diversified audience and consumption base.

The contrasting nature of Spring 2020 seemed to demonstrate the importance of culture, even as some of the key industries *making* culture were under severe threats to their future. Several high-profile voices demanded that there should be no return to the pre-pandemic status quo, shedding light on the inequalities revealed during the pandemic and the crisis it caused for the cultural sector (Giles 2020; Iskander, 2020; White Pube 2020). The sector's deep-rooted inequalities, particularly with regard to its workforce, were out into the spotlight at the point that the social importance of cultural engagement, in the sudden absence of communal, in person, events was clear.

This paper uses these discourses as a starting point for its analysis. Whilst the impact of the pandemic on cultural *production* has been given significant attention (Banks and O'Connor 2020; Banks, 2020; Comunian & England, 2020; Eikhof, 2020; Joffe, 2021; Kay & Wood, 2020), work on *consumption* has seen less attention (Roberts, 2020 on leisure time and NESTA 2020 notwithstanding). Indeed, 2020 seemed to be a moment where the abundance of culture, enabled by digital technology (Beer, 2013; Wright, 2011), *might* have become newly-accessible to a whole range of audiences in ways that were not possible in site-specific and synchronous contexts.

To consider the impact of the pandemic on cultural consumption, the paper presents a comparative analysis of two, nationally representative, surveys of cultural activity in England. We focus our analysis on the cultural and leisure activities, both physical and online, that were available both before and during the pandemic, such as reading, online performances, and art. We ask whether the change in the availability of cultural activities- the decline in physical consumption opportunities and increased supply of online cultural products- affected the cultural lifestyles of the British population.

The analysis demonstrates that, as cultural consumption moved online and to digital modes of delivery and engagement as a result of the pandemic, there was no discernible transformation in the stratification of cultural participation in England. The majority of the population, characterised by the absence of participation in formal, and often state-funded, cultural forms, saw no change to their patterns of engagement. Where cultural consumption did increase, this was among the small minority of people who were already more likely to be highly engaged, while reduction of cultural activities was associated with groups that typically face barriers to cultural consumption. These patterns map closely onto pre-existing inequalities identified by existing research on cultural consumption, in England and beyond.

The analysis is significant for two reasons. For the existing literature it confirms the 'stickiness' of tastes and lifestyles, even in conditions of unexpected social rupture. For the cultural sector, both practitioners and policymakers, it confirms that the inequalities within arts and culture will be unchanged, or even worsened, by the impact of the pandemic. In terms of cultural consumption and the stratification of taste, it seems that the 'new normal' of pandemic life was much like the 'old normal' of an art and cultural audience characterised by significant inequality.

Understanding the stratification of cultural consumption

An extensive literature on cultural consumption, primarily sociological in origin, has identified the differentiation and stratification of cultural preferences and tastes across a range of societies. A prominent intervention is Bourdieu's (1984) *Distinction*, which demonstrated a clear association between social position and taste in France during the 1960s and 1970s.

A substantial body of subsequent research, using a wide range of research methods, has found similar findings in a number of different countries (e.g. Bennett et al., 2009; Lena, 2019), and via cross-national comparisons (Falk & Falk, 2011; Falk et al., 2016; Katz-Gerro, 2017; Lagaert et al., 2018; Reeves, 2019; Van Hek & Kraaykamp, 2013). Extensive, often highly-technical, academic debates have taken place since the first edition of *Distinction* regarding whether and how Bourdieusian theories can be tested. Yet the connection between tastes (as measured by attendance at, participation in, knowledge of, and preferences for, a range of cultural forms), cultural hierarchies, and social inequalities is clear (see, Hanquinet, 2017 for an overview).

The exact nature of these relationships provides much of the motivation for continued sociological research into the social stratification of cultural consumption. These include debates about the importance of different demographic characteristics, including age, gender, and ethnic group (eg DiMaggio & Mukhtar, 2004; Katz-Gerro & Sullivan, 2010; Kraaykamp & Dijkstra, 1999; Meghji, 2019; Patterson, 2020); which measure provides the strongest explanation of tastes and behaviour, whether social class, social status, or education (eg Chan, 2010; Reeves, 2015); and the impact of geographical location (Brook, 2013; Cutts & Widdop, 2017; Leguina & Miles, 2017; Widdop & Cutts, 2012).

For a fuller understanding of the impact of the pandemic on cultural consumption, two additional issues are critical. First, in addition to understanding which variables matter for variation in cultural consumption, researchers must also reflect on how cultural consumption can be measured. Several studies focus on tastes for different musical genres (Bryson, 1996; Katz-Gerro, 1999; Peterson & Kern, 1996), while others address attendance at different events, although limiting analysis to what are sometimes termed 'highbrow' activities, such as classical music concerts, ballets, and visual art museums (Christin, 2012; Kracman, 1996).

Secondly, researchers must consider analytic strategy: whether measures of cultural taste or engagement are treated as distinct from one another, for example, by investigating the social stratification of attendance at different types of event separately; or by analysing such measures jointly, for example, by generating clusters, scales or factors. With regard to cluster analysis, people are grouped together on the basis of shared patterns of cultural consumption. In some cases, this clustering is applied to variables within a broad artform, such as responses to questions about attending different settings exhibiting visual art (Chan & Goldthorpe, 2007); in others, individuals are classified on the basis of their activity across art forms (for example, Bunting et al., 2008). Specific technical debates and competing definitions notwithstanding (de Vries & Reeves, 2021), research findings within this field are remarkably consistent in finding regularities in the social stratification of cultural consumption, regardless of the way that cultural consumption itself is measured.

One consequence of these two issues is that 'cultural consumption' ends up being treated as shorthand for 'the subsidised arts sector'. Descriptors such as 'nonparticipants' or 'non-consumers' are used to describe people who do, in fact, have active lives filled with active leisure, although those activities are not conventionally captured in social surveys or included in formal models (Taylor, 2016). The standard questions used in surveys may not make meaningful sense to those answering the questions, particularly people from minority groups (Novak-Leonard et al., 2015). As a result, the translation to policy can omit key nuances, with groups of 'nonparticipants' constructed as a problem to be solved (Stevenson, 2013). Given these issues, care needs to be taken to ensure that as broad a definition of culture as possible is used to understand changes in participation as a consequence of the pandemic. The publicly-funded sector is only a subset of people's pandemic leisure activities (Roberts, 2020).

The impact of digital

As with the study of the stratification of cultural consumption, there are analogous issues in the digital realm. Much of the research on cultural consumption has, arguably, reflected institutional arrangements and consumption practices premised on a relatively limited range subsidised cultural forms, attendance modes, and broadcasting technologies. The rise of a variety of digital forms of culture, both in terms of consumption and production, suggests a different context from the one shaping *Distinction*'s analysis. Indeed, for many initial theorists of digital culture (e.g. Barlow, 1996), digital engagement and activity offered the possibility of dissolving some of the hierarchies and divisions associated with art and culture. In the English context, from which this paper's data is drawn, various public policy and associated thinktank activity has hailed the potential of digital to transform the cultural sector (Department for Digital, Culture, Media and Sports, 2018).

However, there is a research consensus on need for caution, if not outright scepticism, regarding the impact of digital culture on distinctions, differences, and divisions. These range from critics analysing the limitations of algorithmic recommendations by digital platforms such as Netflix, YouTube, and Spotify (e.g. Beer, 2013; Wright, 2011), through to more general critiques of algorithmic decision-making (Noble, 2018), user experiences online (Carmi, 2020), and personalisation technologies (Kant, 2020). These more general critiques mirror concerns over the impact of digitalisation on cultural workers (e.g. Christin, 2020; Patel, 2020) and social inequalities more generally (Helsper, 2020, Sobande, 2020a, 2020b). Indeed, for scholars of leisure (e.g. Lupton, 2016; Redhead, 2016; Silk et al., 2016), optimistic perceptions of the possibilities offered by digital, such as greater citizen influence over media industries (McGillivray, 2014; McGillivray et al., 2016), are tempered by recognition of the need to attend to the reproduction of existing, alongside the emergence of new, digital inequalities such as barriers to internet access (Ofcom, 2021).

Replication of existing inequalities is clearly demonstrated by Mihelj et al. (2019). Using the UK's Department for Digital, Culture, Media, and Sport's *Taking Part* survey of cultural consumption in England (the same dataset used for part of the analysis in this paper), Mihelj et al. find that, for museums and art galleries, digital modes of engagement mirror 'offline' behaviours; existing inequalities are replicated. Whilst digital activities engage new audiences, these audiences have the sorts of demographic characteristics that form the bulk of the existing audience for museums and galleries. Indeed, as they point out '*Belonging to higher occupational classes, having a degree, not having a disability or longstanding illness, and residing in the capital city all remain strong predictors of participation, while ethnicity has a strong negative effect. Most worryingly, the gaps between the haves and the have nots are even wider online than in the case of physical visits. This means that rather than helping increase the diversity of audiences, online access seems to reproduce, if not enlarge, existing inequalities*'. Mihelj et al. (2019).

This pattern is neither confined to museums and galleries, nor to England. Using Swiss data, Weingartner (2021) found most forms of digital media, excluding television, followed the pattern of reproducing the sorts of stratification patterns, and thus inequalities, commonly found in the cultural consumption literature. In Spain, Montoro-Pons and Cuadrado-García (2020) identified continuing cultural hierarchies in music consumption despite the use of seemingly democratising means of digital engagement.

What, then, should we expect in terms of change to cultural consumption patterns in the context of the Covid-19 pandemic? The unavailability of many in-person cultural and leisure activities, both highbrow and popular, can be expected to drive many consumers to enhance their activity within the limited selection of activities that are still accessible, such as reading and TV watching. They may also exploit the opportunity to take on new activities that were not pursued before, such as art creation or exercise.

Additionally, policy and practitioner voices have faith in digital to engage new audiences and enhance the consumption of existing, already engaged individuals (Department for Digital, Culture, Media and Sports [DCMS], 2018; Ofcom, 2021). Therefore, we could also expect to see a wide increase in online cultural activity. This would be driven by digital newcomers joining previously active consumers who are transferring their consumption habits from the physical to the online realm.

On the other hand, the academic research base suggests we should not expect to see dramatic changes in cultural consumption patterns. Rather we should expect the replication, and perhaps acceleration, of the inequalities and stratification patterns found in what Mihelj et al. (2019) call the 'off-line' cultural world. Cultural lifestyles are embedded behaviours that are not likely to shift abruptly due to changes in external conditions such as those brought by the pandemic. The adoption of new cultural behaviours may be more likely to happen among those already active, while remaining inaccessible to individuals with lower levels of pre- existing cultural engagements. Moreover, online fatigue and increased external constraints aggravated by the pandemic, such as parenting, health, or work, may lead to a reduction of cultural and leisure activity. These constraints are likely to affect those who are already less culturally active, thus exacerbating existing inequalities.

We study these questions empirically by looking at physical and online cultural and leisure activities that were available both before and during the pandemic. The following section describes how we analysed data on changes in consumption of these items between pre-pandemic and pandemic periods, in order to identify patterns of change and resilience in cultural consumption and their corresponding social profiles.

Data and methods

Data

In order to interrogate the impact of the pandemic, the paper uses two data sources: the DCMS Taking Part Web Panel COVID-19, and the Audience Agency COVID-19 Cultural Participation Monitor surveys. The analysis of the two datasets in parallel, helps us to strengthen the validity of our results and serves as a robustness check to the models presented below. The datasets do not have identical scopes, and each contains a slightly different set of questions. Due to the relative complexity of the method and data structure, this difference is beneficial in confirming that our results have general applicability.

The Taking Part Web Panel COVID-19 survey (TPCOVID) was conducted in three waves in May, June and July 2020 (DCMS, 2018). At the conclusion of their interviews for the standard face-to-face surveys, respondents to the Taking Part regular survey are asked if they are willing to participate in further surveys online in subsequent quarters. Our respondents here are drawn from this pool. The survey contains around 1000 respondents in each of the three waves. However, for the analyses in this paper, we pooled all the respondents together. Most of the respondents participated only in one wave of the survey. For respondents that participated in more than one wave, we kept only a single observation that was randomly selected, so as to not include any individuals more than once. The final data file contains 2175 distinct respondents.

We focus on responses to questions about engagement with 41 different activities, where respondents were furthermore asked about the amount of time they have spent on them since the introduction of restrictions by the UK Government in March 2020. These activities cover a wide range, including traditional highbrow cultural activities often studied as part of research into cultural consumption, popular cultural activities, and general leisure activities such as physical exercise or online calls with friends and family. The available response options are 'less time', 'about the same', 'more time', and 'I never do this'. We acknowledge that these categories are imprecise with regards to the magnitude of change, however they capture the most significant aspect of it – its direction (positive or negative). This allows us to investigate the change in respondents' cultural consumption occurring since the start of the pandemic. Table A1 in the online appendix summarises the set of activities by change in frequency of engagement.

Second, the Audience Agency COVID-19 Cultural Participation Monitor survey has been conducted via several waves over the course of the pandemic. Here, we report data collected in the second wave of the survey (TAAW2), which includes questions similar to those drawn from TPCOVID. For TAAW2, a sample of 1,503 respondents, representative of the UK population, was drawn on February 2021.

We analysed questions indicating whether they had done any of a list of 42 leisure activities during the pandemic. Where they provided a positive response for a particular activity, the respondents were also asked about their frequency of engagement. Response options comprised 'fewer times', 'same', 'more times', or 'I did this for the first time during the pandemic'. The category 'I did this for the first time during the pandemic' was, in most cases, very small. These categories were re-coded in order to match those of the TPCOVID data and eliminate inconsistencies in the responses (see figure A1 in the online appendix). TAAW2 also included 15 questions about engagement in in-person activities, such as going to a dance performance or a museum during the pandemic. Since these activities were mostly unavailable at the time, we did not use these questions in our analysis save for those pertaining to outdoor activities (e.g. visiting a historic park or garden) where analogues were available in Taking Part. Table A2 in the online appendix presents the activities and the frequencies of the different responses from TAAW2 after this recoding.

Although the questions that we analysed from both data sources were similar in many respects, they still possess significant differences that encouraged us to examine each dataset as complementary but individually-valuable sources. First, the activities asked about in the two surveys are not phrased in the same way, and many appear on only one of the surveys. Secondly, the TPCOVID questionnaire asks respondents to compare the *amount* of time dedicated to leisure activities during an *unspecified* period before the pandemic, whereas TAAW2 questionnaire asks about the *number* of times in a specific period of *one year* before the pandemic. Thirdly, TAAW2 respondents were asked about their change in an activity only if they indicated earlier that they had done this activity during the pandemic, whereas all TPCOVID respondents were asked to indicate change in level of activity for all items. Crucially, the data collection for the two surveys also took place at different time periods (summer 2020 and February 2021), when restrictions on activity in England were significantly different. While the amount of in-person cultural activity was similarly limited in both, TPCOVID took place in a context where restrictions were being lifted, while TAAW2 survey took place while extensive restrictions had been re-imposed.

Analysis

We ran the same analytic procedure on both data sources. First, we ran a hierarchical cluster analysis of the cultural consumption variables (41/30, depending on the dataset) as a dimension reduction exercise, in order to construct scales for analysis. Since both datasets contain subsets of related activities, the subsequent analysis steps would be affected by the size of those sets and may assign more weight to larger groups of related items. We ran the clustering analysis in the initial step to reduce that bias and ensure that each type of activity gets a similar weight in the following steps. Clustering of cultural activities using statistical methods such as Factor Analysis or Hierarchical Cluster Analysis prior to the analysis of consumption is a common practice in cultural consumption research (Leguina & Miles, 2017; Taylor, 2016; Van Eijck, 2001). In this study, we employ a hierarchical cluster analysis that is suited to handle categorical unordered data by using the ClustOfVar R package (Chavent et al., 2012).

Second, we ran latent class analysis (LCA) on these scales, in order to identify clusters of individuals with similar changes (or lack of change) in their cultural consumption by using the poLCA R package (Linzer & Lewis, 2011). The use of the LCA methodology in the paper is built on the premise that cultural lifestyles are represented in observable patterns of cultural consumption. LCA can specify these groups (classes) by identifying individuals who share the same cultural consumption patterns. For that reason, LCA is often used in cultural and leisure consumption research (e.g. Alderson et al., 2007; Chan & Goldthorpe, 2007; Widdop & Cutts, 2013). In the context of our research, the LCA method aims to identify changes in broad consumption patterns during the pandemic. We are interested in discerning between those that changed the volume of their cultural and leisure consumption during the pandemic, negatively and positively, and those whose consumption modes were not affected by the pandemic situation. Since the initial cultural activities clustering procedure yields several groups of distinct cultural activities, the LCA is more parsimonious and prevents the necessity of running a separate model for each group of activities that would result in a fragmented set of findings. Significant differences in consumers profiles between groups of cultural items will show up as separate latent classes. Since the data only indicates the direction of the consumption change (i.e. less, more, same), we cannot relate to the difference as a continuous scale but rather as categories of change.

Third, we used multinomial regression, with these latent classes as dependent variables, to test whether those variables associated with cultural consumption outside of a pandemic context are equally found to be associated with change in cultural consumption following the introduction of pandemic-related public health restrictions.

Taking Part (TPCOVID) data

We conducted a hierarchical cluster analysis of the activity items in the TPCOVID (see Figure A2 in the online appendix). Employing an adjusted Rand criterion on the resulting hierarchical tree suggested items segmented into 9 clusters of activities. Ranked from the clusters containing more common activities to the most infrequent, we label them as follows: Cluster 1 – TV, Cluster 2 – Outdoor activity, Cluster 3 – Media reading and listening, Cluster 4 – Sports watching, Cluster 5 – Online art and performance, Cluster 6 – Exercise, Cluster 7 – Video games, Cluster 8 – Online heritage and library, Cluster 9 – Creative activities. Table A3 in the online appendix presents the resulting clusters, assigned with labels according to their content. Items allocated to the first cluster all involved cultural creation: writing, performing music, drawing and painting and so on at home. TV watching of different forms – via synchronous broadcasts, or free or subscription-based on demand services – formed cluster 1. Cluster 3 grouped radio-listening with listening to podcasts and audiobooks, alongside items relating to reading books and magazines.

Since the pandemic encouraged seeking out online consumption modes and increased the offering of live online events, we might have expected that clustering of variables capturing change in consumption might yield clusters based on medium of consumption such as online activities, live-streamed events and so on. However, the cluster analysis demonstrated the importance of content over medium. For example, change in watching live music, dance or art events were clustered (i.e. correlated more strongly) with change in watching pre-recorded music, dance or art events cluster 5) rather than watching live TV (cluster 1) or participating in a live exercise or dance class (cluster 6). Cluster 2 encompassed visiting particular sites for exercise, such as parks, historic gardens, places of historic or archaeological interest. Cluster 8 captured taking virtual tours of museums and galleries and sites of historic interest, as well as engagement with historical research online and use of online library services. Cluster 7 grouped together different measures of video gaming, including online betting, and cluster 4 watching pre-recorded sports and eSports events online. The clusters suggest that reported change in engagement were primarily shaped by pre-existing cultural tastes rather than by new consumption opportunities provided as a result of the pandemic, both in terms of availability of consumers' time and the works and resources made newly-available online.

We next conducted a latent class analysis to identify classes of respondents that share similar patterns of change in their leisure activities. We used the clusters stemming from the hierarchical cluster analysis above to generate indicators of change in consumption. We did so by assigning each respondent the modal value regarding change in consumption for the items within each cluster. For example, a respondent that increased her viewing of live arts event and live music or dance performance online, while maintaining the same level of watching pre-recorded arts events and also reducing watching pre-recorded performances, would be classified as increasing consumption of cluster 5 activities. In the case of a multimodal distribution (more than a single mode value) we used the following criterion: if one of the values is 'I never do this', we used is the other value, that is indicating change as the mode, and if both values indicate change, we used the lower value (e.g. 'less' over 'same'). The number of incidents where two of the modes values were 'more' and 'less' at the same time is negligible (for example, 8 out of 2175 respondents in cluster 5 of TPCOVID data). Both BIC and cAIC criteria pointed to a four-class solution as best fitting the data (see Figure A3 online appendix). Figure 1 displays the four classes graphically, summarising the average reported activity pattern for each of the 9 clusters for these four classes in turn.

The first class, consisting of 14% of the sample, is characterised primarily by intensification of activity. The second class (18% of the sample) is characterised by maintaining similar rates of activity both before and during the pandemic: they demonstrate resilience of engagement to the shock. The third class (5% of the sample) is characterised by curtailment of leisure and cultural activity during the pandemic. The fourth class is the largest, consisting of 63% of the sample. Respondents here exhibit low rates of activity overall, and are most likely to not engage across the range of activities

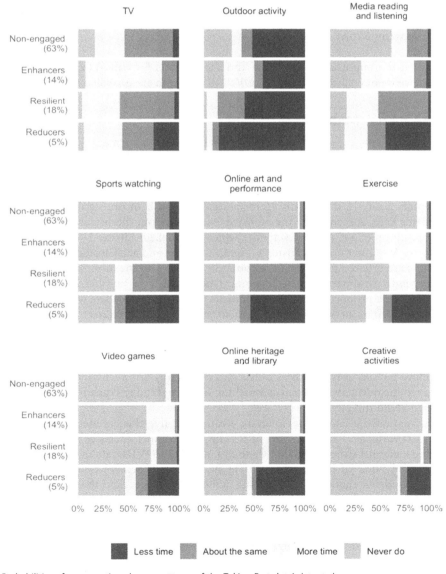

Figure 1. Probabilities of consumption change patterns of the Taking Part data's latent classes.

asked about, whether before or during the pandemic. The exception for this group was TV watching, which they were likely to increase or maintain during the pandemic, and outdoor activities, which they decreased. Accordingly, we termed them 'Enhancers', 'Resilient', 'Reducers' and 'Non-engaged'.

For the next stage of the analysis, we estimated a multinomial logistic regression model to examine the determinants influencing likelihood of being an 'Enhancer', 'Resilient', 'Reducers' or 'Non-engaged' cultural consumer during the pandemic. The dependent variable in the regression was class membership. We used a set of individual variables included in the data and known from the literature to affect cultural consumption and leisure activity as independent variables:

- Sex – male/female
- Ethnicity – White/BAME[1]
- Age group – 16-34/35-45/55 and over
- Work status – Not working/Working/Stopped working
- Parenting – Having children under 16 currently living in your household (yes/no)
- Region – London/North/Midlands/South
- Wave – May/June/July.

Notwithstanding the importance of income and social status for cultural consumption patterns, such variables were not collected in the TPCOVID19 data, and are unavailable for the respondents.

The audience agency (TAAW2) data

We first proceeded with a similar hierarchical cluster analysis of TAAW2 items (see Figure A4 in the online appendix). This source differs in its coverage of cultural engagement, with more detailed measures of consumption of livestreams or recordings of the performing arts, alongside measures of cultural production at home. However, its wide range of measures does allow us to provide a complementary analysis, one which again takes the breadth of potential engagement options seriously. In this case, according to the adjusted Rand criterion, the hierarchical cluster analysis resulted in a partition of 5 clusters of activities which we labelled: Cluster 1 – Outdoor, Cluster 2 – Reading, Cluster 3 – Other online, Cluster 4 – Online culture and art, Cluster 5 – Creative Activity. As before, these are ordered from the more common activities, to the most infrequent. Table A4 in the online appendix summarises these together. Due to the large number of activities surveyed, engaging only a small proportion of the respondents where the sample size was furthermore lower, the clustering proved to be less nuanced than for the TPCOVID source. Nevertheless, clusters identifying distinct segments of activities relating to the respondent's own creative activity, outdoor activity, and reading were replicated. The remaining online activities were clustered into two groups: culture and arts activities (including highbrow genres such as opera and contemporary dance, and more popular forms such as music gigs and family arts events), and 'other activities' – a group likely to include activities such as watching films or standup comedy alongside others that were not asked about directly.

We again conducted a latent class analysis, treating the five clusters identified in the previous stage as manifest variables. Our procedure of selecting the number of classes was driven here by the attempt to find a parallel structure to that we found in the TPCOVID data that resulted in 4 classes. However, probably due to the smaller sample size, the imposed four-class solution failed to distinguish respondents characterised by being active 'fewer times' and those active at 'the same' rate. The four-class solution accordingly lacked face validity. Imposing a five-class solution yielded a more clear-cut separation between those reducing their activity and those maintaining it, while still displaying reasonable fit indices (see Figure A5 online appendix). This solution was more theoretically plausible and we accordingly retained in preference to the four-class solution. Figure 2 presents these five classes and the average change in engagement frequency for each cluster within each class.

Three of the classes share characteristics parallel to those identified in the TPCOVID dataset and were accordingly also termed 'Enhancers', 'Reducers' and 'Resilient'. These classes are very small, together comprising 7% of the sample. The majority belongs to one of the two classes characterised by very infrequent engagement with the activities asked about in the survey. The two classes differ in distinguishing those likely to do outdoor activities before the pandemic who had decreased engagement following its start, and those who were non-engaged outdoors even before the pandemic. For the purpose of this paper, we termed them 'Non-engaged hikers' and 'Non-engaged' accordingly. The difference in the overall size of the non-engaged groups in TAAW2 compared with TPCOVID might be largely explained by the fact that TAAW2asked about participation in the 12-month period before the pandemic, while TPCOVID asked more generally about engagement in the past.

We then estimated a multinomial logistic regression model, similar to that for the TPCOVID data in including as similar a set as possible of explanatory variables. The dependent variable in the model was again class membership, with independent variables comprising:

- Gender – Male/Female/Other
- Ethnicity – White/Other Ethnic Group
- Age group – 16-34/35-45/55 and over

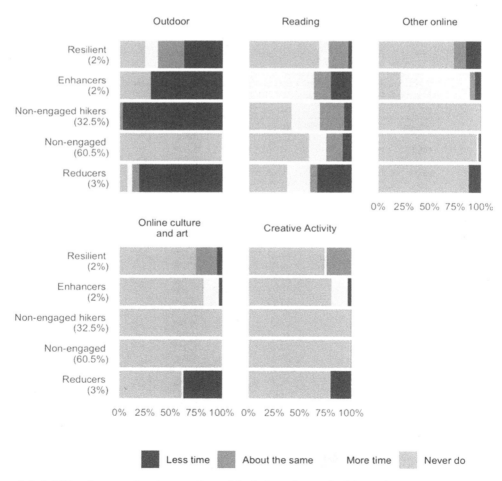

Figure 2. Probabilities of consumption change patterns of the Audience Agency data's latent classes.

- Free time – The impact of Covid-19 on the respondent's amount of free time – more/ same/ less (included as a close substitute for the work status variable in TPCOVID)
- Parenting – Having children under 16 currently living in your household – Yes/No
- Region – London/North/Midlands/South/Scotland/Wales (Northern Ireland was omitted due to technical issues with the data)
- Health – Whether the respondent is limited by a health problem or disability – No/ Yes (where 'a little' and 'a lot' were merged to create a binary variable)

Findings

Taking part (TPCOVID) data

Results of our second multinomial logistic regression model are presented in Table 1. The baseline comparison category in the model is the group of 'Resilient' consumers that showed continuity in their consumption patterns. Since the model presents only comparisons with the 'non-engaged' baseline category, we ran additional post-estimation tests that included comparisons between the other clusters too (see Figure A6 in the appendix).

The findings show the stratification axes shaping change in leisure and cultural consumption in response to the pandemic. We found that women were more likely to be 'Enhancers' than 'Resilient' compared to men. On the other hand, among the two groups that did not change their consumption patterns during the pandemic, we found women were more likely to be non-engaged than resilient active consumers.

Table 1. Multinomial regression of class attribution on personal characteristics of respondents. Baseline category 'Non-engaged'. Taking part data.

	Reducers	Resilient	Enhancers
Female	−0.158	−0.430***	0.044
	(0.204)	(0.118)	(0.134)
BAME	1.510***	0.568*	0.651**
	(0.310)	(0.261)	(0.251)
16–34	0.263	−0.407*	0.168
	(0.260)	(0.190)	(0.161)
55+	0.002	0.249	−0.777***
	(0.292)	(0.166)	(0.193)
Not working	−0.168	−0.289*	−0.126
	(0.256)	(0.147)	(0.171)
Stopped working	0.299	−0.213	0.370*
	(0.266)	(0.181)	(0.169)
Children under 16	0.426	0.123	0.069
	(0.234)	(0.151)	(0.149)
London	−0.419	−0.199	0.117
	(0.371)	(0.210)	(0.220)
North	−0.144	−0.375*	−0.148
	(0.242)	(0.146)	(0.159)
Midlands	−0.241	−0.228	−0.277
	(0.276)	(0.159)	(0.184)
Wave 2	−0.133	−0.094	−0.362*
	(0.238)	(0.143)	(0.160)
Wave 3	−0.211	0.049	−0.109
	(0.249)	(0.145)	(0.156)
Constant	−2.500***	−0.827***	−1.146***
	(0.305)	(0.180)	(0.191)
ll	−2114.18		
chi2	159.027		
N	2132		

Note: Standard errors in parentheses. * p < 0.05, ** p < 0.01, *** p < 0.001

Ethnicity plays a role too in determining consumption patterns. Notwithstanding the relatively small sample of ethnic minorities in the data, we find that members of ethnic minorities had a statistically significant higher propensity than White respondents to be 'less active' during the pandemic compared with membership of all other groups. Controlling for all the other covariates, ethnic minority respondents were more than twice more likely to be a 'Reducer' than an 'Enhancer' or 'Resilient'. However, they were also less likely to be a 'Non-engaged' compared to all other categories (see online appendix).

Most parents, especially those with younger children, had to care for their children more than usual during the lockdowns which may have affected cultural consumption in several ways. On the one hand, taking care of children consumes free time, but it is also plausible that parents will devote increased time spent with their children to cultural and leisure activities. We found that respondents with children in their household were more likely to be a 'Reducer' than members of any other category (see online appendix). However, these differences were not statistically significant.

Age had an intricate effect on the change in consumption patterns. Older respondents, compared to the 35–54 age group, had a much lower propensity (about a third) of increasing their leisure and cultural consumption levels during the pandemic. Younger respondents were more likely to see a change in their consumption pattern during the pandemic than being 'Resilient'. However, there was no statistically significant difference between their propensity of being a 'reducer' or 'Enhancer' (see online appendix). Younger respondents were also more likely be non-engaged than resilient. We can sum this up by saying that while young respondents were more likely to see change in their consumption level over the course of the pandemic conditional on being an active consumer, older respondents were more likely to sustain their consumption level or reduce it than increase it (see online appendix).

Another pandemic-related factor linked to change in time availability is the work status of the respondents. Respondents that were not working both before and during the pandemic were most likely to belong to the non-engaged group, although this difference was only statistically significant compared to the resilient group. However, respondents that had stopped working since the start of the pandemic showed a clear difference compared to working and non-working respondents. Those who stopped working were more likely to increase their level of consumption ('Enhancers'), although we found no significant difference between the propensity to increase or decrease that level. Lastly, in most cases, the geographical location did not have a significant effect on consumption changes. However, between the two non-change groups, residents of the north of the UK were more likely to be 'Non-engaged' rather than 'Resilient', reflecting lower levels of cultural participation in this region in place even before the pandemic.

The audience agency (TAAW2) data

We estimated a similar multinomial logistic model to the one estimated for TPCOVID using TAAW2. Setting aside differences in what was asked, the smaller sample size and smaller sizes of the three active consumption classes was an additional constraint on the power of the model. Nevertheless, we wished to test whether the model's results are generally comparable with those of the previous model. Results are presented in Table 2, with additional comparisons reported in Figure A7 in the online appendix.

Similar to what was found in the TPCOVID data, results here indicate that women are more likely to be non-engagers of both types (previously-active outdoors and previously-non-engaged) than resilient engagers. In this model, we additionally found women more likely to be enhancers than resilient as we had found in the TPCOVID model. In the TAAW2 model, parents are more likely to be 'Reducers' than non-engaged (both types) and 'Enhancers', a finding consistent with that for the TPCOVID model (although it was not statistically-significant there), which underscores parents' struggles during the pandemic (see online appendix). In the TAAW2 model, we did not find a significant effect for respondent ethnicity except for a higher propensity of those other than

White to belong to the 'Non-engaged' category compared to the 'Non-engaged/previously hikers' group. These results are very likely affected by the small proportion of ethnic minorities in the data. The comparison with older did nor yield statistically-significant differences in this model, except for a higher propensity of belonging to the 'Non-engaged/previously hikers' group compared to most other categories (see online appendix). Younger respondents were significantly more likely to be 'Resilient' than 'Non-engaged/previously hikers', which is compatible with our findings in the TPCOVID data.

One advantage of the TAAW2 dataset is its inclusion of measures of self-reported health. Health problems and disabilities are usually linked to consumption barriers. We might therefore expect that during the pandemic consumption differences between those with poorer health and others were attenuated, and that the increase in online content might benefit those traditionally-excluded. Results (see online appendix) suggest that respondents with health issues were more likely during the pandemic to either reduce their consumption (compared to being a non-engaged of both types) or increase it (compared to non-engaged).

Finally, we can examine the effect of increased time availability as a resource for consumption. As found in the TPCOVID model (working status variable), having more free time is associated with change. Respondents that reported having more free time were more likely to increase their level of consumption compared to the two non-engaged categories.

Table 2. Multinomial regression of class attribution on personal characteristics of respondents. Baseline category 'Non-engaged'. Audience Agency data.

	Resilient	Non-engaged hikers	Reducers	Enhancers
Female	−1.210**	−0.063	−0.6	0.011
	(0.417)	(0.116)	(0.319)	(0.378)
BAME	0.113	−0.478**	−0.323	0.198
	(0.487)	(0.183)	(0.438)	(0.497)
16–34	0.601	−0.487***	0.074	−0.355
	(0.428)	(0.143)	(0.343)	(0.428)
55+	−1.844	0.595***	−0.663	−0.382
	(1.075)	(0.147)	(0.552)	(0.507)
Had less free time	−0.395	−0.055	0.457	0.361
	(0.727)	(0.209)	(0.561)	(0.892)
Had more free time	0.161	0.151	0.731	1.446**
	(0.468)	(0.126)	(0.418)	(0.553)
Health limitations	0.088	−0.307*	0.689*	0.532
	(0.428)	(0.128)	(0.317)	(0.377)
Children under 16	0.682	0.094	0.980**	−0.205
	(0.403)	(0.140)	(0.339)	(0.432)
London	0.918	−0.009	0.318	−0.236
	(0.725)	(0.199)	(0.492)	(0.663)
North	0.275	0.173	−0.143	−0.03
	(0.780)	(0.163)	(0.481)	(0.552)
Midlands	1.386*	0.301	−0.395	0.366
	(0.688)	(0.171)	(0.570)	(0.539)
Scotland	0.157	0.059	−0.501	0.345
	(0.935)	(0.221)	(0.685)	(0.656)
Wales	1.328	0.16	0.965*	−0.274
	(0.794)	(0.227)	(0.490)	(0.824)
Constant	−3.714***	0.083	−3.381***	−3.972***
	(0.724)	(0.176)	(0.543)	(0.696)
ll	−1332.047			
chi2	189.601			
N	−1332.047			

Standard errors in parentheses. * p < 0.05, ** p < 0.01, *** p < 0.001

Conclusion: cultural consumption and the Covid pandemic

Writing during the summer of 2020, as re-opening began in the UK (and across many other parts of Europe) Roberts (2020, p. 622) noted that *'the adjustments that people made during lockdown when most out-of-home leisure became inaccessible can be summarised as increasing the amounts of time spent doing things at home that they had done before'*. Using time use data, Roberts demonstrated the *continuities* of leisure practices, rather than a wholesale revolution following the lockdown of March 2020.

Drawing on surveys focused on cultural consumption, our analysis expands on this conclusion. We find that the prevalence of low and non-engagement with cultural consumption was not altered by the pandemic. A majority of respondents reported no involvement with almost any form of cultural consumption other than watching TV and other popular media. The social profile of this group is similar to the known characteristics of low cultural engagement consumers. An additional significant proportion of the population was able to retain their level of cultural consumption through the pandemic but, like the non-engaged, mostly did not exploit the new access opportunities brought by the pivot to digital.

Increasing and diversifying cultural consumption during the pandemic was associated mostly with young age groups and was contingent on having spare time. External constraints such as work and parenting reduced the chances of enhancing consumption. These were also among the risk factors of lowering cultural consumption during the pandemic, along with geographical and health inequalities.

Accordingly, we come to a similar conclusion to Mihelj et al.'s (2019) analysis of *Taking Part*, that finds that the 'offline' patterns of inequality continued into the predominantly digital cultural world of the pandemic. We can see the inequalities associated with race, gender, and age are all still influential on pandemic cultural consumption. There is also striking evidence of the impact of parenting on the change, or lack thereof, in cultural behaviour. Finally, the continuities in the stratification of cultural consumption during the pandemic raises a range of broad questions as to the value of culture and the likelihood of a transformative impact of the pandemic on key aspects of contemporary culture.

Having two sets of data allows for fruitful comparisons, each offering a distinctive perspective with its own strengths and weaknesses. What is striking is the consistency of the story being told by the analysis of both *Taking Part* and *The Audience Agency* survey data, collected at different stages of the pandemic. This consistency between the data sets mirrors the consistency of 'offline' and digital pandemic stratification, whereby the patterns of inequalities demonstrated by the existing literature were not disturbed even by such a major, global, social change.

There are, obviously, limitations to the analysis and the two datasets from which the research is drawn. The demographic variables available in the web panel version of Taking Part are limited. This absence makes it impossible to interrogate the role of social class and education in the social stratification of cultural consumption in this digital context. In addition, it is important to reinforce that our picture of digital participation is limited to the specific digital activities that the surveys ask about. While both surveys draw on a wide range of different activities, and our conclusions are not limited to the publicly-subsidised arts sector, we do not have information on genre within the activities in which people were engaging. We do not know, for example, whether people who increased the number of hours they spent watching on-demand streaming services spent time watching multiple episodes of critically acclaimed dramas in different languages, or if they revisited shows they had already watched multiple times.

These issues notwithstanding, the analysis has important implications for leisure studies and cultural sociology scholars, as well as for policymakers and practitioners. For researchers it reinforces the continuities of stratification and inequality in relation to culture, as well as the need for more detailed and more sophisticated approaches to 'non-engagement'. For policy and practice, as the comments that opened the paper indicated, the struggle for a reformed or reimagined cultural sector continues. The pandemic has, based on our analysis, not disrupted the arts audience, whether in terms of bringing in new engagement or in terms of key demographics of existing consumers. 'Digital' will not be enough to change the arts; rather, the core lesson of the pandemic is the need for real vision as to what a representative and fair cultural sector would look like in order to reach a truly representative, and thus diverse, audience.

Note

1. We acknowledge the limitation of the BAME category and the fact that it represents an heterogenous group. However, the sample size does not allow us a finer distinction between ethnic groups. Therefore we use of the BAME category congruently with other research works in the field (e.g. Oakley & O'Brien, 2015; Roberts, 2020).

Disclosure statement

No potential conflict of interest was reported by the author(s).

Funding

This work was supported by the Arts and Humanities Research Council [AH/V00994X/1].

References

ACE. (2020). *Covid-19: More information*. https://www.artscouncil.org.uk/covid-19/covid-19-more-information#section-1

Alderson, A. S., Junisbai, A., & Heacock, I. (2007). Social status and cultural consumption in the United States. *Poetics*, *35*(2–3), 191–212.

Banks, M. (2020). The work of culture and C-19. *European Journal of Cultural Studies*, *23*(4), 648–654. https://doi.org/10.1177/1367549420924687

Banks, M., & O'Connor, J. (2021). "A plague upon your howling": Art and culture in the viral emergency. *Cultural Trends*, 30(1), 3–18. https://doi.org/10.1080/09548963.2020.1827931

Barlow, J. P. (1996). A Declaration of the Independence of Cyberspace. Retrived June 14, 2022 from: https://www.eff.org/cyberspace-independence.

Beer, D. (2013). *Popular culture and new media: The politics of circulation*. Palgrave.

Bennett, T., Savage, M., Silva, E. B., Warde, A., Gayo-Cal, M., & Wright, D. (2009). *Culture, class, distinction*. Routledge.

Bourdieu, P. (1984). *Distinction: A social critique of the judgment of taste*. Routledge.

Brook, O. (2013). Reframing models of arts attendance: Understanding the role of access to a venue. The case of opera in London. *Cultural Trends*, 22(2), 97–107. https://doi.org/10.1080/09548963.2013.783175

Brown, M. (2020). Arts Council England promises £160m to buoy the public during lockdown. *The Guardian*. Retrieved August 21, 2021, form https://www.theguardian.com/world/2020/mar/24/arts-council-england-promises-160m-to-buoy-public-during-lockdown

Brown, M. (2020a). National Theatre to broadcast shows online. *The Guardian*. Retrieved August 21, 2021, form https://www.theguardian.com/stage/2020/mar/26/national-theatre-to-broadcast-shows-online-on-thursdays

Bryson, B. (1996). 'Anything but heavy metal': Symbolic exclusion and musical dislikes. *American Sociological Review*, 61(5), 884–899. https://doi.org/10.2307/2096459

Bunting, C., Chan, T. W., Goldthorpe, J., Keaney, E., & Oskala, A. (2008). *From indifference to enthusiasm: Patterns of arts attendance in England*. Arts Council England.

Carmi, E. (2020). *Media distortions: Understanding the power behind spam, noise, and other deviant media*. Peter Lang International Academic Publishers.

Chan, T. W., & Goldthorpe, J. H. (2007). Social stratification and cultural consumption: The visual arts in England. *Poetics*, 35(2–3), 168–190. https://doi.org/10.1016/j.poetic.2007.05.002

Chan, T. W. (ed.). (2010). *Social status and cultural consumption*. Cambridge University Press.

Chavent, M., Kuentz-Simonet, V., Liquet, B., & Saracco, J. (2012). ClustOfVar: An R package for the clustering of variables. *Journal of Statistical Software*, 50(13), 1–16. https://doi.org/10.18637/jss.v050.i13

Christin, A. (2012). Gender and highbrow cultural participation in the United States. *Poetics*, 40(5), 423–443. https://doi.org/10.1016/j.poetic.2012.07.003

Christin, A. (2020). *Metrics at work*. Princeton University Press.

Comunian, R., & England, L. (2020). Creative and cultural work without filters: Covid-19 and exposed precarity in the creative economy. *Cultural Trends*, 29(2), 112–128. https://doi.org/10.1080/09548963.2020.1770577

Cutts, D., & Widdop, P. (2017). Reimagining omnivorousness in the context of place. *Journal of Consumer Culture*, 17(3), 480–503. https://doi.org/10.1177/1469540516634413

de Vries, R., & Reeves, A. (2021). What does it mean to be a cultural omnivore? Conflicting visions of omnivorousness in empirical research. *Sociological Research Online*, 27(2), 292–312. https://doi.org/10.1177/2F13607804211006109

Department for Digital, Culture, Media and Sports. (2018). *Culture is digital*.

DiMaggio, P., & Mukhtar, T. (2004). Arts participation as cultural capital in the United States, 1982– 2002: Signs of decline? *Poetics*, 32(2), 169–194. https://doi.org/10.1016/j.poetic.2004.02.005

Eikhof, D. (2020). COVID-19, inclusion and workforce diversity in the cultural economy: What now, what next? *Cultural Trends*, 29(3), 234–250. https://doi.org/10.1080/09548963.2020.1802202

Falk, M., & Falk, R. (2011). *An ordered probit model of live performance attendance for 24 E.U. countries*. Austrian Institute of Economic Research (WIFO).

Falk, M., & Katz-Gerro, T. (2016). Cultural participation in Europe: Can we identify common determinants? *Journal of Cultural Economics*, 40(2), 127–162. https://doi.org/10.1007/s10824-015-9242-9

Giles, J. (2020). I woke up and the arts was gone. Retrieved from https://harryjosephine.com/2020/03/20/i-woke-up-and-the-arts-was-gone/

Hanquinet, L. (2017). Inequalities: When culture becomes a capital. In: Durrer, V., Miller, T., & O'Brien, D. (Eds.), *The Routledge Handbook of Global Cultural Policy* (pp. 327–340). London: Routledge.

Helsper, E. (2020). *The digital disconnect*. Sage.

Iskander, T. (2020). "The arts after Covid-19: Let's fix the things that weren't right before" The Stage. Retrieved from https://www.thestage.co.uk/opinion/the-arts-after-covid-19-lets-fix-the-things-that-werent-right-before

Joffe, A. (2021). Covid-19 and the African cultural economy: An opportunity to reimagine and reinvigorate? *Cultural Trends*, 30(1), 28–39. https://doi.org/10.1080/09548963.2020.1857211

Kant, T. (2020). *Making it personal: Algorithmic personalization, identity, and everyday life*. Oxford University Press.

Katz-Gerro, T. (1999). Cultural consumption and social stratification: Leisure activities, musical tastes, and social location. *Sociological Perspectives*, 42(4), 627–646. https://doi.org/10.2307/1389577

Katz-Gerro, T., & Sullivan, O. (2010). Voracious cultural consumption: The intertwining of gender and social status. *Time & Society*, 19(2), 193–219. https://doi.org/10.1177/0961463X09354422

Katz-Gerro, T. (2017). Cross-national differences in the consumption of non-national culture in Europe. *Cultural Sociology*, 11(4), 438–467. https://doi.org/10.1177/1749975517725637

Kay, J., & Wood, H. (2020). Culture and commoning in a time of coronavirus: Introduction to a cultural commons special section on COVID-19. *European Journal of Cultural Studies*, 23(4), 630–634. https://doi.org/10.1177/1367549420928360

Kraaykamp, G., & Dijkstra, K. (1999). Preferences in leisure time book reading: A study on the social differentiation in book reading for the Netherlands. *Poetics*, 26(4), 203–234. https://doi.org/10.1016/S0304-422X(99)00002-9

Kracman, K. (1996). The effect of school-based arts instruction on attendance at museums and the performing arts. *Poetics*, 24(2–4), 203–218. https://doi.org/10.1016/S0304-422X(96)00009-5

Lagaert, S., & Roose, H. (2018). Gender and highbrow cultural participation in Europe: The effect of societal gender equality and development. *International Journal of Comparative Sociology*, 59(1), 44–68. https://doi.org/10.1177/0020715217753271

Leguina, A., & Miles, A. (2017). Fields of participation and lifestyle in England: Revealing the regional dimension from a reanalysis of the taking part survey using multiple factor analysis. *Cultural Trends*, 26(1), 4–17. https://doi.org/10.1080/09548963.2017.1274356

Lena, J. (2019). *Entitled: Discriminating tastes and the expansion of the arts*. Princeton University Press.

Linzer, D. A., & Lewis, J. B. (2011). poLCA: An R package for polytomous variable latent class analysis. *Journal of Statistical Software*, 42(1), 1–29. https://doi.org/10.18637/jss.v042.i10

Lupton, D. (2016). Foreword: Lively devices, lively data and lively leisure studies. *Leisure Studies*, 35(6), 709–711. https://doi.org/10.1080/02614367.2016.1216582

McGillivray, D. (2014). Digital cultures, acceleration and mega sporting event narratives. *Leisure Studies*, 33(1), 96–109. https://doi.org/10.1080/02614367.2013.841747

McGillivray, D., McPherson, G., Jones, J., & McCandlish, G. (2016). Young people, digital media making and critical digital citizenship. *Leisure Studies*, 35(6), 724–738. https://doi.org/10.1080/02614367.2015.1062041

Meghji, A. (2019). *Black middle-class Britannia: Identities*. Manchester University Press.

Mihelj, S., Leguina, A., & Downey, J. (2019). Culture is digital: Cultural participation, diversity and the digital divide. *New Media & Society*, 21(7), 1465–1485. https://doi.org/10.1177/1461444818822816

Montoro-Pons, J. D., & Cuadrado-García, M. (2020). Analyzing online search patterns of music festival tourists. *Tourism Economics*, 27(6), 1276–1300. https://doi.org/10.1177/1354816620945440

Noble, S. (2018). *Algorithms of oppression*. NYU Press.

Novak-Leonard, J. L., O'Malley, M. K., & Truong, E. (2015). Minding the gap: Elucidating the disconnect between arts participation metrics and arts engagement within immigrant communities. *Cultural Trends*, 24(2), 112–121. https://doi.org/10.1080/09548963.2015.1031477

Oakley, K., & O'Brien, D. (2015). *Cultural value and inequality: A critical literature review*. Arts and Humanities Research Council.

Ofcom. (2021). *Adults' media use and attitudes report 2020/2021*. Ofcom. https://www.ofcom.org.uk/__data/assets/pdf_file/0025/217834/adults-media-use-and-attitudes-report-2020-21.pdf

Patel, K. (2020). *The politics of expertise in cultural labour*. Rowman and Littlefield.

Patterson, N. D. (2020). Who goes to shows? Race-ethnicity and the visual and performing arts. *Cultural Sociology*, 14(1), 22–41. https://doi.org/10.1177/1749975519885467

Peterson, R. A., & Kern, R. M. (1996). Changing highbrow taste: From snob to omnivore. *American Sociological Review*, 61(5), 900–907. https://doi.org/10.2307/2096460

Redhead, S. (2016). Afterword: A new digital Leisure studies for theoretical times. *Leisure Studies*, 35(6), 827–834. https://doi.org/10.1080/02614367.2016.1231832

Reeves, A. (2015). Neither class nor status: Arts participation and the social strata. *Sociology*, 49(4), 624–642. https://doi.org/10.1177/0038038514547897

Reeves, A. (2019). How class identities shape highbrow consumption: A cross-national analysis of 30 European countries and regions. *Poetics*, 76, 101361. https://doi.org/10.1016/j.poetic.2019.04.002

Roberts, K. (2020). Locked down leisure in Britain. *Leisure Studies*, 39(5), 617–628. https://doi.org/10.1080/02614367.2020.1791937

Silk, M., Millington, B., Rich, E., & Bush, A. (2016). (Re-)thinking digital leisure. *Leisure Studies*, 35(6), 712–723. https://doi.org/10.1080/02614367.2016.1240223

Sobande, F. (2020a). 'We're all in this together': Commodified notions of connection, care and community in brand responses to COVID-19. *European Journal of Cultural Studies*, 23(6), 1033–1037. https://doi.org/10.1177/1367549420932294

Sobande, F. (2020b). *The digital lives of Black Women in Britain*. Palgrave.

Stevenson, D. (2013). What's the problem again? The problematisation of cultural participation in Scottish cultural policy. *Cultural Trends*, 22(2), 77–85. https://doi.org/10.1080/09548963.2013.783172

Taylor, M. (2016). Nonparticipation or different styles of participation? Alternative interpretations from taking part. *Cultural Trends*, 25(3), 169–181. https://doi.org/10.1080/09548963.2016.1204051

Van Eijck, K. (2001). Social differentiation in musical taste patterns. *Social Forces*, 79(3), 1163–1185. https://doi.org/10.1353/sof.2001.0017

Van Hek, M., & Kraaykamp, G. (2013). Cultural consumption across countries: A multi-level analysis of social inequality in highbrow culture in Europe (2013). *Poetics*, *41*(4), 323–341. https://doi.org/10.1016/j.poetic.2013.05.001

Weingartner, S. (2021). Digital omnivores? How digital media reinforce social inequalities in cultural consumption. *New Media & Society*, *23*(11), 3370–3390. https://doi.org/10.1177/1461444820957635

White Pube. (2020). Ideas for a new art world. Retrieved from https://thewhitepube.co.uk/art-thoughts/ideasforanewartworld/

Widdop, P., & Cutts, D. (2012). Impact of place on museum participation. *Cultural Trends*, *21*(1), 47–66. https://doi.org/10.1080/09548963.2012.641775

Widdop, P., & Cutts, D. (2013). Social stratification and sports' participation in England. *Leisure Sciences*, *35*(2), 107–128.

Wright, D. (2011). Making tastes for everything: Omnivorousness and cultural abundance. *Journal for Cultural Research*, *15*(4), 355–371. https://doi.org/10.1080/14797585.2011.613222

Time use, work and leisure in the UK before, during, between and following the Covid-19 lockdowns

Ken Roberts

ABSTRACT

This paper presents findings from time-use surveys in the UK, which were conducted prior to, during and following the Covid-19 lockdowns in 2020 and 2021. These findings are set against the background of evidence from similar surveys in the UK and globally from 1920s onwards. Movements into and out of successive lockdowns between 2020 and 2021 disrupted former temporary routines with consequences that endured in 2022. There has been no return to the old normal, or even towards that normal. The new normal was a population with more leisure time than pre-pandemics but which was also spending more time doing paid work. There were differences in sex, age and income, but overall time had been released for other uses by people doing less travelling, less studying and less unpaid child care. Extra leisure time was being filled mainly by the media.

Introduction

This paper presents data on time use in the UK before, during, between and following the Covid-19 lockdowns in 2020 and 2021. The significance of a series of stop-start lockdowns, a period of turbulence in time use unprecedented since the Second World War, can be grasped only when set against the background of changes and continuities in time use throughout the preceding decades. Evidence from the lockdown years is therefore preceded by a history and major findings from earlier time use studies, mainly but not only, in the UK. The big question in the discussion and conclusions that follow concerns whether post-lockdown time use has been returning to the old normal, or whether we are now in a period when a new normal is being constructed and, if so, exactly what has changed.

Background: the development of time use research

Time use research was pioneered in Russia between the World Wars (see Moskoff, 1984), and after 1945 these studies were repeated in the Soviet Union and launched in most other countries in the enlarged Soviet bloc. Similar studies also began in Western countries. Thus, in the 1960s Alexander Szalai, a Hungarian though then based in Vienna, was able to assemble the findings from time-use studies in Hungary, the German Democratic Republic, Czechoslovakia, Bulgaria, Poland and Yugoslavia together with the USA, France, Belgium and the Federal Republic of Germany, plus Peru. The outcome was a book (Szalai, 1972) with contributions from each country's researchers who reported their national findings. There was no attempt to compare or to draw any conclusions.

Comparisons were difficult since researchers in each country had adopted their own idiosyncratic methods of classifying time use, and rapid harmonisation was impossible in the pre-digital era. The analyses presented by the country teams were the first, and for many years the only outputs from these studies.

The early interest of communist regimes in their people's uses of time was a response to labour shortages and a desire to identify whose time could be diverted into production. Subsequently, an additional concern was to discover how free time was being used. Communist regimes had firm ideas on what was good and what was bad leisure. Heavy television viewing, which took-off in Russia from the mid-1960s, was in the latter category. Collective activities were preferred (by the authorities) to those that were privately organised. There was an overarching expectation that in uses of time and other aspects of life, there would be a historical convergence between men and women, urban and rural dwellers, and occupational strata. The point of convergence was to be a common socialist way of life. Such change was never discovered, but this should not be treated as evidence of a failure of communism. We now know, as we shall see below, that in every country temporal routines usually change slowly if at all, and over decades rather than years. Communist authorities repeatedly found that their populations were dissatisfied with their quantity of free time: they wanted more which was delivered in a five-day work-week and holiday entitlement that varied from industry to industry, while throughout the economy workers took more holidays than their official entitlement with or without the approval of managements. Time use studies also recorded widespread dissatisfaction with provisions for out-of-home leisure from day-to-day, and for holidays away from home (Moskoff, 1984). Time use studies in Western countries have served the interests of various government departments and independent research communities with interests in age, sex and social class differences, and changes and continuities over time.

Technical difficulties in harmonising findings from different countries' time use studies have now been resolved at the Centre for Time Use Research at University College London which stores harmonised data sets from surveys conducted over 60 years in 25 countries. Basic methods for conducting these studies are now standard worldwide. Samples of a population are issued with diaries with each hour divided into 10-min episodes. Respondents are asked what they were doing in each of these periods. Sometimes they are asked about main and any secondary activities, where they were and with whom. The main categories of time use into which respondents' answers are collapsed always include sleeping, self-maintenance (eating, washing, dressing), paid work, travelling (unpaid), domestic work and child care, leaving activities most of which can be treated and labelled as leisure. In early time-use studies, samples were handed paper diaries that they were asked to fill-in several times each day. Printed instructions were accompanied by advice from fieldworkers, who checked that the diaries were completed correctly when visiting to collect. Nowadays the surveys are always online.

UK time use surveys

The first UK time-use surveys were conducted by the BBC in 1961 and 1975, after when it was several years before the first public release of the findings (British Broadcasting Corporation, 1978; Gershuny & Thomas, 1980). The BBC was interested in who was watching and listening to its output, and precisely when. In these surveys, respondents were asked to complete diaries for two full weeks. There were problems with the drop-out and compliance. In more recent UK time use surveys commissioned by the Office for National Statistics in 2000, 2005 and 2015, then during and following the pandemic lockdowns, individuals have been asked to complete diaries for just 2 days, a weekday and a weekend day. Results are weighted to give mean minutes of time spent on different activities on an average day.

The reason why time-use studies in the UK and elsewhere have been conducted infrequently is that one of the first findings was that aggregate uses of time change slowly, if at all. This was evident in comparisons between the BBC's results in 1961 and 1975, and in the surveys conducted in 2000 then 2005, so the next survey was not until 2015.

Comparative studies

Inter-country comparisons have produced many interesting, sometimes surprising and puzzling findings. In all countries where time use surveys have been conducted, and whenever the surveys took place, men and women, over their lifetimes, have spent similar proportions of their lives doing paid or unpaid work (Bittman & Wajcman, 1999). Americans spend fewer hours at work than East Asians, but more than Europeans (Robinson & Godbey, 1999). The UK is closer to America than Europe in this respect. A five-country European study at the beginning of the 21st century found that Swedes were managing with just 486 min of sleep per day, whereas the French slept for 531 min. Swedes completed their daily housework in 186 min while Hungarians took 231 min (MacInnes, 2006).

Rather than time-use data, inter-country comparisons in leisure studies have normally focussed on specific activities, especially physically active recreation and cultural consumption, and have used participation rates – percentages of a population taking part each week or monthfor example. The proportions of time spent on specific sports, visits to cinemas and theatres, are extremely low, and for most respondents, even regular (maybe weekly) participants, the amount is usually nil on the days when they completed their time diaries. However, whether time use or reported participation rates are used, explanations of inter-country differences can rarely be found within this kind of evidence. Veal's study has been exceptional in starting with, and accessing data that was suitable to test, a specific hypothesis. Veal followed Wilkinson and Pickett's earlier demonstration that economically more equal countries usually do better on health and other well-being indicators and (low) crime rates. Veal was able to add that the same countries tend to have the highest rates of participation in physically active leisure and attending cultural performances (Veal, 2016; Wilkinson & Pickett, 2009). Other explanations of country specifics in time use usually need to be in terms of geography, national traditions and cultures.

Studies of change over time within countries have yielded clearer results. In the UK, the five-day working week spread gradually up to the 1970s, but was reversed from the 1990s as Sunday became another shopping day and night-time economies created weekend fun for some and work for others (Gershuny & Sullivan, 2019). There has been a long-term trend towards genderless time use, admittedly at snail's pace with men doing a minute more housework per day each year (Sullivan, 2000), but over 50 years the change has been substantial.

Up to now time use surveys have made only minor contributions in leisure studies. Throughout the pre-digital and pre-broadband eras the surveys were expensive to conduct, cumbersome to analyse, and usually showed little or no change over time. Also and in this case enduringly, the surveys are most useful for measuring large blocks of time, not specific leisure activities, where the most common participation reported by respondents on the survey days is 'nil'. However, time-use researchers can plausibly claim that entries in time diaries are more accurate than answers to questions, such as 'How often do you ... ? and 'When did you last do ... ?' (Chase & Godbey, 1983). People are said typically to double the time when they engage in physically active recreation. Gershuny and Harris (2019) make a case for relying on the different proportions reporting 'any' and 'nil' time in the diary days as offering the most accurate estimates available of differences between socio-demographic groups. Also, time use studies have the merit of scanning 'Big Leisure' (Roberts, 2013), all of it, and situating their uses of leisure in the context of the rest of people's everyday lives.

Notwithstanding their serious limitations, there can be no dispute that time-use studies excel in periods of major disruption to time routines, as during the Covid-19 lockdowns. The following section shows that time lost from then only partly regained by other uses enabled leisure time to expand and shrink during and between the lockdowns in 2020 and 2021, from which the population emerged with a historically unusual large gain in leisure time in just over 2 years.

Time use in the UK, 2015–2022

The pandemic surveys

If there had been no pandemic, the next UK time-use survey following 2014/15 (Table 1, column 1) would probably have been in 2025. Fieldwork in the pre-pandemic surveys had been spread over 12 months to take account of seasonal differences. The pandemic surveys were completed in just 1 month, and this should be borne in mind when noting relatively small changes over time.

Table 1 column 1 gives the findings from the 'regular' 2014–15 time use survey. The initial pandemic survey (Table 1, column 2) was conducted during the first month of the first national lockdown, which began on 23 March 2020 (Office for National Statistics, 2020). This was the most severe of all the lockdowns. The headline instruction was to 'stay at home' except for essential purposes, basically essential shopping (only retailers selling foodstuffs were allowed to remain open), daily exercise and essential work, plus other work in which social distancing could be maintained. Face masks were mandatory in indoor public spaces, and seating on public transport was socially distanced. By mid-March, infections were spreading rapidly. There was no vaccine or effective treatments. No-one knew when infections would peak. Subsequently, we found that deaths with Covid-19 peaked in mid-April. By mid-May, when the Office for National Statistics' infection survey began to publish weekly reports of results (www.ons.gov.uk. Coronavirus [COVID-19] Infection Survey pilot, weekly data releases), the infection rate was one in 370 and declining, and continued to decline to one in 2000 in mid-August and early-September.

The lockdown began to be eased from May 28. Restaurants and bars operated but only with all customers seated at tables at least 2 m apart, with no more than six at each table. Spectator sports resumed but only in stadiums empty or with tiny numbers of spectators until the Euro football finals in June and early-July 2021. International travel remained heavily restricted. Cinemas and theatres were allowed to reopen, but only with socially distanced audiences. Some cinemas opened, but theatres and concert halls remained closed: their reduced capacities meant that they would operate at a loss. Nevertheless, in August 2020 the country was 'eating out to help out', enjoying government-subsidised meals in a bid to accelerate the revival of an economy that had lost 20% of its output. The country hoped that the virus was disappearing. GDP was still 8% down at the end of 2020.

Table 1. Average daily time in minutes, whole population age 18 and over.

	1 2014/2015	2 March/April 2020	3 Sept/Oct 2020	4 March 2021	5 March 2022
Travelling and transport, including walking	84	17	54	30	52
Working not from home	150	98	115	93	116
Working from home	15	55	73	74	65
Total work	*165*	*153*	*188*	*167*	*181*
Study	14	9	8	8	9
Unpaid childcare	31	35	25	26	27
Unpaid housework	147	144	132	157	151
Sleep and rest	533	551	533	534	531
Personal care, including eating and drinking	146	133	138	135	144
Keep fit	19	23	25	30	25
Gardening and DIY	16	39	28	28	20
Entertainment and socialising	277	321	295	308	297
Total leisure	*312*	*383*	*348*	*366*	*362*
Other	8	15	15	17	5

The second pandemic time use survey (Table 1, column 3) was conducted over a month from mid-September 2020 (Office for National Statistics, 2020b). When planned it was possible to hope that this would be the post-pandemic survey. The country had been out of full lockdown since May 28 albeit with the continuing restrictions noted above. However, infections had begun rising by the time that this survey was launched. At the end of October, the infection rate was one in 100. Deaths with Covid-19 were also rising and would reach 1000 a day in January 2021. September and October 2020 were months of hope, then worry. No vaccine trials had produced positive results.

A second lockdown was imposed in November 2020. This time there were variations in details and timing between the regions of England and the four countries of the UK. Restrictions were eased to permit gatherings within households from early December until Christmas and New Year had passed, then re-imposed. The infection rate peaked at one in 50 in early-January. Vaccinations had begun in early-December 2020 and by February 2021 were hauling down infection and death rates. The third pandemic survey month of March 2021 (Table 1, column 4) opened with an infection rate of one in 145 and ended with a rate of one in 340 (Office for National Statistics, 2021). The decline continued to one in 1300 in mid-May 2021 by when gradually lifting restrictions had started. The March 2021 survey was conducted at a time of tight restrictions, but hope that vaccinations would bring the pandemic to an end (Office for National Statistics, 2021).

In the event, as restrictions on social contact were lifted a highly contagious Delta variant of Covid had begun to spread. From mid-May onwards infections started to rise again and had reached one in 50 by the end of October. However, this infection rate was leading to less than 200 deaths with Covid per day, not over 1000 as in January 2021.

During January 2022 an even more contagious but less lethal Omicron Covid variant was sweeping through the country. Vaccines and improved treatments were not eliminating the virus or reducing transmissions but were reducing the likelihood of infections becoming hospital cases and deaths. The UK was trying to live normally with the virus, and by March 2022 (Table 1, column 5, Office for National Statistics, 2022) all restrictions had been lifted including international travel for the fully vaccinated, but amid an infection rate of around one in 25, much higher than in the winter of 2020–21. This final pandemic survey was conducted before global economic recovery in 2022 had led to rising demand for commodities leading to steep price rises, and before the February 24 Russian invasion of Ukraine, sanctions imposed on and countermeasures by Russia pushed price inflation even higher. Subsequent time use surveys will be able to use the final pandemic survey as a baseline from which to measure the effects on time use of the squeeze on household budgets and living standards that began in 2022.

Time use before, during, between and following the 2020 and 2021 lockdowns

Table 1 splits paid work into work done at or from home and work done elsewhere, like at the respondents' normal workplaces. 'Keep fit' (which alternatively might be regarded as personal care), and DIY and gardening (which could be treated as unpaid housework) are included in 'total leisure'.

Within this table our primary interest is which if any time uses were jolted out of the pre-pandemic normal (column 1) by the first national lockdown (column 2), whether any changes were wholly or partly maintained in the between lockdown survey (column 3), whether any previous changes were re-asserted during the third lockdown (column 4), and sustained into the post-lockdown period (column 5). Our focus is on total leisure time, which was enlarged, especially during lockdowns, and what proves to be its main covariates which are the relocation of paid work time and an associated drop in travelling time, with additional contributions from declines in time spent studying and unpaid child care.

Changes between 2014/15 and the first lockdown survey in March–April 2020 have been reported in detail elsewhere (Roberts, 2020). There had been a substantial increase in leisure time from 312 to 383 min per day. This was less due to a decline in total paid work time, than to a major shift of paid work from elsewhere into people's homes and a related decline in travelling time, which was also reduced by the lack of opportunities to engage in out-of-home leisure. People were spending 67 fewer minutes per day travelling, roughly 8 hours per week. Total leisure time increased by 71 min per day, again roughly 8 hours per week. Total work time declined by just 12 min per day.

The second pandemic survey, conducted in September–October 2020, which was between the first and second lockdowns (though this was not known at the time), recorded shifts in time use back towards, but remaining short of pre-pandemic norms. Travelling time rose from 17 to 54 min per day. Working away from home increased from 98 to 115 min per day. The surprising finding is that the time spent working at home also rose from 55 to 73 min per day. So total work time rose to 188 min per day, in excess of the pre-pandemic level. It seemed that people were over-compensating for the loss of work time during the first lockdown. Total leisure time fell back from 383 to 348 min per day, but remained higher than the pre-pandemic 312 min.

The March 2021 pandemic survey, conducted during the final national lockdown, found that travelling time had fallen back to just 30 min per day. Time spent working away from home fell from 115 to 93 min. Time spent working at home remained stable from the September/October 2020 finding. The net effect was that total work time was at the pre-pandemic norm – 167 min per day compared with 165 in 2014/15. Total leisure time rose from 348 min during the Autumn 2020 to 366 min in March 2021, well above the pre-pandemic 312 minutes. This was the reward for the drop in travelling time from 84 to 30 min per day.

Post-lockdown time use (Table 1, column 5) is best compared with pre-pandemic time use (Table 1, column 1). The turbulence of the lockdown years did not end with a reduction but an increase in total paid work time from 165 to 181 min by the average citizen per average day. There had been a decline from 150 to 116 min in time working away from home, and over-compensation with an increase from 15 to 65 min in time spent working at or from home. This enabled travelling time to decline from 86 to 52 min per day. Time spent studying, which was mainly by the younger age group who would have been in tertiary education, declined when teaching went online and did not return post-lockdowns to the pre-pandemic level. Time spent on unpaid child care declined overall, mainly in the older age group. Grandparents who were unable to offer child care during lockdowns had not resumed in March 2022. Time spent on sleep and rest, and on personal care, never left or had returned to pre-pandemic norms by 2022. The main beneficiary of all time saved on other uses was total leisure time. This increase in just 2 years by a massive 70 min per day is remarkable given the pre-pandemic year-to-year stability. There were differences by gender, age and income bands, but total leisure time rose in them all. All these groups recorded rises in total work time, its relocation from workplaces to homes, and reduced travelling time.

Up to now reductions in work time have usually been seen as a necessary condition for leisure time to expand (see Veal, 2022). The UK pandemic surveys confound this former assumption. An increase in total work time does not necessarily mean that employees and the self-employed are working longer. It could be due to an increase in the proportion of a population that is economically active. However, this did not happen in the UK during or following the lockdowns. More young people were extending their educational careers (see Roberts, 2021). More workers in their fifties and sixties began retiring (Office for National Statistics, 2021b). A clue to exactly who was responsible for the increase in total work time in the UK may be found in an American study of time use by 577 managers conducted in August 2019 and repeated in August 2020 when most were working wholly or partly from home (Teodorovicz et al., 2022). Time saved from travelling was being used not for leisure but for work, specifically for online meetings. The shift of work into homes in the UK during, and sustained following lockdowns, occurred among all socio-demographic groups, but was strongest among young males in the higher income band. These young managers and professionals, like their American counterparts, are likely to have used time saved from commuting to start work earlier and/or finish later.

Overall, comparing time use pre-pandemic with 2022, time had been lost mainly from travel (32 min by the average adult on an average day), in smaller amounts from studying and unpaid child care, plus statistically insignificant amounts from sleep and rest and personal care. Time released from elsewhere went mainly to leisure (50 min) and a much smaller amount to paid work (16 min). Leisure time was the big winner but, contrary to assumptions in the previous leisure studies literature, not at the expense of working time.

Triangulating time use with other leisure evidence

Time-use data become more meaningful when set alongside other types of leisure evidence on what happened to people's lives during and following the pandemic lockdowns. As acknowledged above, plausible explanations, even hypotheses requiring further investigation, can rarely be found solely within time-use data sets. Time use is just one dimension, casting a narrow beam across people's lives. Triangulation with other types of quantitative evidence offers a more rounded picture. Qualitative evidence illuminates how people experience changes and continuities in their routines, and can distinguish where the actors' behaviour was agentic rather than enforced. Quantitative data excels in describing what large numbers of people did – their actions. The large numbers are usually representative samples of even larger populations, as in the ONS time-use surveys.

Actions

We cannot be certain that the differences from time-to-time in Table 1 were due to the imposition and relaxation of lockdowns. This interpretation of the evidence is certainly plausible, and becomes even more plausible when set alongside trends in participation recorded in the *Active Lives* and *Taking Part* surveys that have been conducted annually starting long before 2014/15. Neither survey recorded major changes in participation from 2014 up to 2020 (see Department for Digital, Culture, Media and Sport, 2020; Feder et al., 2022; Sport England, 2020*Sport England*, 2020b, 2021, 2022).

In the case of physically active leisure, triangulation suggests strongly that the increased amount of time accounted for during the pandemic lockdowns was not due to more people becoming active. Sport England's measurements from self-reports indicate that the proportion judged 'active' dipped by 3% during 2020 from the former 61% of the adults who were exercising for at least 150 min per week, and only partly recovered in 2021 (Sport England, 2020*Sport England*, 2020b, 2021, 2022). Set alongside the time-use evidence, this suggests that some who were already active became even more active, specifically from the Sport England data by increasing their walking for exercise and cycling. The percentage of adults leading active leisure lives in the UK has remained stable since the late-1980s, alongside a shift from playing large team sports outdoors, towards indoor sport, lifestyle sports and individual exercise, initially in gyms, but during lockdowns on footpaths, pavements and roads (see van & Salome, 2010; Wheaton, 2013). In other words, the pandemic tweaked longer-term trends and the tweaks endured post-pandemic alongside stability in the proportion of the UK population leading active leisure lives.

A point to stress here that there are more than just two different ways (time diaries and self-estimates), of measuring the population's levels of 'exercise'. A study in the UK's Bristol region based on 10–11 year olds attending 50 schools and their parents who were all fitted with accelerometers found that post-lockdowns, in December 2021, levels of exercise among the children were beneath 2017–2018 levels, whereas parents' levels of activity were unchanged (Salway et al., 2022). There were no signs in these data of some adults who were already active becoming more so or less so. Such a change may have happened but was not picked-up in the aggregated accelerometer evidence, or the Bristol region could be different from other parts of the UK.

The rises in time spent gardening and do-it-yourself that occurred during the first lockdown are similar to those that often occur when people become unemployed, and when they retire (see Bhatti, 2006; Sinfield, 1981). However, in these cases time spent in the garden and on home improvements usually falls back to former levels when outstanding jobs are done, money for tools and materials is exhausted or, in the case of unemployment, when people regain jobs. Time spent gardening and on DIY remained well above the pre-pandemic level throughout the lockdowns, but appeared to be returning to its pre-pandemic level in 2022.

Entertainment and socialising accounted for an average of 277 min per day in 2014–15 and 30 min in March 2022. In Table 1 these figures are exceeded only by time spent sleeping and resting. Entertainment and socialising alone exceeded paid work time by wide margins in all the pandemic surveys. This large category within total leisure needs to be disaggregated, and this is possible within the time-use evidence. Researchers who construct time series see advantages in maintaining constant categories and measurements between sweeps. At the same time, researchers wish to identify the appearance of new ways of using time. These purposes are reconciled in the time-use surveys by gathering evidence in lower- and upper-level categories. Table 1 uses upper-level categories that remain constant from the pre-pandemic 2014/15 survey then throughout all the pandemic series. There are 11 of these categories in Table 1. Respondents fill in electronic time sheets using lower level categories of which there were 78 in the pandemic series. Most of these categories were not distinguished in the 2014–15 and earlier UK time use studies, so Column 1 in Table 2 is blank. The pandemic surveys distinguished time spent streaming, playing computer games, video-calling, browsing the internet, constructing a website, writing a blog and using social media. Many of these lower-level categories, including those just named with the exceptions of streaming, games and social media, accounted for under a minute per day of the average adult's time, but will have accounted for much more of the time of the minorities who were involved. Lower-level categories are bundled into the upper-level categories in Table 1 which permits comparisons between time use before, during and following the pandemic lockdowns.

Table 2 has evidence from time use on lower-level categories from the lockdown and post-lockdown years only. The specific forms of entertainment and socialising in Table 2 include the largest forms that were recorded, Time spent watching television, DVDs and blue-rays dipped between and following the lockdowns, as did time spent watching streamed content though in this case the dips were relatively small. Time spent on social media and playing games, including electronic games, declined steadily from a highpoint (in this time series) during the first lockdown in 2020. Time spent socialising face-to-face with family members, friends, neighbours and colleagues dipped inversely, peaking between and following the lockdowns. So did visits to cinemas and other places of out-of-home entertainment, but at a much lower level. Reading peaked (in this time series) during the first 2020 lockdown, fell-back during the remainder of 2020 and 2021, and dipped more steeply post-lockdowns in 2022.

A problem when introducing new lower level categories in the pandemic series is that we are unable to tell which of these new time uses increased, stayed the same or diminished between 2014/15 and March 2020. Fortunately, as with physically active recreation, time-use data on entertainment and socialising during and following the lockdowns can be interpreted alongside other sources of evidence, and the annual reports of Ofcom offer comprehensive evidence from well

Table 2. Average daily time in minutes, whole population age 18 and over.

	1 2014–2015	2 March/ April 2020	3 Sept/ Oct 2020	4 March 2021	5 March 2022
TV. Blue-ray, DVDs		128	108	121	106
Streaming		45	40	45	43
Social media		11	7	5	4
Playing games, computer games		28	27	22	16
Reading books, magazines, newspapers		36	28	28	17
Time with family, friends, neighbours, colleagues		6	34	12	31
Cinema, theatre, concerts, events, galleries, museums		<1	2	<1	5

before, throughout and following the pandemic lockdowns (Ofcom, 2015, 2018, 2020, 2021, 2022). Ofcom gathers its data from self-reports in online and telephone surveys, and comparisons with the ONS data, when possible, confirm the tendency of self-estimates to exaggerate. For example, Ofcom reports adults (aged 16 and over) spending 240 min online per average day in 2022 whereas the ONS evidence shows that no more than 228 min could possibly have been spent online plus watching television. However, the two sources of evidence agree that screen time peaked in 2021 rather than falling back post-lockdowns in 2022. The Ofcom data show a massive rise in total screen time from 171 to 298 min per day between 2015 and 2021, then a drop to 240 min in 2022. In the ONS time use data the drop is from 171 min to 153 min of watching television, Blue-ray, DVDs, streamed content and using social media. We must rely on Ofcom data for the overall trend from 2015–2022, but the ONS diaries are the best estimates of total screen time at any point in time.

The lockdown rises in time spent being entertained and socialising must have been entirely via the media. The media were the major winners during the lockdowns. The long-term rise in time spent watching a screen began when the most watched screens moved from cinemas to homes as the age of television dawned. There was a steady rise in tele-viewing when television became multi-channel with 24/7 programming, and a further rise when broadband added streaming to the existing air and satellite signals. As this happened, the most watched screens ceased to be television sets and became mobile devices. Lockdowns turbo-charged the rise in time spent online (Ofcom, 2021, 2022). The big commercial winners during lockdowns were streaming services such as Netflix, Disney and Amazon Prime, plus YouTube (Armstrong, 2021), and TikTok began to challenge Facebook as the dominant social networking site. Capitalism had found ways to profit from time spent aimlessly (Zizek, 2019), and held on to most of its pandemic gains post-lockdowns.

Suggestions that interactive social media can come close to compensating for in-person interaction are difficult to reconcile with the evidence from time diaries. Out of lockdowns (Table 2, columns 3 and 5), people spent 34 and 31 min on an average day on in-person socialising. During lockdowns (columns 2 and 4) they spent just 11 and 5 min using social media. In and out of lockdown was dominated by TV, Blue-ray, DVDs, and streamed services, not interactive social media.

Out-of-home leisure had begun to recover its audiences, spectators and participants, but had not regained pre-pandemic levels in 2022. The pandemic time use surveys included only persons age 18 and above. The surveys omitted children, the very group whose future lives are likely to be most affected. School attendance was interrupted for most pupils from spring 2020 and throughout the subsequent academic year. Ofcom research shows that children and young people are the heaviest consumers of and contributors to social media sites and other online services, and became even more heavily involved while locked down in their homes. In 2021 a half of all children owned a mobile phone by age 10 and nearly all children by age 13. Fifteen and sixteen year olds were self-reporting nearly 5 hours a day online in 2021 (Ofcom, 2021). The development of tastes and skills in out-of-home leisure during childhood and youth that was suppressed during lockdowns may never recover, and these are the uses of leisure time that are known to promote well-being. Future leisure research must be alert to possible profound cohort effects. Among the first cohorts of children who grew up in the age of television in the UK, there was a stepwise drop in memberships of clubs and associations, and this drop remained visible 40 years later when the cohorts were approaching retirement (McCulloch, 2014). There is already evidence of a similar broadband effect (Geraci et al., 2022). Older members may drift back to clubs that closed or went online during lockdowns (for example, Scouts Association, 2021), but the cohorts of new young recruits may be slimmer than older cohorts. This applies to all kinds of associations including political parties and movements. A likely net result will be a weakening of civil society and the perpetuation of low trust (Office for National Statistics, 2021c). All this is reminiscent of Putnam's account of how Americans going 'bowling alone' signalled profound and depressing changes in the country's socio-political fabric ((D, 2000).

Experiences

Time-use data illuminate just one dimension of people's lives at work and leisure. Fortunately, leisure research was one of the occupations that remained alive throughout the pandemic and with a broader vision than the narrowly focused time use surveys. Researchers circumvented lockdowns with qualitative projects using telephone and online contacts, usually with sub-populations in specific countries. They uncovered tales of remarkable enterprise and ingenuity in keeping leisure tastes and relationships alive throughout lockdowns. Forms of leisure activity that could be maintained often became more important than ever in lives that were otherwise heavily constrained (see Lashua et al., 2022).

That said, the big story is that opportunities to engage in out-of-home leisure were severely limited during the lockdowns in 2020 and 2021. The closure of all places and cessation of activities that could draw together people from different households was unprecedented in Britain, even in wartime when it had been considered essential to keep the home population entertained. Most people observed the 'stay at home' command issued in March 2020. Feelings of loneliness and liminality, having been thrust from normal places and activities, became widespread (see Shir-Wise, 2021). People resented being shut in and locked out from places and people they wanted to visit. These changes in time use were enforced, not agentic. Levels of mental health deteriorated (Sehmi & Slaughter, 2021). People who consumed alcohol heavily prior to the lockdowns drank even more at home (Holmes, 2020). There was no upsurge in national unity in a common effort to defeat the virus despite the ritual doorstep hand clapping for heroic health and social care staff, which was orchestrated by the government in summer 2020. There was an all-round decline in trust towards virtually everyone other than family, from neighbours to government, especially when members of the government and its senior staff were suspected of breaking rules that were set for all (Borkowska & Laurence, 2020; Office for National Statistics, 2021c).

There were some bright spots. People began to make greater use and became more appreciative of local parks, playgrounds and beauty spots (Office for National Statistics, 2021d). Time devoted to DIY and gardening increased during lockdowns, but possibly only temporarily, whereas the increase time spent exercising looks likely to be sustained. Visits to places of out-of-home entertainment and socialising had recovered from their lockdown lows in 2020 and 2021, but had still not regained pre-pandemic levels in the spring 2022.

Conclusions

The pandemic series of time-use studies has shredded the earlier narrative of temporal routines in the UK changing slowly if at all from year-to-year. During 2020 and 2021 successive lockdowns disrupted former routines. The population did not enjoy the experiences of being barred from places that they wished to visit, denied access to out-of-home entertainment and other places for in-person socialising, and being stuck in their homes. Nevertheless, in 2022 there had been no rush back to, or even towards, the old normal. Why not, if the lockdown changes had been enforced and disliked, not agentic? The lockdowns accelerated some pre-pandemic trends: more flexible hybrid work schedules, and more time accounted for by the media. Other post-lockdown trends were new: the UK population was studying less, travelling less, spending less time on unpaid child care, enjoying more leisure time, but also doing more paid work. Some of these changes may have been agentic, but not the restrictions on 'going out'. Yet hospitality business was still 30% beneath pre-pandemic levels at the end of 2021 (McAllister, 2021). In 2022, the Cineworld chain considered filing for bankruptcy.

A boost in media use was probably inevitable when people were locked down in their homes, and when extra leisure time was gained by not having to travel to and from work. What else could people do but log-on or switch something on? What else could they do during lockdowns when there were prohibitions on visiting other households and when leisure facilities were closed? New technologies can give people greater control of their time: when to answer emails, texts and voicemails, and when to watch broadcasts (Wajcman, 2015). However, during and post-lockdowns people have found that this control is bounded by obligations to perform paid and domestic work (Roberts, 2019).

Media use has been rolled back from its high point during the 2020 lockdown but has consolidated its already dominant position in leisure time use. The new normal looks less like the leisure utopias that some leisure scholars once envisaged (for example, Best, 1978; Neulinger, 1990). Rather it resembles the dystopia of people stranded in a wilderness of free time, rescued from boredom only by the constantly available media (Glasser, 1970). The post-pandemic normal resembles a 21st century version of the American culture industry spreading a state of passive contentment that the Frankfurt School experienced before, during and following the Second World War (see Adorno, 1996).

The leisure studies literature is full of examples of how wellbeing is enhanced by activities that pull people from their armchairs and preferably out of their homes into in-person contact with others. The challenge to public, voluntary sector and commercial providers is to innovate and create offers that can out-compete switching on. If the UK and other countries are exiting the lockdown years into a decade of economic stagnation, high inflation and squeezes on household budgets, and if public sector austerity is perpetuated in the UK and imposed elsewhere, all providers of out-of-home leisure will need to innovate and compete with low-cost products or disappear completely from 21st century leisure markets.

Disclosure statement

No potential conflict of interest was reported by the author(s).

References

Adorno, T. (1996). *The culture industry: Selected essays on mass culture*. Routledge.
Armstrong, M. (2021), *Leisure in Lockdown: The Biggest Winners and Losers*, www.statista.com.
Best, F. (1978). The time of our lives. *Loisir Et Société / Society and Leisure*, *1*(1), 95–114. https://doi.org/10.1080/07053436.1978.10715091
Bhatti, M. (2006). When I'm in my garden I create my own paradise": Homes and gardens in later life'. *The Sociological Review*, *54*(2), 318–341. https://doi.org/10.1111/j.1467-954X.2006.00616.x
Bittman, M., & Wajcman, J. (1999), *The rush hour: The quality of leisure time and gender equity*, SPRC Discussion Paper 97, University of New
Borkowska, M., & Laurence, J. (2020). Coming together or coming apart? Changes in social cohesion during the Covid-19 pandemic in England. *European Societies*, *23*(sup1), S618–636. https://doi.org/10.1080/14616696.2020.1833067
Chase, D. R., & Godbey, G. (1983). The accuracy of self-reported participation rates. *Leisure Studies*, *2*, 231–235.
D, P. R. (2000). *Bowling alone: The collapse and renewal of American community*. Simon and Schuster.
Department for Digital, Culture, Media and Sport. (2020). *Taking part2019/20: Statistical release*. Department for Digital, Culture Media and Sport.
Feder, T., McAndre, S., O'Brien, D., & Taylor, M. (2022). Cultural consumption and Covid-19: Evidence from the taking part and COVID-19 cultural participation monitor surveys. *Leisure Studies*. https://doi.org/10.1080/02614367.2022.2088831
Geraci, A., Nardotto, M., Reggiani, T., & Sabatini, F. (2022). Broadband internet and social capital. *Journal of Public Economics*, *206*(3), 104578. https://doi.org/10.1016/j.jpubeco.2021.104578
Gershuny, J., & Harris, T. (2019). Time and physical activity. In J. Gershuny & O. Sullivan, *What We Really Do All Day* (pp. 189–206.l). Pelican.
Gershuny, J., & Sullivan, O. (2019). *What we really do all day*. Pelican.

Gershuny, J. I., & Thomas, G.S. (1980). *Changing patterns of time use: UK activity patterns 1961 and 1975*. Science Policy Research Unit, University of Sussex.
Glasser, R. (1970). *Leisure: Penalty or prize?*. Macmillan.
Holmes, L. (2020) *Drinking During Lockdown: Headline Findings* www.alcoholchange.org.uk/blog/2020/covid19-drinking. Accessed 02.06.2020
Lashua, B., Johnson, C. W., & Parry, D. C. (2022). *Leisure in the time of coronavirus*. Routledge.
MacInnes, J. (2006). Work–life balance in Europe: A response to the baby bust or reward for the baby boomers? *European Societies*, 8(2), 223–249. https://doi.org/10.1080/14616690600644988
McAllister, J. (2021). Hospitality revenue remains at less than 70% of pre-pandemic levels, ONS reveals. *BigHospitality*. www.bighospitality.co.uk
McCulloch, A. (2014). Cohort variations in the membership of voluntary associations in Great Britain, 1991–2007. *Sociology*, 48(1), 167–185. https://doi.org/10.1177/0038038513481643
Moskoff, W. (1984). *Labour and leisure in the soviet union*. Macmillan.
Neulinger, J. (1990). *Eden After All*. Giordano Bruno.
Ofcom (2015), *Adults' media use and attitudes report*, Ofcom,
Ofcom (2018), *Communications market report*, Ofcom,
Ofcom. (2020). *Online nation*. Ofcom.
Ofcom (2021), *Online nation: 2021 report*, Ofcom,
Ofcom (2022), *Online nation: 2022 report*, Ofcom,
Office for National Statistics. (2020). *Coronavirus and how people spent their time under lockdown: 28 march to 26 April 2020*. Office for National Statistics.
Office for National Statistics. (2020b). *A new normal? how people spent their time after the march 2020 coronavirus lockdown*. Office for National Statistics.
Office for National Statistics. (2021). *How people with a vaccine spent their time – one year on from the first lockdown, march 2021*. Office for National Statistics.
Office for National Statistics. (2021b). *Living longer: Older workers during the coronavirus (COVID-19) Pandemic*. Office for National Statistics.
Office for National Statistics. (2021c). *Coronavirus and the social impacts on Great Britain: 14 may 2021*. Office for National Statistics.
Office for National Statistics. (2021d). *How has lockdown changed our relationship with nature?*. Office for National Statistics.
Office for National Statistics. (2022). *How people spent their time after coronavirus restrictions were. March 2022*, Office for National Statistics.
Roberts, K. Leisure: The importance of being inconsequential. (2013). *Leisure Studies*, 30(1), 5–20. ISSN 0261-4367. https://doi.org/10.1080/02614367.2010.506650
Roberts, K. (2019). A future for UK leisure studies. *International Journal of the Sociology of Leisure*, 2(3), 239–253. https://doi.org/10.1007/s41978-018-0020-z
Roberts, K. (2020). Locked down leisure in Britain. *Leisure Studies*, 39, 617–628. https://doi.org/10.1080/02614367.2020.1791937
Roberts, K. (2021). Education-to-work transitions during the Covid-19 lockdowns in Britain, 2020-2021. *Advances in Applied Sociology*, 11, 564–584. https://doi.org/10.4236/aasoci.2021.1111049
Robinson, J. P., & Godbey, G. (1999). *Time for life: The surprising ways Americans use their time*, 2nd edition. Pennsylvania: Pennsylvania State University Press.
Salway, R., Foster, C., Vocht, F., de Tibbitts, B., Emm-Collison, L., House, D., Williams, J. G., Breheny, K., Reid, T., Walker, R., Churchward, S., Hollingworth, W., & Jago, R. (2022). Accelerometer-measured physical activity and sedentary time among children and their parents in the UK before and after COVID-19 lockdowns: A natural experiment. *The International Journal of Behavioral Nutrition and Physical Activity*, 19, 51. https://doi.org/10.1186/s12966-022-01290-4
Scouts Association (2021), *Good For You*, www.scouts.org.uk_Posted_26.5.21, accessed 27.5.21.
Sehmi, R., & Slaughter, H. (2021). *Double trouble: Exploring the labour market and mental health impact of covid-19 on young people*. Resolution Foundation.
Shir-Wise, M. (2021). Melting time and confined leisure under COVID-19 lockdown. *World Leisure Journal*, (3), 221–233. https://doi.org/10.1080/16078055.2021.1944296
Sinfield, A. (1981). *What unemployment means*. Oxford: Martin Robertson.
Sport England (2020), *Active lives adult survey may 2019/2020 report*, Sport England,
Sport England (2020b), *Active lives adult survey mid-march-mid May 2020. coronavirus (COVID-19) Report*, Sport England,
Sport England (2021), *Active lives adult survey, may 2020/21 report*, Sport England,
Sport England (2022), *Active lives adult survey november 2020-21 report*, Sport England,
Sullivan, O. (2000). The division of domestic labour: Twenty years of change. *Sociology*, 34(3), 437–456. https://doi.org/10.1177/S0038038500000286

Szalai, A. (1972). *The use of time*. The Hague: Mouton.
Teodorovicz, T., Sadun, R., Kun, A. L., & Shaer, O. (2022), *How does working from home during covid-189 affect what managers do? Evidence from time use studies*, Discussion Paper 1844, Centre for Economic Performance, London School of Economics,
van, B. M., & Salome, L. (2010). The indoorisation of outdoor sports: An exploration of the rise of lifestyle sports in artificial settings. *Leisure Studies, 29*, 143–160. https://doi.org/10.1080/02614360903261479
Veal, A. J. (2016). Leisure, income inequality and the Veblen effect: Cross-national analysis of leisure time and sport and cultural activity. *Leisure Studies, 35*(2), 215–240. https://doi.org/10.1080/02614367.2015.1036104
Veal, A. J. (2022). The 4-day work-week: The new leisure society? *Leisure Studies*, 1–16. https://doi.org/10.1080/02614367.2022.2094997
Wajcman, J. (2015). *Pressed for time: The acceleration of life under digital capitalism*. University of Chicago Press.
Wheaton, B. (2013). *The cultural politics of lifestyle sports*. Routledge.
Wilkinson, R., & Pickett, K. (2009). *The spirit level: Why more equal societies almost always do better*. Allen Lane.
Zizek, S. (2019). *The relevance of the communist manifesto*. Polity Press.

CrossFit during lockdown. The promises and pitfalls of digitally mediated training for leisure-time physical activity

Verena Lenneis, Jeppe Klarskov Hansen and Sine Agergaard

ABSTRACT

The COVID-19 pandemic led to nationwide lockdowns and rigid measures of social distancing in Denmark. Such a situation provides the unique opportunity to study interruptions in training routines and scrutinise the significance of physical attendance, face-to-face interactions and collective engagement for sport and leisure-time physical activity. Drawing on Randall Collins' micro-sociological theory of 'Interaction Ritual Chains', this article focuses on CrossFit – an activity, which is not only known for members' high-intensity workouts but also for a tight-knit community. Specifically, we explored how CrossFitters in Denmark made sense of and experienced the changes of their leisure practices throughout the COVID-19 pandemic. Semi-structured interviews with 20 CrossFitters recruited from different CrossFit boxes showed that not only activity levels but also emotional energy and group solidarity dropped considerably during COVID-19 as members lacked interactions within the CrossFit boxes which had been crucial for their participation before the pandemic. Notably, new training situations, specifically online workouts, could not replace the highly successful interaction rituals in the CrossFit box, which stresses the significance of face-to-face interactions for continuous leisure-time physical activity. In so doing, this article contributes to discussions about whether online workouts and digitally mediated communities can complement or replace physical training.

Introduction

In the last two years, the COVID-19 pandemic has greatly affected individuals' everyday lives, including different aspects of their leisure such as opportunities for leisure-time physical activity (LTPA). For example, such opportunities were and are altered by closed sports facilities or measures of social distancing and assembly bans. Consequently, several review studies have reported decreases in LTPA during various forms of lockdowns in different countries (Caputo & Reichert, 2020; Stockwell et al., 2021). Also in Denmark, participation rates in sports and LTPA have declined during COVID-19 (Schmidt & Pawlowski, 2021). Even in April 2021 when the Danish government started to lift some restrictions that gradually allowed for organised outdoor sports participation, only 54% of the Danish adult population engaged in LTPA, which is 10% less compared to pre-pandemic levels (Eske, 2021).

Not only have LTPA participation rates decreased, but there have also been significant changes in the ways in which different groups of the population engage in sports and LTPA. For example, due to the COVID-19 government measurements affecting different kinds and forms of LTPA and sports unequally, some activities (e.g. exercising in a gym) have dropped in popularity, whereas others (e.g. outdoor walking) have become more popular. Likewise, the use of digital media and technologies for home-based exercise has grown during the lockdown (Kirkegaard et al., 2020; Mutz et al., 2021).

Although survey results give important insights into COVID-19 induced changes in LTPA participation rates, research about how individuals made sense of and experienced the impact of the COVID-19 lockdown on their LTPA lives is scarce. However, qualitative studies may help us scrutinise digitally mediated training and detail how COVID-19 has affected participants' processes of meaning and identity making. Furthermore, whilst a number of studies have examined elite athletes' perspectives (Bowes et al., 2021; Souter et al., 2022; Whitcomb-Khan et al., 2021), research focusing on the experiences of groups that engage in recreational sport and LTPA is limited.

One of the groups whose opportunities to exercise have been particularly affected by COVID-19 are those participating in organised fitness activities. After all, gyms in many countries have been closed during the different waves of the COVID-19 pandemic. Yet, at the time of writing, only few studies have given voice to such individuals. One of the few studies is Kaur et al. (2020), who explored the lockdown experiences of gym goers in India. This study showed how the closure of gyms initially led to a lack of motivation as participants missed their gym mates. However, with time and help of social media, online training and music, Kaur et al.'s (2020) informants managed to develop new training routines. In addition, Carter and Alexander (2021) emphasise the importance of social and emotional support for regular participation in fitness activities. For many of the study's informants, digital workouts made it difficult to connect to the community and could not replace face-to-face interactions. These findings are congruent with a study with fitness instructors who experienced online classes as an insufficient substitute for face-to-face teaching as digital platforms impeded socio-emotional connectedness with participants (Andersson & Andreasson, 2021).

Contributing to the sparse socio-cultural literature on LTPA and COVID-19, the aim of this article is to shed light on the significance of physical attendance, face-to-face interactions and collective engagement for participation in LTPA. We have chosen to focus on CrossFit, one of the fastest growing fitness trends in the world as it is not only known for participants' intense exercise regimes but also for a strong community among members (Crockett & Butryn, 2018; Dawson, 2017; Edmonds, 2020; Lautner et al., 2021; Pickett et al., 2016). To investigate the impact that COVID-19 restrictions and changed training routines have had on CrossFitters' experiences and the CrossFit community, we will draw on Collins' (2014a, 2020) theory on Interaction Ritual Chains. Collins ascribes great importance to face-to-face interactions as successful rituals pump up individuals with emotional energy and create group solidarity. This makes Collins' theory highly relevant in times of a pandemic where otherwise well-established conditions and forms of social interaction have been disrupted. Consequently, this article will not only provide insights into the experiences and perspectives of the 20 interviewees but will also contribute to more general discussions about whether virtual communities and online workouts can complement or replace physical communities. Such insights will help to identify not only the promises but also the pitfalls of digitally mediated training.

We begin by providing background information about the COVID-19 lockdown in Denmark before describing the socio-cultural literature on CrossFit.

CrossFit during lockdown in Denmark

There are no official numbers on individuals engaging in CrossFit in Denmark, but out of the more than 15,000 affiliated CrossFit gyms (so-called CrossFit boxes),[1] in the world, 33 are located in Denmark.[2] As part of the nationwide COVID-19 lockdown in March 2020, all CrossFit boxes were closed. Consequently, CrossFit boxes started to share online workouts for which little equipment was needed. Members could choose whether to suspend their membership or support their CrossFit box, with some boxes offering members to borrow equipment in exchange. In April 2020, CrossFit boxes were allowed to offer outdoor classes. However, these were limited to five, later ten participants, required class reservations, and were characterised by social distancing and sanitisation of hands, equipment and surfaces.

Whereas CrossFit boxes could reopen in summer 2020 (however, members had to wear a face mask before getting dressed for training), they were again closed in December 2020 during the pandemic's second wave. In February 2021, CrossFit boxes were able to offer outdoor classes; again with several COVID-19 restrictions such as social distancing, sanitisation, etc. In May 2021 CrossFit boxes could reopen. However, members had to show a 'COVID-19 passport' (meaning that one must either be vaccinated, have recovered from COVID-19, or show a negative COVID-19 test). Due to the Omicron variant, several restrictions such as the 'COVID-19 passport' were reintroduced in December 2021. However, in February 2022 COVID-19 was no longer classified as a critical disease in Denmark and (nearly) all restrictions were lifted (Figure 1).

Socio-cultural research on CrossFit

Whilst a relatively large body of physiological research exists on the benefits as well as the risks of injury in CrossFit (Meyer et al., 2017; Montalvo et al., 2017; Rodríguez et al., 2022), there has been less focus on CrossFit from a socio-cultural perspective. Existing socio-

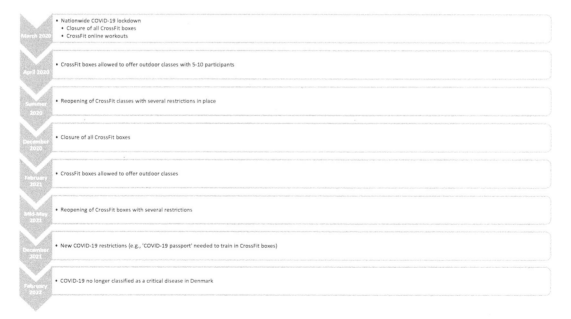

Figure 1. A timeline of CrossFit opportunities in Denmark during the COVID-19 pandemic.

cultural studies have explored gender constructions and negotiations, including how CrossFit might give women the opportunity to challenge dominant gender norms and body ideals (e.g. Nash, 2018; Schrijnder et al., 2021; Washington & Economides, 2016). Additionally, several studies have focused on the fitness culture of CrossFit highlighting that despite CrossFit's competitive environment, in which a whiteboard ranking participants pushes individuals to their physical limits, CrossFit is characterised by a supportive atmosphere with caring and engaged coaches, cheering, bonding and socialising (Bailey et al., 2019; Crockett & Butryn, 2018; Edmonds, 2020; Gipson et al., 2021; Lautner et al., 2021; Pickett et al., 2016; Woolf & Lawrence, 2017). Furthermore, research indicates that participation in CrossFit may provide members with a greater sense of community belongingness and higher levels of social capital compared with 'traditional' gym participation (Pickett et al., 2016; Whiteman-Sandland et al., 2018). Indeed, accountability and responsibility towards the community ensured regular participation (Lautner et al., 2021).

The literature explains these differences with CrossFit's class structure and CrossFit boxes' open layout that facilitate interaction and cooperation between members. Such a setup does not provide participants with the possibility to claim their own space and be anonymous or autonomous. This is contrary to traditional gyms where members frequently listen to music or watch TV while exercising, thus creating 'virtual boundaries between themselves and others' (Edmonds, 2020, p. 364; see also, Crockett & Butryn, 2018; Woolf & Lawrence, 2017). Consequently, CrossFit is often described as an accepting and inclusive space regardless of age, fitness level or experience although research also points to an underlying social hierarchy based on the precondition of pushing oneself to the limit (Edmonds, 2020) or on exercise ability (Crockett & Butryn, 2018). Indeed, Woolf and Lawrence (2017) argue that CrossFit's increasing focus on competitive events may undermine inclusivity and lead to greater hierarchies between members. Likewise, research emphasises that CrossFit and its culture may not appeal to everyone (Dawson, 2017; Lautner et al., 2021). However, those who stay 'align themselves with the institution's discourses and regard its principles as an extension of their own values and beliefs' (Dawson, 2017, p. 372).

Not surprisingly then, CrossFit has been characterised as an environment where individuals can shape and self-transform their bodies and (re)construct individual and collective identities (Dawson, 2017; Edmonds, 2020; Gipson et al., 2021; Woolf & Lawrence, 2017). Specifically, the tight-knit community and relations to others seem to affect such identity constructions. Woolf and Lawrence (2017) have found that even CrossFitters participating in competitions have a stronger sense of social identity than athletic identity, which is remarkable given that CrossFit brands itself as a competitive sport. Indeed, due to CrossFitters' great training frequency, specific exercise and diet practices as well as a tight-knit community with members showing high levels of trust and loyalty, CrossFit has been compared with a cult or a religion. Scrutinising the culture of CrossFit, Dawson (2017, p. 366) labels CrossFit an 'exercise-military-religion nexus'. Likewise, in her examination of Christian CrossFitters, Ornella (2019) draws a parallel between a CrossFit box and a church, highlighting similarities such as a close community, hard work and dedication as central values.

In sum, previous research highlights the great importance that social relations and the CrossFit community have for CrossFitters' regular participation and their identity constructions. This makes CrossFit a specifically relevant leisure setting in which to investigate the consequences of the COVID-19 pandemic on leisure communities. To be able to explore CrossFit members' experiences of the changes afflicted to their regular leisure time participation in the CrossFit box, we will now introduce Collins' (2014a) theory on Interaction Ritual Chains.

Interaction Ritual Chains

Interaction ritual theories originate from Émile Durkheim's (1915) theory of religious rituals, which describes mechanisms that ultimately hold society together. The second major influence is Erving Goffman (1967), who basically extended Durkheim's approach to secular life by examining mini-rituals of everyday life. Collins' (2014a) micro-sociological theory on 'Interaction Ritual Chains', on which we draw in this article, combines and further develops Durkheim and Goffman's approaches to a formal theory of ritual interaction (Summers-Effler, 2007). Unlike common parlance that uses 'ritual' in a more restricted sense, rituals in interaction ritual theory describe all focused interactions which occur in various contexts. Hence, for Collins (2014a) situations are the centre of micro-sociological explanation; the repeated enactment of rituals forms individuals and their identity along with creating solidarity in a group and (re)producing social structures.

Collins (2014a) formalised Goffman's work on interaction rituals using a rather mechanistic approach similar to Durkheim (Summers-Effler, 2007). Consequently, according to Collins (2014a, pp. 47–48), four conditions must be present to initiate interaction rituals. Firstly, there must be *bodily co-presence* so that two or more people are physically present; they are close to each other and can hear, watch and feel what the others are doing. Secondly, there are *barriers to outsiders* that mark who is taking part and who is excluded from the interaction ritual. Thirdly, there must be a *mutual focus of attention*: a common focus on either an activity or an object, and finally, interaction rituals are initiated by a *shared mood* described as an emotional state between those present.

An interaction ritual only takes place when all these four components are fulfilled, and the different components such as the mutual focus of attention and shared mood may feedback upon each other. Indeed, 'as the persons become more tightly focused on their common activity, more aware of what each other is doing and feeling, and more aware of each other's awareness, they experience their shared emotion more intensely, as it comes to dominate their awareness' (Collins, 2014a, p. 48). Accordingly, the different ingredients can reinforce each other and create so-called 'rhythmic entrainment', a highly coordinated form of social interaction in which individuals' bodies or voices get into the same rhythm (e.g. chanting, dancing or clapping; Collins, 2014a, 2014b, 2020). Such collective action can generate what Durkheim (1915) has termed 'collective effervescence' – an intensification of a mutual emotional experience of excitement. Feeling such emotional arousal, 'a sort of electricity' (Durkheim, 1915, p. 247 as cited in Collins, 2014a, p. 35) is highly enjoyable for the individual and can unify the group as such collective movements create intersubjectivity. For example, sports events may facilitate feeling rhythmic entrainment and collective effervescence:

> The attraction of being in a live audience at a sports event is not that one can see the action on the field better (visibility is usually worse than on TV), but it is being pumped up by the excitement of the crowd when they hold their breath together, rise to their feet together, jump up and down, and hug each other together as they respond to the action. (Collins, 2020, p. 482)

Notably, collective effervescence is a momentary state which, however, can lead to different long-term outcomes. Firstly, the outcome of a successful interaction ritual is *group solidarity* which is described as the feeling of belonging to a particular group. Secondly, *emotional energy*, a feeling of confidence, strength, elation, enthusiasm and drive to act. Thirdly, *collective symbols* representing the group (e.g. physical objects, specific gestures or icons) – hereby drawing a clear parallel to Durkheim's (1915) 'sacred objects' – and fourthly, *feelings of morality* defining what is considered right and wrong in the group.

Among these outcomes of interaction rituals, which can vary in strength, emotional energy is of particular importance as it is the main motivator of social life. Indeed, according to Collins (2014a, 2014b) individuals have a basic motivation to maximise their levels of emotional energy albeit such strategies of maximisation mostly operate on an intuitive and subconscious level. Collins (2014a, 2014b) describes that emotional energy ranges on a continuum from high to low; individuals experiencing high emotional energy are self-confident, enthusiastic and proactive, whilst persons with low emotional energy feel passive, withdrawn or depressed. Consequently, individuals are more likely to repeat rituals during which they have felt collective effervescence and which have generated high emotional energy and a heightened sense of social connectedness. As the term interaction ritual *chains* emphasises, individuals move from one interaction ritual to the next taking the consequences which the interaction had on their emotional energy levels with them (Collins, 2014b). Hence, as described by Summers-Effler (2007, p. 139), although the 'interaction order has independent situational demands, past interaction determines the level of emotional energy and symbolic capital available to us to deal with these demands'.

Importantly, interaction rituals can also be mediocre or even fail with the consequence that such long-term emotions are absent and do not contribute to a strengthening of the group solidarity, identity, etc. However, as 'life is structured around the contrast between successful, socially magnetic ritual situations with their high degree of emotion, motivation, and symbolic charge, and situations of lesser ritualism' (Collins, 2014a, p. 51), it is important in an analysis of situations to also look at failed interaction rituals and examine *what* makes the difference between weak and strong outcomes.

As Collins (2014a, 2020) focuses on emotions rather than cognitive processes and frequently refers to sports (fandom) in his articles and books (see also, Collins, 2016), Interaction Ritual Chains theory has been described as a fruitful approach to study sports and leisure contexts in which embodied experiences, relations with others and communities are decisive (Simons, 2020; Spaaij & Schaillée, 2021). Indeed, Collins (2020, p. 482) has described embodied experiences caused by rhythmic entrainment and collective effervescence as 'the glue that creates moments of social solidarity'. However, opportunities for these kinds of embodied experiences have been scarce during the COVID-19 pandemic. This makes it particularly relevant to draw on Collins' (2014a, 2020) micro-sociological theory that emphasises the importance of face-to-face-interactions to explore what happens to a leisure community such as CrossFit when the ingredients of interaction rituals are curtailed.

Methods

This article is based on individual, semi-structured interviews with 20 members of different CrossFit boxes in Denmark. We decided to use interviews as we were particularly interested to hear members' perspectives and descriptions related to the lack of face-to-face interactions during the COVID-19 pandemic. We recognise that participant observation of new training opportunities (e.g. outdoor classes) during COVID-19 could have contributed to our analysis by taking the situation as an analytical starting point (Collins, 2014a). However, due to the COVID-19 restrictions which limited the number of participants allowed to participate, this has not been possible.

Drawing on criterion-based sampling (Patton, 2015; Sparkes & Smith, 2014), we sought to recruit informants who prior to COVID-19 had trained at least three times a week and who had been active members of a CrossFit box for a year or longer (thereby making sure that our informants were able to compare different training situations before and after the lockdown). To have a varied perspective of CrossFitters' experiences during COVID-19, we addressed CrossFitters from six different boxes in four Danish cities (Copenhagen, Silkeborg, Aarhus and Aalborg). The 20 informants were aged 23–49, with the majority being in their twenties. Most interviewees were either pursuing or had obtained a higher level of education (Table 1). We strived for an equal gender balance, but due to drop-outs we ended up interviewing fifteen male and five female CrossFitters. To protect the personal information provided by our informants, we removed identifying information and used pseudonyms throughout the research process.

Table 1. The interviewees.

Pseudonym	Gender	Age	Occupation	Experience with CrossFit prior to COVID-19 (years)
Anders	Male	29	Project consultant	1.8
Anne	Female	26	Health professional	5
Christian	Male	26	Carrier	1.5
Fie	Female	23	Public employee	2
Jens	Male	27	Health professional	7
Jes	Male	26	Student	4.5
Kirsten	Female	23	Student	2.6
Lars	Male	25	HR-consultant	2
Mads	Male	26	Bricklayer	3
Michael	Male	25	IT-consultant	5
Mille	Female	25	Health professional	3
Morten	Male	28	Health/sports professional	4
Per	Male	48	Salesperson	9
Peter	Male	28	Primary school teacher	7
Pia	Female	26	Office clerk	3
Rasmus	Male	38	HR manager	6.5
Ryan	Male	49	Educator	7
Simon	Male	47	Salesperson	7
Søren	Male	28	Student	5
Thomas	Male	27	Project coordinator	11

The interviews were semi-structured and conducted along the guidelines of Brinkmann and Kvale (2015). Due to the COVID-19 restrictions when conducting the interviews in April-May 2021 (this was just before CrossFit boxes were allowed to reopen, albeit with several restrictions; see, Figure 1), all interviews were conducted online and lasted between 30–75 minutes. The online format provided participants with greater flexibility to choose a convenient time and day (Iacono et al., 2016). As two groups of graduate students, including the second author, who were supervised by the first and the last author, acted as interviewers, two slightly different interview guides were employed. However, all interviews were centred around the interviewees' CrossFit biographies including the importance they ascribed to their participation, the CrossFit community, and particularly how COVID-19 lockdown(s) and restrictions had affected their participation.

All 20 interviews were recorded and then transcribed by different students. Next, the first author (VL) analysed the material drawing on to the six-phase model of reflexive thematic analysis (Braun & Clarke, 2019, 2022; Braun et al., 2016), which emphasises the role of the researcher and the importance of reflective and thoughtful engagement with the data. After VL (re)read all the transcripts to become familiar with the data (phase 1), the coding process started in phase 2 during which both data-driven (e.g. 'friendships' or 'outdoor classes') and theory-driven codes (e.g. 'shared mood' or 'collective symbols') were generated. In phases 3–4, VL started to cluster the numerous codes and develop subthemes and candidate themes such as 'group cohesion and solidarity', 'identity constructions' or 'decrease in motivation'. In phase 5, in which the other authors were involved as well, we compiled and edited our notes and formed three final theory-inspired themes: 'Highly successful interaction rituals in the CrossFit box before the pandemic', 'Loss of emotional energy and one's identity as a CrossFitter' and 'New strategies to gain emotional energy', which also structured our analytical narrative in phase 6.

We applied a 'relativist approach' employing study-specific criteria when evaluating the study's quality (Burke, 2016; Sparkes & Smith, 2014). Taking Tracy's (2010) criteria as a point of departure, we considered 'worthy topic', 'rich rigor', 'meaningful coherence', 'ethics' and 'sincerity' as particularly relevant. As the first and the last author were CrossFit 'outsiders', whilst the second author and some of the other students who had conducted the interviews were CrossFit 'insiders' (Sparkes & Smith, 2014), it was important to reflect on how these different positions impacted the knowledge construction throughout the research process. Here, discussions among CrossFit insiders and outsiders, for example, about CrossFit's inclusive potential, which is often taken for granted in CrossFit, helped to negotiate these positions and maintain a 'critical distance' (Thorpe, 2011).

Results and discussion

Drawing on Collins (2014a, 2020), it is also crucial to explore the interaction rituals in the CrossFit box before COVID-19 to understand how the lack of face-to-face interactions influenced the experiences of CrossFitters during the pandemic. We will therefore first examine (previous) interactions in the CrossFit boxes before focusing on the consequences of the altered training situations.

Before the COVID-19 pandemic: Highly successful interaction rituals in the CrossFit boxes

All informants used to be regular goers who had exercised 3–7 times per week in their respective CrossFit boxes. For Fie and others CrossFit was 'more than just training [...]; it's as much about the community'. Accordingly, the informants would meet before training to drink coffee and chat with each other; also, after training they would eat an energy bar, evaluate the 'Workout of the Day' (WOD in CrossFit parlance) and make new training appointments. During training, CrossFit members would help and cheer on each other, giving high fives or fist bumps.

To characterise the CrossFit community, almost all interviewees compared CrossFit with exercising in what they depicted as 'traditional' gyms, which they had found lonely. For example, Simon emphasised that in a gym members would work out wearing headphones 'being in their own small world while they exercise'. Contrary, in CrossFit 'everybody talks to each other; there are no mirrors; nobody wears headphones ... it's a really positive environment' (Ryan). Such descriptions are congruent with several studies which stress that CrossFit is more committed to community building than conventional fitness gyms (Pickett et al., 2016; Whiteman-Sandland et al., 2018). Drawing on Collins (2014a, 2014b), it can be assumed that individual gym goers often lack the mutual focus of attention and a shared mood that are crucial for a successful interaction ritual. Here, gym goers' movements are not synchronised, their focus is spread towards different orientations and they are not likely to feel collective effervescence (Dawson, 2017).

In contrast, Christian talked about a strong 'we-feeling' experienced during training,

> We always support and motivate each other where we say, 'We are gonna do it'. It feels like a great victory when we survive the training session. But you don't feel that it's your victory but that you have completed this super hard WOD together. It's a joint victory.

This quote highlights the strong mutual focus of attention in the CrossFit boxes, followed by outcomes that with the perspective of Collins (2014a) appear as group solidarity and emotional energy; a feeling that Christian described as a 'great victory', a state of euphoria caused by completing the hard WOD together. Similar dimensions of emotional energy developing through the interactions in the CrossFit boxes were described by other interviewees as 'a mental boost' and 'lifting their spirits'. Notably, Christian and others used negative expressions such as '*surviving* the training session', 'a workout *hurts*', 'the training was *terrible*' or 'experiencing *pain* together' when talking about a WOD, which according to the interviewees was characteristic of the practices in the CrossFit boxes (see also, Ornella, 2019). Drawing on Collins (2014a, 2020), a strong mutual focus of attention (on the WOD) and a shared emotional state (enduring pain and suffering together) feedback upon and intensify each other. Furthermore, such a terminology mirroring a strong work ethic indicates that participants in CrossFit boxes develop feelings of morality sharing responsibility that the group workout is successful for everyone (Edmonds, 2020; Woolf & Lawrence, 2017).

Such a shared focus of attention and emotions also appeared in other practices in the box, e.g. when cheering on each other, writing training results on a whiteboard, or ringing a specific bell to mark and celebrate a personal record. The characteristic whiteboard or the bell hanging on the wall in each CrossFit box appear as group symbols or Durkheimian 'sacred objects' (Collins, 2014a; Durkheim, 1915) that represent the common values in the CrossFit boxes. Whilst high fives and fist bumps may represent group cohesion, the whiteboard and the bell stand for hard work and pushing oneself to the limits, which appears as a premise for being recognised as a CrossFitter with a high standing (Collins, 2014a; see also, Edmonds, 2020; Woolf & Lawrence, 2017). However, our informants described not only pushing oneself but also open-mindedness and inclusion as central values that were dominant in CrossFit. Supporting other studies, our interviewees experienced 'a strong sense of community that extended beyond the gym' (Bailey et al., 2019, p. 197) and told us about friendships and social gatherings in and outside the box. Here, participants used strong expressions such as 'family' or 'a second home' when referring to a tight-knit CrossFit community.

Although probably affected by the COVID-19 lockdown, all interviewees provided detailed descriptions of (previous) practices in the CrossFit boxes that appear as highly successful interaction rituals resulting in strong outcomes such as group solidarity between participants, high emotional energy, use of group symbols and feelings of morality (Collins, 2014a). However, the COVID-19 lockdown and restrictions made it impossible to repeat such training situations over a longer period. This leads us to explore what happens when it is no longer possible for the CrossFit community to reproduce such successful interaction rituals in the CrossFit box.

Loss of emotional energy and one's identity as a CrossFitter during the COVID-19 pandemic

Due to the nationwide lockdown and other COVID-19 restrictions, the interviewees' training situations were altered considerably, which for many led to a major decline in motivation. For example, Mille had previously trained four hours six times a week, whilst she only trained half an hour during the pandemic, 'I started to run, but also quickly lost my motivation. It's because you're doing it alone. This also goes for starting a workout [alone] – it's just really demotivating'. Anne's activity levels also dropped considerably during COVID-19,

> It's been difficult for me to find the motivation and keep training. [...] We actually got the opportunity to borrow some equipment from our box, but I've just had such a hard time to find something that worked for me. [...] I tried a training programme where I should train three times a week and do these exercises. But I just couldn't. It was as if my basement was 20km away.

For Mille, Anne and others it was the absence of physical training communities that became a barrier for their participation in CrossFit during the lockdown.

This was also the main problem with the digitally mediated forms of CrossFit training such as online workouts, which CrossFit boxes offered during the first lockdown. Admittedly, a few interviewees found that online training did have a positive influence on their motivation although they missed 'looking into each other's eyes and talk ... seeing whole bodies, not only a computer screen' (Rasmus). Fie also enjoyed online workouts but acknowledged that 'most members probably sat and ate chips while watching the workout. But seeing each other's comments created a feeling of being together, although none of us really were'.

However, many informants criticised that training in a virtual community was simply not fun and could not foster a sense of working out together. Consequently, they soon dropped online workouts,

> When you are used to throw barbells and dumbbells around, it's difficult to find the motivation [...]. Because you were used to exercise together with your group. That's what has motivated me. [...] And then, to stand in your own living room, and others standing in front of a webcam ... that wasn't the same. (Lars)

Lars and others' experiences are congruent with research that found that online fitness events could not provide coaches and participants with the same amount of group cohesion and feelings of belonging. Here, Collins' (2014a, 2020) theoretical framework can further contribute to explore online training and its limitations. Accordingly, physical co-presence is crucial in interaction rituals as it facilitates a mutual focus of attention, a shared mood, rhythmic entrainment and collective effervescence. Indeed, Collins (2020, p. 482) elaborates that individuals feel rhythmic entrainment and collective effervescence most intensely when all bodily channels (and not only seeing or hearing) are involved, i.e. when an experience becomes *embodied*.

Hence, although digitally mediated training also seeks to direct participants' focus of attention to the WOD, their focus and common emotional experience are impaired as it is difficult to see other participants' facial expressions and gestures and, specifically, feel and share a form of emotional arousal and excitement with other CrossFitters. As indicated by Rasmus' statement above, online workouts made it difficult to see whether others were exhausted or out of breath or, as expressed by Fie, if participants actually worked out or only watched the livestream. Likewise, it was mostly the coach who gave one-way instructions whilst the participants could not help each other. No physical hugs, cheers, high-fives or fist bumps could be exchanged during online training, and unlike during working out in the CrossFit box, the interviewees felt no emotional arousal evoked by the digitally mediated training. Hence, contrary to previous training situations in the CrossFit box before COVID-19, no feedback loop between a common focus of attention and a shared emotional state arose. In sum, online workouts can be characterised as failed interaction rituals. Many interviewees found the new online training situations rather energy draining than exhilarating. On the output side, no collective emotions were created and participants' emotional energy declined with the result that they felt unmotivated to exercise. This might explain why the interviewees refrained from repeating these interaction rituals during the second lockdown or even took a break from CrossFit.

Not surprisingly, independent of their exercise behaviour during the pandemic, all interviewees agreed that they greatly missed training in their local CrossFit box, with several informants explaining that the lockdowns had shown them how much the community and training with others meant to them. Even those who had continued to train at home during lockdown acknowledged that CrossFit was so much of a social activity for them that their identity as a CrossFitter was affected. Rasmus stated, 'I didn't have the opportunity to be a CrossFitter at all. I trained on the floor in my living room with a little kettlebell when my children were in bed'. Likewise, Thomas and Kirsten, who had both taken a break from CrossFit during the pandemic, described that they lacked a big part of their everyday lives and their identity as CrossFitters; not being able to train regularly left an empty space in their lives.

> I can feel that I need to be part of a community. [...] That everybody has a common interest ... [...] that defines me in some way [...]. And I can really feel now where I don't have that anymore [...], that something's missing. [...] I think what's challenging right now is that I lack something where I can thrive [...], something I can talk with others about [...]. I miss these moments of satisfaction, but also these adrenaline rushes [...], a feeling of happiness. (Kirsten)

Thus, not being able to work out in the CrossFit box and/or taking a break from CrossFit during the COVID-19 pandemic was linked with losing out on the identity as a CrossFitter and the emotional energy it provided in the form of enthusiasm, excitement, motivation and happiness (Collins, 2014a). Ryan described the emotional consequences of lacking face-to-face training situations, 'I won't say that I broke down, but it was almost like getting a winter depression in the middle of spring'. Mads even argued that the lack of successful interaction rituals in the box had a negative impact on his ability to interact with others,

> Now that I don't exercise anymore [...] I can feel how I don't have the same amount of self-confidence. [...] I feel that corona has made me less confident in social relations than I was before when I was in a good shape and trained CrossFit with my friends.

Likewise, although the owners of one CrossFit box actively tried to strengthen the group cohesion during the lockdown by using a cobblestone painted with the box's logo that members should pass on to others – a new collective symbol representing hard work and strength – all interviewees reported a drop in group solidarity in the CrossFit community during the pandemic (Collins, 2014a).

Strategies to gain emotional energy: new (semi-)successful interaction rituals during the COVID-19 pandemic

During the pandemic other new training situations were initiated, such as training in small, informal groups and outdoor training. Contrary to digitally mediated workouts these settings provided the participants with the possibility to gain emotional energy (albeit lower amounts than in the CrossFit boxes).

First, eight of the 20 interviewees formed small training groups with other CrossFit members during COVID-19. Notably, those who trained with others tended to keep up with their training regimes, whilst those who did not were declined to take a break from CrossFit. The interviewees exercising in small groups emphasised the social aspect of this form of training during lockdown,

> During the second lockdown, I was offered to train in one member's basement, which we called 'The Armpit'. We've trained down there during the lockdown. [...] But the amount of training we got done, compared to the time we were there, was ridiculous. We definitely spent most time talking to each other and just hanging out. (Anders)

In Collins' (2014a) terms, the naming of the basement can be described as a collective symbol that represents the training group, pointing to close physical contact that fosters group solidarity. Similarly, Simon explained the difference between working out alone and training in his small 'bubble',

> When I should train alone at home, I tend to find excuses for why I can't train. [...] It's much easier if I have an appointment. [...] It's the social part that gets me going [...]. What's helped me through the pandemic was this little training bubble of us four.

Several interviewees told us that they only managed to train when they arranged to meet with others. For Jes, this was coupled with a realisation that training should be fun; consequently, he cut back on the overall amount of training during COVID-19 and exclusively trained with others,

> CrossFit's always been a leeway in my life; something that gives me energy and a boost; it's something that I enjoy. I did not want CrossFit to become a duty, a negative thing in my life. [...] So, I realized – when I'm not motivated and don't think it's fun, that's not something I want to do. I'll get in a good shape again when we [his local CrossFit box] reopen.

Drawing on to Collins (2014a), Jes' statement shows how he refrained from training situations (i.e. training alone at home without a mutual focus of attention and a shared mood) that provided him with low emotional energy or even draining of energy. Rather, he sought social training situations (i.e. training in the co-presence of others, with clear barriers to outsiders, a common focus and shared emotions) that provided him with high levels of emotional energy. Notably, Jes did not only talk about enjoyment, an immediate good feeling during the workout, but also about a leeway, energy and a boost in his everyday life, which demonstrates how positive short-time feelings might get transformed to long-lasting emotional energy (Collins, 2014a). This was also evident when Simon quoted above stated that training with others helped him to get through the pandemic. In sum, face-to-face training in these small CrossFit communities can be considered quite successful interaction rituals that resulted in emotional energy, group solidarity and collective symbols. Nevertheless, it must be emphasised that far from all interviewees managed to form small training groups. As one of our informants described, joining such groups required planning and 'drawing on the friendships you had' (Fie). Hence, it may be assumed that CrossFitters with a higher standing in the CrossFit community had greater possibilities to navigate through the pandemic and maintain their lifestyle.

Secondly, when the CrossFit boxes were allowed to offer outdoor classes, the great majority, both those who had continued to train CrossFit and those who had taken a break, participated in outdoor training, which in general was described positively. For example, Ryan had stayed physically active during COVID-19 mostly training at home with his wife and children but really missed the bigger CrossFit community,

> I was the very first one who was ready to join outdoor training. [...] It's meant a lot to me [...]. It's because I have missed the community and training with others. Even when it was 2°C outside and it was frigging cold in the morning, I managed to.

Still, participants yearned for more equipment as available in the CrossFit box, the previous flexibility that CrossFit had offered them (where they did not have to register for certain classes), and especially to be able to socialise with others before and after training. Although many informants were happy to train with others again, they did not think that 'outdoor training was the same, although it still gives you something' (Per). Rasmus also 'still missed a lot that CrossFit boxes could reopen [...]. Physically it's fine, but for the social part we are not there at all yet'. Kirsten elaborated on the differences between the new and old training situations,

> You must stand on your own little square where you must keep distance to others. It's a bit like ten individualists who are just there to train. I like when you show up and have a good chat. But you can't do that here, so the community gets lost. It's a lot like you stand on your own tile, do your thing, go home. [...] You aren't allowed to move into others' private sphere. You can't even look into each other's eyes because all squares point in the same direction. [...] It gives me something to come close to people; I miss that.

Despite outdoor training taking place in the physical co-presence of other members, it is in Collins' (2014a, 2014b, 2020) terms more difficult to feel rhythmic entrainment and collective effervescence as participants only marginally can see each other's facial expressions or body language and are not allowed to have body contact (e.g. to give high-fives or hug each other). This makes it harder to feel a mutual emotional experience of excitement and achieve a state of synchrony with others where a mutual focus of attention and a shared mood feedback upon each other. Notably, Kirsten's description of outdoor training resembled the other interviewees' experiences with exercising in a 'traditional' gym, which they characterised as much less social than CrossFit training (Pickett et al., 2016; Whiteman-Sandland et al., 2018). Participants' accounts revealed how the four initiating conditions of interaction rituals are present but not as strong as before the pandemic. Consequently, outdoor training can be described as a less successful interaction ritual with weaker outcomes than training in the CrossFit box.

Nevertheless, it must be emphasised that outdoor training attracted most of the interviewees, which suggests that the (moderate) amount of emotional energy gained may still have been important in terms of preventing long-term dropout among CrossFit members. Still, it is an open question whether outdoor training would have been replaced by more successful interaction rituals that provided members with higher levels of emotional energy and group solidarity if the COVID-19 lockdown and restrictions had lasted longer (Collins, 2014a, 2020). Likewise, it must be emphasised that 19 out of 20 interviewees continued to financially support their CrossFit box by not cancelling their membership, which is notable given that CrossFit is an LTPA offered by a profit-oriented company. This highlights high levels of loyalty among members and to their local CrossFit box, which supports analogies between religion and CrossFit (Dawson, 2017; Ornella, 2019). Furthermore, a brief follow-up in July 2021 showed that all interviewees took up training CrossFit again when the CrossFit boxes reopened. This indicates that participants' previous interaction rituals in CrossFit had been strong enough to not lose their emotional appeal throughout the pandemic (Collins, 2014a, 2020).

Conclusion

This article provides insights into how CrossFit members in Denmark made sense of and experienced their greatly changed training routines during the COVID-19 pandemic. Drawing on Collins' (2014a) theory on Interaction Ritual Chains, we specifically explored how a lack of face-to-face interactions in the CrossFit box and altered training situations affected CrossFitters' (leisure) lives. In so doing, this article adds new knowledge to general discussions about whether digitally mediated training and online communities can complement or replace face-to-face encounters and interactions.

Indeed, all interviewees emphasised the social aspect of CrossFit, which is in line with the pre-COVID-19 literature that describes CrossFit as a LTPA with a tight-knit community (Bailey et al., 2019; Crockett & Butryn, 2018; Edmonds, 2020; Gipson et al., 2021; Lautner et al., 2021; Pickett et al., 2016; Whiteman-Sandland et al., 2018). Yet, due to the pandemic and the subsequent lockdowns and measures of social distancing, the interviewees could no longer reproduce the successful interaction rituals in the CrossFit box with various strong outcomes (group solidarity in the form of feeling a belonging to the local CrossFit community, emotional energy in the form of joy, passion, initiative, motivation, etc., collective symbols such as high fives or a personal record bell that represented the group's values and moralities such as pushing oneself to the limits). Accordingly, the COVID-19 restrictions and lockdowns appeared to affect members' activity levels and their motivation to train, their identities, levels of emotional energy as well as feelings of group solidarity, which related to new training situations only created weaker interaction ritual chains (Collins, 2014a).

Further, it was striking that online CrossFit workouts were almost exclusively used during the first lockdown where no other opportunities were available. A lack of physical co-presence coupled with a weak mutual focus of attention and shared mood did not result in rhythmic entrainment and collective effervescence and hence did not result in group solidarity or emotional energy. Consequently, online workouts could mostly be described as failed interaction rituals that were energy draining and which members did not want to repeat (Collins, 2014a, 2020; see also, Andersson & Andreasson, 2021; Carter & Alexander, 2021). In contrast, there was a clear tendency that members preferred training in small groups or outdoor training during the second COVID-19 wave where face-to-face interactions were possible if social distancing was kept.

Collins (2020) argues that interaction rituals can die if they are challenged by other rituals or lose their emotional appeal. However, despite two lockdowns and several COVID-19 related restrictions that made it impossible to repeat the interaction rituals in the CrossFit box over a longer period, all but one interviewee continued to pay membership fees. Furthermore, a brief-follow up in July 2021 showed that all participants had taken up CrossFit again when their box reopened. This indicates that the interaction rituals in the CrossFit boxes were so strong and successful that they endured the pandemic and managed to pull members back to their previous training regimes.

Supporting Collins' (2014a, 2020) position, our results highlight the importance of regular face-to-face LTPA interactions with physical co-presence, which digital training opportunities could not replace. However, as Collins (2020, p. 496) asks, 'But what if technology is tweaked so that it better mimics the ingredients and feedback processes that generate successful interaction rituals?' In future, technological advances may succeed in mimicking strong interaction rituals (e.g. by better transmitting emotions) and hence provide a real alternative to physical leisure communities. Furthermore, it must be emphasised that the social aspect of CrossFit and the close interaction between members had played a crucial role for the informants' participation in CrossFit before the pandemic, which might explain why online workouts could not compete with training in the CrossFit box. It would, therefore, be interesting to explore whether the perspectives of other ('traditional') gym goers differ from our interviewees' experiences. If the community plays a less important role for individuals' participation in LTPA, does that make online workouts, which are time-efficient, cheap and flexible, more attractive? Future research is needed to provide answers to these questions.

Notes

1. CrossFit boxes are gyms in often large, former industrial buildings. Instead of fitness machines, TV's or mirrors they are equipped with medicine balls, bars, rings, tires, weights, kettlebells, ropes etc.
2. As per February 2022; see https://www.crossfit.com/affiliate-list

Acknowledgement

The authors would like to thank Cille Bundgaard Holst, Jannik Unger, Jesper Seemann Serritzlew, Jonas Thorøe Olesen, Morten Bak Falkenskov and Patrick Bæk Rasmussen for their help with interviewing CrossFit participants.

Disclosure statement

No potential conflict of interest was reported by the author(s).

References

Andersson, K., & Andreasson, J. (2021). Being a group fitness instructor during the covid-19 crisis: Navigating professional identity, social distancing, and community. *Social Sciences*, *10*(4), 118. https://doi.org/10.3390/socsci10040118
Bailey, B., Benson, A. J., & Bruner, M. W. (2019). Investigating the organisational culture of CrossFit. *International Journal of Sport and Exercise Psychology*, *17*(3), 197–211. https://doi.org/10.1080/1612197X.2017.1329223
Bowes, A., Lomax, L., & Piasecki, J. (2021). A losing battle? Women's sport pre- and post-COVID-19. *European Sport Management Quarterly*, *21*(3), 443–461. https://doi.org/10.1080/16184742.2021.1904267
Braun, V., Clarke, V., & Weate, P. (2016). Using thematic analysis in sport and exercise research. In B. Smith & A. C. Sparkes (Eds.), *Routledge handbook of qualitative research in sport and exercise* (pp. 191–205). Routledge. https://doi.org/10.4324/9781315762012.ch15
Braun, V., & Clarke, V. (2019). Reflecting on reflexive thematic analysis. *Qualitative Research in Sport, Exercise and Health*, *11*(4), 589–597. https://doi.org/10.1080/2159676X.2019.1628806
Braun, V., & Clarke, V. (2022). Conceptual and design thinking for thematic analysis. *Qualitative Psychology*, *9*(1), 3–26. https://doi.org/10.1037/qup0000196
Brinkmann, S., & Kvale, S. (2015). *Interviews: Learning the craft of qualitative research interviewing*. Sage.
Burke, S. (2016). Rethinking 'validity' and 'trustworthiness' in qualitative inquiry: How might we judge the quality of qualitative research in sport and exercise sciences? In B. Smith & A. C. Sparkes (Eds.), *Routledge handbook of qualitative research in sport and exercise* (pp. 330–339). Routledge.
Caputo, E. L., & Reichert, F. F. (2020). Studies of physical activity and COVID-19 during the Pandemic: A scoping review. *Journal of Physical Activity & Health*, *17*(12), 1275–1284. https://doi.org/10.1123/jpah.2020-0406

Carter, A., & Alexander, A. C. (2021). "It's a whole different atmosphere": A qualitative examination of social support as a facilitator of exercise during the COVID-19 pandemic. *Health Promotion Practice, 22*(5), 622–630. https://doi.org/10.1177/15248399211013005

Collins, R. (2014a). *Interaction ritual chains*. Princeton University Press.

Collins, R. (2014b). Interaction ritual chains and collective effervescence. In C. von Scheve & M. Salmela (Eds.), *Collective emotions* (pp. 583–605). Oxford Scholarship Online. https://doi.org/10.1093/acprof

Collins, R. (2016). Micro-sociology of sport: Interaction rituals of solidarity, emotional energy, and emotion al domination. *European Journal for Sport and Society, 13*(3), 197–207. https://doi.org/10.1080/16138171.2016.1226029

Collins, R. (2020). Social distancing as a critical test of the micro-sociology of solidarity. *American Journal of Cultural Sociology, 8*(3), 477–497. https://doi.org/10.1057/s41290-020-00120-z

Crockett, M. C., & Butryn, T. (2018). Chasing Rx: A spatial ethnography of the CrossFit gym. *Sociology of Sport Journal, 35*(2), 98–107. https://doi.org/10.1123/ssj.2017-0115

Dawson, M. C. (2017). CrossFit: Fitness cult or reinventive institution? *International Review for the Sociology of Sport, 52*(3), 361–379. https://doi.org/10.1177/1012690215591793

Durkheim, É. (1915). *The elementary forms of religious life*. Free Press.

Edmonds, S. E. (2020). Geographies of (Cross)fitness: An ethnographic case study of a CrossFit Box. *Qualitative Research in Sport, Exercise and Health, 12*(2), 192–206. https://doi.org/10.1080/2159676X.2019.1602559

Eske, M. (2021). *Danskernes motions- og sportsvaner under endnu en gradvis genåbning. Notat 5: [Danish people's physical activity and sports habits during another gradual reopening]*. https://idan.dk/vidensbank/downloads/danskernes-motions-og-sportsvaner-under-endnu-en-gradvis-genaabning-notat-5/59e860ee-743a-4e44-9050-ad1700a16b77

Gipson, C., Bennett, H., Malcom, N., & Trahan, A. (2021). Social innovation and fitness sports: A case of the Crossfit movement in North America. In A. Tjønndal (Ed.), *Social Innovation in Sport* (pp. 189–208). Palgrave Macmillan.

Goffman, E. (1967). *Interaction ritual: Essays on face-to-face behavior*. Pantheon.

Iacono, V. L., Symonds, P., & Brown, D. H. K. (2016). Skype as a tool for qualitative research interviews. *Sociological Research Online, 21*(2), 1–15. https://doi.org/10.5153/sro.3952

Kaur, H., Singh, T., Arya, Y. K., & Mittal, S. (2020). Physical fitness and exercise during the COVID-19 pandemic: A qualitative enquiry. *Frontiers in Psychology, 11*. https://doi.org/10.3389/fpsyg.2020.590172

Kirkegaard, H., Eske, M., & Rask, S. (2020). *Danskernes motions- og sportsvaner [Danish people's physical activity and sports participation]*. https://idan.dk/vidensbank/downloads/danskernes-motions-og-sportsvaner-under-coronanedlukningen-del-1/6515aeed-a9ef-437e-89b3-abb400822dd8

Lautner, S. C., Patterson, M. S., Spadine, M. N., Boswell, T. G., & Heinrich, K. M. (2021). Exploring the social side of CrossFit: A qualitative study. *Mental Health and Social Inclusion, 25*(1), 63–75. https://doi.org/10.1108/MHSI-08-2020-0051

Meyer, J., Morrison, J., & Zuniga, J. (2017). The benefits and risks of CrosSfit: A systematic review. *Workplace Health & Safety, 65*(12), 612–618. https://doi.org/10.1177/2165079916685568

Montalvo, A. M., Shaefer, H., Rodriguez, B., Li, T., Epnere, K., & Myer, G. D. (2017). Retrospective injury epidemiology and risk factors for injury in CrossFit. *Journal of Sports Science & Medicine, 16*(1), 53–59.

Mutz, M., Müller, J., & Reimers, A. K. (2021). Use of digital media for home-based sports activities during the covid-19 pandemic: Results from the German spovid survey. *International Journal of Environmental Research and Public Health, 18*(9), 4409. https://doi.org/10.3390/ijerph18094409

Nash, M. (2018). Let's work on your weaknesses': Australian CrossFit coaching, masculinity and neoliberal framings of 'health' and 'fitness. *Sport in Society, 21*(9), 1432–1453. https://doi.org/10.1080/17430437.2017.1390565

Ornella, A. D. (2019). 'Jesus Saves' and 'Clothed in Christ': Athletic religious apparel in the Christian CrossFit community. *Sport in Society, 22*(2), 266–280. https://doi.org/10.1080/17430437.2017.1360580

Patton, M. Q. (2015). *Qualitative research & evaluation methods* (4th ed.). SAGE Publications.

Pickett, A. C., Goldsmith, A., Damon, Z., & Walker, M. (2016). The influence of sense of community on the perceived value of physical activity: A cross-context analysis. *Leisure Sciences, 38*(3), 199–214. https://doi.org/10.1080/01490400.2015.1090360

Rodríguez, M., García-Calleja, P., Terrados, N., Crespo, I., Del Valle, M., & Olmedillas, H. (2022). Injury in CrossFit®: A systematic review of epidemiology and risk factors. *Physician and Sportsmedicine, 50*(1), 3–10. https://doi.org/10.1080/00913847.2020.1864675

Schmidt, T., & Pawlowski, C. S. (2021). Physical activity in crisis: The impact of COVID-19 on Danes' physical activity behavior. *Frontiers in Sports and Active Living, 2*. https://doi.org/10.3389/fspor.2020.610255

Schrijnder, S., Van amsterdam, N., & McLachlan, F. (2021). 'These chicks go just as hard as us!' (Un)doing gender in a Dutch CrossFit gym. *International Review for the Sociology of Sport, 56*(3), 382–398. https://doi.org/10.1177/1012690220913524

Simons, I. (2020). Changing identities through collective performance at events: The case of the redhead days. *Leisure Studies, 39*(4), 568–584. https://doi.org/10.1080/02614367.2020.1768281

Souter, G., Tonge, A., & Culvin, A. (2022). The impact of Covid-19 on the mental health of professional footballers. *Managing Sport and Leisure*, 27(1–2), 168–171. https://doi.org/10.1080/23750472.2021.1877569

Spaaij, R., & Schaillée, H. (2021). Inside the black box: A micro-sociological analysis of sport for development. *International Review for the Sociology of Sport*, 56(2), 151–169. https://doi.org/10.1177/1012690220902671

Sparkes, A. C., & Smith, B. (2014). *Qualitative research methods in sport exercise and health: From process to product*. Routledge. https://doi.org/10.4324/9780203852187

Stockwell, S., Trott, M., Tully, M., Shin, J., Barnett, Y., Butler, L., McDermott, D., Schuch, F., & Smith, L. (2021). Changes in physical activity and sedentary behaviours from before to during the COVID-19 pandemic lockdown: A systematic review. *BMJ Open Sport and Exercise Medicine*, 7(1), e000960. https://doi.org/10.1136/bmjsem-2020-000960

Summers-Effler, E. (2007). Ritual theory. In J. E. Stets & J. H. Turner (Eds.), *Handbook of the sociology of emotions* (pp. 135–154). Springer. https://doi.org/10.1007/978-0-387-30715-2

Thorpe, H. (2011). *Snowboarding bodies in theory and practice*. Palgrave Macmillan.

Tracy, S. J. (2010). Qualitative quality: Eight "big-tent" criteria for excellent qualitative research. *Qualitative Inquiry*, 16(10), 837–851. https://doi.org/10.1177/1077800410383121

Washington, M. S., & Economides, M. (2016). Strong is the new sexy: Women, CrossFit, and the postfeminist ideal. *Journal of Sports and Social Issues*, 40(2), 143–161. https://doi.org/10.1177/0193723515615181

Whitcomb-Khan, G., Wadsworth, N., McGinty-Minister, K., Bicker, S., Swettenham, L., & Tod, D. (2021). Critical pause: Athletes' stories of lockdown during COVID-19. *The Sport Psychologist*, 35(1), 43–54. https://doi.org/10.1123/tsp.2020-0106

Whiteman-Sandland, J., Hawkins, J., & Clayton, D. (2018). The role of social capital and community belongingness for exercise adherence: An exploratory study of the CrossFit gym model. *Journal of Health Psychology*, 23(12), 1545–1556. https://doi.org/10.1177/1359105316664132

Woolf, J., & Lawrence, H. (2017). Social identity and athlete identity among CrossFit members: An exploratory study on the CrossFit open. *Managing Sport and Leisure*, 22(3), 166–180. https://doi.org/10.1080/23750472.2017.1415770

COVID-19 and outdoor recreation in the post-anthropause

Jacob J. Bustad, Samuel M. Clevenger and Oliver J.C. Rick

ABSTRACT
The lockdown measures instituted during the early months of the COVID-19 pandemic resulted in a moment of restricted human activity and mobility that researchers have called the 'anthropause'. Along with accounts of the widespread suspension or disruption of various industries, including sport, recreation, and tourism, media reported on the anthropause's positive impact on wildlife and environments, evidenced by accounts of animals returning to their previously displaced habitats and thriving in spaces typically marked by human activity. However, the period following these lockdown measures witnessed the re-opening of disrupted industries, and also a marked increase in outdoor human activity, particularly via engagement with forms of outdoor recreation at national and state parks and other protected areas. This analysis asserts that during this post-anthropause, the renewal and increase in outdoor recreation practices within protected areas re-demonstrated the ecological impacts of human activity within those spaces. Utilising media reports regarding outdoor recreation and US national and state parks during the pandemic, this essay explores the implications of leisure after lockdown, arguing that the post-anthropause represents an important conceptual tool for better understanding the complex relations between physical cultures, environments, and the anthropocentric dictates of contemporary 'burnout society'.

Introduction

The early months of 2020 saw the emergence of the COVID-19 pandemic and a corresponding disruption to various industries around the world, including the leisure, recreation, and tourism industries as well as a wave of postponed or cancelled events and suspended seasons in the global sport industry (Hall, 2020). With rising positive cases, national governments closed their borders in response to the pandemic (McClanahan, 2020) and instituted 'lockdown' measures that entailed quarantining, mask wearing, and social distancing requirements, travel restrictions, and an overall restriction of human mobility and disruption of people's pre-pandemic work and leisure routines (Katella, 2021).

The lockdown measures described above were part of a 'considerable global slowing of modern human activities', leading scholars (Rutz et al., 2020) to propose the term 'anthropause' to refer to the general interruption of contemporary patterns of human action and interaction during these pandemic policies and mobility and travel restrictions. This brief anthropause period of decreased or restricted human activity and mobility included media reports of animals reclaiming environments and habitats and returning to areas they had been forced from, or encroaching within urban spaces. The British Broadcasting Corporation (BBC), for example, reported in April 2020 that animals were 'exploring emptied streets and waterways' in urban areas and 'delighting human inhabitants along the way' (BBC, 2020). The lockdown measures and their correspondence restrictions on human activity seemingly gave 'animals the confidence to go deeper into our cities and stay for longer' as well as enjoy the 'nature reserves and parks all to themselves ... while tourists are away' (BBC, 2020). The same B.B.C. report highlighted various examples of animals around the world moving into traditionally human-centred spaces during the lockdown period: dolphins in shipping channels in the Bosphorus; wild hogs in the streets of Haifa, Israel; and, cougars prowling in neighbourhoods in Santiago, Chile, while also reporting that decreased human activity within national parks was having a positive impact on pink flamingos in Albania and dugong (sea cows) in Thailand. Taken together, these stories came to reflect a particular mediated narrative of animals and nonhumans thriving *sans* humans during the anthropause, suggesting an unintended, yet seemingly positive by-product of the lockdown measures. This period of the anthropause, however, was temporary and limited. With the relaxing of lockdown measures in the U.S. and elsewhere by the spring of 2020, there was a resumption of pre-pandemic human activity, including a renewed pursuit of forms of outdoor recreation in national parks, state parks, and other protected areas in the U.S. context. The outdoor recreation patterns and rates reported during this period after lockdown, which we are calling the *post-anthropause*, re-demonstrated the ecological impacts of ecological impacts of human activity within those spaces. As humans sought refuge and adventure in outdoor spaces during the prolonged pandemic, their renewed recreational consumerism also renewed forms of environmental disturbance and damage, including the modification of animal habitats and ecological landscapes within national and state parks (Chow, 2020), and the enactment of policies aimed at making public lands and outdoor spaces available for resource production and extraction (Miller, 2020).

This essay thus introduces and explores the post-anthropause period of physical culture, in regard to the resumption of human activity after the initial lockdown measures of 2020, as well as the relations between this resumed human activity and its environmental and nonhuman implications within the historical context of the Anthropocene. Though this focus on outdoor recreation and leisure practices and experiences during the COVID-19 pandemic, our analysis contributes to the study of physical activity as interconnected with both human and non-human elements, including the 'nature-society' dimensions of leisure (Rose & Carr, 2018) and the 'more-than-human' elements of social relations (Searle et al., 2021), in order to apprehend the ongoing transformation of leisure and tourism in the Anthropocene age (Fletcher, 2019). Moreover, this analysis contributes to research focused on physical culture within the COVID-19 context, and the relationship between the pandemic and recreation and leisure activities (Easterbrook-Smith, 2021; Liu et al., 2022; Rice et al., 2020; Sivan, 2020). In particular, our project works to connect discussions of 'multispecies' leisure during this period (King, 2022) with questions of how social and cultural responses to the pandemic, and more specifically the anthropause and post-anthropause phases, might lead to different approaches to researching leisure, tourism, and physical culture (Katz-Rosene, 2021; Lawton, 2020; Soto et al., 2021).

In this analysis, we focus on the resumption and increase in outdoor recreation and recreation-based tourism during the post-anthropause, and the ways in which such consumer-oriented forms of recreation re-articulated and re-promoted the anthropocentric logics of the pre-pandemic capitalist regime. Utilising media reports of outdoor recreation within protected areas in the spring and summer of 2020, the essay explores the ways in which the activity-driven and consumer-focused impulses of twenty-1st century capitalism were arguably re-energised during the post-anthropause, evidenced by increased human engagement in outdoor recreational forms and practices following the relaxing of lockdown measures. The aim of this analysis is to present the post-anthropause as a conceptual tool that can help examine the complex relations between the active bodies and the Anthropocene, in order to both critically interrogate this relationship and simultaneously provoke consideration for how we might transform associations between physical cultures and the environment, specifically in regard to outdoor recreation and protected areas.

The anthropocene and the post-anthropause

While the global scale and scope of the COVID-19 pandemic has resulted in unprecedented disruptions to human activity and industry, there has been considerable debate surrounding the idea that this disruption was accompanied by the potential for societal transformations that acknowledge the fragility of humanity's relationship with the planet. These arguments have centred on whether or to what degree the pandemic might result in changes to our everyday lives, specifically in regard to the interrelationship between consumerism, socioeconomic 'growth', and environmental sustainability (Hickel, 2021). Yet we might recognise that the COVID-19 crisis has not only demonstrated the interconnectivity of a globalised world, but also has emphasised the importance of situating these forms of interconnectivity within the broader context of the Anthropocene as a distinct era of planetary development. Following Heyd (2021), we can understand the Anthropocene as 'a new geologic epoch characterised by the overarching impact of human activities on the planet, its processes and species' (23). The question of the degree to which humans impact the planet, and the precise timeline of this impact, has been the subject of ongoing research, however the general notion that the practices and movements of human beings has a primarily deleterious effect on the environment is now increasingly accepted:

> we are increasingly finding that activities that at first seem innocuous, such as heating our homes, travelling to our places of work and leisure, industrially exploiting resources to supply ourselves with useful products, and so on, cumulatively are having global and long-lasting effects, including climate change, habitat destruction and environmental contamination, with important negative repercussions for endangered species as well as for human health and wellbeing ... we humans have already become 'a geological force' in virtue of our overall impact on Earth systems. *(Heyd, 2021, p. 23).*

In framing the COVID-19 virus less as a singular biological and cultural phenomenon, and instead as characteristic of the contemporary social and geological age, we might therefore address the implications of the pandemic as a result of the cumulative effects of global human activity. In referring to COVID-19 as 'the disease of the Anthropocene', O'Callaghan-Gordo and Antó (2020) cite the impact of human activity in disrupting natural habitats and ecosystems and the consequent transformation to interactions between human and non-human species, including the transmission of infectious diseases. Accordingly, as a disease of the Anthropocene, COVID-19 'follows a complex sequence involving disruption of the natural, social, economic and governance systems':

> The destruction of natural habitats and the extinction of species, the poorly regulated capture, marketing and consumption of non-human animals, the influence of lobbies to nullify or delay measures to protect natural and social systems, the limitation of current scientific knowledge and the contempt by governments and companies of the available evidence, have all worked in an orchestrated sequence to facilitate the current COVID-19 pandemic. This sequence of distal causes is closely related to the global climate crisis and the rest of environmental disruptions of the Anthropocene. Consumption of fossil fuels for energy, deforestation and the conversion of natural habitats into farmland or extensive livestock are among the main sources of greenhouse gas emissions, and at the same facilitate the emergence of new zoonosis, such as SARS-CoV-2, with a pandemic potential *(O'Callaghan-Gordo & Antó, 2020, p. 2).*

COVID-19 therefore demonstrates the implications of human activity within natural habitats, and emphasises the inextricable association between natural and social systems as characteristic of the Anthropocene. Moreover, this approach enables a critical examination of particular social and cultural responses to the pandemic, including during the period of lockdown and the anthropause. In this analysis, we focus on the relationship between protected areas and outdoor recreation in the post-anthropause, referring to a phase of the pandemic after initial lockdowns and quarantines in which humans re-turned (in varying degrees) to aspects of daily life, including nature-based leisure practices. The linkages between protected areas and tourism practices – including visitors engaging in forms of outdoor recreation – have been an important area of study in the context of the Anthropocene. As Saarinen (2019) explains, the impacts of human activity on and in nature have been the driving force for the creation of conservation policies, including protected areas; yet at the same time, many of these areas are still considered endangered due to human activity. This means that while larger-scale processes such as global warming result in a general decrease in biodiversity across the world, it is often more local forms of anthropocentric action and interaction that 'filter in' to protected areas via park visitation and tourism (Saarinen, 2019, p. 480). Indeed, the more recent development of the tourism industry has featured an increasing focus on nature-based tourism, including in regard to adventure tourism, eco-tourism, and other experiences often involving forms of outdoor recreation. While these types of tourism have often drawn on a historical connection between travel, leisure, and natural or 'wilderness' spaces, they have also been characterised by the increased scale and scope of contemporary tourism, wherein improved access to protected areas has meant that these spaces are increasingly embedded within national and regional tourism markets (Frost & Hall, 2010). In turn, protected areas have been incorporated into models of commercialisation and consumption, including 'marketing and visualising natural environments and staging wilderness settings for touristic purposes ... creating and using global imaginaries of wildernesses as commercialised wild spaces where a consumer is a visitor who does not remain' (Saarinen, 2019, p. 481).

In our analysis, these interconnections between protected areas and tourism – and more specifically, tourism practices involving outdoor recreation within these spaces – provide a unique context in which to examine the implications of leisure during and after the COVID-19 lockdown. In particular, we extend this critical study of the impacts of human activity within natural spaces to analyse the re-turn of humans to national and state parks in the United States during the post-anthropause, referring to the period following lockdown and beginning (approximately) in the summer of 2020. The following section therefore provides empirical detail to the environmental implications of increased human activity after the anthropause, in regard to outdoor recreation and overtourism in US national and state parks, as well as the targeting of protected areas for the extraction of natural resources during this period. We then discuss these implications within the framework of Han (2015) 'burnout society', interrogating the connections between outdoor recreation and the notion of the 'self-project' predicated on productivity and positivity. In short, we argue that the post-anthropause of the COVID-19 pandemic provokes concerns regarding the current and future development of outdoor recreation and protected areas in the epoch of the Anthropocene.

Research design

The present study is part of a broader research project on the ideological and ontological meaning of physical cultural forms, practices, and experiences in the post-anthropausem as this context offers a generative lens into the complex intersections linking human physical culture, anthropogenic capitalist activity, and the more-than-human in this age of the Anthropocene. The purpose of the present study is to develop said project by specifically examine and analyse the online and mainstream media coverage of one particular aspect of post-anthropause: outdoor recreation in protected areas in the United States and Western Europe during the period in 2020 in which various governmental bodies instituted, and subsequently relaxed, lockdown measures restricting human activity as part of responses to COVID-19. Scrutinising available reports on the outdoor recreation attendance and consumer patterns at parks and other protected areas allowed us to cultivate a clearer, though incomplete and limited to certain geopolitical locales, idea of how and why recreation consumers engaged in certain practices and spaces following the easing of lockdown measures.

Our approach to studying the media coverage is informed by an understanding of published media articles as constructed narratives that, following the late cultural studies scholar Stuart Hall, use language as their 'principal medium' for articulating and distributing 'different ideological discourses' (Hall, 2021, p. 180). Following Hall, the media's 'main sphere of operations', unintentionally or otherwise, 'is the production and transformation of ideologies' (p. 180), with media texts reproducing ideas of race, gender, sexuality, class, disability, and other social phenomena, as well as the more-than-human, through the deployment of linguistic representation. The goal of the essay, following the tradition of critical cultural studies in the field of the sociology of sport (McDonald & Birrell, 1999), is to 'read' the media narratives and analyse the ways in which they circulated the ideological significance of outdoor recreation patterns in the post-anthropause period.

As our analysis focuses primarily on the United States, the post-anthropause context explored in this study reflects an assortment of differing American policies, practices, and procedures following the initial lockdown response to COVID-19 in March 2020. The rest of this year following lockdown, as spring turned summer turned fall and winter 2020, was characterised by the implementation of varying US state guidelines related to masking, social distancing, travel restrictions, and testing and tracing, as well challenges to these guidelines often involving a lack of clear planning and policy from the US federal government (Hanage et al., 2020). At the same time, the process of developing potential treatments and a possible vaccine for COVID-19 highlighted both scientific innovation and coordination, as well as contemporary forms of disinformation and conspiracy theories (Pereira et al., 2020). Against this backdrop of mixed guidelines and a lack of knowledge and communication about the disease, health and medical organisations increased recommendations for physical activity in outdoor settings throughout 2020, as these activities would meet any guidelines for social distancing and minimise the indoor spread of the virus.

The media articles examined were therefore collected in a period between March and December of 2020, and were acquired using a broad online search, with particular attention to organisations and government agencies associated with state and national parks, recreation-related online magazines and websites, and newspapers of record covering attendance rates and trends at protected areas. Articles were also acquired using Google News and broad search terms such as 'outdoor recreation' and 'recreation parks' to cast a wide net and access as many published reports as were available. We then studied the accumulated media reports on outdoor recreation rates in May-December 2020 in terms of their relation to the politics of consumption and anthropogenic activity in protected spaces during the post-anthropause.

Protected areas and post-anthropause recreation

As two key examples of protected areas in the United States, national and state parks function as institutionally supported and governed spaces of human-nature interaction. The parks are 'landscapes' (Maher, 2008), meaning environmental spaces altered and transformed by human physical labour into designated spaces of 'nature' and 'wilderness' for human enjoyment (for example, the creation of hiking trails, campgrounds, and facilities for recreational activity). Over the past century, these landscapes have been celebrated as landmarks, tourist destinations, as well as sites for visitors to (re)connect with 'the outdoors' through human-devised recreational opportunities (such hiking trails, campgrounds, as well as swimming and other sporting activities) (O'Dell, 2017). However, over the last decade there has been a marked increase in both the levels of visitation at many parks, as well as the accompanying effects of human traffic in and through these spaces. For example, the National Parks Service reported over 330,000 recreation visits in 2016 and 2017, compared with over 275,000 in 2007 (National Park Service, 2022). As Finnessey (2012) explains, the depletion of national resources, pollution, and physical changes to the environment constitute three major sources of ecological impact via tourism practices and policies within US national parks, meaning that in general 'tourism generates land degradation, air and noise pollution, littering, trampling and the alteration of ecosystems ... these areas of impact not only risk the well being of the land, but also the species that call these areas home' (p. 13). Manning et al. (2017)

also recognise the effects of human visitors in regard to the administration of parks services, as management problems often include:

> impacts to park resources (soil, vegetation, water, air, wildlife, historical/cultural resources, soundscapes, night skies), impacts to the quality of the visitor experience (crowding, conflict, depreciative behaviour), and impacts to park facilities (trails, campsites, attraction sites, roads/parking lots, and interpretive facilities/programs) (p. 158).

Importantly, these studies emphasise the environmental modifications caused by both the active bodies of visitors, as well as the infrastructure developed in order to make protected areas accessible to those visitors. Following Monz et al. (2016), protected areas can be impacted by the incorporation of facilities intended to service visitors – bathrooms, lodging, visitor centres, nature centres, park ranger stations, etc. – and also by the construction of road networks needed to access these facilities. At the same time, humans contribute to ecological change through outdoor recreational pursuits, as activities such as 'walking, hiking, backpacking, rock climbing, horseback riding, camping, and biking have great negative impacts on national parks as well' (Finnessey, 2012). A particular example of this direct impact of active human bodies within these spaces could include trampling, wherein visitors use specific paths or routes repeatedly and without periods of rest, leading to damage to animal and plant ecosystems (Tenenbaum, 2000). This research indicates that the significance of national and state parks as sites for human engagement in outdoor recreation practices ultimately contributes to increased numbers of park visitors and, consequently, an increase in the ecological impacts on these protected areas as a result of the human activity. The environmental stresses wrought by human activity is further accentuated within particularly popular national and state parks, as 'the pressures placed on well-loved and accessible national parks ... lead to severe conflicts of visitor numbers, activities and the protection and management of natural resources' (Bell et al., 2007, p. 29). These issues are often further exacerbated by temporal overtourism (Cheer et al., 2019), referring to the process where seasonal changes in visitors means that parks face even greater challenges due to increased traffic and decreased available capacity.

Conceptually, the post-anthropause, in contrast to the reduced presence of humans in cities during the lockdown phase of many nations' response to COVID-19, allows us to highlight how the summer of 2020 witnessed a dramatic increase in visitors to outdoor spaces, including US national and state parks. The initial reaction to COVID-19, entailing self-isolation and social distancing, served as a temporary disruption to park visitation and tourism. Following lockdown, "visitors flocked to national parks as a means to 'safely' 'social distance' in the outdoors" (Templeton et al., 2021). Moreover, these conditions provided a context in which outdoor recreational activities were 'one of the few things that people could do ... [and] that has just created this massive spike in public lands use since March [2020]' (Chrobak, 2020). Spenceley et al. (2021) state that while visitors to national parks decreased during March and April, corresponding with the initial period of lockdown during the pandemic, by August 2020 normal levels of visitation had returned or were being exceeded, as some parks including Glacier, Yellowstone, and Joshua Tree 'reported rapid increases in visitation when they were re-opened' (p. 105). Overall, the U.S. National Parks Service stated that over 237 million people visited national parks in 2020, a 28% decrease from the previous year but with a corresponding 26% decrease in visitor hours, including many parks that were temporarily closed during the initial lockdown period (National Park Service, 2022). Despite these measures, 15 parks set a new recreation visitation record in 2020, including 5 parks that had set a record in 2019 (National Park Service, 2022).

At the same time, the increased concentration of visitors in the months following lockdown – during the post-anthropause – meant that several parks were experiencing higher than usual levels of litter, vandalism, and overcrowding; as Time magazine reported, 'National Parks are getting trashed by COVID-19': 'Many of these spaces, supposed to be untouched swaths of time-proof wilderness, have been overrun by first-time visitors seeking refuge from quarantine, joblessness, or the inability to take far-flung vacations' (Chow, 2020). Increased traffic in Zion National Park in

Utah and Grand Canyon National Park in Arizona during this period resulted in trail and campground closures due to overcrowding, and the accompanying problems related to human activity in these protected areas. A Parks Service staff member at Grand Canyon National Park reported that the increase in visitors corresponded with damage to and in park facilities: 'They're dealing with vandalism, they're dealing with out-of-bounds camping ... People are stealing toilet paper, and ripping (hand) sanitiser off the wall, and if you don't have the vault toilets open, then people are taking a poop right next to the toilet' (Repanshek, 2020). Problems related to overcrowding during this period were often compounded by other effects of the pandemic, notably a loss in funding and issues regarding the availability of park staff and park volunteers. In reviewing visitor experiences at popular US national parks during the pandemic, Taff et al. (2022) assert that 'nature- and wildlife-based tourism destinations may be hit particularly hard by the pandemic through the loss of funding and inability to employ rangers and other staff, which has resulted in increased illegal activities and degradation of resources during this time' (p. 146).

These trends were also reflected within state and regional parks, with some states recording much higher numbers of park visitors during the summer of 2020. The Maryland Department of Natural Resources reported a 45% increase in state park visitors compared to 2019, with attendance surpassing the previous annual record in September 2020, and the number of 'capacity closures' (when a park has reached full capacity) reaching 260 in 2020, in comparison to 80 in 2019 (Himes, 2020). As one example of this increase, Maryland's Assateague Island National Seashore – home to the island's famous wild horses – saw 500,000 visitors in June 2020, with the previous monthly record being 170,000; the park then saw nearly 500,000 visitors in both July and August, breaking records for those months as well (Prensky, 2020). As a result, the OSV (over the sand vehicle zone) in the park typically reached capacity by 6 a.m. on weekends and the wait time to access the zone could exceed 3 h, with traffic to enter the park on weekend also sometimes backed up about 3 miles (Prensky, 2020). In Wisconsin, state parks were faced with the temporary closure of 40 sites in April 2020, yet the number of overall visitors increased 15% from 2019 to 2020 (Jacques & Stout, 2020). As demonstrated in national parks, this rise in visitors was accompanied by various issues related to human activity in protected areas, including environmental damage, vandalism and littering, and capacity closures due to limited facilities (Jacques & Stout, 2020).

These examples demonstrate two key points: first, that any environmental benefits of the anthropause might be best understood as limited and temporary, in that humans emerged from COVID-19 lockdown with seemingly increased levels of energy and attention towards outdoor recreation. Second, attendance at national and state parks are only two aspects of this dimension of the post-anthropause, as evidenced by the rise in RV sales (Brunell, 2020) or bicycle sales (Bernhard, 2020), or the record number of hunting permits and licences that were issued in many states during this same period (Hayes, 2020). Yet while the pandemic provided opportunities for some to rediscover nature and outdoor activities, it also set the backdrop for the enactment of policies that focused on the production and extraction of natural resources, with the accompanying deleterious effects of these initiatives on animal habitats and populations. As Buckley (2020) explains, many large private resource extraction companies have developed long-term strategies aimed at gaining access to resources within publicly owned conservation reserves, with a particular focus on opportunities to gain access during periods of social and political instability. In this mode, any 'social or civil disruption, including the current pandemic, provides an opportunity' for the advancement of arguments for corporate access to resources on publicly owned protected areas (Buckley, 2020). Within the context of US national and state parks, these strategies were further entangled with the politics of the US federal government during the initial period of response to the pandemic. As Hempel (2018) explains, from his election in 2016 the administration of Donald Trump worked towards the general rolling back of environmental policies and reduction of programmes, yet within the 'whack-a-mole world of Trump agenda setting, environmental problems are lost in a fog and flurry of competing issues' (p. 186). This approach towards environmental policies reflects an era of 'anthropotrumpism' (Hempel, 2018), in which:

> The aim of the Trump normalisation process appears to be socially orchestrated acceptance of poverty – both economic and ecological – in the service of obscenely concentrated wealth. Protected areas become expendable environmental luxuries, while consumer luxuries become entitlements of inheritance, shrewd investment, and lower taxes. Ecological services give way to plutocracy in the service of greed (p. 87).

Thus during the same period following the anthropause in spring 2020, the Trump administration continued a specific strategy of weakening environmental protections and enabling industrial polluters within U.S. protected areas. As Holden (2020) explains, during the COVID-19 lockdown:

> US federal agencies eased fuel-efficiency standards for new cars; frozen rules for soot air pollution; proposed to drop review requirements for liquefied natural gas terminals; continued to lease public property to oil and gas companies; sought to speed up permitting for offshore fish farms; and advanced a proposal on mercury pollution from power plants that could make it easier for the government to conclude regulations are too costly to justify their benefits.

A former official for the Environmental Protection Agency (EPA) described the situation in the summer of 2020 by saying 'Trump is burning down the house ... We're in a period of massive biodiversity loss and increasing chemical and toxic burdens on individuals, and the EPA is not responding to the crises at hand' (Gillam, 2020). Since taking office in January 2021, the Biden administration has moved to reverse or remove many of these policies, as part of an 'uphill battle' to restore the EPA as a credible and effective federal agency involved in actual environmental protection, and to address the impacts of the Trump administration in relation to environmental issues more broadly (Sadasivam, 2021).

Following Perkins et al. (2022), understanding the COVID-19 anthropause as a social 'perturbation' entails examining the scientific and social implications of the phases of the pandemic. In this analysis, drawing attention to the renewed ecological impacts of human activity during the period following COVID-19 lockdown enables a recognition of the relationships between outdoor recreation and protected areas, and the meanings of these relationships for these spaces within the era of the Anthropocene. In particular, this includes both the more direct impacts of human engagement with the outdoors through the active bodies of runners, hikers, bikers, campers, climbers, and other physical cultures – these moving bodies correspond with issues related to overcrowding, vandalism and littering, and the general degradation of national and state parks, along with the development of park infrastructure designed to accommodate these bodies. At the same time, these protected areas continue to be the target for resource extraction, including through strategies aimed at gaining corporate access to resources in publicly owned lands, with a particular focus on opportunities for policy-shaping actions during periods of social and political disruption. Our analysis therefore frames the COVID-19 post-anthropause by emphasising that any environmental benefits of the early lockdown phase should be understood as superficial and temporary, in that the 'great quietening' of reduced human activity (Lecocq et al., 2020) was a short-lived phenomenon that was ended by the resumption of the travel, tourism, and recreation and leisure industries. Moreover, critically examining these dimensions of the post-anthropause also allows for a discussion of the re-permutation of interconnections between outdoor recreation, protected areas, and consumer capitalism. In the following section, we explicate the post-lockdown association between recreation, leisure, and consumption, exploring how forms of outdoor recreation relate to contemporary 'burnout society' (Han, 2015).

Outdoor recreation and the post-anthropause "burnout society"

After the initial lockdown in the spring and summer of 2020, a number of reports appeared in popular media outlets reiterating the physical and mental health benefits of outdoor recreation practices within the context of the pandemic. This was in part a response to the clearly deleterious effects of the pandemic and restricted human mobility on mental health, with increasing numbers of people suffering from anxiety, depression, and other maladies during lockdown. The

Organisation for Economic Co-operation and Development (OECD) reported a marked uptick in depression and anxiety in multiple countries around the world since March of 2020 (OECD, 2021), while researchers noted a link between the experience of lockdown restrictions and significantly higher rates of anxiety and depression (Fiorillo et al., 2020). As a result, some underscored the importance of outdoor recreation as a palliative for mental health. On March 20th, the CEO of a national parks and recreation management group, in a blog post for the National Recreation and Park Association, wrote:

> As park and recreation professionals, we know in our hearts that good mental health is often related to having access to the outdoors and greenspace. Research over the years has shown that when people are more stressed, anxious and socially isolated, as we are right now due to the global COVID-19 pandemic, having access to parks, trails and natural areas becomes even more important *(Penbrooke, 2020).*

In late April, the environmental scholar Laurence Smith wrote a piece for *Scientific American* arguing that increased time in park and natural settings was an 'unexpected benefit' of the lockdown measures and 'restorative' for people's mental health (Smith, 2020). As a June 2020 article in *The New York Times* declared, 'Numerous studies have shown the mental and physical benefits of spending time in nature', and 'it took a pandemic and stay-at-home orders for that desire to spend more time outdoors to feel like a necessity' (St-Esprit McKivigan, 2020).

This re-energised discussion of the healthful qualities of outdoor recreation was accompanied by renewed attention to the racial and social inequalities associated with access to parks and green spaces. A report published in June by the Center for American Progress found that communities of colour in the U.S. were up to three times more likely than their white counterparts to live in neighbourhoods with little to no access to park and green space (Borunda, 2020). The 'coronavirus pandemic', the report explains, 'has exposed an uneven and inequitable distribution of nearby outdoor spaces for recreation, respite, and enjoyment' (Rowland-Shea et al., 2020). The report focused on the problem of unequal access to parks and green spaces on account of racial, class, and geographical divisions, while recapitulating the point already established by published research that the ability to visit and enjoy parks and protected areas plays a key role in the maintenance of human health and well-being (Romagosa et al., 2015).

The mediated discussion that appeared in 2020 concerning the healthful benefits of recreational pursuits in parks and protected areas was often coupled with references to outdoor recreation as tools for self-management and improvement. Early in the pandemic, some media outlets, usually while referencing recently published research on the subject, told their readers that visiting green spaces safely, even doing an outdoor activity as simple as walking, 'may be a particularly helpful strategy' for managing one's stress levels (Sgobba, 2020). The Rails-to-Trails Conservancy noted in September of 2020 that millions of Americans were 'addressing their mental health needs during the coronavirus ... through frequent activity in the outdoors' (Matteson, 2020). The article also cited a recent Conservancy survey that found that 46% of the respondents linked their pursuit of outdoor recreation in protected areas to a reduction of their stress levels, while 66% said that they were visiting parks and protected areas 'at the same level or greater than before the coronavirus' (Matteson, 2020). In other words, the renewed discussion of outdoor recreation during the pandemic, occurring as attendance figures at parks and protected areas significantly increased, entailed presenting the recreational pursuits as tools for self-management.

Though we do not dispute that engaging in forms of outdoor recreation in park spaces and protected areas can improve one's overall health and alleviate stress and anxiety (Olafsdottir et al., 2018), we do contend that the post-anthropause can help researchers closely attend to the relations between the pursuit of outdoor recreation and the reproduction of capitalist ideals of self-improvement. The increased popularity of recreational practices at parks and protected areas during the post-anthropause seems at least partly linked with the capitalist dictates of personal 'productivity' and managing one's capacity to be productive, even during times of great stress. This dictate is at the core of what philosopher Han (2015) terms the twenty-first-century 'burnout society': a society in which the individual is not so much compelled by external forces to be productive in the appropriate manners, but instead is driven and exploited by internal pressures as one compulsively seeks achievement in all endeavours and the maximisation of one's performance in life. Han explains that the human subject of the postindustrial 'burnout society' contrasts with those of Foucault's industrial disciplinary society in that humans are transformed into 'projects' who pathologically engage in 'voluntary self-exploitation' by pursuing the maximisation of themselves (p. 44). The twenty-first-century postindustrial society has become an achievement-centred society, in which human projects constantly seek to re-brand themselves and their skillsets to maintain their competitiveness and productivity in the burnout economy. 'The late modern achievement-subject is subject to no one', Han writes. 'It positivizes itself; indeed, it liberates itself into a project. Achievement society is the society of self-exploitation' (p. 46).

Relating the post-anthropause to the context of the capitalist 'burnout society' provokes philosophical and ethical consideration of outdoor recreation and leisure practices as anthropocentric and wedded to capitalist dictates of compulsive activity linked to the consumption of 'nature' as a commodity and a spatialised tool for self-management. While we can recognise that those who enjoy and pursue forms of outdoor recreation may be opposed or antagonistic towards policies that destroy the environment in favour of natural resource production and extraction, it is also important to recognise that the lifestyle of the modern runner, biker, hiker, or hunter is dependent on global capitalist and consumer processes that seeks continual market growth and perpetuate the exploitation of natural spaces as 'resources' necessary to fuel (sometimes literally) such growth. In a study on the environmental impacts of sport and outdoor recreation in Sweden, McCullough et al. (2018) note that outdoor recreation practices often pose specific challenges to the protection and preservation of the environment due to their close connection to anthropocentric consumption. From the transport, equipment, sporting good, and apparel consumption that takes place in conjunction with outdoor recreation, to the altering of rural environments for the purposes of planning recreational spaces and facilities, such human-centred activities can serve to contradict environmental sustainability efforts. This is perhaps why scholars including philosopher Soper (2020) have called for alternative ways of living and recreating that are potentially more sustainable than the consumer and growth-oriented forms that endure in the contemporary global sporting, recreation, and leisure industries.

If we apply Han (2015) notion of the burnout society to the context of the anthropause and the initial lockdown measures of the pandemic, we are compelled to recognise that perhaps the predominant reaction by consumers and industries to the temporary restriction of human activity and mobility was to subsequently find other means of re-asserting our personal productivity, and continuing to devote our energies towards activities that fit with the logic of self-management, self-improvement, and the 'self-project'. The post-anthropause, in other words, witnessed the reinforcement of the self of the productive project and a further embedding, rather than challenging, of the consumer and commodification processes of the burnout society. Indeed, a critical reflection on many forms of outdoor recreation available in the marketplace would demonstrate how these activities often lend themselves to this ongoing project of self-commodification and objectification, as we seek out new achievements to celebrate: parks to visit, trails to conquer, PRs to be set. At the same time, viewing the renewed growth in outdoor recreation consumption through the lens of the post-anthropause and Han's burnout society underscores that the never-ceasing concern for personal productivity is fuelled by and feeds into the imperative for socioeconomic growth. This continues to result in the degradation and destruction of environments and animal habitats, all within a consumer-capitalist order dependent on the endless extraction of resources from the global ecosystem.

Conclusion

Our goal in introducing and exploring the period of post-anthropause physical culture is to underscore the environmental and social implications in the resumption and resurgence of human physical and consumer activity following the initial lockdown measures in 2020, specifically the renewed ecological impacts in regard to outdoor recreation in protected areas in the United States. As Horn (2021) explains, the 'reduced traffic and halted industry' during the initial lockdown measures represented an opportunity for a 'new and more appropriate approach to environmental policy', and 'an experimental space in which to test out how things might be done differently' to limit or reduce the impact of consumer, tourist, recreation, and leisure activities on the global environment (p. 124). However, following mediated accounts of the collective stoppage of the anthropause and its positive impact on environmental spaces and wildlife, consumers flocked to mountains, beaches, rivers, and other outdoor spaces, taking up old and new recreational and leisure practices, often with the material support of well-timed Amazon packages (Weise, 2021). The increase in outdoor recreation rates and consumerism occurred alongside other environmentally destructive developments during the pandemic, including the Trump administration's efforts to relax or remove environmental protections at national parks and other protected areas in order to increase corporate access to resources within those publicly owned spaces (Holden, 2020). Framing the increase in outdoor recreation rates within the period of the post-anthropause highlights the ways in which such developments are often folded into and following the anthropogenic logic of the prevailing consumer capitalist regime. These considerations also point to possible future research related to outdoor recreation and leisure in the various phases and stages of the COVID-19 pandemic, both within the United States and other local, national, and regional contexts.

At the same time, considering outdoor recreation practices during the post-anthropause also underscores the need to envisage post-anthropocentric forms of physical culture in this age of the Anthropocene, engaging with points of interconnections between human (physical) activities and environmental change, and emphasising the ties between recreation, leisure, tourism and processes of ecological damage and disruption. For example, the environmental implications of post-anthropause recreation illustrates the need for alternative forms of tourism such as 'proximity tourism' (Rantala et al., 2020), emphasising 'local destinations, short distances and lower-carbon modes of transportation' as a particular strategy to minimising the planetary impacts of tourist activity. At the same time, the post-anthropause underscores the immense challenges entailed in fundamentally altering the relationship between human populations and outdoor recreation and tourism as cultural and consumer-based industries. As one example, this discussion of post-anthropause outdoor recreation dovetails with Fletcher (2019) discussion of the ongoing shift towards new forms of ecotourism and 'Anthropocene tourism', in which tourism entrepreneurs seek new opportunities for consumer activity and revenue generation through the commodification of environmental destruction. Thus, tourists visit receding glaciers in protected areas as part of a commercial industry reorienting itself from 'selling an encounter with the glacier per se to selling an experience of its imminent disappearance' (Fletcher, 2019, p. 522). While it is possible to view such analyses as another indication of the inevitable environmental consequences of anthropocentric recreational, leisure, and tourist consumerism within twenty-1st century capitalism, we would suggest that we might consider the period of COVID-19 lockdown as not merely a pause, but as a potential 'portal', in regard to a 'passage to an alternative period or configuration of space – time' that provides us with a 'fruitful intellectual arena for considering the reconfigurations which may be offered by anthropause events' (Searle et al., 2021, p. 74). This approach thus emphasises the anthropause as a rupture that holds the potential for social change, a notion that Beck (2015) extends to the broader context of climate change during the Anthropocene:

> Seen this way, climate change risk is far more than a problem of measures of carbon dioxide and the production of pollution. It does not even only signal a crisis of human

self-understanding. More than that, global climate risk creates new ways of being, looking, hearing and acting in the world – highly conflictual and ambivalent, open-ended, without any foreseeable outcome (Beck, 2015 p. 83).

In our view, the post-anthropause might similarly be conceptualised as a portal to an intellectual area for imagining post-anthropocentric forms of outdoor recreation, via practices that emphasise more ecologically balanced relations between active human bodies and the environment.

Disclosure statement

No potential conflict of interest was reported by the author(s).

References

BBC. (2020, April 29). *Coronavirus: Wild animals enjoy freedom of a quieter world*. bbc.com. https://www.bbc.com/news/world-52459487

Beck, U. (2015). Emancipatory catastrophism: What does it mean to climate change and risk society?. *Current Sociology*, *63*(1), 75–88.

Bell, S., Tyrväiinen, L., Sievänen, T., Pröbstl, U., & Simpson, M. (2007). Outdoor recreation and nature tourism: A European perspective. *Living Reviews in Landscape Research*, *1*(2), 2–46. https://doi.org/10.12942/lrlr-2007-2

Bernhard, A. (2020). *The great bicycle boom of 2020*. bbc.com. https://www.bbc.com/future/bespoke/made-on-earth/the-great-bicycle-boom-of-2020.html

Borunda, A. (2020, July 29). *How 'nature deprived' neighborhoods impact the health of people of color*. nationalgeographic.com. https://www.nationalgeographic.com/science/article/how-nature-deprived-neighborhoods-impact-health-people-of-color

Brunell, D. (2020, October 17). *Coronavirus stimulates RV sales and rentals*. spokesman.com. https://www.spokesman.com/stories/2020/oct/17/don-brunell-coronavirus-stimulates-rv-sales-and-re/

Buckley, R. (2020). Conservation implications of COVID19: Effects via tourism and extractive industries. *Biological Conservation*, *247*, 108640. https://doi.org/10.1016/j.biocon.2020.108640

Cheer, J. M., Milano, C., & Novelli, M. (2019). Tourism and community resilience in the Anthropocene: Accentuating temporal overtourism. *Journal of Sustainable Tourism*, *27*(4), 554–572. https://doi.org/10.1080/09669582.2019.1578363

Chow, A. R. (2020, July 22). *National Parks Are Getting Trashed During COVID-19, Endangering Surrounding Communities*. time.com. https://time.com/5869788/national-parks-covid-19/

Chrobak, U. (2020, March 25). *A guide to safe outdoor activities during the coronavirus pandemic*. popsci.com. https://www.popsci.com/story/environment/lockdown-coronavirus-covid-go-outside/

Easterbrook-Smith, G. (2021). By bread alone: Baking as leisure, performance, sustenance, during the COVID-19 crisis. *Leisure Sciences*, *43*(1–2), 36–42. https://doi.org/10.1080/01490400.2020.1773980

Finnessey, L. (2012). The negative effects of tourism on national parks in the United States. *Bachelor of Science Honors Thesis, Johnson & Wales University* [Online] http://www.scholararchive. jwu. edu/cgi.

Fiorillo, A., Sampogna, G., Giallonardo, V., Del Vecchio, V., Luciano, M., Albert, U., Carmassi, C., Carrà, G., Cirulli, F., Dell'Osso, B., & Nanni, M.G. (2020). Effects of the lockdown on the mental health of the general population during the COVID-19 pandemic in Italy: Results from the COMET collaborative network. *European Psychiatry, 63*(1), 1–28. https://doi.org/10.1192/j.eurpsy.2020.89

Fletcher, R. (2019). Ecotourism after nature: Anthropocene tourism as a new capitalist "fix". *Journal of Sustainable Tourism, 27*(4), 522–535. https://doi.org/10.1080/09669582.2018.1471084

Frost, W., & Hall, C. M. (Eds.). (2010). *Tourism and national parks*. Routledge.

Gillam, C. (2020, October 25). *While We Focus on COVID-19, Trump's EPA Is Quietly Killing Us*. ecowatch.com. https://www.ecowatch.com/trump-epa-rollbacks-covid-2648440328.html

Hall, S. B. (2020, April 9). *This is how COVID-19 is affecting the world of sports*. World Economic Forum. https://www.weforum.org/agenda/2020/04/sports-covid19-coronavirus-excersise-specators-media-coverage/

Hall, S. (2021). *Writings on media* (C. Brunsdon, Ed.). Duke University Press.

Han, B.-C. (2015). *The burnout society*. Stanford Briefs.

Hanage, W. P., Testa, C., Chen, J. T., Davis, L., Pechter, E., Seminario, P., Santillana, M. Santillana, M., Krieger, N. (2020). COVID-19: US federal accountability for entry, spread, and inequities—lessons for the future. *European Journal of Epidemiology, 35*(11), 995–1006. https://doi.org/10.1007/s10654-020-00689-2

Hayes, J. (2020, October 31). *Hunting numbers surge during COVID — but will the sport's popularity last?* thehill.com. https://thehill.com/opinion/energy-environment/523207-hunting-numbers-surge-during-covid-but-will-the-sports-popularity

Hempel, M. (2018). AnthropoTrumpism: Trump and the politics of environmental disruption. *Journal of Environmental Studies and Sciences, 8*(2), 183–188. https://doi.org/10.1007/s13412-018-0491-8

Heyd, T. (2021). Covid-19 and climate change in the times of the Anthropocene. *The Anthropocene Review, 8*(1), 21–36. https://doi.org/10.1177/2053019620961799

Hickel, J. (2021). What does degrowth mean? a few points of clarification. *Globalizations, 18*(7), 1105–1111. https://doi.org/10.1080/14747731.2020.1812222

Himes, H. (2020, October 5). *Maryland Park Service reports new attendance record in state parks*. fredricknewspost.com. https://www.fredericknewspost.com/news/economy_and_business/services/maryland-park-service-reports-new-attendance-record-in-state-parks/article_0d84c914-447d-5ffe-9ee1-d6f2be9fa0da.html

Holden, E. (2020, May 11). *Trump dismantles environmental protections under cover of coronavirus*. theguardian.com. https://www.theguardian.com/us-news/2020/may/10/trump-environmental-blitzkrieg-coronavirus

Horn, E. (2021). Tipping points: The Anthropocene and Covid-19. In G. Delanty, *Pandemics, politics, and society: critical perspectives on the Covid-19 crisis* (pp. 124). Berlin: De Gruyter.

Jacques, M., & Stout, J. (2020). *Wisconsin State Parks and the COVID-19 Pandemic*. University of Wisconsin.

Katella, K. (2021, March 9). *Our Pandemic Year—A COVID-19 Timeline*. Yale Medicine. https://www.yalemedicine.org/news/covid-timeline

Katz-Rosene, R. (2021). The pandemic, the economy, and environmental change: six implications for the study of international political economy. *Global Perspectives, 2*(1), 24409. https://doi.org/10.1525/gp.2021.24409

King, S. (2022). Of companionship, curfew, and conflict: Multispecies leisure in the age of COVID. *Leisure Studies, 41*(3), 301–309. https://doi.org/10.1080/02614367.2021.1989018

Lawton, G. (2020). Life in the anthropause. *New Scientist, 247*(3292), 21. https://doi.org/10.1016/S0262-4079(20)31284-7

Lecocq, T., Hicks, S.P., Van Noten, K., Van Wijk, K., Koelemeijer, P., De Plaen, R.S., Massin, F., Hillers, G., Anthony, R.E., Apoloner, M.T., & Arroyo-Solórzano, M. (2020). Thumbnail Global quieting of high-frequency seismic noise due to COVID-19 pandemic lockdown measures. *Science, 369*(6509), 1338–1343. https://doi.org/10.1126/science.abd2438

Liu, H. L., Lavender-Stott, E. S., Carotta, C. L., & Garcia, A. S. (2022). Leisure experience and participation and its contribution to stress-related growth amid COVID-19 pandemic. *Leisure Studies, 41*(1), 70–84. https://doi.org/10.1080/02614367.2021.1942526

Maher, N. (2008). *Nature's new deal*. Oxford University Press.

Manning, R. E., Anderson, L. E., & Pettengill, P. (2017). *Managing outdoor recreation: Case studies in the national parks*. Cabi.

Matteson, C. (2020, September 2). *How Trails and Outdoor Access Provide Important Mental Health Benefits*. railstotrails.org. https://www.railstotrails.org/trailblog/2020/september/02/how-trails-and-outdoor-access-provide-important-mental-health-benefits/

McClanahan, P. (2020, March 29). *I'm a U.S. Citizen. Where in the World Can I Go?* The New York Times. https://www.nytimes.com/article/coronavirus-travel-restrictions.html

McCullough, B. P., Bergegard, N. A., Collins, A., Muhar, A., & Tyrväinen, L. (2018). *The impact of sport and outdoor recreation (Friluftsliv) on the natural environment*. The Swedish Foundation for Strategic Environmental Research.

McDonald, M. G., & Birrell, S. (1999). Reading sport critically: a methodology for interrogating power. *Sociology of Sport Journal, 16*(4), 283–300. https://doi.org/10.1123/ssj.16.4.283

Miller, J. (2020, April 30). *Trump seizes on pandemic to speed up opening of public lands to industry*. theguardian.com. https://www.theguardian.com/environment/2020/apr/30/public-lands-sale-trump-coronavirus-environmental-regulations

Monz, C., D'Antonio, A., Lawson, S., Barber, J., & Newman, P. (2016). The ecological implications of visitor transportation in parks and protected areas: Examples from research in US National Parks. *Journal of Transport Geography, 51*, 27–35. https://doi.org/10.1016/j.jtrangeo.2015.11.003

National Park Service. (2022, Februrary 16). *Visitation Numbers*. nps.gov. https://www.nps.gov/aboutus/visitation-numbers.htm

O'Callaghan-Gordo, C., & Antó, J. M. (2020). COVID-19: The disease of the Anthropocene. *Environmental Research, 187*, 109683. https://doi.org/10.1016/j.envres.2020.109683

O'Dell, P. (2017). Redefining the National Park Service role in urban areas: bringing the parks to the people. *Journal of Leisure Research, 48*(1), 5–11. https://doi.org/10.18666/jlr-2016-v48-i1-7168

OECD. (2021) . *Tackling the mental health impact of the COVID-19 crisis: An integrated, whole-of-society response*. OECD.

Olafsdottir, G., Cloke, P., Schulz, A., van Dyck, Z., Eysteinsson, T., Thorleifsdottir, B., & Vögele, C. (2018). Health benefits of walking in nature: a randomized controlled study under conditions of real-life stress. *Environment and Behavior, 52*(3), 248–274. https://doi.org/10.1177/0013916518800798

Penbrooke, T. L. (2020, March 20). *Access to Parks and the Outdoors is Crucial for Mental Health in Our Communities*. nrpa.org. https://www.nrpa.org/blog/access-to-parks-and-the-outdoors-is-crucial-for-mental-health-in-our-communities/

Pereira, P. S., Silveira, A. D. S., & Pereira, A. (2020). Disinformation and conspiracy theories in the age of COVID-19. *Frontiers in Sociology, 5*, 96.

Perkins, S. E., Shilling, F., & Collinson, W. (2022). Anthropause opportunities: experimental perturbation of road traffic and the potential effects on wildlife. *Frontiers in Ecology and Evolution, 192*, 1–7. https://doi.org/10.3389/fevo.2022.833129

Prensky, M. (2020, October 13). *Maryland state parks, Assateague smash attendance records thanks in part to COVID-19*. delmarvanow.com. https://www.delmarvanow.com/story/news/local/maryland/2020/10/13/md-state-parks-assateague-national-smash-attendance-records-thanks-covid/5910144002/

Rantala, O., Salmela, T., Valtonen, A., & Höckert, E. (2020). Envisioning tourism and proximity after the anthropocene. *Sustainability, 12*(10), 3948. https://doi.org/10.3390/su12103948

Repanshek, K. (2020, March 24). *Coronavirus Leading To Vandalism, Illegal Camping, Short Staffing In National Parks*. nationalparkstraveler.org. https://www.nationalparkstraveler.org/2020/03/coronavirus-leading-vandalism-illegal-camping-short-staffing-national-parks

Rice, W. L., Mateer, T. J., Reigner, N., Newman, P., Lawhon, B., & Taff, B. D. (2020). Changes in recreational behaviors of outdoor enthusiasts during the COVID-19 pandemic: Analysis across urban and rural communities. *Journal of Urban Ecology, 6*(1), juaa020. https://doi.org/10.1093/jue/juaa020

Romagosa, F., Eagles, P. F., & Lemieux, C. J. (2015). From the inside out to the outside in: Exploring the role of parks and protected areas as providers of human health and well-being. *Journal of Outdoor Recreation and Tourism, 10*, 70–77. https://doi.org/10.1016/j.jort.2015.06.009

Rose, J., & Carr, A. (2018). Political ecologies of leisure: A critical approach to nature-society relations in leisure studies. *Annals of Leisure Research, 21*(3), 265–283. https://doi.org/10.1080/11745398.2018.1428110

Rowland-Shea, J., Doshi, S., Edberg, S., & Fanger, R. (2020, July 21). *Confronting Racial and Economic Disparities in the Destruction and Protection of Nature in America*. americanprogress.org. https://www.americanprogress.org/article/the-nature-gap/

Rutz, C., Loretto, M.-C., Bates, A. E., Davidson, S. C., Durate, C. M., Jetz, W., Johnson, M., Kato, A., Kays, R., Mueller, T., & Rb, P. (2020). COVID-19 lockdown allows researchers to quantify the effects of human activity on wildlife. *Nature Ecology and Evolution, 4*, 1156–1159. https://doi.org/10.1038/s41559-020-1237-z

Saarinen, J. (2019). What are wilderness areas for? Tourism and political ecologies of wilderness uses and management in the Anthropocene. *Journal of Sustainable Tourism, 27*(4), 472–487. https://doi.org/10.1080/09669582.2018.1456543

Sadasivam, N. (2021, March 01). *Inside Biden's uphill battle to restore the EPA after Trump*. grist.org. https://grist.org/politics/epa-joe-biden-environmental-law-enforcement-trump/

Searle, A., Turnbull, J., & Lorimer, J. (2021). After the anthropause: Lockdown lessons for more-than-human geographies. *The Geographical Journal, 187*(1), 69–77. https://doi.org/10.1111/geoj.12373

Sgobba, C. (2020, May 13). *12 Outdoor Activities for When You Need to Get Out of the House*. self.com. https://www.self.com/story/safe-outdoor-activities-coronavirus

Sivan, A. (2020). Reflection on leisure during COVID-19. *World Leisure Journal, 62*(4), 296–299. https://doi.org/10.1080/16078055.2020.1825260

Smith, L. C. (2020, April 26). *More Time Out in Nature Is an Unexpected Benefit of the COVID-19 Sheltering Rules*. scientificamerican.com. https://blogs.scientificamerican.com/observations/more-time-out-in-nature-is-an-unexpected-benefit-of-the-covid-19-sheltering-rules/

Soper, K. (2020). *Post-Growth living: for an alternative hedonism*. Verso.
Soto, E. H., Botero, C. M., Milanés, C. B., Rodríguez-Santiago, A., Palacios-Moreno, M., Díaz-Ferguson, E., Velázquez, Y. R., Velázquez, Y. R., Abbehusen, A., Guerra-Castro, E., Simoes, N., Muciño-Reyes, M., Filho, J. R. S. (2021). How does the beach ecosystem change without tourists during COVID-19 lockdown? *Biological Conservation*, 255, 108972. https://doi.org/10.1016/j.biocon.2021.108972
Spenceley, A., McCool, S., Newsome, D., Báez, A., Barborak, J. R., Blye, C.-J., Bricker, K., Sigit Cahyadi, H., Corrigan, K., Halpenny, E., Hvenegaard, G., Malleret King, D., Leung, Y.-F., Mandić, A., Naidoo, R., Rüede, D., Sano, J., Sarhan, M., Santamaria, V., Zschiegner, A.-K. (2021). Tourism in protected and conserved areas amid the COVID-19 pandemic. *Parks*, 27(27), 103–118. https://doi.org/10.2305/IUCN.CH.2021.PARKS-27-SIAS.en
St-Esprit McKivigan, M. (2020, June 23). '*Nature Deficit Disorder' Is Really a Thing*. nytimes.com. https://www.nytimes.com/2020/06/23/parenting/nature-health-benefits-coronavirus-outdoors.html
Taff, B. D., Thomsen, J., Rice, W. L., Miller, Z., Newton, J., Miller, L., & McCormick, M. (2022). US national park visitor experiences during COVID-19: Data from Acadia, Glacier, Grand Teton, Shenandoah, and Yellowstone National Parks. *Parks Stewardship Forum*, 38(1), 145–159. https://doi.org/10.5070/P538156128
Templeton, A., Goonan, K., & Fyall, A. (2021). COVID-19 and its impact on visitation and management at US national parks. *International Hospitality Review*, 35(2), 240–259. https://doi.org/10.1108/IHR-08-2020-0039
Tenenbaum, D. J. (2000). Trampling paradise: Dream vacation–environmental nightmare? *Environmental Health Perspectives*, 108(5), A214–A219. https://doi.org/10.2307/3454371
Weise, K. (2021, April 29). *Amazon's profit soars 220 percent as pandemic drives shopping online*. The New York Times. https://www.nytimes.com/2021/04/29/technology/amazons-profits-triple.html

Sports participation during a lockdown. How COVID-19 changed the sports frequency and motivation of participants in club, event, and online sports

Erik Thibaut, Bram Constandt, Veerle De Bosscher, Annick Willem, Margot Ricour and Jeroen Scheerder

ABSTRACT

The impact of the COVID-19 crisis and its related measures on how people practice and experience leisure continues to be significant. In the current study, a survey measuring sport participation during the third week of the first lockdown, that started on the 18th of March 2020 and has been gradually loosened as of the 18th of April 2020, was carried out among 13,515 Flemish citizens. Through a canonical correlation analysis, four clusters of COVID-19-sports-participants are distinguished, i.e. people who experience restrictions when it comes to (i) time and sports infrastructure, (ii) closed sports clubs and cancelled event activities, (iii) time and fear/sickness, and (iv) those who experience no impact. Logistic regression results indicate that participants with online sports experience have a (more) positive effect on their sports participation behaviour, while less missing and having to adapt their previous sports behaviour. The opposite is found for sports club members, while former sports event participation has a positive effect on sports frequency, but a negative effect on their motivation. The results of both analyses give insight into the role that different policy instruments (i.e. sports clubs, events, type of sports) play in keeping different clusters of sports participants motivated to stay sports-active.

1. Introduction

The COVID-19 crisis has a major impact on people's behaviour. To prevent the virus from spreading among the population and thus overloading the healthcare system, most countries in the world have been forced to impose social restrictions and stay-at-home measures (e.g. through a lockdown). Nevertheless, a consequence of these restrictions is that this seriously affects how citizens practice their leisure activities (Mackenzie & Goodnow, 2020), as they deprive people of engaging in sports settings such as leisure centres, gyms, and sports clubs (Lashua et al., 2020), and in sports activities that are practised away from home and with fellow sports companions (Constandt et al., 2020).

The scientific consensus is that practicing sports is beneficial for physical and psychological health and that it also benefits social well-being (Caputo & Reichert, 2020; Eime et al., 2013; Son et al., 2020; Xie et al., 2020). Carter et al. (2020) argue that the importance and potential of physical activity and sports should not be marginalised during a pandemic, given the overall health risks that are associated with obesity and the specific figures that indicate that obesity increases mortality rates due to COVID-19. These risks should not be neglected, as Zhu et al. (2021) demonstrate that obesity rates in China increased during the COVID-19 outbreak.

While the above studies suggest that COVID-19 has a mainly negative impact on general sports participation figures, they fail to explain why certain groups of people are less sports-active, and how policymakers can deal with the increased sports inactivity. Therefore, the current study investigates how different types of sports participants change their sports behaviours and motivation due to COVID-19 and the lockdown. In particular, the study analyses the determining factors of how the COVID-19 measures (i) prevent people from taking part in sports, (ii) whether they (have to) adapt their sports participation, (iii) and whether they miss their usual way of sports participation behaviour. One of the determinants that the current study will focus on, is how different popular sports participation settings experience the impact of restrictions imposed by COVID-19 and related policy measures (Borgers et al., 2018; Eime et al., 2020).

The reason why participants in different settings can be expected to experience a different impact is based on the serious leisure perspective (SLP) of Elkington and Stebbins (2014). They stipulate that leisure activities can and should be grouped into three categories, i.e. casual, project-based, and serious leisure. People can be expected to face more difficulties in engaging in sports activities that can be thought of as serious leisure activities/settings (e.g. sports club and group sports) compared to project-based activities/settings such as mass sports participation events (Evans et al., 2020; Filo et al., 2013) or casual sports activities/settings. A first setting is thus offered by the sports club members, as opposed to participants that prefer to sport where, when, how, and with whom they want (i.e. light organised sports settings) (Borgers et al., 2018). Second, a large number of people prefer to take part in structured mass participation sports events (Xie et al., 2020). Research concerning these two settings is important, as both settings often contain sports activities and contexts that are not adapted to the COVID-19 related social distance measures (e.g. running in large groups). More precisely, these activities and settings often entail high-spread risks (e.g. indoor contact sports) that are not appropriate during a pandemic (Halabchi et al., 2020). Online sports participants (i.e. people who practice sports on online platforms including, but not limited to, myfitnesspal®, Runkeeper®, Strava®, Tiktok®, and Swift®), represent the third setting under scrutiny, especially as they can be seen as casual leisure activities that nevertheless allow staying in touch with fellow sports companions (see e.g. Hayes, 2020). These online participants can be expected to feel less restricted in their sports participation behaviour due to the implied social distance measures. These variables will be investigated in a multivariate way along with the (more traditional) socio-demographic variables age, sex, education, and having children or not.

Gaining information about how different types of sports participants are affected by COVID-19 helps policymakers to better understand how lockdown restrictions affect specific groups of sports participants. Such information is useful for post-COVID-19 sports policy. First, the results offer insights into which sports participation settings are affected most by COVID-19, and thus which clusters policy should focus most on. Second, COVID-19 is an interesting, and hopefully once in a lifetime, opportunity to semi-experimentally investigate the effect of closed organised sports settings on sports participation behaviour and on the motivation to stay sports-active.

2. Literature review

Leisure is one of the most strongly affected industries due to the outbreak of COVID-19 (Lachance, 2020; Lashua et al., 2020), as the popularity of many leisure activities is based on the ability to socially interact with others (Xie et al., 2020). As a consequence, these 'social' leisure activities are often unable to adapt themselves to the imposed rules of social distancing due to COVID-19 and have been suspended in many countries until the coronavirus was under control. In this light, sports participation presents itself as an interesting case to enhance our knowledge about the trade-off between leisure's benefits and risks during an international health crisis. During COVID-19 lockdowns, many public authorities have encouraged physical activity through sports to strengthen one's immune system against viral infections. At the same time, many forms of sports participation and especially those that entail close physical interaction with others, have been temporarily forbidden due to the risk of mass dispersion of the new coronavirus.

2.1. Sports participation in times of COVID-19-related restrictive measures

Worldwide, different measures have been implemented to prevent COVID-19 from spreading among the population. Overall, governments face the challenging task to find a balance between keeping the mortality rate as low as possible on the one hand, and mitigating the detrimental effects of COVID-19 on economic welfare and other health indicators such as (in)sufficient physical activity on the other hand (Anderson et al., 2020). Numerous countries have implemented a restrictive quarantine (i.e. a national lockdown) to prevent COVID-19 from infecting the population as much as possible. In the first half of 2020, in some countries and regions such as China, France, Spain, Italy, and Tyrol (Austria), a very strict lockdown was imposed by the government, implying that most physical (outdoor) activities during the outbreak of COVID-19 in Europe were prohibited. For example, the Austrian region of Tyrol implemented a 'very early and very harsh lockdown' (Miner & Wright, 2020), by which all outdoor activities (including jogging and hiking) were forbidden. Figures of Tyrol indicate that people engaged less in sports during the stay-at-home order (Schnitzer et al., 2020). In Italy, the strict lockdown resulted in a significant decrease in physical activity (see Mattioli et al., 2020).

Other countries opted for a partial lockdown during the COVID-19 wave at the beginning of 2020. For instance, on the 18th of March 2020 Belgium (i.e. the research context of the current study) opted for a so-called 'lockdown light'. While schools were closed and people had to work from home, Belgian citizens were allowed to practice a limited number of sports activities: i.e. running, walking, equestrian sports, cycling, and other non-motorised activities on wheels (e.g. skateboarding, inline skating) (Constandt et al., 2020). Also, the context in which citizens could practice sports was strongly regulated. Sports activities had to be practised alone, or with other household members, or with a maximum of one friend outside the family (i.e. a sports buddy). Although people were allowed to go as far from home as they would to engage in sports activities, people had to start the activity from home as it was forbidden to use a car or other motorised transport vehicles. Citizens were not permitted to take a rest during their sports activities, nor to visit others at their homes. Furthermore, other forms of sports such as sports club activities and mass leisure activities (e.g. sports events) were not allowed (Lachance, 2020). Fitness centres (and other kinds of sports infrastructure) also had to close their doors. A month after the start of the first lockdown (18th of March), the restrictions were gradually loosened, by e.g. opening gardening and do-it-yourself stores (18th of April), allowing outdoor physical activity with two persons from outside the household (4th of May), outdoor social contact with 4 people (10th of May), outdoor sports club activities with 20 people (18th of May). Nevertheless, even before the unleashing of the above restrictions, physical activity and sports participation among adults increased in Flanders in that period, as 36% of the respondents indicated to have exercised more and 41% as much as before (Constandt et al., 2020).

In summary, the above highlights that different social restrictions result in different effects on sports participation (behaviour). To gain full insight into sports participation since the outbreak of COVID-19, additional knowledge is not only needed concerning how attitudes and behaviours have changed but also about the evolving interests and opinions (AIO's) of the sport participants themselves. The current study will therefore whether people had to change their sports participation behaviour and whether they miss their previous behaviour. Or, put differently, the current study offers into whether the increase in sports participation in Flanders during the lockdown is due to positive aspects of the lockdown (e.g. having more time, discovering sports activities from outside the comfort zone), or rather rooted in negative drivers (e.g. no alternative leisure activities available).

2.2. Sports-specific clusters

The SLP framework of Elkington and Stebbins (2014) distinguishes serious leisure, project-based leisure, and casual leisure. Specific to serious leisure activities is that people invest effort (e.g. training) to gain skill and knowledge, resulting in durable benefits, while also forming a strong identification and shared values with other participants. Project-based leisure is more about short-term and infrequent leisure, although it still involves significant planning, effort, and skill/knowledge. The latter is less the case for casual leisure.

The current study builds on Sharon Shen and Yarnal's (2010) notion that a dichotomisation between serious and casual leisure is not appropriate. Practicing sports in sports clubs club (in contrast to so-called light-organised sports participation) (e.g. Borgers et al., 2016, 2018; Scheerder et al., 2020) and during sport events sports (e.g. Funk et al., 2011; Helsen et al., 2021) are popular sports contexts in the categories of serious leisure and project-based leisure respectively. These two categories are especially interesting when it comes to COVID-19-related sports participation research, as Evans et al. (2020) indicate that both settings can be expected to have experienced a significant impact. Based on the SLP framework, one would expect that participants in serious leisure activities (i.e. sports clubs) are impacted more when compared to participants in activities that contain more project-based characteristics (i.e. mass sports events) or that are more casual. Therefore, the current study will also investigate whether the organisational setting at hand has an impact on how sports participants are affected by the lockdown measures. One of the main reasons to focus on sports club membership is linked with its alleged benefits. Membership of a sports club is shown to increase the frequency of, and time spent on sports (Borgers et al., 2016; Downward et al., 2014; Lera-López et al., 2015), life satisfaction (Eime et al., 2010), learning and leadership skills (Tsigilis et al., 2009), and mental well-being and social-connectedness (Eime et al., 2010). The annulation of sports club membership can thus be expected to have a negative effect on the motivation and the sports participation frequency of sports club members.

In addition to the sports setting at hand, the current study distinguishes between activities that are practised alone versus activities that require other people to join. In Austria, people engaged more in outdoor sports during the COVID-19 lockdown (Schnitzer et al., 2020). This type of sports activities is typically practised alone and outside specific sports infrastructures. On the one hand, people who were already taking part in solitary sports activities pre-COVID-19 can be expected to be able to continue their usual sports behaviour. On the other hand, people who engaged in sports for which – at least – one opponent is needed will have to switch to other (variants of their) activities if they want to remain sports active. Accordingly, the behaviours and perceptions of sports club members and people who (normally) need team-mates and/or opponents for their sports activities are expected to be affected more strongly by the COVID-19 lockdown compared to so-called individual 'light-organized' sports participants.

Until recently, online sports participation was a less popular activity. Nonetheless, the current study will also test whether people who – to some extent – practised sports online/virtually pre-COVID-19 are less impacted by the COVID-19 measures. Also, the COVID-19-measures of social distancing and cancellations of events could create a momentum for a switch towards online/virtual leisure activities (Lachance, 2020). The usage of online sports platforms can serve as an important driver towards a healthier and more sports-active lifestyle (Glynn et al., 2014). Moreover, during a lockdown, these platforms can serve as one of the sole options that still allow for social contact and competition, while aligning with the obliged distance measures. Therefore, people who are already familiar with online/virtual sports participation are expected to be better positioned to (partially or fully) switch to online forms of sports participation.

2.3. Sociodemographic variables

Research has extensively investigated the effect of the sociodemographic variables sex, age, education, and having children on sports participation. The current study integrates these variables in its scope to examine their effect on changes in sports participation attitudes, interests, and opinions during the time of COVID-19 restrictions. When individuals and households face challenging times, the abovementioned sociodemographic variables are expected to significantly impact how people are (un)able to continue their former sports participation behaviour during the COVID-19 lockdown. Most studies on sports participation pre-COVID-19 report that men spend more time on sports than women (e.g. Downward et al., 2014). A negative relationship between the frequency of sports participation since COVID-19 broke out and having school-aged children is likely, as schools were shut down and parents thus had to take care of their children (e.g. childcare and/or assisting pre-teaching) without much external support. For age, the majority of existing studies found decreasing sports activity with increasing age (e.g. Borgers et al., 2016). As people above a certain age are more vulnerable to COVID-19 (Carter et al., 2020), they might be more restricted and/or hesitant to engage in sports during a pandemic (Constandt et al., 2020; Son et al., 2020). Although no adapted advice towards older and/or vulnerable groups was given in Belgium (i.e. shielding guidance), the above rationale suggests that a negative relationship between age and changes in sports participation behaviour during the COVID-19 lockdown can be expected.

3. Method

The focus of the current study is on Flanders, which is the Dutch-speaking part of Belgium. While Flanders is the competent authority for sports, in the first lockdown, all COVID-19 measures were applied on the whole Belgian territory and were thus the same for Flanders, Brussels, and Wallonia (i.e. Belgium's three geographical regions).

A newly-developed, online questionnaire was distributed through email, newspapers, and social media and was open for responses in the third week after the COVID-19 measures were implemented in Flanders/Belgium, namely from the 30th of March until the 5th of April, 2020. As of the 27th of March, the measures were prolonged until at least the 19th of April (and it was communicated that at that moment the measures could be prolonged), and given that only at the 6th of April a task force was created to develop an exit strategy, all respondents of the questionnaire had very little information and/or perspective about how long the lockdown would last eventually.

The questionnaire resulted into a sample of 13,515 respondents, aged between 18 and 75 years old. From this sample, only those people who took part in sports since the start of the lockdown are included because (i) the research question focuses on sports participation habits (i.e. setting, kinds of sports activities) and thus on people who have been sports active, (ii) almost all sports-specific variables are 'blank' for the non-participants, and (iii) there is an overrepresentation of sports-active people. Finally the data are also weighted for sex, age, and education, such that a representative dataset of 11,763 sports-active respondents is given.

Logistic regressions are used to investigate the factors that influence the three dependent variables, namely respondents (i) who maintained or increased their sports participation frequency versus respondents that reduced the frequency of their engagement in sports (i.e. sport_more), (ii) who adapted the nature of their sports participation versus those who had not (i.e. adapted_sports), and (iii) who missed their usual sports participation versus those who did not miss it (i.e. missing_sports). The latter was only asked from the respondents who answered affirmatively on the previous question (adapted_sports). The descriptive results in Table 1 demonstrate that overall,

Table 1. Descriptive statistics of the dependent and independent variables (in %).

Dependent variables		Sport_more (N = 11,646)		Sport_adapt (N = 11,763)		Missing_sports (N = 8,802)	
		Equal or increased (1)	76.8	Yes (1)	79.6	Yes (1)	79.4
		Reduced (0)	23.2	No (0)	20.4	No (0)	20.6

Independent variables	Operationalization	Categories	Percentages
Online_SP	Took part in online sports participation before COVID-19	Yes	11.2
		No	88.8
Club_SP	Was a sports club member before COVID-19	Yes	42.3
		No	57.7
Event_SP	Was preparing for a sports event before COVID-19	Yes	34.0
		No	66.0
Solo_sport	Practised solo sports (sports activity for which no opponent is needed, e.g. running, cycling, etc.)	Yes	94.7
		No	5.3
Duo_sport	Practised duo sports (sports activity for which at least one opponent is needed, e.g. racket sports and martial arts)	Yes	8.2
		No	91.8
Team_sport	Practised team sports (sports activity for which at least two opponents are needed, e.g. basketball, soccer, etc.)	Yes	8.6
		No	91.4
Children	Has children living in their household	Yes	38.7
		No	61.3
Age	Age of the respondent	Age 18–34	25.5
		Age 35–54 (ref.)	38.8
		Age 55–74	35.7
Education	Degree of education, with people who are still at school, and people who finished school (lower) versus people who finished college or university	Educ_student	5.2
		Educ_lower (ref.)	59.3
		Educ_higher	35.5
Sex	Sex of the respondent	Male	52.6
		Female (ref.)	47.4

Obstacles	The following was an obstacle in practising sports:	Categories	Percentages
Obst_infr	Closed sports infrastructure	Yes	40.2%
		No	59.8%
Obst_club	No sports club activities	Yes	31.2%
		No	68.8%
Obst_friend	No friends to sport with	Yes	24.5%
		No	75.5%
Obst_event	Cancelled sports events	Yes	25.8%
		No	74.2%
Obst_env	No adequate environment to practice sports	Yes	14.6%
		No	85.4%
Obst_fear	Fear for COVID-19	Yes	9.3%
		No	90.7%
Obst_time	Lack of time	Yes	3.2%
		No	96.8%
Obst_intr	No interest (anymore)	Yes	2.2%
		No	97.8%
Obst_sick	Sickness	Yes	1.9%
		No	98.1%
Obst_no	No obstacles experienced	Yes (i.e. no obstacles experienced)	28.9%
		No (i.e. obstacles experienced)	71.1%

approximately 3 out of 4 adults in Flanders fill out that they were able to be equally or more active when compared to the period before the COVID-19 social restrictions. Nevertheless, 4 out of 5 indicate that they had to adapt their sports behaviour, while they reported missing certain aspects of their usual pre-COVID-19 sports participation.

The first group of independent variables are the sports-specific variables that indicate how people participated in sports before the COVID-19 measures. These variables indicate whether the respondents previously practised sports online (Online_SP), in a club-organised sports context (Club_SP), and/or whether they were training to take part in a mass sports event (Event_SP). Also, the variables Sport_solo, Sport_duo and Sport_team indicate the kind of sports activities that respondents took part in. This categorisation is in line with De Haan and Breedveld (2000), who divide sports activities into (i) sports for which no opponent is needed such as running and fitness (Solo_sport), (ii) sports activities for which at least one opponent is needed according to the formal rules of the game, such as racquet sports and martial arts (Duo_sport), and (iii) team sports that typically involve two teams of at least two players, such as basketball and soccer (Team_sport). The second group of variables includes four sociodemographic variables, having children or not (Children), the level of education (Education), age (Age), and sex (Sex).

Additional to the logistic regressions, a non-linear categorical canonical correlation analysis with optimal scaling (OVERALS) is used. This method provides a graphical solution to describe the relationship between variables and is therefore useful for segmentation purposes in the field of leisure and sports (e.g. Alén et al., 2017; Scheerder et al., 2005; Taks & Scheerder, 2006). This OVERALS-method suits the data well, as it is designed to cope with ordinal and nominal data (Alén et al., 2017; Van der Burg et al., 1994). In the analysis, the regression variables are included, although an additional set of variables is added to gain further understanding about the motives why people were seen to adapt their behaviour and perceptions. More particularly the obstacles that hindered sports participants in their sports participation were added (see also Table 1, second part). In the canonical correlation analysis, the reference categories of the independent variables (see Table 3) and of the dependent variables (people who did not adapt sports participation 'Sport_noadapt'; practised sports to a lesser extent 'Sport_less') are also added. Compared to the regression, two (sets of) variables are excluded, namely 'Missing_Sports' and the sports setting variables (Online_SP, Club_SP, Event_SP). Regarding the former, the 'Missing_sports' question was only asked to the people who answered 'Adapted_sports' positively. Including this variable in the OVERALS procedure, would therefore result in dropping a large number of the observations. The sports setting variables are not included because of multicollinearity with the obstacles.

4. Results

First, the overall change in sports participation behaviour and perception for the sports-specific groups is given (see Table 2). Although the bivariate statistics do not control for other variables, they offer a view on the data structure. A first overall result is that for all sports participant categories, on average, people have not downsized their sports participation behaviour since the start of the COVID-19 lockdown, but that they nevertheless had to adapt their sports behaviour, and that they experienced a feeling of missing their pre-COVID-19 sports behaviour. Table 2 also makes clear that certain clusters (e.g. sports club members) experience a less pronounced increase in sports participation behaviour compared to others (e.g. sports event participants). Moreover, a more significant downfall in motivation is found regarding the clusters that have had a less positive rise in sports activity behaviour. For example, sports club members miss their previous sports participation behaviour more when compared to event sports participants, who in their turn miss it more compared to online sports participants.

Table 2. Overview of the bivariate statistics for the dependent variables by the sports-specific independent variables (in %).

	Overall	Sportclub	Event	Online	Solo	Duo	Team
Sport_more	76.8	71.6	80.5	86.1	77.9	51.9	66.5
Sport_adapt	79.6	90.7	81.9	79.3	78.1	95.9	93.9
Missing_sports	79.4	88.1	81.2	75.7	77.1	80.6	85.8

Table 3. Logistic regression results for the determining factors of maintaining, adapting, and missing sports participation behaviour pre- versus post-COVID-19 restrictions.

	Maintained or increased sports participation	Adapted their sports participation behaviour	Miss their sports participation behaviour
Online_SP	0.572***	−0.231**	−0.225*
Club_SP	−0.407***	1.191***	1.111***
Event_SP	0.24***	0.081	0.174**
Sport_solo	0.107	0.060	−0.302*
Sport_duo	−0.960***	1.596****	0.479***
Sport_team	−0.418***	0.620***	0.122
Children	0.104	−0.084	0.125
Age 18–34	0.074	0.169*	−0.003
Age 55–74	0.014	−0.387***	0.271***
Educ_student	0.028	0.075	0.060
Educ_higher	0.018	0.256***	−0.046
Male	0.195***	−0.162***	−0.096
Constant	0.949***	−0.267	−0.204

Reference categories: Age 35–54, Educ_lower, Female
Significance levels: *p < .05; **p < .01; ***p < .001

Second, the categories in Table 2 are not mutually exclusive, as one individual can indicate to have practised sport in each of the listed settings (club, event, online, solo, duo, and team) pre-COVID-19. Therefore, logistic regression results are needed to investigate the so-called net effect of these independent variables on the dependent variables 'Sport_more', 'Sport_adapt', and 'Missing_sports'. The regression results for the three independent variables are listed in Table 3. It is clear that being a sports club member is negatively related to sports participation behaviour post-COVID-19, while they also change and miss their behaviour more when compared to non-sports club members. For people with online sports experience, the exact opposite is found, as they are more sports-active while adapting and missing their behaviour less than people with no experience in online sports. Mixed results are reported by people who were preparing for a sports event, as they answer to sport more frequently and that they have not adapted their previous behaviour that much, but they nevertheless indicate to miss their previous behaviour more compared to people who were not preparing for a sports event.

Practicing a sports activity for which (an) opponent(s) are needed, also results in a more moderate rise in sports participation behaviour and a higher perception of missing and adapting previous sports participation behaviour. This especially is the case for people who took part in duo sports before the COVID-19 measures, as both the statistical significance and the odds ratios are higher when compared to team sports. For the sociodemographic variables, several significant effects (with relatively low odds ratios) can be noted. A paradox is that older people feel that their participation differs less when compared to younger people, although at the same time they are found to miss their previous sports participation behaviour more when compared to their younger counterparts. The higher the education, the higher the perception that sports habits are different compared to the past. Finally, male sports participants adapt their sports participation behaviour less and experience a bigger increase in frequency compared to women.

Third, Figure 1 depicts the canonical correlation results. Variables close to the origin of the coordinate system do have little discriminatory power, while the opposite goes for variables at the top/down or the far left/right. Also, graphically close variables are related to each other. The first group of variables consist of the variables 'having to adapt sports habits' (sport_adapt) and a 'decrease in sports participation behaviour since COVID-19 lockdown started' (sport_less). This appears to apply to participation in duo sports (sport_duo) before COVID-19 started, and COVID-19 related obstacles like no fitting environment (obst_env) and/or sports infrastructure (obst_infr). Second, there is a segment of variables practicing team sports pre-COVID-19 that are restricted because of the closure of the sports clubs (obst_club) and cancelled sports events (obst_event). Mostly younger people (age_yng, ed_stdnt) belong to

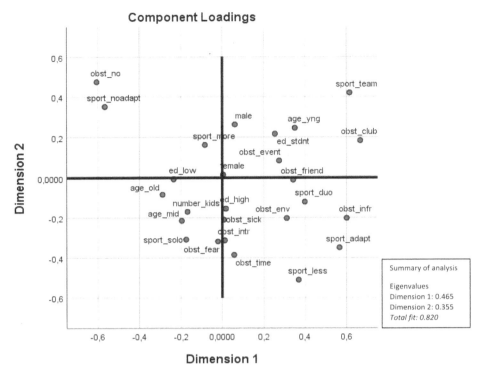

Figure 1. Component loadings of the canonical correlation analysis for COVID-19 sports participants (N = 11,927). The abbreviations are explained in Table 1, the obstacles ('obst') in the last paragraph of the method section. Sport_more OR sport_less (sport more OR less since CIVID-19); sport_noadapt OR sport_adapt (had to adapt their sports participation since/due to COVID-19); age_yng OR age_mid OR age_old (age 19–34 OR 35–54 OR 55+); male OR female (gender); number of kids (numeric value of number of kids); ed_student OR ed_low OR ed_high (still a student OR highest level of education); sport_solo/ sport_duo /sport_team (practice sport that typically involves no/one/more other people); obst_no (no obstacles) OR obst_club (no more club activities is obstacle)/obst_event (no more events is obstacle)/obst_friend (no friends to practice sports with is obstacle)/obst_infr (closed infrastructure is obstacle)/obst_intr (no interest anymore)/obst_fear (fear of COVID-19 is obstacle)/ obst_sick (being sick is obstacle)/obst_time (lack of time is obstacle)/obst_env (no adequate environment is obstacle)

this group. A third cluster, although less pronounced, consists of the constraints fear (obst_fear), sickness (obst_sick), and a lack of time (obst_time). These constraints are linked to people who are often older (age_mid, age_old) and have kids. The final cluster consists of the people who do not experience obstacles when practicing sports (obst_no), mainly because they did not have to adapt their sports participation behaviour (sport_noadapt). This segment is relatively close to the people who maintained or increased their sports frequency.

5. Discussion

The current study exposes that, during the first Belgian COVID-19 lockdown initiated in March 2020, people on average report a rise in sports frequency. Constandt et al. (2020) attribute the positive change in sports participation frequency to the lockdown-light and the fact that safe forms of outdoor exercising in public spaces were allowed and even encouraged in Belgium. Indeed, a negative effect is found in countries with strict lockdowns, such as in Tyrol in Austria (Schnitzer et al., 2020) and in Italy (Mattioli et al., 2020).

Nevertheless, the results of the current study demonstrate that an improved understanding of the changes in sports participation requires to dig deeper into associated motivations and the behaviours. First, the respondents in this study report negative feelings about their changed sports participation practices. This is especially interesting, as research demonstrates that reduced sports participation perceptions and motivation are essential in endorsing long-term exercise persistence (Rodrigues et al., 2020). This argument is in line with the self-determination theory, that stipulates that the psychological need for autonomy, support and satisfaction results into manifold advantages such as a higher motivation and thus better perseverance and maintenance (Vansteenkiste & Ryan, 2013). In their review study, Vansteenkiste and Ryan (2013) also demonstrate that a controlled environment can have a positive impact on behaviour, but that in the long run a more autonomous setting is (more) beneficial and should thus be preferred. This rationale can be underpinned by the results outlined in Figure 1 of the current study, as Sport_adapt and Sport_less are close (and thus related) to each other. The current results thus indicate that the change in motivation is more negative compared to the change in behaviour. Given that the survey was taken in the first weeks of the lockdown, it can be expected that this also induced a more negative change in behaviour in the long term. Second, the average positive change since/due to COVID-19 does not mean that all sports participants' behaviour and perceptions have improved accordingly. Indeed, the results suggest that the positive change in behaviour does not paint the whole picture and that other aspects than 'sports frequency' have to be taken into consideration when assessing the long-term evolution. The results are in line with what could be expected based on the SLP approach of Elkington and Stebbins (2014), namely that several leisure types can be detected, that these activities have differing characteristics, and thus that these activities and participants are affected differently by the COVID-19-measures. It is indeed clear from the results that participants in certain settings (i.e. club sport, mass event sports, duo, and team sports) experience a more severe impact from the COVID-19 measures when compared to their counterparts. Also, regarding leisure and sports participation, an explanation for this difference can be found in the studies of Glynn et al. (2014) and Xie et al. (2020) on the one hand, and Menheere et al. (2020)on the other hand. While the former authors argue that in most leisure activities social interactivity is essential, the latter authors find that runners (i.e. solo sports participants) seldomly quit for social reasons. Chacón Cuberos et al. (2018) highlight that fun and social contact are, along with health, the three most important reasons for people to take part in sports. It is thus needless to say that forcing people to practice sports alone or within a limited company, severely impacts serious and project-based sports activities. Thus, policymakers need to pay attention to how serious (i.e. club) and also project-based (i.e. event) sports participants' behaviour further evolves during and after lockdowns, as well as to develop strategies to further support these sports participants in meeting their previous sports participation behaviour and motivation.

In this matter, and on the other side of the spectrum, this study suggests that existing experience with online sports participation results in both a higher sports participation frequency and in less negative feelings about the changed sports habits during lockdown. This finding highlights the benefits of low threshold online sports participation options. Not that we suggest that this innovative online approach should replace 'regular' sports participation, but the results of the current study indicate that additional online sports participation tools could help motivate certain clusters of people to stay physically active such that in the future these sport participant clusters can benefit from online complements of traditional sports forms (Westmattelmann et al., 2020). Online sports participation can, for example, add a social and/or a fun aspect (see also Dallinga et al., 2018) and thus help people to increase their sports participation (Ehrlén, 2021). As argued before, the contrast between casual and serious leisure is not dichotomous, and online sports participation can also contribute to serious forms of leisure. Lupton (2013) for example, demonstrates the engaging capacity of digital technologies, while Ehrlén (2021) concludes that sharing these online exercise data is self-motivational. The recent COVID-19 crisis created momentum for digital and virtual sports practices (Lachance, 2020), as sports participants that wanted interaction had to appeal on online form of sports participation, while also the developers of online sports applications were almost forced to improve their supply.

Figure 1 demonstrates that having to adapt previous sports participation behaviour is closely related to diminishing sports participation frequency. The segmentation of the sports population into different clusters of sports participants exposes how different clusters of the so-called COVID-19 sports participant can be detected, and thus how policymakers can target these clusters (Alén et al., 2017; Scheerder et al., 2005; Taks & Scheerder, 2006).

The first cluster groups (often male) sports participants who do not have to adapt their participation behaviour, thus logically do not experience many obstacles, and tend to be more physically active than before COVID-19. Second, people who had to adapt their sports participation are found to sport less, as they are often restricted by a lack of time. A third cluster can be situated around (typically younger) club sports participants, as they practice team sports (but also duo sports), miss their sports companions, and lack a place to practice their sports. Finally, middle-aged to older sports participants (often with children) have to deal with a lack of time, decreased interest in sports participation, and/or even fear for COVID-19. It is in line with expectations that these people already opt for solo sports activities pre-COVID-19, as these activities can be considered as health-enhancing activities that can be practised where and when people want, i.e. so-called 'light' sports participation settings (see also Borgers et al., 2016). For sports policymakers, the latter three clusters are of particular interest, as these three clusters all experienced a positive impact on behaviour since COVID-19, although they face different difficulties and barriers in maintaining their sports frequency and/or sports interest.

6. Conclusion

The current study investigates how sports participation was impacted in the period after the first COVID-19-related lockdown in Flanders, thereby demonstrating that different sports participants reacted differently to the lockdown, and this both in relation to their behaviour and their subjective perception. Experience with online sports participation seems to foster physical activity, while the social restrictions had a more severe impact on sports club members, but also on people who were preparing for a sports event.

It is important to acknowledge the context of the study, as it has been carried out three weeks after the first COVID-19 lockdown started. Given the positive behaviour change, but the negative sentiment of people missing their previous behaviour, the question how the figures evolved in the weeks and months after the current study arises. Although it will be very difficult to deduce causal insights (as the lockdown measures in Flanders also changed in the period after the current research), future research should focus further on how COVID-19 influenced sports participation behaviour, and which clusters were impacted most. As of 23 October 2020, Belgium implemented a new, partial lockdown. As of this moment, people had to work from home again. Additionally, almost all leisure activities (e.g. sports clubs, fitness centres, swimming pools, theatres, events), and non-necessary shops were closed, and the weather was much colder compared to the first lockdown. Nevertheless, the measures taken by government were less strict compared to the first lockdown, as each household was allowed to have one 'cuddle contact' outside of the household, schools remained open, and people were allowed to practice outdoor sports activities (e.g. walking, cycling, running, tennis) with maximum four persons and with a social distance of 1.5 metres. It could be worthwhile to investigate the effect of the second lockdown on sports participation in Flanders. In this regard, Scheerder and Helsen (2020) point out that in Flanders walking, cycling, and other outdoor sports were the only allowed social activities, which could have led to similar increases in sports participation again. Other drivers of the rising popularity of these sports activities are that they fit in the escapism trend towards leisure activities as a counterweight for the hasty society (especially when taking obliged home-office in mind), that they can be practised alone (solo), while at the same time new sensations can be added by staying connected through screens and smart (social media) innovative attributes.

The current study clearly demonstrates that closing sports clubs and cancelling sports events has a negative impact on the motivation and sports frequency of certain sports participants. Despite the risen popularity of so-called 'light sports', policymakers still need a mix of traditional and innovative sports settings to alter sports participation rates and frequencies. Concerning the latter, the current research enhances our understanding about the ways in which the accelerated and almost forced adoption of certain innovations in sports participation (through smart and online applications), could foster the quest for increasing sports participation figures, also when COVID-19 will (hopefully) be a distant ghost from the past. It will be important to further investigate whether these changes were temporary due to the circumstances, and to what extent they inducted a lasting change in the sports participation behaviour.

Disclosure statement

No potential conflict of interest was reported by the author(s).

ORCID

Erik Thibaut http://orcid.org/0000-0002-5831-6433
Bram Constandt http://orcid.org/0000-0002-5630-0745
Annick Willem http://orcid.org/0000-0003-3753-2919

References

Alén, E., Losada, N., & de Carlos, P. (2017). Profiling the segments of senior tourists throughout motivation and travel characteristics. *Current Issues in Tourism*, *20*(14), 1454–1469. https://doi.org/10.1080/13683500.2015.1007927

Anderson, R. M., Heesterbeek, H., Klinkenberg, D., & Hollingsworth, T. D. (2020). How will country-based mitigation measures influence the course of the COVID-19 epidemic? *The Lancet*, *395*(10228), 931–934. https://doi.org/10.1016/S0140-6736(20)30567-5

Borgers, J., Breedveld, A., Tiessen-Raaphorst, A., Thibaut, E., Vandermeerschen, H., Vos, S., & Scheerder, J. (2016). A study on the frequency of participation and time spent on sport in different organisational settings. *European Sport Management Quarterly*, *16*(5), 635–654. https://doi.org/10.1080/16184742.2016.1196717

Borgers, J., Pilgaard, M., Vanreusel, B., & Scheerder, J. (2018). Can we consider changes in sports participation as institutional change? A conceptual framework. *International Review for the Sociology of Sport*, *53*(1), 84–100. https://doi.org/10.1177/1012690216639598

Caputo, E. L., & Reichert, F. F. (2020). Studies of physical activity and COVID-19 during the pandemic: A scoping review. *Journal of Physical Activity and Health*, *17*(12), 1275–1284. https://doi.org/10.1123/jpah.2020-0406

Carter, S. J., Baranauskas, M. N., & Fly, A. D. (2020). Considerations for obesity, vitamin D, and physical activity amid the COVID-19 pandemic. *Obesity*, *28*(7), 1176–1177. https://doi.org/10.1002/oby.22838

Chacón Cuberos, R., Chacón Borrego, F., Zurita Ortega, F., Cachón Zagalaz, J., Zagalaz Sánchez, M. L., & Chinchilla Mira, J. J. (2018). Characterization of motivation and type of physical-sport practice in adults through COMPASS profiles. *Journal of Human Sport and Exercise*, *13*(1), 161–173. https://doi.org/10.14198/jhse.2018.131.16

Constandt, B., Thibaut, E., De Bosscher, V., Scheerder, J., Ricour, M., & Willem, A. (2020). Exercising in times of lockdown: An analysis of the impact of COVID-19 on levels and patterns of exercise among adults in Belgium. *International Journal of Environmental Research and Public Health*, *17*(11), 4144. https://doi.org/10.3390/ijerph17114144

Dallinga, J., Janssen, M., van der Werf, J., Walravens, R., Vos, S., & Deutekom, M. (2018). Analysis of the features important for the effectiveness of physical activity-related apps for recreational sports: Expert panel approach. *JMIR*, *6*(6), e143. https://doi.org/10.2196/mhealth.9459

De Haan, J., & Breedveld, K. (2000). *Trends en determinanten in de sport. Eerste resultaten uit het AVO 1999 (SCP Paper 68)* [Trends and determinants of sport participation. The first results of the AVO 1999 (SCP Paper 68)]. The Hague: Social & Cultural Planning Office.

Downward, P., Lera-López, F., & Rasciute, S. (2014). The correlates of sports participation in Europe. *European Journal of Sport Science*, *14*(6), 592–602. https://doi.org/10.1080/17461391.2014.880191

Ehrlén, V. (2021). Tracking oneself for others: Communal and self-motivational value of sharing exercise data online. *Leisure Studies*, *40*(4), 545–560. https://doi.org/10.1080/02614367.2020.1869289

Eime, R. M., Harvey, J. T., Brown, W. J., & Payne, W. R. (2010). Does sports club participation contribute to health-related quality of life? *Medicine & Science in Sports & Exercise*, *42*(5), 1022–1082. https://doi.org/10.1249/MSS.0b013e3181c3adaa

Eime, R. M., Harvey, J. T., & Charity, M. (2020). Sport participation settings: Where and 'how' do Australians play sport? *BMC Public Health*, *20*(1), 1344. https://doi.org/10.1186/s12889-020-09453-3

Eime, R. M., Young, J. A., Harvey, J. T., Charity, M. J., & Payne, W. R. (2013). A systematic review of the psychological and social benefits of participation in sport for children and adolescents: Informing development of a conceptual model of health through sport. *International Journal of Behavioral Nutrition and Physical Activity*, *10*(98), 1-21. https://doi.org/10.1186/1479-5868-10-98

Elkington, S., & Stebbins, R. (2014). *The serious leisure perspective. An introduction*. Routledge.

Evans, A. B., Blackwell, J., Dolan, P., Fahlén, J., Hoekman, R., Lenneis, V., McNarry, G., Smith, M., & Wilcock, L. (2020). Sport in the face of the COVID-19 pandemic: Towards an agenda for research in the sociology of sport. *European Journal for Sport and Society*, *17*(2), 85–95. https://doi.org/10.1080/16138171.2020.1765100

Filo, K., Spence, K., & Sparvero, E. (2013). Exploring the properties of community among charity sport event participants. *Managing Leisure*, *18*(3), 194–212. https://doi.org/10.1080/13606719.2013.796179

Funk, D., Jordan, J., Ridinger, L., & Kaplanidou, K. (2011). Capacity of mass participant sport events for the development of activity commitment and future exercise intention. *Leisure Sciences*, *33*(3), 250–268. https://doi.org/10.1080/01490400.2011.564926

Glynn, L. G., Hayes, P. S., Casey, M., Glynn, F., Alvarez-Inglesias, A., Newell, J., Ólaighin, G., Heaney, D., O'Donnell, M., & Murphy, A. W. (2014). Effectiveness of a smartphone application to promote physical activity in primary care: The SMART MOVE randomized controlled trial. *British Journal of General Practice*, *64*(624), 384–391. https://doi.org/10.3399/bjgp14X680461

Halabchi, F., Ahmadenijad, Z., & Selk-Ghaffari, M. (2020). COVID-19 Epidemic: Exercise or not to exercise; that is the question! *Asian Journal of Sports Medicine*, *11*(1), e10263. https://doi.org/10.5812/ajsm.102630

Hayes, M. (2020). Social media and inspiring physical activity during COVID-19 and beyond. *Managing Sport and Leisure*, 1–8. https://doi.org/10.1080/23750472.2020.1794939

Helsen, K., Derom, I., Corthouts, J., De Bosscher, V., Willem, A., & Scheerder, J. (2021). Participatory sport events in times of COVID-19. Analysing the (virtual) sport behaviour of event participants. *European Sport Management Quarterly*, 1–20. https://doi.org/10.1080/16184742.2021.1956560

Lachance, E. L. (2020). COVID-19 and its impact on volunteering: Moving towards virtual volunteering. *Leisure Sciences*, *43*(1-2), 104-110. https://doi.org/10.1080/01490400.2020.1773990

Lashua, B., Johnson, C. W., & Parry, D. C. (2020). Leisure in the time of coronavirus: A rapid response special issue. *Leisure Sciences*, *43*(1-2), 6-11. https://doi.org/10.1080/01490400.2020.1774827

Lera-López, F., Wicker, P., & Downward, P. (2015). Does government spending help to promote healthy behaviour in the population? Evidence from 27 European countries. *Journal of Public Health*, *38*(2), e5–e12. https://doi.org/10.1093/pubmed/fdv071

Lupton, D. (2013). Quantifying the body: Monitoring and measuring health in the age of mHealth technologies. *Critical Public Health*, *23*(4), 393–403. https://doi.org/10.1080/09581596.2013.794931

Mackenzie, S. H., & Goodnow, J. (2020). Adventure in the age of COVID-19: Embracing microadventures and locavism in a post-pandemic world. *Leisure Sciences*, *43*(1-2), 62-69. https://doi.org/10.1080/01490400.2020.1773984

Mattioli, A. V., Puviani, M. B., Nasi, M., & Farinetti, A. (2020). COVID-19 pandemic: The effects of quarantine on cardiovascular risk. *European Journal of Clinical Nutrition*, *74*(6), 852–855. https://doi.org/10.1038/s41430-020-0646-z

Menheere, D., Janssen, M., Funk, M., van der Spek, E., Lallemand, C., & Vos, S. (2020). Runner's perception of reasons to quit running: influence of gender, age and running-related characteristics. *International Journal of Environmental Research and Public Health*, *17*(17). https://doi.org/20.3390/ijerph17176046

Miner, L., & Wright, R. (2020, April 20). Austria begins reopening after 'very early and very harsh' lockdown. *Euronews*. https://www.euronews.com/2020/04/20/austria-begins-reopening-after-very-early-and-very-harsh-lockdown

Rodrigues, F., Teixeira, D. S., Neiva, H. P., Cid, L., & Monteiro, D. (2020). The bright and dark sides of motivation as predictors of enjoyment, intention, and exercise persistence. *Scandinavian Journal of Medicine & Science in Sports*, *30*(4), 787–800. https://doi.org/10.1111/sms.13617

Scheerder, J., Helsen, K., Elmose-Østerlund, K., & Nagel, S. (2020). Exploring pan-European similarities and club-organised Sports. A cross-national and cross-temporal comparison. In S. Nagel, K. Elmose-Østerlund, B. Ibsen, & J. Scheerder (Eds.), *Functions of Sports Clubs in European Societies. A cross-national comparative study* (pp. 315–343). Springer. Sport Economics, Management & Policy. https://doi.org/10.1007/978-3-030-48535-1

Scheerder, J., & Helsen, K. (2020). *The rise of slow sport? Trends in loop- en wandelsport [The rise of slow sport]*. Online presentation at the KU Leuven conference 'Loop- en Wandelsport in Vlaanderen: Trends, participatie en uitdagingen' [Running and walking sports in Flanders: trends, participation and challenges], 19 november 2020. Flanders: KU Leuven.

Scheerder, J., Vanreusel, B., Taks, M., & Renson, R. (2005). Social stratification patterns in adolescents' active sports participation behaviour. A time trend analysis 1969-1999. *European Physical Education Review*, *11*(1), 5–27. https://doi.org/10.1177/1356336X05049822

Schnitzer, M., Schöttl, S. E., Kopp, M., & Barth, M. (2020). COVID-19 stay-at-home order in Tyrol, Austria: Sports and exercise behaviour in change? *Public Health*, (185), 218–220. https://doi.org/10.1016/j.puhe.2020.06.042

Sharon Shen, X., & Yarnal, C. (2010). Blowing open the serious leisure-casual leisure dichotomy: What's in there? *Leisure Sciences*, *32*(2), 162–179. https://doi.org/10.1080/01490400903547179

Son, J. S., Nimrod, G., West, S. T., Janke, M. C., Liechty, T., & Naar, J. J. (2020). Promoting older adults' physical activity and social well-being during COVID-19. *Leisure Sciences*, *43*(1-2), 287-294. https://doi.org/10.1080/01490400.2020.1774015

Taks, M., & Scheerder, J. (2006). Youth sports participation styles and market segmentation profiles. Evidence and applications. *European Sport Management Quarterly*, *6*(2), 85–121. https://doi.org/10.1080/16184740600954080

Tsigilis, N., Masmanidis, T., & Koustelios, A. (2009). University student's satisfaction and effectiveness of campus recreation programs. *Recreational Sports Journal*, *33*(1), 65–77. https://doi.org/10.1123/rsj.33.1.65

Van der Burg, E., De Leeuw, J., & Dijksterhuis, G. (1994). Overals: Nonlinear canonical correlation with k sets of variables. *Computational Statistics & Data Analysis*, *18*(1), 141–163. https://doi.org/10.1016/0167-9473(94)90136-8

Vansteenkiste, M., & Ryan, R. M. (2013). On psychological growth and vulnerability: Basic psychological need satisfaction and need frustration as a unifying principle. *Journal of Psychotherapy Integration*, *23*(3), 263–280. https://doi.org/10.1037/a0032359

Westmattelmann, D., Grotenhermen, J. G., Sprenger, M., & Schewe, G. (2020). The show must go on – Virtualisation of sport events during the COVID-19 pandemic. *European Journal of Information Systems*, *30*(2), 119–136. https://doi.org/10.1080/0960085X.2020.1850186

Xie, H., Chen, Y., & Yin, R. (2020). Running together is better than running alone: A qualitative study of a self-organised distance running group in China. *Leisure Studies*, *39* (2), 195–208. Advance online publication. https://doi.org/10.1080/02614367.2019.1698647

Zhu, Q., Li, M., Ji, Y., Shi, Y., Zhou, J., Li, Q., Qin, R., & Zhuang, X. (2021). "Stay-at-home" lifestyle effect on weight gain during the COVID-19 outbreak confinement in China. *International Journal of Environmental Research and Public Health*, *18*(4), 1813. https://doi.org/10.3390/ijerph18041813

Nearby nature in lockdown: Practices and affordances for leisure in urban green spaces

Katherine King and Janet Dickinson

ABSTRACT
During the Covid-19 pandemic, urban green spaces provided a route to connect with everyday 'nearby natures'. The paper explores the reconfiguration of leisure practices during restrictions, utilising theory on affordances and social practices to explore what people valued in urban green spaces and what can be learnt from a period when relationships with these spaces were in sharp focus. The study participants utilised Mobile Instant Messaging Diaries to present their lived experiences first-hand. Participants developed routines that involved engaging with urban green spaces as part of their daily structure, and this brought practices based around meaningful actions in these spaces to the fore. Urban green spaces became meaningful when they served a purpose, when they built knowledge and skill, and when they supported social needs. During lockdown, a patchwork of urban green spaces became useful. The findings call for more attention to be paid to small pockets of urban green space to afford nature connectivity and to the value of a social practice lens as a tool for providers to explore affordances and exclusions.

Introduction

The Covid-19 pandemic and resulting lockdown has seen locally accessible urban green spaces emerge as a route to connect with everyday nearby natures. During May 2020, as the first lockdown was under way, 60% of adults in England said that they had spent time outside in green and natural spaces in the previous two weeks. Urban green space (including parks, fields and playgrounds) was the most visited type of space, and 74% of adults reported more time to notice and engage with everyday nature (Natural England, 2020). Ten months later in March 2021, monitoring shows the continued importance of these spaces, with 43% of adults reporting visits to green and natural spaces as even more important to their wellbeing since coronavirus (Natural England, 2021).

Multiple studies argue access to nature benefits mental and physical health (Britton et al., 2020; Hartig et al., 2014; Pretty et al., 2005). With national and international concerns about stress during the crisis (Office for National Statistics, 2020; World Health Organisation, 2020), and an emphasis on outdoor environments as safer than those indoors for minimising risk of transmission, green spaces have played an important role in supporting everyday leisure practices during the pandemic. Crucially, during national lockdowns in the UK, access to formally managed and honeypot sites such as National Parks, formal gardens, and nature reserves in the wider countryside were limited by travel restrictions, social distancing measures and advice to avoid public transport. Urban green spaces, near to people's homes, therefore, became important tools for facilitating nature connectivity (Lovell et al., 2020; Venter et al., 2021).

The UK Government's 25 year Environment Plan (Department for Environment, Food and Rural Affairs, 2018) aims for more people, from all backgrounds, to engage with and spend time in green and blue spaces in their everyday lives, and prioritises urban green spaces as valuable opportunities to reconnect people with nature (also see, J. Glover, 2019). Greener living environments are considered to be beneficial for health and wellbeing, but quality and access is variable (Lovell et al., 2020). Policy agendas seek to increase access for all people, under a green infrastructure framework, which views urban green spaces as part of an integrated network encompassing a broad a range of green spaces of different sizes, types and value. At the same time, the UK has committed to a legally binding target of net zero carbon emissions by 2050 and achievement of this goal assumes significant individual behaviour change towards decreasing travel and low carbon leisure (Committee on Climate Change, 2019).

Based on data collected during the first UK lockdown when leisure became localised, this paper utilises theory on affordances and social practices to draw out insight into what people valued in local urban green spaces, and the actions and engagement that emerged. It also highlights the challenges of negotiating shared urban green space, and the knowledge and skill development required by users to realise potential benefits. The paper therefore reflects on how reconfigurations of practice will continue to alter people's relationship with urban green spaces and the implications for post-pandemic policy and practice, as access to nature is positioned 'front and centre' (Lovell et al., 2020, p.ii) of plans for recovery.

Leisure and urban green space

Urban green spaces are areas within the urban environment comprised largely of vegetation, ranging from private gardens and balconies, to allotments, infrastructural green such as roadside verges, to recreation grounds, fields, or woodlands (Swanwick et al., 2003). As leisure spaces, urban green spaces have been explored in relation to the wellness benefits they offer to those who live nearby. Urban green spaces are considered beneficial to health as spaces which are easily accessible and supportive of a range of physical leisure activities (Pietilä et al., 2015), for social wellbeing through leisure activities such as socialising with others, or feeling part of a community (Peschardt et al., 2012), but also through cultural ecosystem benefits such as feelings of relaxation or inspiration people assign to leisure experiences amongst nature (Edwards et al., 2022).

Work on pocket parks identifies the role accessible urban green spaces can play in filling the need for people's everyday contact with nature (Nordh & Østby, 2013). Nature connectivity describes a perception of sameness between the self, others, and the natural world (Dutcher et al., 2007) and holds a positive relationship to psychological wellbeing, environmental concern and environmental behaviour (Mayer & Frantz, 2004; Nisbet et al., 2009). Frequent use of urban green spaces such as access to gardens, proximity to tree cover, or visits to local parks can increase nature connectivity (Nisbet et al., 2020; Richardson et al., 2015). It is claimed nearby nature can also buffer against feelings of low social connection (Cartwright et al., 2018) and play an important role in developing a sense of place (Žlender & Gemin, 2020)

These environments found close to home are often referred to as 'mundane' through their positioning as part of the ordinary experiences of everyday life. According to Hollenhorst et al. (2014) local places are often overlooked or are perceived to underperform in favour of more exotic experiences, which can lead to a cycle of limited attachment, disinvestment, and further desire for escapism. Locavism revisits these narratives by embracing slow leisure behaviours which can create community connections to local places 'by going "deeper" not further' (Houge Mackenzie & Goodnow, 2021, p. 66).

Dobson et al. (2021) refer to the 'magic of the mundane' (p. 5) when considering the effects routine or incidental encounters with urban nature can have in enhancing individuals' wellbeing. Even small pieces of urban green spaces have potential to act as restorative environments for local residents (Hadavi et al., 2015; Peschardt et al., 2012). Yet despite the benefits of encounters with nearby nature, research by Nisbet and Zelenski (2011) identifies behavioural avoidance of contact with urban nature and a general disconnect from the potential benefits of these environments. It is important therefore to examine the different values that are placed on urban green spaces and to explore the ways in which they are used as part of mundane engagements with them. This paper utilises theory on affordances and social practices as a framework for this.

Affordances, social practices and urban green space

Affordance theory is commonly applied within environmental psychology as part of studies relating to place attachment or human place bonds. For Kyle et al. (2004), human place bonds comprise of: place identity; the connection between self and environment; place dependence; how well a setting may serve a purpose or desired experience. The concept of place identity or sense of place has a strong emotional component whilst the concept of place dependence has a strong activity or use dimension (Kyle et al., 2004; Stokowski, 2002).

Belonging to a place provides security and stability, often referred to as rootedness (Tuan, 1980) or insideness (Relph, 1976) capturing the symbolic nexus of meanings, emotions, identities and memories which comprise human place bonds. Place ballet refers to the repeated mobilities which occur as part of everyday time space routines, and bring a profound sense of place (Seamon, 1980). Thus, mundane spaces and the routine interactions with them, can facilitate connections which are meaningful and significant. The very idea of neighbourhood is not inherent in any arrangement of streets, parks or houses, but is rather an ongoing practical and discursive social process (Gieryn, 2000). 'The space most intimately inhabited, traversed and practised is that familiar, often homely space that forms the all too unnoticed backdrop to the unreflexive habits' (Binnie et al., 2007, p. 166).

Places are therefore made as people ascribe qualities to the material and social phenomena gathered there (Gieryn, 2000). J. J. Gibson's (1977) theory of affordances focuses on the physical and social function of the environment. Affordance theory states that objects have detectable functions which are perceived in terms of what they afford as opposed to what qualities they have (Clark & Uzzell, 2002). This helps to understand the behaviours the environment supports and positions spaces as opportunities for 'meaningful action' (Kaplan & Kaplan, 2003, p. 1484).

Social practices theory places attention on routine social practices that constitute an individual's everyday existence, whereby the practice itself, as opposed to the individual, or the social structures which surround it, is the focus (Hargreaves, 2011). Reckwitz (2002) defines practices as 'a routinised type of behavior which consists of several elements, interconnected to one another: forms of bodily activities, forms of mental activities, "things" and their use, a background knowledge in the form of understanding, know-how, states of emotion and motivational knowledge' (p. 249). Shove et al. (2012) refine this to three elements of social practices: materials, skills, and meaning. Materials refer to the physical properties or things used to perform a practice; skills refer to acquired knowledge and 'the regular skillful performance of human bodies' (Reckwitz, 2002, p. 251); whilst meanings refer to the interpretations and ways of wanting and feeling within a practice. Social practice theory situates human behaviour with the wider social environment. It is also important for understanding everyday life as the setting for practices to be created, re-created or repeated and enabling individuals to understand the world around them and their place within it (Hargreaves, 2011; Reckwitz, 2002).

Practice theory and affordance theory can be drawn upon reciprocally to explore human-nature relations in the context of urban green space use. Urban park use is often explored in the context of a park's functions, qualities, and components, and the types of activities and experiences provided. Environmental affordances can be the perceptual foundation for preference judgements about the quality of urban green space (Hadavi et al., 2015). Research by Richardson et al. (2015) found people identify positive attributes of nearby nature in the context of activities they took part in. Nordh and Østby (2013) identify specific activities and components which supported restorative experiences in urban pocket parks. Thus, previous work has explored the social, physical and emotional affordances of the environment (Hadavi et al., 2015). Practice theory, however, can account for the meanings which extend beyond these affordances. Users may be motivated by recreational affordance, however, the meaning they derive may relate to the social, identity or spiritual dimensions that enhance their experience beyond the recreational component (Kyle et al., 2004). According to Lepoša (2018), the combination of these approaches can show how the affordances of these elements can shape the meaning of practices and how these elements matter through the creation of 'action possibilities' (p. 20). Confinement to nearby urban green spaces through the lockdown restrictions on travel made different practices and different affordances possible. Taking account of these practices and the affordances these spaces provide can help to identify the types of urban green spaces that people want to use, and the meanings they convey (Hadavi et al., 2015).

Methodology

The study was instigated at the start of the first UK lockdown in March 2020 and sought an approach that would capture participant reflections on their practices in urban green spaces as they were lived. Restrictions of the COVID 19 pandemic, however, saw access to people and their everyday experiences for research become increasingly complex and research transitioned to socially distant methods and the digital domain (Lobe et al., 2020). Therefore, the study looked to the role of mobile instant messaging methods as part of a lay geographies approach (Crouch, 2000; Dashper & Brymer, 2019) to conducting qualitative research. Specifically, mobile instant messaging (MIM) diaries were utilised as a discursive practice to capture qualitative data remotely in the form of text, photographs, video or voice recordings, maps and screenshots shared through WhatsApp. Mobile methods are well established in tourism (Bærenholdt et al., 2004; Buscher & Urry, 2009) and transport research (Sheller & Urry, 2006). However, the challenge of physically being with participants in contexts that have a degree of spontaneity and where researcher presence is intrusive has led to the development of alternative methods (Dickinson et al., 2013). These include performative methods such as the diary-photograph, diary-interview method (Latham, 2003; Line et al., 2011). The MIM diaries developed for this study built on these methods to focus in on everyday experiences. The approach not only reconfigures the dynamics of the researcher-subject relationship but also provides intimate access to power and knowledge dynamics in ordinary spaces. In this respect, the lack of direct access to participants was fortuitously overcome.

The methodological advantages of using MIM as digital tools in qualitative research have been rarely acknowledged, despite the familiarity, ease of use and multimedia data they can generate (Gibson, 2022; Kaufmann et al., 2021). WhatsApp, the most popular mobile instant messenger app is accessed by two billion users on a monthly basis (Statista, 2021) and can support the submission of written entries, voice recordings, videos, photos and location tags. Visualisation is an essential component of mobile methodologies (Murray,2009) and the visual element of the MIM diaries enabled access to tacit and experiential content researchers were unable to participate in themselves (Milne & Muir, 2020; Pink, 2007). Users could also post on-the-go, and immediacy of communication between the researcher and participant enabled near real time interaction, and the opportunity to seek clarification from the participant, enhancing the validity of the findings as part of an ongoing conversation.

Participants were sent instructions to submit WhatsApp entries reflecting upon their encounters with local spaces and communities over a 2-week period between 9th April and 12 May 2020. Participants were given some suggestions for entries such as the documentation of daily exercise, or face to face encounters within the local community, and examples of topics for reflection such as what spaces are available to use in your local area? And how are you encountering people from your local community? Entries could be submitted as frequently/infrequently as participants wished, though it was suggested participants completed one entry per day, where possible. This approach sought to capture participants lived experiences first-hand, which in turn facilitated the examination of practices described by Kaufmann and Peil (2020) as 'deeply rooted in everyday life' (p. 242).

Twelve participants' completed diaries, of which ten participants used WhatsApp and two participants chose to use email. Research ethics approval was secured prior to data collection. All prospective participants were provided with an information sheet explaining the purpose of the project, what taking part would involve, and how data would be used, stored and shared. Participant agreement forms were completed prior to taking part.

Participants were recruited from the Bournemouth, Christchurch, Poole (BCP) and Brighton to Shoreham urban conurbations, both on the south coast of England. Both conurbations provide a range of green spaces within and around the urban setting which include beaches and riverside settings, urban parks and forested areas, alongside smaller pockets of green spaces within neighbourhood settings. Whilst privileged in terms of access to some high quality green spaces within and beyond the urban setting, the conurbations have areas of dense housing with very limited or no garden space and significant areas considered socially disadvantaged according to the indices of multiple deprivation. The choice of these locations was opportunistically linked to the researchers who lived in the conurbations and were therefore well placed to understand participant comments on locations.

Participants were recruited through existing online groups hosted on Facebook in the two conurbations. The researchers were members of these communities and sought permission from moderators to post messages seeking participants to take part. Participants therefore self-selected based on their interest in the research topic. There was no incentive for participation and the MIM diary method involved a high degree of commitment from participants. These factors are likely to have affected who participated and the sample may represent individuals who were active in community social media groups at the time and were able to commit the time during lockdown to take on the collection of data on a voluntary basis.

The final sample consisted of 12 participants ranging in age from early twenties to late seventies. Five participants were retired, whilst others were all in work, education, or were full-time parents. Eight participants were women and four were men. Due to the reliance on untrained volunteers creating lay geographies, the usefulness of the data varied, but significant insights were gained from all participants. Entries were diverse, highly personal, and at times intimate. Some participants focused predominantly on activities and places visited, while others were more reflective. Feedback indicated that most participants valued the experience and some sought to continue their own diaries following participation.

Analysis of the data was performed through thematic analysis. Where WhatsApp was used, text entries and photographs were downloaded and collated for each participant, noting any video and audio recordings which were stored alongside. This generated a large volume of material from participants, with one participant's diary leading to over 90 pages of text and photo data. This organisational stage was followed by an initial coding exercise where both authors read and reread transcripts independently and applied process codes to capture action and descriptive codes to summarise the data (Saldana, 2011). Visual data was submitted by all participants and was usually directly captioned or referred to in the longer text entries. Writers on visual methodologies note that analysis of visual content alone is not enough without locating the social, cultural and personal contexts which give it meaning, and the subjective agendas through which they are produced (Jupp, 2006; Pink, 2007). Visual data was subject to coding, using questions proposed by Banks and Zeitlyn (2015) such as what is the image content? when, how and why is it made, and for whom? to guide interrogations of the these elements. Visual data was therefore coded alongside the written entries to add validity by offering an additional layer of meaning (Glaw et al., 2017).

Coding lists were initially compiled independently and then shared and compared between authors through an iterative process of critical reflexivity and refinement (Rose & Johnson, 2020) across three separate meetings. This process drew attention to author positionalities in their interpretations and representation of the findings such as their social markers as white, middle-

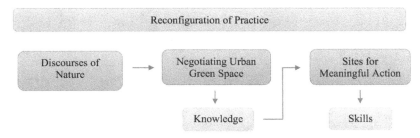

Figure 1. Diagram of Thematic Relationships.

class women, and their own unique experiences and observations of lockdown and the Covid-19 pandemic, in and around their own geographically separate communities. This first meeting reviewed and interrogated this coding process and resulted in the development of an agreed list of five broad themes. Further read throughs of the transcripts ensued and a second meeting closely scrutinised the legitimacy of connections between codes in the initial data analysis stage (Fereday & Muir-Cochrane, 2006). Merging and reframing of two sets of themes produced three overarching themes. A final meeting sought to explore both the outlying and inconsistent data that ran counter to the three themes (Rose & Johnson, 2020). This also identified that the development of knowledge and skills to use urban green spaces was a subtheme and further repositioned the core themes. Figure 1 shows the relationship which emerged between the themes as a result of this process.

Findings

Lockdown restrictions universally interrupted daily life routines. This led to the restructuring of routines that included participants engaging with and (re)discovering urban green spaces. Daily walking or another outdoor activity, such as cycling or jogging, was a commonly discussed, for example, 'daily walk as part of a new routine' (P. 4) or 'Daily walk ... down river, across Adur Recreation ground to Shoreham Beach' (P. 8). Many participants identified these as new behaviours, for example, Participant 2 notes '7:30 cycle to start the day/not usual activity'. Urban green spaces provided materials for these repeated and routinised bodily performances that constituted new practices (Reckwitz, 2002).

While the discovery of urban green spaces as part of new localised routines was not surprising, closer engagement with the data provided more insight into practices that has resonance beyond the distinct moment-in-time capture in participants' diaries. Conceptually the data was organised into three themes: discourses of nature; navigating and negotiating urban green space; and sites for meaningful actions.

Discourses of nature

The findings draw attention to the normative value afforded to nature. Participants accounts demonstrated more time and motivation for spending outdoors in their local area. They spoke of noticing more, of 'walking with no purpose' (P. 7), time for taking stock and contemplating, and that they have 'deliberately been more observant' as lockdown had created 'time to dwell' (P. 4). Without prompt by researchers or the diary instructions, most participants referred to nature and natural settings. Many of the images and videos participants shared were of material natures; images of flowers, plants and trees, sunrises, and skyscrapers (see Figure 2), videos and audio recordings of the sound of water in local waterways or coastal areas. Captions documented the scent of the flowers, or hearing the birds singing (P. 9) and demonstrated an attention to the sensual affordances of nature.

Figure 2. Example of capturing material natures (Participant 9).

Participants presented this in relation to the contribution contact with nature made to their own physical, psychological and social wellbeing. Participant 2 described a routine woodland walk that provided scenic views and had become 'our favourite destination and also the dog's favourite', while Participant 6 described connecting with nature as a source of comfort in times of difficulty, using her doorstep as a setting for repose.

> I burst into tears and just went outside and sat on the front doorstep. I listened to the birds, sat in the sun looking into the blue sky and did some deep breathing. Knowing that the evidence is that nature is soothing and de stressing I sat for as long as I could manage. It helped.. (P. 6)

Participant 9 photographed her home working space, commenting that she had repositioned her desk so she could see the outdoors as she was working, whilst another photographed some roadside vegetation whilst taking the 'scenic route' home (P. 10). This reflected wider practices of sharing attractive images on social media. It chimes with media reports about a resurgence of interest in nature during lockdown (BBC, 2020) and a discourse of nature pervaded. However, this discourse did not resonate with all, and several participants did not refer to nature at all, despite living in locations with ready access to urban green space and documenting its use. These participants did not perform a narrative of nature nor overtly instil naturalness with meaning. Other, potentially conflicting, values were present.

Navigating and Negotiating Urban Green Space

In tourism settings, Germann Molz (2010) suggests tourists anticipate daily rhythms of a place which can lead to anxiety of visiting places at the right time. During lockdown these place ballets (Seamon, 1980) of everyday spaces brought the complexities of intersecting with other people's life routines to the fore. Regular landscapes became a setting for a 'changing same' (Binnie et al., 2007) where sights were familiar but experienced with a differing perspective.

In many instances, the routines linked to urban green space use during lockdown reflected anticipated crowding associated with the natural rhythms of places. For example, Participant 1 notices the visiting pattern at a local river is different: 'Water sports users launch and land here so seeing it deserted on the water side was strange really'. Participants drew on tacit knowledge of when to visit and some participants developed their routines of using urban green spaces at quieter times. For example, Participant 1 walked every evening while Participant 2 walked, cycle or jogged in the early morning. Visiting once at a later time, Participant 2 wrote 'It was different going out later in the day. More people especially by the river'. This alertness to other users is noted by Participant 6 who describes how her family became 'acutely aware of occasional people we see. Do we know them, do they look friendly, are they going to cross over for us, or do we need to'. This is not a new problem, but one made more obvious during the pandemic.

The availability of space appeared to be felt strongly, and diary entries included assessments of the material provision in urban green spaces such as the width of footpaths, the distribution of passing places, or parking, to accommodate the flow of people.

> Went for a long walk in Stamner [an urban fringe park in Brighton] to the downs. Extremely busy, no parking spaces in the virtually all carparks and so many families out.. (P. 5)

Participant 11 reported being particularly mindful of her dog's needs for space outdoors since it is afraid of other dogs: 'I walked A**** [the dog] out from home as usual since lockdown. This is not great for him, he's used to Wareham Forest [10 miles east of BCP], often a quiet bridleway alongside the road where there are no other dogs'. For another participant, her disabled daughter's fear of dogs made accessing local spaces as a family feel 'a bit tricky, as there are a lot of dogs out ALL the time at the moment locally' (P. 6). Some entries documented overt tensions in people's interactions with non-household members in outdoor spaces. Participant 8 shares several photographs commenting 'Social distance the correct way' or 'Too many sitting around in Buckingham Park'.

> Feels like too many people are out and about and I think road traffic has increased. People are being a bit more complacent I think which is disappointing. (P. 4)

The noting of who was sharing the space, the number of people around, social distancing, and who was doing what represent what T. D. Glover (2021), refers to as the 'more complicated moments of neighbouring' (p. 285), which emerged as a result of the pandemic. According to Binnie et al. (2007), there is a tendency for banal mobility to become sites of contestation and regulation, and conflict commonly occurs between and within recreational groups in shared spaces. These issues were more noticeable in lockdown where the behaviour of others caused feelings of fear, and where people were restricted to their local area, and therefore experiencing locally specific issues. Nevertheless, there were many examples of positive comments about low key social interaction with strangers where the socio-material environment of these spaces facilitated this (T. D. Glover, 2021).

> Plenty of people to talk with either with a dog or a child. Noticed everyone does keep their distance. Noticing that people in general have got time for the time of day with others that is a positivity of this crisis.. (P. 3)

> Great Hengistbury walk with the socialisation of good mornings from everyone as we passed in single file.. (P. 4)

Whilst the data reports on a unique moment in time, it also reflects the general tensions of using urban green space and concerns about other users, their intentions, and whether these might result in conflict (Santos et al., 2016). Some participant accounts demonstrated the accumulation of new place knowledge and skills to avoid issues highlighting the complexity of navigating and negotiating urban green space more broadly, including the tensions between different users, navigating where to go, when to go, what to avoid, and crucially, what to do. Inevitably some users of urban green space self-exclude, especially those with particular needs or those who are more wary of negative encounters. We see this in the parent of a disabled child who assesses spaces and departs if a point of tension is apparent.

> All was fine - but then a couple of dogs were headed our way and [daughter] freaked out., She scrambled on her bottom away and sort of slid and landed in the brown sludge. She panicked and I got cross with the guy who said what everyone always says. ' they are the friendliest dogs you could meet!' I said it didn't matter as she was still terrified of them! He realised from her reaction that it was a big problem for us. [Daughter] was in tears now and we had to quickly put shoes etc on and head off home. The man called out that he was sorry he had disturbed us., I smiled feeling quite defeated - saying don't worry - it didn't matter. When it clearly did. So many times our nice trips end in tears. Not just because of dogs.sadly (P. 6)

Another participant who visited urban green spaces to walk with an anxious dog documented her avoidance of places that were too busy with people or other dogs.

> We aimed for a local piece of grass only the size of a large garden but it overlooks Poole Harbour in the distance and is big enough for him to be on the long flexi lead if no other dogs around plus he then does his rolling around on his back which I always think relaxes him and oils his joints! There were 2 other dogs there off lead running around so we didn't go in (P. 11)

Through practices such as daily exercise, participants increased understanding of the rhythms, and social realities of urban green spaces which acted to nurture their own sense of place (Wunderlich, 2008). The functions of spaces changed throughout the day, and time-space routines which afforded positive social interactions were learnt, enacted, and repeated, whilst those that were problematic were dismissed. The sharing of space became an important part of the knowledge-building surrounding use of urban green space as the Covid-19 pandemic put negotiating and co-existing with others in the community into the spotlight (Mayers, 2021). In this way, the practices of visiting urban green spaces became routinised ways of coming to understand the world (Reckwitz, 2002). These examples show the development of a place literacy as a practice-based knowledge about the rhythms and flows of urban green spaces, their users, and their capacity to afford human and non-human potentialities. This demonstrates the potential for social practice theory to provide a new lens to examine urban green space use, through which providers can reflect on the intersection of the material provision, with user skills and meanings, and how this might provide opportunities for some, but prove exclusionary for others.

Sites for meaningful actions

People's time sovereignty (Cass et al., 2004) was altered during lockdown and leisure activities in urban green space became important for the structuring and passing of time. Consistency and repetition in the use of urban green space during lockdown was positive for some: 'Taking pleasure in your surroundings has always been part of my life as a retired person who is out and about in the countryside all the time' (P. 4), but less so for others, for example: 'We are fortunate that we have access to river, beach, countryside or town but even these become repetitive in the 1 hr time constraint' (P. 8). Participants described participation in a range of activities whilst using urban green spaces to alleviate boredom associated with lockdown. To this end, urban green spaces became spaces for meaningful actions (Kaplan & Kaplan, 2003, p. 1484); whereby participants pursued activities that achieved a goal or resulted in a tangible output.

Participant 3 indicated her use of urban green space contributed to 'busyness': 'Kept myself busy today cutting the grass and making the back garden look good'. For others, urban green spaces offered the opportunity for the development of leisure for health, which provided a sense of purpose.

> a short walk for health reasons yet again tonight. Motivation could be higher - but onward. (P. 1)

Creative projects were a focus for some. Participant 8, a keen photographer, described how the restrictions on visiting other destinations forced him to 'look at things differently' in his local area. 'I have rediscovered micro and looking at smaller things, previously I took mainly landscape and seascape' (P. 8). Another participant created themes for walks such as spot all the colours of the rainbow in seven days: 'yellow was my rainbow colour today and it is amazing how observant you get to spot the colour' (P. 4). Figure 3 shows a photograph taken by a participant as part of a social media project where people painted rocks and left them for others to find. These individual projects provided a focus for accessing urban green spaces and connection to a wider community of users (also see, Figures 4 and 5).

Further to this, entries also described a renewed sense of interest in the local people and places around them as they began daily walks. For example, Participant 4 'took some photos with a view to finding out more about history in the area'. Two others reflected on their personal histories and connections to their local area.

> We have revisited the roads we used to walk a lot down when I was doing local school runs with the buggy. The nursery both the kids went to *** primary school and [son] went there for one year before moving full time to a special needs school. The house we nearly bought on the Green. It has brought back a lot of memories of times we haven't thought about for a long time. Without this time to spend walking around our neighbourhood-we might not have had those conversations. (P. 6)

> After lunch did a nearly 5 mile walk with dogs. Interesting walked down the road where I lived when I was little. Noticed one house still had old windows. (P. 3)

Accounts also showed how participants adapted to the spaces available and looked for different material attributes of urban green spaces to meet their needs, whilst access to their usual leisure spaces and routines were limited. Some talked of (re)discovering places through microadventures, using urban green spaces in a reconceptualisation of adventure from remote and exotic to local and attainable (Houge Mackenzie & Goodnow, 2021). For example, Participant 10 captioned a photo as 'trying out our new cycle path' or as Participant 2 comments:

Figure 3. Rock finding project (Participant 4).

Figure 4. Left messages (Participant 2).

Up early for a walk/thought we would try Canford Sang[1] never been there before but it is just about possible to do in the time constraints. An interesting place that I didn't know was there prior to this situation.

Participant 1 photographed a local street he captioned 'The Hill' (see, Figure 5) which he discovered during lockdown when his usual incline walk became too busy, demonstrating the development of acquired knowledge relevant to the affordance of a space. He described it as: 'New venue to walk instead of [access path] at beach. Found this one nearby which is steep enough to get me into the oxygen dept'.

Participants' perspectives zoned in on the offering the local environment provided, reframing urban green spaces previously overlooked, for the material affordances they now required. For example, Participant 11 describes 'trying to visit new roads each day. But focusing on roads with grassy verges for the dog!' so he can roll (see, Figure 6). She describes 'finding lovely hidden tiny patches of green in alleyways we didn't know were there' (see, Figure 7). These findings demonstrate that practices were also multispecies (Dashper & Brymer, 2019), with non-humans playing an important role in the leisure use of urban green spaces and the assessment of their affordances. The role of animals in animating walks or providing shared moments for social connection (also see, Mayers, 2021) enhanced individuals' interactions with urban green space.

According to Kaplan and Kaplan (2003) people are attracted to environments that permit exploration, such as those which provide interesting, safe and diverse routes, but also those that provide reasons for being outside. This led to a sense of rediscovery of urban green spaces which offer 'action possibilities' (Lepoša, 2018, p. 20). The restriction of movement and activity imposed by lockdown created disorder in participants' usual leisure time-space routines and mundane mobilities. These disruptions create both insecurity, but also productivity, in the constructing of

Figure 5. 'The Hill' (Participant 1).

Figure 6. Grass verges for dog rolling (Participant 11).

Figure 7. :'Hidden patches of green' (Participant 11).

life worlds differently (Binnie et al., 2007). An interest in the past was a focus for some (also see, Gammon & Ramshaw, 2021), whilst for others, creative projects or health and wellbeing pursuits, provide a focus for using these spaces.

From this we can see that many participants felt the need to productively do things in urban green spaces. Participants adapted to the potentialities offered by urban green spaces, part of which was to create a sense of purpose. Urban green spaces became sites of action potential, and skills needed to be developed or re-discovered to enable their use (Kaplan & Kaplan, 2003, p. 1484). Though capturing a moment in time, the data highlights that while urban green spaces have some intrinsic value, for many people, though not all, there is a skill to realising the full potential.

Conclusion

This paper has drawn on theories of affordances and social practices to draw out insight into the use and value of urban green spaces during the first UK lockdown. According to Binnie et al. (2007, 'the perforation of the ordinary by the extraordinary can bring forth transformative or even enchanting moments or situations' (pg. 168). In this case, the 'stay at home' restrictions created space for explorations of urban green spaces and the (re)formation of perspectives and practices attached to these.

Urban green space use in lockdown manifest itself in three ways. First, participants developed a place literacy to understand where they could go and when best to visit to meet their needs. Second, beyond gardens and other private spaces, urban green space was shared with others, and therefore users were required to successfully negotiate use with others whose practices may be different and conflicting. Third, not all, but many participants needed a reason to be in urban green spaces to avoid boredom, and therefore developed skills or interests during lockdown to make visits purposeful.

Our findings bring to the fore aspects of negotiating and navigating urban green spaces that resonate beyond the lockdown experience, and have implications for post-pandemic policy and practice. Findings highlight the importance of making spaces inviting, providing clarity the public can access through signage, and designing welcoming access points to build confidence in users. It also flags the significance of initiatives, such as health walks in the UK, that initiate people into urban green space use and build their skills in using these spaces. Here, social practice theory offers a tool for providers to analyse the use of urban green spaces through the material provision, knowledge of users' skills, and the diverse meanings attached to urban green spaces. This has potential to flag the structural constraints and cultural influences that may exclude some users or afford participation by others. The tensions in lockdown also draw attention to the need to design defensible spaces where there are territorial concerns about who has access, what activities are permitted and who has control (Stodolska et al., 2013). As a result of lockdown conditions, the sharing of space became an important determinant in the selection of space. The concentration of people in urban green spaces added to tensions already present between user groups (See, Santos et al., 2016). In high use areas open vistas, widened paths or alternative routes, so users can see and anticipate actions of others, and take avoidance action may help to meet the demands on use.

Previous work has identified that urban green spaces will not be used if they do not meet the needs and preferences of local people (Hadavi et al., 2015). This data has shown how 'being' and 'doing' is important in nature-place connectivity. 'Action possibilities' (Lepoša, 2018, p. 20) help us to think that these spaces become meaningful when they serve a purpose, when they help us to acquire knowledge and skills, and when they support social needs, particularly in challenging times. Nature-place connectivity should be viewed in relation to action potential. Urban green spaces can be planned and managed to actively encourage activities which provide a sense of purpose for users. Examples include providing grassy sites by suitable rivers to encourage swimming or strategically sited cafes that provide focal points for visits. Our participants engaged in social media projects (for example, leaving painted rocks and sharing to a Facebook group) which might be harnessed by managing organisations, such as local authorities, to encourage continued engagement.

Aligning with Kaplan and Kaplan (2003), this research shows that even small pockets of urban green space can afford opportunities for restoration. Even simple spaces, such as back alleys or small pieces of grass had qualities which supported the needs of human and non-human users, yet these were often for short periods, as places to use, for a purpose, and move on from. Participants showed that often very mundane urban green spaces can offer opportunities for (re)discovery, exploration and the reframing of these spaces according to their action potential. A diversity of green spaces became important as people sought to meet different needs.

To conclude, the findings present a patchwork of urban green spaces becoming useful to those who lived near them, as places to pay attention to, as opposed to passing by. There is scope to develop these everyday practices of engagement as sustainable alternatives to places of national significance, or congested sites in the wider countryside, in providing the benefits of nature connectivity. The potential for significant and long-term material change in working practices through home working may create a further reconfiguration of practices towards short engagements with nearby urban green spaces as part of the breaks in the working day. As such, post pandemic investment should focus on the suburban social infrastructure which enable these affordances (T. D. Glover, 2021). Paying attention to the small pockets of urban nature and making sure these permeate the urban fabric rather than being tucked away in more formal spaces (also see, Nisbet & Zelenski, 2011) would provide more diversity and access to the types of nature engagements which may be more widely sought in future. If leisure use of these smaller spaces continues, then these spaces will develop new meaning and in turn become better protected.

Note

1. SANG stands for Suitable Alternative Natural Greenspace created as part of new housing developments in the UK.

Disclosure statement

No potential conflict of interest was reported by the author(s).

ORCID

Katherine King http://orcid.org/0000-0002-9679-3142
Janet Dickinson http://orcid.org/0000-0003-3310-2882

References

Bærenholdt, J. O., Haldrup, M., Larsen, J., & Urry, J. (2004). *Performing Tourist Places*. Ashgate.
BBC (2020). *The New Normal: Back to Nature*. https://www.bbc.co.uk/sounds/play/p08kmpxv
Binnie, J., Edensor, T., Holloway, J., Millington, S., & Young, C. (2007). Mundane mobilities, banal travels. *Social & Cultural Geography*, 8(2), 165–174. https://doi.org/10.1080/14649360701360048
Britton, E., Kindermann, G., Domegan, C., & Carlin, C. (2020). Blue care: A systematic review of blue space interventions for health and wellbeing. *Health Promotion International*, 35(1), 50–69. https://doi.org/10.1093/heapro/day103
Buscher, M., & Urry, J. (2009). Mobile methods and the empirical. *European Journal of Social Theory*, 12(1), 99–116. https://doi.org/10.1177/1368431008099642
Cartwright, B. D. S., White, M. P., & Clitherow, T. J. (2018). Nearby nature 'buffers' the effect of low social connectedness on adult subjective wellbeing over the last 7 days. *International Journal of Environmental Research and Public Health*, 15(6), 1238. https://doi.org/10.3390/ijerph15061238
Cass, N., Shove, E., & Urry, J. (2004). Transport infrastructures: A social-spatial-temporal model. In D. Southerton, H. Chappells, & B. Van Vliet (Eds.), *Sustainable Consumption: The implications of changing infrastructures of provision* (pp. 113–129). Edward Elgar.
Clark, C., & Uzzell, D. (2002). The affordances of the home, neighborhood, school and town center for adolescents. *Journal of Environmental Psychology*, 22(1–2), 95–108. https://doi.org/10.1006/jevp.2001.0242
Committee on Climate Change, 2019. *Net Zero: The UK's contribution to stopping global warming*. https://www.theccc.org.uk/publication/net-zero-the-uks-contribution-to-stopping-global-warming/
Crouch, D. (2000). Places around us: Embodied lay geographies in leisure and tourism. *Leisure Studies*, 19(2), 63–76. https://doi.org/10.1080/026143600374752
Dashper, K., & Brymer, E. (2019). An ecological-phenomenological perspective on multispecies leisure and the horse-human relationship in events. *Leisure Studies*, 38(3), 394–407. https://doi.org/10.1080/02614367.2019.1586981
Department for Environment, Food and Rural Affairs (2018). *A Green Future: Our 25 Year Plan To Improve The Environment*. https://assets.publishing.service.gov.uk/government/uploads/system/uploads/attachment_data/file/693158/25-year-environment-plan.pdf
Dickinson, J. E., Filimonau, V., Cherrett, T., Davies, N., Norgate, S., Speed, C., & Winstanley, C. (2013). Understanding temporal rhythms and travel behaviour at destinations: Potential ways to achieve more sustainable travel. *Journal of Sustainable Tourism*, 21(7), 1070–1090. https://doi.org/10.1080/09669582.2013.802328
Dobson, J., Birch, J., Brindley, P., Henneberry, J., McEwan, K., Mear, M., Richardson, M., & Jorgenson, A. (2021). The magic of the mundane: The vulnerable web of connections between urban nature and wellbeing. *Cities*, 108, 1–11. https://doi.org/10.1016/j.cities.2020.102989
Dutcher, D., Finley, D., Luloff, J. C., & Buttolph Johnson, J. (2007). Connectivity with nature as a measure of environmental values. *Environment and Behavior*, 37(4), 474–493. https://doi.org/10.1177/0013916506298794
Edwards, R. C., Larson, B. M. H., & Church, A. (2022). A "magic teleportation machine": Ethnically diverse green space users derive similar cultural ecosystem benefits from urban nature. *Urban Forestry & Urban Greening*, 67. https://doi.org/10.1016/j.ufug.2021.127409

Fereday, J., & Muir-Cochrane, E. (2006). Demonstrating Rigor Using Thematic Analysis: A Hybrid Approach of Inductive and Deductive Coding and Theme Development. *International Journal of Qualitative Methods*, *5*(1), 80–92. https://doi.org/10.1177/160940690600500107

Gammon, S., & Ramshaw, G. (2021). Distancing from the Present: Nostalgia and Leisure in Lockdown. *Leisure Sciences*, *43*(1–2), 131–137. https://doi.org/10.1080/01490400.2020.1773993

Germann Molz, J. (2010). Performing Global Geographies: Time, Space, Place and Pace in Narratives of Round-the-World Travel. *Tourism Geographies*, *12*(3), 329–348. https://doi.org/10.1080/14616688.2010.494684

Gibson, J. J. (1977). The theory of affordances. In R. Shaw & J. Bransford (Eds.), *Perceiving, acting, and knowing: Toward an ecological psychology* (pp. 67–82). Erlbaum.

Gibson, K. (2022). Bridging the digital divide: Reflections on using WhatsApp instant messenger interviews in youth research. *Qualitative Research in Psychology*, *19*(3), 611–631. https://doi.org/10.1080/14780887.2020.1751902

Gieryn, F. (2000). A Space for Place in Sociology. *Annual Review of Sociology*, *26*(1), 463–496. https://doi.org/10.1146/annurev.soc.26.1.463

Glaw, X., Inder, K., Kable, A., & Hazelton, M. (2017). Visual Methodologies in Qualitative Research: Autophotography and Photo Elicitation Applied to Mental Health Research. *International Journal of Qualitative Methods*, *16*(1), 1–8. https://doi.org/10.1177/1609406917748215

Glover, J. 2019 *Landscapes Review*, Department for Environment, Food and Rural Affairs. (Final Report). https://assets.publishing.service.gov.uk/government/uploads/system/uploads/attachment_data/file/833726/landscapes-review-final-report.pdf

Glover, T. D. (2021). Neighboring in the Time of Coronavirus? Paying Civil Attention While Walking the Neighborhood. *Leisure Sciences*, *43*(1–2), 280–286. https://doi.org/10.1080/01490400.2020.1774014

Hadavi, S., Kaplan, R., & Hunter, M. C. R. (2015). Environmental affordances: A practical approach for design of nearby outdoor settings in urban residential areas. *Landscape and Urban Planning*, *134*, 19–32. https://doi.org/10.1016/j.landurbplan.2014.10.001

Hargreaves, T. (2011). Practice-ing behavior change: Applying social practice theory to pro-environmental behavior change. *Journal of Consumer Culture*, *11*(1), 79–99. https://doi.org/10.1177/1469540510390500

Hartig, T., Mitchell, R., de Vries, S., & Frumkin, H. (2014). Nature and Health. *Annual Review of Public Health*, *35*(1), 207–228. https://doi.org/10.1146/annurev-publhealth-032013-182443

Hollenhorst, S. J. S., Houge Mackenzie, S., & Ostergren, D. M. (2014). The Trouble with Tourism. *Tourism Recreation Research*, *39*(3), 305–319. https://doi.org/10.1080/02508281.2014.11087003

Houge Mackenzie, S. H., & Goodnow, J. (2021). Adventure in the Age of COVID-19: Embracing Microadventures and Locavism in a Post-Pandemic World. *Leisure Sciences*, *43*(1–2), 62–69. https://doi.org/10.1080/01490400.2020.1773984

Jupp, V. (2006). Visual Methods. *The SAGE Dictionary of Social Research Methods*, 321–322. https://doi.org/10.4135/9780857020116.n222

Kaplan, S., & Kaplan, R. (2003). Health, Supportive Environments and the Reasonable Person Model. *American Journal of Public Health*, *93*(9), 1484–1489. https://doi.org/10.2105/AJPH.93.9.1484

Kaufmann, K., & Peil, C. (2020). The Mobile Instant Messaging Interview (MIMI): Using WhatsApp to enhance self-reporting and explore media usage in-situ. *Mobile Media & Communication*, *8*(2), 229–246. https://doi.org/10.1177/2050157919852392

Kaufmann, K., Peil, C., & Bork-Hüffer. (2021). Producing In Situ Data From a Distance With Mobile Instant Messaging Interviews (MMIs): Examples From the COVID-19 Pandemic. *International Journal of Qualitative Methods*, *20*, 160940692110296. https://doi.org/10.1177/16094069211029697

Kyle, G., Graefe, A., Manning, R., & Bacon, J. (2004). Effects of place attachment on users' perceptions of social and environmental conditions in a natural setting. *Journal of Environmental Psychology*, *24*(2), 213–225. https://doi.org/10.1016/j.jenvp.2003.12.006

Latham, A. (2003). Research, performance, and doing human geography: Some reflections on the diary-photograph, diary-interview method. *Environment & Planning A*, *35*(11), 1993–2017. https://doi.org/10.1068/a3587

Lepoša, N. (2018). When sea becomes home. *Annals of Tourism Research*, *72*, 11–21. https://doi.org/10.1016/j.annals.2018.06.001

Line, T., Jain, J., & Lyons, G. (2011). The role of ICTS in everyday mobile lives. *Journal of Transport Geography*, *19*(6), 1490–1499. https://doi.org/10.1016/j.jtrangeo.2010.07.002

Lobe, B., Morgan, D., & Hoffman, K. A. (2020). Qualitative Data Collection in an Era of Social Distancing 19. *International Journal of Qualitative Methods*, *19*, 1–8. https://doi.org/10.1177/1609406920937875

Lovell, R., White, M. P., Wheeler, B., Taylor, T., & Elliott, L. (2020). *A rapid scoping review of health and wellbeing evidence for the Green Infrastructure Standards*. European Centre for Environment and Human Health, University of Exeter Medical School. Natural England, Department for the Environment, Food and Rural Affairs, Public Health England, and Ministry for Housing, Communities and Local Government.

Mayer, F., & Frantz, C. M. (2004). The connectedness to nature scale: A measure of individuals' feeling in community with nature. *Journal of Environmental Psychology, 24*(4), 503–515. https://doi.org/10.1016/j.jenvp.2004.10.001

Mayers, R. (2021). Dogs Unleashed: The Positive Role Dogs Play during COVID-19. *Leisure Sciences, 43*(1–2), 252–259. https://doi.org/10.1080/01490400.2020.1774010

Milne, E.-J., & Muir, R. (2020). Photovoice: A Critical Introduction. In L. Pauwels & D. Mannay (Eds.), *The SAGE Handbook of Visual Research Methods* (2nd ed.). SAGE Publications. 282–296.

Murray L. (2009). Looking at and looking back: visualization in mobile research. *Qualitative Research, 9*(4), 469–488. 10.1177/1468794109337879

Natural England, (2020). *The People and Nature survey* (May 2020). https://www.gov.uk/government/statistics/the-people-and-nature-survey-for-england-monthly-interim-indicators-for-may-2020-experimental-statistics

Natural England, (2021). *The People and Nature survey* (March 2021). https://www.gov.uk/government/statistics/the-people-and-nature-survey-for-england-monthly-interim-indicators-for-march-2021-experimental-statistics

Nisbet, E. K., Zelanski, J. M., & Murphy, S. A. (2009). The nature relatedness scale: Linking individuals' connection with nature to environmental concern and behaviour. *Environment and Behavior, 41*(5), 715–740. https://doi.org/10.1177/0013916508318748

Nisbet, E. K., & Zelenski, J. M. (2011). Underestimating Nearby Nature: Affective Forecasting Errors Obscure the Happy Path to Sustainability. *Psychological Science, 22*(9), 1101–1106. https://doi.org/10.1177/0956797611418527

Nisbet, E. K., Shaw, D. W., & Lachance, D. G. (2020). Connectedness with nearby nature and well-being. *Frontiers in Sustainable Cities, 2*. https://doi.org/10.3389/frsc.2020.00018

Nordh, H., & Østby, K. (2013). Pocket parks for people—A study of park design and use. *Urban Forestry & Urban Greening, 12*(1), 12–17. http://dx.doi.org/10.1016/j.ufug.2012.11.003

Office for National Statistics. (2020). *Coronavirus and the social impacts on Great Britain: 16 April 2020*. https://www.ons.gov.uk/peoplepopulationandcommunity/healthandsocialcare/healthandwellbeing/bulletins/coronavirusandthesocialimpactsongreatbritain/16april2020

Peschardt, K. K., Schipperijn, J., & Stigsdotter, U. (2012). Use of small public urban green space (SPUGS). *Urban Forestry & Urban Greening, 11*(3), 235–244. https://doi.org/10.1016/j.ufug.2012.04.002

Pietilä, M., Neuvonen, M., Borodulin, M., Korpela, K., Sievänen, T., & Tyrväinen, L. (2015). Relationships between exposure to urban green spaces, physical activity and self-rated health. *Journal of Outdoor Recreation and Tourism, 10*, 44–54. https://doi.org/10.1016/j.jort.2015.06.006

Pink, S. (2007). *Doing Visual Ethnography.* (2nd ed.). SAGE Publications. https://doi.org/10.4135/9780857025029

Pretty, J., Peacock, J., Sellens, M., & Griffin, M. (2005). The mental and physical health outcomes of green exercise. *International Journal of Environmental Health Research, 15*(5), 319–337. https://doi.org/10.1080/09603120500155963

Reckwitz, A. (2002). Toward a theory of social practices: A development in culturalist theorizing. *European Journal of Social Theory, 5*(2), 243–263. https://doi.org/10.1177/13684310222225432

Relph, E. (1976). *Place and placelessness.* Pion.

Richardson, M., Hallam, J., & Lumber, R. (2015). One thousand good things in nature. Aspects of nearby nature associated with improved connection to nature. *Environmental Values, 24*(5), 603–619. https://doi.org/10.3197/096327115X14384223590131

Rose, J., & Johnson, C. W. (2020). Contextualizing reliability and validity in qualitative research: Toward more rigorous and trustworthy qualitative social science in leisure research. *Journal of Leisure Research, 51*(4), 432–451. https://doi.org/10.1080/00222216.2020.1722042

Saldana, J. (2011). *Fundamentals of Qualitative Research.* Oxford University Press.

Santos, T., Nogueria Mendes, R., & Vasco, A. (2016). Recreational activities in urban parks: Spatial interactions among users. *Journal of Outdoor Recreation and Tourism, 15*, 1–9. https://doi.org/10.1016/j.jort.2016.06.001

Seamon, D. (1980). Body-subject, Time-space routines, and Place-Ballets. In A. Buttimer & D. Seamon (Eds.), *The Human Experience of Space and Place*. Croom Helm. 148–165.

Sheller, M., & Urry, J. (2006). The new mobilities paradigm. *Environment & Planning A, 38*(2), 207–226. https://doi.org/10.1068/a37268

Shove, E., Pantzar, M., & Watson, M. (2012). *The Dynamics of Social Practice: Everyday Life and How it Changes.* Sage.

Statista (2021). *Whatsapp Statistics & Facts.* https://www.statista.com/topics/2018/whatsapp/#dossierKeyfigures

Stodolska, M., Shinew, K. J., Acevedo, J. C., & Roman, C. G. (2013). I Was Born in the Hood": Fear of Crime, Outdoor Recreation and Physical Activity Among Mexican-American Urban Adolescents. *Leisure Sciences, 35*(1), 1–15. https://doi.org/10.1080/01490400.2013.739867

Stokowski, P. A. (2002). Languages of place and discourses of power: Constructing new senses of place. *Journal of Leisure Research, 34*(4), 368–382. https://doi.org/10.1080/00222216.2002.11949977

Swanwick, C., Dunnett, N., & Woolley, H. (2003). Nature, Role and Value of Green Space in Towns and Cities: An Overview. *Built Environment, 29*(2), 94–106. https://doi.org/10.2148/benv.29.2.94.54467

Tuan, Y. F. (1980). Rootedness versus Sense of Place. *Landscape, 24*(1), 3–8.
Venter, Z. S., Barton, D. N., Gundersen, V., Figari, H., & Nowell, M. S. (2021). Back to nature: Norwegians sustain increased recreational use of urban green space months after the COVID-19 outbreak. *Landscape and Urban Planning, 214,* 1–10. https://doi.org/10.1016/j.landurbplan.202.104175
World Health Organisation. (2020). *Mental health and psychosocial considerations during the COVID-19 outbreak.* https://www.who.int/docs/default-source/coronaviruse/mental-health-considerations.pdf
Wunderlich, F. M. (2008). Walking and Rythmicity: Sensing Urban Space. *Journal of Urban Design, 13*(1), 125–139. https://doi.org/10.1080/13574800701803472
Žlender, V., & Gemin, S. (2020). Testing urban dwellers' sense of place towards leisure and recreational peri-urban green open spaces in two European cities. *Cities,* 98. https://doi.org/10.1016/j.cities.2019.102579

"I felt there was a big chunk taken out of my life": COVID-19 and older adults' library-based magazine leisure reading

Nicole K. Dalmer, Dana Sawchuk and Mina Ly

ABSTRACT
Reading is a central leisure activity among older adults, serving as a means of entertainment, escape, connection, and/or education. COVID-19 public library closures drastically altered this activity. Based on interviews with 21 older adults across Ontario, Canada, this study explores how library closures in the province affected older adults' magazine leisure reading practices. Analysis yielded three themes: COVID-19 transforming experiences of library as place, COVID-19 as time of loss, and COVID-19 as catalyst for adaptation. Participants voiced the many ways COVID-19 has shaped (often restricting) their choices related to magazine reading (where, how, and what they read, and where they located their magazines). While libraries remained virtually open during the pandemic, many participants chose not to switch to digital platforms (despite their technical proficiency to do so). As a result, they often stopped reading magazines completely, despite the loss this stoppage represented. At the same time, pandemic restrictions compelled others to use the online library services they had previously avoided. Ultimately, participants' experiences of magazine reading during the COVID-19 pandemic further our understanding of reading as leisure in later life and also trouble prevailing assumptions that older adults' resistance to digital media engagement is merely a reflection of age-related incompetence.

Introduction

Public libraries and leisure reading

Social institutions, including public libraries, have had to shift and pivot with the many changes associated with and caused by COVID-19. For public libraries in particular, changes associated with COVID-19 were especially jarring: 'shuttering the library in a crisis is new territory' (Jones, 2020, p. 954). In previous disaster situations (natural disasters, civil unrest, etc.), public libraries have been able to be physically open, to connect and support library patrons. COVID-19 physical distancing mandates and closures have therefore brought about challenges for library workers, library patrons, and the communities that library branches serve. As the pandemic evolves in unpredictable ways, public library staff and public library patrons continue to negotiate the changing roles and expectations of public libraries, particularly as public libraries are taking up hybrid practices in response to different patrons' leisure needs.

Closures were especially difficult to navigate given the multiple ways that communities engage with their public libraries. As key 'third places' (Oldenburg, 1989), people seek out and use their local public library branch as a space for learning, play, refuge, social connection, and leisure (Houghton et al., 2013). Indeed, public libraries are intimately linked with leisure, providing space, materials, staff, and programmes to support and sustain a wide range of different community members' leisure needs. Libraries offer a needed space for relaxation, escapism and socialisation, and are a space where those with restricted financial means can access leisure-related materials, devices, and events that might otherwise be unavailable to them (Hayes & Morris, 2005, 2005b; Hider, 2022; Stebbins, 2009).

While libraries provide access to a myriad of resources and collections (including kitchen spaces, makerspaces, and seed libraries, among others), public libraries are perhaps best (and most traditionally) known for the reading materials they offer. The relationship between reading and leisure is well documented. Ross, McKechnie, and Rothbauer's (2006; 2018) pioneering edited collections on reading detail the many reasons why individuals read for leisure. For many, reading is a beneficial and essential activity in their everyday lives, being both educational and entertaining, and providing, overall, pleasure (Billington, 2016; Wolf, 2018). As Ross (2018) elaborates, reading can fulfil many, seemingly contradictory, needs for adults: 'to escape from the world and to connect with other people, to be relaxed and to be stimulated, to be solitary and to be social, to confirm ideas you already have and to be opened up to new ideas' (p. 158).

Gibson and Singleton (2012) report that media use (including reading) is the most time-consuming leisure activity among older individuals. While reading is typically a solitary activity, Luyt and Ho (2011) confirm Smith's (1993) earlier work, in that paradoxically, solitary reading helps connect older readers with society at large and is often used as a mechanism to cope with loneliness and stress. Studies about reading as leisure specifically among older adults are both dated (e.g. Smith, 1993, 1996) and sparse, often relying on general surveys that collapse and/or over-simplify older adults' experiences of reading. Rothbauer & Dalmer (2018) pilot study of interviews with five older readers is a notable exception to the existing body of literature in this area. In-depth conversations with older readers revealed that reading for leisure supported resilience and a reflective stance on life, enabling older readers to navigate and celebrate their own lived experiences. Findings revealed that reading 'infused daily life with pleasurable escape or mindful engagement', and 'buil[t] bridges to resilient attitudes and behaviours' (Rothbauer & Dalmer, 2018, p. 171).

Reading research, however, seldom focuses on magazine reading.[1] Perhaps unsurprisingly then, very little is known about the role magazine reading as leisure plays in older adults' everyday lives. In past general reading surveys, periodicals, such as newspapers and magazines, were reported as preferred reading materials for people 65 years of age and older (Scales & Rhee, 2001; Smith, 1993), with Smith (1996) relaying that as compared to younger readers, 'older adults are more likely to read books, religious materials, correspondence, and magazines for personal use' (p. 216). In their overview of media use patterns among older adults, Robinson et al. (2004) note that older magazine (and newspaper) readers are motivated by a desire to increase their knowledge whereas older book readers are more likely to read for pleasure. Drawing on research from the 1970s, these authors report that magazine readership tends to decline with age, dropping dramatically after 70 years of age (Robinson et al., 2004). As is evident, updated research on magazine leisure reading among older adults is desperately needed.

Very recent research in the field of ageing studies does explore how and why older adults read magazines. Sawchuk and Ly's research (2022), for example, explored not only how older women used the information in women's magazines to bolster and convey their confidence and competence in an ageist world but also how they viewed reading magazines as a significant and undemanding form of relaxation and entertainment. Nonetheless, most magazine studies in this field have been content analyses concerned with dissecting the nature and implications of visual and textual representations of ageing or older adults in magazines (e.g. Marshall, 2018; Ylänne, 2021). Much of this research, then, with its focus on magazine content as opposed to consumption, does not directly engage with older readers themselves.

In light of these multiple domains of research, our present study is in response to the scant scholarship available at the intersection of later life, public libraries, reading/readers and leisure. Furthermore, our conversations with older readers explore a type of reading, magazine reading, that is itself underexplored in relation to the above topics. Finally, to our knowledge, this is the only available study that explores and articulates the role of magazine reading in relation to the COVID-19 pandemic. As such, we turn next to a description of the pandemic-related library closures in Ontario, Canada, the site of our research. We then follow with a description of our methods and, finally, an elaboration and discussion of our findings.

Ontario public libraries' COVID-19 lockdown

Shortly after the World Health Organisation declared COVID-19 a global pandemic on March 11th, 2020, the Ontario government, mirroring similar decisions made in other provinces and territories in Canada, mandated a series of closures in the public and private sectors, beginning with the closure of public schools on March 12th (Ranger, 2021). Public libraries were ordered to close as part of the provincial state of emergency announced on March 17th, though some had already closed a few days prior. The City of Toronto (Canada's largest city), for example, closed its 100 library branches on March 13th (Klingbeil, 2020). By the end of March, most Canadian public libraries had shuttered their doors (Klingbeil, 2020) and, according to one literature review (McMenemy et al., 2022), most libraries worldwide also closed at some point during March and April 2020. In June 2020, Ontario public library systems began to reopen their physical spaces, albeit gradually and with certain restrictions (Ontario Library Association, 2020). These included capacity limits and restrictions to a narrow range of activities for patrons such as picking up holds, computer and printer usage, and limited browsing (Rosales, 2021).

During this time, library spokespeople made clear through traditional and social media outlets that libraries remained accessible to their users (Dalmer & Griffin, 2022). As the Ontario Library Association (2020) emphasised,

> while physical branches have been closed to members of the community ... they have continued to operate virtually, providing access to a wide array of services and resources for people of all ages, 24 hours a day, 7 days a week (p. 1).

Hence virtual programming (e.g. storytimes, book clubs, craft activities) and new innovations in the provision of physical materials (e.g. curbside pickup, lending Wi-Fi hot spots) were widely developed, with a few libraries developing patron outreach initiatives ('care calls') to help reduce social isolation among vulnerable community members (including older adults) and connect them with social services, if needed. Among the most significant developments, however, was the expansion of e-resources, in which 96% of surveyed Ontario libraries were engaged (Ontario Library Association, 2020). As such, libraries put much time, energy, and finances into expanding, promoting, and providing tutorials on how to use their e-collections as one of their main adaptations to the pandemic. With this focus on online resources, however, some have questioned the underlying assumption that libraries' digital offerings can somehow maintain or foster the social connection that libraries provided in-person, pre-pandemic (Dalmer & Mitrovica, 2022).

Beginning in late December 2020, libraries were again closed to most in-branch services as part of another province-wide lockdown intended to curb virus transmission amidst Ontario's second pandemic wave (CBC News, 2020). Throughout 2021, the year when the interviews for this study were conducted, various provincial plans for phased-in reopening were announced. However, given the repeated fluctuations in the state of the pandemic, progression towards reopening was punctuated by periods of reversals to increased restrictions and even stay-at-home orders in the first half of the year, and by various pauses in reopening schemes in the latter half (Elliot, 2022). It is difficult to generalise about Ontario library closures, given that restrictions sometimes varied according to region-specific COVID-related metrics (such as virus incidence and test positivity rates). Nonetheless, all library systems in the province experienced at least some closures and operating restrictions during the year.[2]

Materials and methods

This article is based on an extension of earlier research on older women and women's magazines (Sawchuk & Ly, 2022), during which several interviewed participants commented on the importance of public libraries for providing access to the magazines they read. The current study is based on 21 semi-structured interviews. Following university research ethics board approval (from Wilfrid Laurier University and McMaster University), we sought to recruit magazine readers (of any gender) over the age of 55 who used the library to access magazines (of any type). We began by contacting interviewees from the earlier study to invite them to participate in this new project. We then moved to contacting public libraries in cities and towns in Ontario (the most populous province in Canada); fliers advertising the study were posted in hard copy in library buildings and on various library systems' websites.

Eighteen women and three men participated in the study. Among them, they frequented libraries in ten different public library systems. Participants ranged in age from 56 to 81 (see Table 1). Although there were exceptions, they were a relatively educated group, with the majority completing at least one university degree and holding a professional (current or former) occupation. Despite efforts to enhance sample diversity (by posting our flyer in library branches located in neighbourhoods with a significant racialised population and by sharing our recruitment poster with diverse older adult cultural groups), the sample was also a relatively homogeneous one, with two participants identifying as Asian and the remainder as White. To preserve participant anonymity, we use pseudonyms throughout this article (and ages are provided the first time a participant is mentioned).

The first and second authors conducted the interviews between July and November 2021. Due to concerns related to COVID-19, no interviews were held in person. Instead, interviews were held

Table 1. Sample profile.

		N
Gender:		
	Female	18
	Male	3
Age range:		
	55-59	3
	60-64	6
	65-69	5
	70-74	4
	75-79	1
	80-84	2
Race:		
	White	19
	Asian	2
Marital status:		
	Married	12
	Separated/divorced	5
	Widowed	1
	Single	3
Educational Attainment:		
	High school	2
	College	2
	Some university	1
	University degree	8
	Graduate/professional degree	8

over the phone or Microsoft Teams, per each participant's preference. The interview guide consisted of questions related to magazine reading preferences and habits; library usage to access magazines; and the effect of COVID-19 on library usage and magazine reading. Participants were also asked whether they had any advice or comments for library staff related to magazines and libraries. Interviews lasted between 30 and 62 minutes. All interviews were recorded, either with digital recorders or via the recording function in Teams, and then were transcribed by the third author and a research assistant.

Inductive thematic analysis proceeded as inspired by Mayan (2009) and Braun and Clarke (2006). Following each interview, the respective interviewer wrote up a brief memo on the overall tone and notable features of the interaction. These observations and other initial ideas about the data were discussed during regular research team meetings, occasionally leading to slight changes to the guide for subsequent interviews. Once all interviews were conducted and transcribed, all authors independently generated codes for the first five interviews and composed their own lists of categories under which their codes could be collated. We next compared our lists and discussed whether to expand, combine or otherwise refine category names and contents, resulting in an agreed upon series of categories contained within a shared online document. After dividing up the remaining transcripts, we coded our respective data and continued with the process of assigning codes to categories while discussing potential revisions to our scheme as necessary (reflecting our assumption that qualitative research is an iterative as opposed to linear process). In the process, interviews were reread multiple times and illustrative quotations for the categories were excerpted by all three authors and shared in another joint document. These categories and quotations were then used as the basis to develop the three themes (COVID-19 transforming experiences of library as place, COVID-19 as a time of loss, and COVID-19 as a catalyst for adaptation) as described and discussed below.

Results

As participants spoke more generally about their magazine preferences and related reading practices, nearly all participants (18 of the 21 participants) indicated that they had been enjoying and reading magazines for many decades. Several detailed the evolution of magazine reading throughout their life course, with preferred magazine titles changing in relation to their evolving stage of life, interests, and lifestyles. Perhaps unsurprisingly, then, magazine reading was integral to a number of participants' experiences of leisure.

Indeed, participants' accounts of how magazine reading fulfilled a variety of their reading, and relatedly, leisure needs correspond to previous research on magazine readers, including older adults (e.g. Sawchuk & Ly, 2022; Smith, 1996; Stevens et al., 2007; Winship, 1987; Ytre-Arne, 2011a). As such, magazine reading for our participants was a decidedly pleasurable experience, a treat and/or something enjoyable they engaged in, often to unwind. As Joyce (age 73) expressed,

> It's relaxing.... It's like a comfort moment in my life. It's like comfort food... And, I just think, I just – it gives me a chance to go out and do something and pick up some things. Rather, it's just a fast pick up. It's like going in and having a cup of coffee. You go in and get yourself a magazine from the library.

Linked to the pleasurable nature of magazine reading for Joyce and others was the fact that, unlike books, magazines do not require as much sustained or deep concentration (Hermes, 1995). Sophia (age 65) talked about the appeal of magazines' *'entertaining side and light side'* and the reader's ability to

> Just sorta dip in and dip out" from them. Barbara (age 64) elaborated that, if she were *"feeling not well ... I really don't want to get into a book. You know, I want to be able to, you know, just pick something up and read it and be able to put it down.*

In addition, special-interest magazines were sought as a source of information related to some of the other leisure pursuits our participants mentioned, for example by providing practical information about gardening or cooking or introducing them to new destinations for vacationing.

As each interview progressed, participants illuminated how vital the library was in meeting and sustaining their magazine reading needs and, therefore, how disruptive the COVID-19 pandemic was to their magazine reading (and leisure) routines. As participants voiced their experiences of public library-supported magazine reading throughout the pandemic, reading practices clearly shifted and evolved, intimately linked to public library closures. The reactions and adaptations to this shift, though, varied significantly between participants. Three clear themes emerged:

COVID-19 transforming experiences of library as place

A number of participants highlighted the library *as place* as being central to their experiences of leisure pre-pandemic. Library 'as place', a concept from Library and Information Science, draws attention to libraries as 'culturally constructed places [that] have an important role to play in fostering and developing varying senses of community and providing services to different communities' (Leckie & Buschman, 2007, p. 13). Participants viewed the library as a place of leisure, as a place where they could read, rest, and socialise – a place, that is, as captured beautifully by Betty (age 73): 'a library-esqe living room'. As a place that was expected to be warm in the winter and cool in the summer, participants' local public library branches served as appealing destinations, as convenient places that participants could walk, drive, or bike to. In some cases, the mode of transportation itself, such as walking, could be classed as a component of library-related leisure, as in the case of Amelia (age 68), who routinely combined her walking for exercise with a stop at her local library. Interviews focused on the library as a place for supporting magazine reading (with nearly all participants commenting on the pleasurable ritual of browsing magazine stacks for issues and articles that 'piqued' their interest), and several reported that they enjoyed sitting in a comfortable chair or near a window to read their finds on site. However, what emerged from conversations was that visits to the library simultaneously facilitated the enjoyment of *multiple* forms of leisure: participants also mentioned finding DVDs or boardgames, using a laptop in a quiet corner, attending library programmes, 'hanging out' with a spouse on a weekend afternoon, and taking grandchildren to library activities.

As the role of library as place as a *physical* place was key to so many of the participants, for many, physical distancing mandates, concerns around personal safety and hygiene, and limited library hours (or library closures) that accompanied the COVID-19 pandemic collectively restricted the pleasure that many library patrons experience when using the library. Sophia elaborated about her experiences with the library branch during the pandemic:

> *It's more of a – to me now more of an in and out kind of place, the way I look at it. I don't know how other people feel. That's how I feel. It's a more of an in and out. Not go in and browse around. Not that I'd be in there for hours or anything, but it was more of a relaxed place where you could go in and look at things and I don't have that kind of feeling about it now. . . . I mean I would not linger [during the pandemic], look at them [magazines], I just see if I could grab it, kind of. My goal was just to be in and out as quickly as I could. Particularly before being vaccinated.*

As the public library during the COVID-19 pandemic shifted to a predominantly *digital* place (Dalmer & Griffin, 2022), participants had to revise their understandings of library as place, grappling with the 'implications of a public library that [was] simultaneously physically closed and virtually open' (p. 136).

For many months, with libraries closed, the only way to gain access to magazines was through libraries' different online portals (e.g. PressReader, OverDrive, hoopla, etc.). But, while public libraries emphasised being virtually open, this digital expansion was not embraced by a majority of our participants. Their reticence was not necessarily due to a lack of knowledge surrounding digital access or a technophobic attitude. In fact, many of our participants reported knowing how to access magazines online and revealed considerable comfort with digital technology in other realms of their lives. Instead, electing to avoid online magazines stemmed from a clear dislike of the digital magazine format and thus a clear dislike of the experience of reading magazines digitally.

Participants differently described elements that rendered digital magazine reading incompatible with their own interpretation of a leisurely reading experience: wanting less screen time, limited Internet access at home, difficulty navigating the platform, tablets or phones being too heavy to hold over a sustained period, and frustrations related to scrolling and trying to adjust the font size. Several participants also mentioned that digital magazines were less aesthetically or tangibly pleasing than their print counterparts. As Catherine (age 56) summarised,

> *There is no substitute for [print]. I don't care how amazing, hyperlinked, beautiful, pixelated, whatever, digital – it's never going to compete with print for me ever, ever ... the kinaesthetic, the aesthetic experience, the feel and the smell of the paper, everything matters to me, and I get none of that from digital, like none.*

Overall, the experience of reading digital magazines was overwhelmingly viewed as less satisfying than having a magazine in hand and being able to physically turn the pages. As such, participants' preferences aligned with previous research that has reported a significant positive association between older age and heavy print media usage (Nossek et al., 2015), as well as with research that highlights how readers of women's magazines prefer to experience magazines as physical and aesthetic, and not digital, objects (Ytre-Arne, 2011b).

As a number of participants chose not to engage with their virtual library during COVID-19, it was soon clear that the magazines borrowed from local public library branches were also intimately linked with their broader leisure experiences and routines. As captured by Carol (age 64), the shift to the library experienced as a predominantly *digital* place had profound implications for participants' experiences of the library as place for social interaction:

> *prior to COVID, it was quite a social place. You know, people of like mind knew each other and the only reason we knew each other is because we were, you know, we were within the library system. We were looking. We were reading. We were – you know, so that was the basis of our connection. And that's slipping a little bit because of COVID, certainly, but I think that it's really limiting down to my generation because I think you know, certainly your generation and younger is doing everything online. You are very comfortable with digital access and I'm – it's not that I couldn't do it. I'm not interested in doing [it].*

Significantly, Carol's latter point, which was echoed by other participants, is also substantiated by previous research which highlights older adults' beliefs that younger people are more intuitively able to use digital technologies (Vaportzis et al., 2017). Overall, and despite library branches' emphasis on being virtually open, when it came to magazine reading, our participants' informed aversion to digital formats meant that libraries as place (and the magazine-related leisure associated with them) were effectively closed.

COVID-19 as a time of loss

The pandemic closure of public libraries, as far as our participants' intentions and purposes were concerned, had additional implications. Participants expressed frustrations and disappointments related to the restrictions of their magazine reading routines as a result of the pandemic. As magazine reading routines were stilted, so too were all of participants' other leisure-related schedules and rhythms linked to visiting the library. Collectively, participants, much like Betty, conveyed a deep sense of loss experienced with library closures:

> *I felt there was a big chunk taken out of my life ... I felt like it was a big chunk taken out of my life 'cause there was shorter hours. I loved the library staff, but it was – part of my mental health was diminished.*

Participants differently expressed this sense of loss through various affective tones, noting an overarching sense of missing the library as place. As Catherine revealed, *'I miss going, I miss looking through the magazines and finding something'*. For these participants and others, the pandemic-related library lockdowns represented a dual loss: as elaborated above, not only were participants unable to physically visit the library (thus stripping them of leisure experiences linked to library visits), but unexpectedly, despite the importance that participants placed on magazine reading, a majority of participants reported that they completely ceased reading magazines during the pandemic.

Stopping magazine reading during the pandemic should not be viewed as a reflection of the importance of magazine reading for participants. In fact, some participants explained why magazines were especially crucial leisure materials during the pandemic. Sophia, for example, in alignment with research on leisure as a stress-buffering distraction in the face of negative life events and conditions (e.g. Kleiber et al., 2002; Mannell, 2007), shared how she used magazines to escape from the relentless distressing news in the broader media about COVID-19. Instead, such stoppage was frequently reported by participants to be related to magazine cost, availability, and their disinclination to accessing and reading digital magazines, factors that in turn compounded their feelings of loss.

For over 70% of our sample (n = 15), public libraries were the *only* source of magazines; purchasing magazines, either from retail outlets or via subscription, was relatively rare. By and large, this was due to the emphasis participants placed on getting magazines for free at the library and/or the perceived costliness of magazines. For many on a budget, they described buying magazines or having a magazine subscription as a luxury they could no longer afford. As a result, the available collection at their public library branch often dictated what could be read. As a result, when libraries closed, hard copies of magazines became unavailable altogether to participants who could not buy them.

In addition, notable in the interviews was the number of interviewees who arrived at their library without a particular magazine title in mind. For many, browsing the collection, which included discovering new titles and having a wide choice in titles, was a key component of their experiences of leisure at the library. In the pandemic, then, library closures or restrictions meant that every branch had a limited or even eliminated collection. Barbara further elaborates how the disorganising impact of the pandemic wreaked havoc with her magazine reading (or lack thereof):

> *They shut the magazines down completely during COVID.... They took magazines completely off the shelf and there was nothing. You could not get a magazine. I'm not entirely sure if you couldn't have gotten one from hold online, but because there was no browsing in the library, you couldn't point and say, 'I'd like that magazine over there'. There was none.*

This sense of loss related to feeling removed from or disconnected from the library's magazine collection throughout the pandemic was exacerbated for those participants who could not or would not access magazines using the libraries' online portals – whether due to a dislike or lack of experience of engaging with digital products or due to, as Catherine emphasised, their allegiance with print materials: *'I like print. I live for print, right?'* Dorothy (age 73) explains how the lack of library-provided instructions regarding digital magazine access precluded her from being able to access magazines altogether and the affective impact this then wrought:

> *So you can't get any kind of hands on instruction on how to do anything, right. Same as downloading books in library. Same thing. I don't know how to do that because I never wanted to do it. So I just bit the bullet and didn't do anything. Well, I could still ... like I said when it was closed, I was devastated pretty much. Well, not devastated, but ... it was a big change.*

With the multiple forms of disruption that COVID-19 introduced, some participants looked to their leisure experiences of magazine reading for a sense of normalcy. As part of maintaining that sense of normalcy, participants held an underlying expectation that public libraries would or should provide, as Dorothy outlined above, instructions or support to enable patrons to use the library as they had pre-pandemic. Without this support, accessing magazines from the library was more cumbersome during the pandemic and as a result, some participants simply elected to stop accessing magazines from the library:

> But I was not looking at magazines at all that whole time, not even once. And like, yeah, we couldn't go in and then even once we were allowed in, we weren't allowed to sit down. It's just like, you go in for five minutes and then you're gone. So I just – I was all completely looking at books . . . [I] just sort of dropped out. Like I just – yeah, once the library was kind of not making it easy for me, I just forgot about [i.e. reading magazines at the library]"
> (Cecilia, age 65).

COVID-19 as a catalyst for adaptation

In contrast to those who reluctantly abandoned magazine reading while libraries were closed, the sense of loss outlined in the previous section provoked some participants to modify their library-related leisure routines. A smaller proportion of our participants (n = 4) adapted to the COVID pandemic (whether by choice or by necessity) by integrating digital access into their magazine reading repertoire. Perhaps best encapsulated by Shirley (age 62), who throughout her interview, spoke to the many reasons why she was now accessing and reading magazines online using her public library system:

> I just became more aware. And with COVID, it forced me to act, you know, forced me to use it better, I guess the technology and what availability that they have. And so I just became more and more of a user.

She went on to comment that as a result of accessing her library digitally, she was using her library even more than before the pandemic and felt more comfortable using the library via this medium given the health and hygiene concerns she had about physically visiting the library and using and flipping through print versions of magazines.

Even those participants who maintained a strong preference for print acknowledged the advantages to reading magazines digitally as a means to keep up this leisure activity throughout COVID-19:

> Probably in a pre-pandemic world I probably would prefer the print. But I can see – one advantage of using the digital, using these formats I mentioned is that I can see all these topics and titles that I just had no idea were available
> (Sophia).

A number of other hybrid readers' (readers whose reading repertoires drew on both digital and print platforms [Adoni & Nimrod, 2020]) comments also revealed that their hybrid reading practices were the direct result of the constraints of the COVID-19 pandemic.

Nonetheless, as the research of Quan-Haase et al. (2016) suggests, participants' combination of familiar (print) and novel (digital) reading practices were not solely a result of pandemic need; an evaluation of the relative merits of digital access also factored into participants' reading practices. A majority of the advantages that participants listed regarding digital magazine access dealt with availability and accessibility. Some participants noted that it was easier to access magazines digitally during the pandemic (whether because libraries were closed or because some library systems removed magazines from circulation entirely during the pandemic). Others, much like Sophia, noted that they benefited from the increase in variety when they moved online – there were far more magazine topics and titles to explore through the library's virtual portal than were available in the physical stacks. Lastly, some noted and applauded the accessibility features that were available to them when they read magazines online (cf. Nimrod, 2019). Linda (age 61), for example, noted that reading magazines online was a necessary way to deal with certain health issues. She noted that a print magazine wouldn't be backlit, so I can't read it at night when my husband's sleeping and I can't sleep. So as I get insomnia, then I can't pick them up and I used to have a little light and that's just not convenient.

The ability to enlarge text size, easily take screenshots, and click through hyperlinks were some of the other digital features that appealed to some participants.

Adaptation took many forms among our participants. In addition to those participants who had the means and the desire to partake in digital magazine reading, other participants adapted their magazine leisure through other methods: swapping magazines with friends and family or sharing magazines with informal libraries in their apartment buildings or condominiums. Again, however, other participants were quick to note that pandemic restrictions and stay-at-home orders sometimes interfered with such exchanges.

As we spoke with participants about the adaptations they had made to their magazine reading as a direct result of the pandemic, we asked which changes to their magazine reading they could foresee keeping. Participants were quite mixed with their responses and their expectations of the future. Some, such as Shirley, predicted that their digital magazine reading would continue post-pandemic and their physical visits to the library would subsequently diminish:

> To be honest with you, I think that habit of some of the things I used to do, I probably won't do anymore, like just going, visiting, hanging around, browsing. I don't think I'll probably do that anymore when I can browse online.

Others, however, could not wait to return to their public library branch as soon as they were safely able to begin borrowing print magazines. As Miranda (age 75) notes,

> Yes, that's one of the things that I really miss the most, was being able to go to the library. And one of the things that was at the top of my list for doing as soon as the restrictions were lifted, I went to the library.

Recent research at the intersection of ageing and technology draws on media displacement theory, which suggests that the use of traditional media will decline over time and be replaced by new media (Loos & Ivan, 2022; Nimrod, 2019). Participants' varied experiences of library use during the pandemic and expectations of library use post-pandemic (including print and digital magazine access and use) challenge the seemingly unidirectional nature of this theory. The COVID-19 pandemic context has strongly influenced a number of participants' use or integration of new media – though this displacement of print magazines with digital magazines is not necessarily permanent. Participants' engagement with print and/or digital magazines oscillates over time and is likely to evolve with time, context, and individual participants' comfort level and desire to engage with digital devices.

Discussion

Previous research has reported that older readers are a heterogeneous group, whose reading practices are informed by a complex medley of factors (Adoni & Nimrod, 2020; Rothbauer & Dalmer, 2018). To these existing studies, our research confirms a similar heterogeneity among older magazine readers, in terms of magazine reading preferences and practices. Conversations with older magazine readers revealed their reading habits were shaped by multiple, and sometimes competing, factors: available time, finances, interests, technological comfort, and availability at their library, with the COVID-19 pandemic as an overarching, permeating factor. In discussing their magazine reading habits, it was clear that across participants, magazine reading played a central role in their experiences of and need for leisure. As a result, our results call into question earlier findings by Robinson et al. (2004) who reported that older magazine readers were motivated by more instrumental needs (the desire to increase their knowledge) whereas older book readers were more likely to read for pleasure. As participants demonstrated, and consistent with more recent research (Sawchuk & Ly, 2022), interviewed older magazine readers' motivations, while they may involve instrumental information seeking, are also undeniably centred on seeking pleasure.

Across the three themes (COVID-19 transforming experiences of library as place, COVID-19 as a time of loss, and COVID-19 as a catalyst for adaptation), the concept of choice emerged as an influential factor in participants' experiences of magazine reading for leisure. Indeed, a preference for choice and the freedom to choose are recurring themes in broader leisure research with and about older adults (Craike & Coleman, 2005; Guinn, 1999). Across interviews, participants made clear the degree to which the COVID-19 pandemic had constrained their choices related to magazines: where they read, how they read, what they read, and where they located their magazines. What ultimately appeared to dictate these experiences of choice (or lack thereof) are threefold: public library closures, the perceived costliness of magazines, and the tension between the allure and dislike of digital magazine access.

First, as public libraries closed their doors or reopened with severe restrictions, participants were unable to access print magazines and/or were unable to sit in the library to enjoy their reading. For those who were unable or unwilling to access magazines through libraries' virtual portals, even if virtually 'open', physically closed libraries removed all semblance of choice with regards to their magazine reading.

Second, a majority of participants discussed the high costs of purchasing magazines or magazine subscriptions, a cost that was unpalatable, out of reach, or considered too luxurious for many. As a result, the public library was the sole location participants could access magazines without needing to pay. Cavanagh and Robbins (2012) have previously discussed the importance older adults – especially those for whom discretionary spending is diminished – place in being able to use library services without cost. The severe impact of library closures is again revealed, with participants' only source of magazine access completely severed.

Finally, and third, while public libraries promoted their online catalogue and virtual offerings as a means for patrons to stay connected with the libraries' collections and programs, participants overwhelmingly voiced their dislike for reading magazines digitally. This is in keeping with previous survey research that found that older Canadians have relatively low rates of digital magazine consumption (Magazines Canada, 2017). Some participants who did adapt to virtual magazine reading noted their reluctance at doing so. Nimrod (2017) uncovered similar results in their cross-European study of older Internet users, finding that those older adults who were tech-savvy were still inclined to use traditional mass media as opposed to newer digital media devices. Ultimately, as Quan-Haase et al. (2016) also found, our participants' decision of whether or not to adopt digital devices to read their magazines was not a simple binary. Instead, their decisions reflect contexts and choices that revolve around preferences and convenience of use and not necessarily, as stereotypes would suggest, around technical skill level. Indeed, stereotypes of older adults as being technologically slow, anxious, or inept continue (Birkland, 2022). While some participants demonstrated that their experiences with technology are shaped by societal and internalised ageism (Barrie et al., 2021), other participants clearly demonstrated that their decision to not engage with technology was not borne out of fear or a lack of knowledge, but arose from a conscious choice, often tied to an aesthetic dislike of the digital platform. As a result, while the pandemic undeniably constrained many participants' reading and leisure choices, in other ways it showcased participants' agency with regards to choice (including a choice to *not* engage) in relation to digital technologies. Accordingly, in keeping with the tenets of socio-gerontechnological research (Peine et al., 2021), our findings can help inform future research with older readers, underscoring the importance of engaging directly with older adults about their experiences with and about digital devices as a means of respecting and highlighting their own agency in relation to technologies.

These findings can also provide a window into the complex interactions of coexisting digital and offline worlds of leisure for older adults, which expands existing research on digital leisure studies (one that has been previously discussed largely in relation to younger adults; e.g. Silk et al., 2016) throughout the life course. Indeed, interviewing older readers directly about their magazine reading practices and preferences is one way to give voice to older adults, who are often only indirectly studied via their representation in magazines. The present study thus similarly expands audience-centred work on magazines, which also has tended to focus predominantly on younger readers (e.g. McDonnell, 2014; Stevens et al., 2007; Ytre-Arne, 2011a, 2011b).

This library patron-centred study is a notable departure from the majority of existing library-focused pandemic research, which has tended to focus either on analyses of public library websites and social media posts for COVID-related announcements (e.g. Alajmi & Albudaiwi, 2021; Lund et al., 2022; Wang & Lund, 2020) or on public library staff's perspectives of the changes that COVID has wrought (e.g. Garner et al., 2021; Haasio & Kannasto, 2020; Robinson et al., 2022). While a post-pandemic future of the public library looms in the distance, in the interim, as library staff negotiate post-lockdown contexts and juggle patrons' and communities' needs and expectations (including decisions related to the expansion of digital offerings), (re)imagining how to best navigate the upcoming months and years is most fulsomely done through direct engagement with library patrons (Smith, 2020). Looking, then, to implications for library studies and practice more broadly, our findings highlight the need to engage directly with older library patrons as the pandemic continues to evolve in unpredictable ways, particularly as libraries continue to negotiate which programs and services to keep in online formats. This intentional incorporation of older adults into library planning and practice also aligns with a number of governing documents and mandates from library associations (e.g. the American Library Association, 2008; the Canadian Federation of Library Associations, 2016).

In closing, given the little research at the intersection of reading and later life and the even smaller pool of research that specifically examines magazine reading among older adults, this study represents an important point of departure for future research in this area. We encourage reading-focused researchers to include and highlight magazines as a significant reading material in their research and suggest separating newspaper from magazine reading when engaging with older readers. Not only can these results contribute to what little is known about older adults in public library practice and education (guiding, for example, readers' advisory services for older library patrons), but these findings also highlight the complexities and broader, intersecting factors that influence and shape older adults' reading for leisure.

Notes

1. For example, the *Canadian Leisure & Reading Study: 2021* published by BookNet Canada (2021), a non-profit organisation that serves the book industry, focuses on books, ebooks and audiobooks only, making no mention of magazines.
2. For an example of the varying service levels at one small, rural Ontario public library system over the course of 2021, see their chronological list at https://www.thebluemountainslibrary.ca/service-updates-and-covid-19.cfm?is=10.

Acknowledgments

(1) This work was supported by the Social Sciences and Humanities Research Council of Canada under Insight Development Grant number 430-2018-00150.
(2) The authors are grateful for the time and contributions of all the participants in the study, for the recruitment and transcription assistance of Samantha Pinckney, and for the helpful comments from the anonymous reviewers
(3) Some sections of this paper, in earlier form, were presented at the Ontario Libraries Association Super Conference (held online in February 2022).

Disclosure statement

No potential conflict of interest was reported by the authors.

Funding

This work was supported by the Social Sciences and Humanities Research Council of Canada under Insight Development Grant number 430-2018-00150.

ORCID

Nicole K. Dalmer http://orcid.org/0000-0002-0326-4293
Dana Sawchuk http://orcid.org/0000-0002-3728-5682
Mina Ly http://orcid.org/0000-0001-6868-2384

References

Adoni, H., & Nimrod, G. (2020). The emergence of the hybrid older reader: A cross-national study. *Communications*, 45(4), 414–439. https://doi.org/10.1515/commun-2019-2033
Alajmi, B. M., & Albudaiwi, D. (2021). Response to COVID-19 pandemic: Where do public libraries stand? *Public Library Quarterly*, 40(6), 540–556. https://doi.org/10.1080/01616846.2020.1827618
American Library Association. (2008). Guidelines for library and information services to older adults. *Reference & User Services Quarterly*, 48(2), 209–212. https://doi.org/10.5860/rusq.48n2.209
Barrie, H., La Rose, T., Detlor, B., Julien, H., & Serenko, A. (2021). "Because I'm old": The role of ageism in older adults' experiences of digital literacy training in public libraries. *Journal of Technology in Human Services*, 39(4), 379–404. https://doi.org/10.1080/15228835.2021.1962477
Billington, J. (2016). *Is literature healthy?*. Oxford University Press.
Birkland, J. L. (2022). How older adult information and communication technology users are impacted by aging stereotypes: A multigenerational perspective. New Media & Society, 146144482211089. https://doi.org/10.1177/14614448221108959
Braun, V., & Clarke, V. (2006). Using thematic analysis in psychology. *Qualitative Research in Psychology*, 3, 77–101. https://doi.org/10.1191/1478088706qp063oa
Canada, B. (2021). Canadian leisure & reading study: 2021. *BookNet Canada Research & Education Report*. https://www.booknetcanada.ca/canadian-leisure-and-reading-2020
Canadian Federation of Library Associations. (2016, August 26). *Canadian guidelines on library and information services for older adults*. http://cfla-fcab.ca/en/guidelines-and-position-papers/canadian-guidelines-on-library-and-information-services-for-older-adults/
Cavanagh, M. F., & Robbins, W. (2012). Baby boomers, their elders and the public library. *Library Review*, 61(8/9), 622–640. https://doi.org/10.1108/00242531211292114
CBC News. (2020, December 21). *Here's what's allowed and not allowed under Ontario's provincewide lockdown*. https://www.cbc.ca/news/canada/toronto/ontario-shutdown-details-pdf-1.5850224
Craike, M., & Coleman, D. (2005). Buffering effects of leisure self-determination on the mental health of older adults. *Leisure/Loisir*, 29(2), 301–328. https://doi.org/10.1080/14927713.2005.9651333
Dalmer, N., & Griffin, M. (2022). "Still open and here for you": News media's framing of Canadian public libraries during COVID-19. *The Library Quarterly*, 92(2), 129–150. https://doi.org/10.1086/718599
Dalmer, N. K., & Mitrovica, B. L. (2022). The public library as social infrastructure for older patrons: Exploring the implications of online library programming for older adults during COVID-19. *Library & Information Science Research*, 44(3), 101177. https://doi.org/10.1016/j.lisr.2022.101177
Elliot, S. (2022, January 21). *Ontario's COVID-19 response: A history of announced measures, 2020-2022*. https://www.jdsupra.com/legalnews/ontario-s-covid-19-response-a-history-1280608/
Garner, J., Hider, P., Jamali, H. R., Lymn, J., Mansourian, Y., Randell-Moon, H., & Wakeling, S. (2021). 'Steady ships' in the COVID-19 crisis: Australian public library responses to the pandemic. *Journal of the Australian Library and Information Association*, 70(2), 102–124. https://doi.org/10.1080/24750158.2021.1901329
Gibson, H. J., & Singleton, J. F. (Eds.). (2012). *Leisure and aging: Theory and practice*. Human Kinetics.
Guinn, B. (1999). Leisure behaviour motivation and the life satisfaction of retired persons. *Activities, Adaptation & Aging*, 23(4), 13–20. https://doi.org/10.1300/J016v23n04_02
Haasio, A., & Kannasto, E. (2020). Covid-19 and its impact on Finnish public libraries. *Qualitative and Quantitative Methods in Libraries*, 3–19. http://78.46.229.148/ojs/index.php/qqml/article/view/639
Hayes, E., & Morris, A. (2005). Leisure role of public libraries: User views. *Journal of Librarianship and Information Science*, 37(3), 131–139. https://doi.org/10.1177/0961000605057480
Hayes, E., & Morris, A. (2005b). Leisure role of public libraries: A historical perspective. *Journal of Librarianship and Information Science*, 37(2), 75–81. https://doi.org/10.1177/0961000605055358
Hermes, J. (1995). *Reading women's magazines: An analysis of everyday media use*. Polity Press.

Hider, P. (2022). 'I can't afford to buy all the books I read': What public libraries offer leisure readers. *Journal of the Australian Library and Information Association*, *71*(2), 1–17. https://doi.org/10.1080/24750158.2022.2069640

Houghton, K., Foth, M., & Miller, E. (2013). The continuing relevance of the library as a third place for users and non-users of IT: The case of Canada Bay. *The Australian Library Journal*, *62*(1), 27–39. https://doi.org/10.1080/00049670.2013.771764

Jones, S. (2020). Optimizing public library resources in a post COVID-19 world. *Journal of Library Administration*, *60*(8), 951–957. https://doi.org/10.1080/01930826.2020.1820281

Kleiber, D. A., Hutchinson, S. L., & Williams, R. (2002). Leisure as a resource in transcending negative life events: Self-protection, self-restoration, and personal transformation. *Leisure Sciences*, *24*(2), 219–235. https://doi.org/10.1080/01490400252900167

Klingbeil, C. (2020, March 25). Canadian libraries respond to COVID-19. *Library Journal*. https://www.libraryjournal.com/story/canadian-libraries-respond-to-covid-19.

Leckie, G. J., & Buschman, J. E. (2007). Space, place, and libraries: An introduction. In J. E. Buschman & G. J. Leckie (Eds.), *The library as place: History, community, and culture* (pp. 3–25). Libraries Unlimited.

Loos, E., & Ivan, L. (2022). Not only people are getting old, the new media are too: Technology generations and the changes in new media use. *New Media & Society*, 146144482211017. https://doi.org/10.1177/14614448221101783

Lund, B. D., Wang, T., & Alenezi, A. (2022). Bookending a pandemic and its impact on public libraries: Policy and announcement information provided by libraries throughout the coronavirus (COVID-19) response. *Public Library Quarterly*, 1–13. https://doi.org/10.1080/01616846.2022.2102844

Luyt, B., & Ho, S. A. (2011). Reading, the library, and the elderly: A Singapore case study. *Journal of Librarianship and Information Science*, *43*(4), 204–212. https://doi.org/10.1177/0961000611418813

Magazines Canada. (2017). *Vividata's latest report shows Canadians love magazines*. https://magazinescanada.ca/news/vividatas-latest-report-shows-canadians-love-magazines/.

Mannell, R. C. (2007). Leisure, health and well-being. *World Leisure Journal*, *49*(3), 114–128. https://doi.org/10.1080/04419057.2007.9674499

Marshall, B. L. (2018). Happily ever after? 'Successful ageing' and the heterosexual imaginary. *European Journal of Cultural Studies*, *21*(3), 363–381. https://doi.org/10.1177/1367549417708434

Mayan, M. J. (2009). *Essentials of qualitative inquiry*. Left Coast Press.

McDonnell, A. (2014). *Reading celebrity gossip magazines*. Polity Press.

McMenemy, D., Robinson, E., & Ruthven, I. (2022). The impact of COVID-19 lockdowns on public libraries in the UK: Findings from a national study. *Public Library Quarterly*, 1–19. https://doi.org/10.1080/01616846.2022.2058860

Nimrod, G. (2017). Older audiences in the digital media environment. *Information, Communication & Society*, *20*(2), 233–249. https://doi.org/10.1080/1369118X.2016.1164740

Nimrod, G. (2019). Selective motion: Media displacement among older Internet users. *Information, Communication & Society*, *22*(9), 1269–1280. https://doi.org/10.1080/1369118X.2017.1414865

Nossek, H., Adoni, H., & Nimrod, G. (2015). Is print really dying? The state of print media use in Europe. *International Journal of Communication*, *9*, 365–385.

Oldenburg, R. (1989). *The great good place: Cafés, coffee shops, community centers, beauty parlors, general stores, bars, hangouts, and how they get you through the day*. Paragon House Publishers.

Ontario Library Association. (2020). *Ontario public library response to COVID-19*. https://accessola.com/wp-content/uploads/2020/08/2020-06-PLResponsetoCOVID-19-SurveyReport.pdf

Peine, A., Marshall, B. L., Martin, W., & Neven, L. (2021). *Socio-gerontechnology: Interdisciplinary critical studies of ageing and technology*. Taylor & Francis.

Quan-Haase, A., Martin, K., & Schreurs, K. (2016). Interviews with digital seniors: ICT use in the context of everyday life. *Information, Communication & Society*, *19*(5), 691–707. https://doi.org/10.1080/1369118X.2016.1140217

Ranger, M. (2021, March 11). "Timeline: A year of pandemic life in Toronto." *CityNews Toronto*. https://toronto.citynews.ca/2021/03/11/timeline-a-year-of-pandemic-life/.

Robinson, E., Ruthven, I., & McMenemy, D. (2022). Delivering services in the new normal: Recording the experiences of UK public library staff during the COVID-19 pandemic. *Journal of Librarianship and Information Science*, 096100062210933. https://doi.org/10.1177/09610006221093371

Robinson, J. D., Skill, T., & Turner, J. W. (2004). Media usage patterns and portrayals of seniors. In J. Coupland & J. F. Nussbaum (Eds.), *Handbook of communication and aging research* (pp. 443–466). Routledge.

Rosales, N. (2021). Public library responses to COVID-19: An investigation & reflection of Canadian experiences. *Emerging Library & Information Perspectives*, *4*(1), 169–185. https://doi.org/10.5206/elip.v4i1.13852

Ross, C. S. (2018). Adult readers. In C. S. Ross, L. McKechnie, & P. M. Rothbauer (Eds.), *Reading matters: What the research reveals about reading, libraries, and community* (pp. 137–146). ABC-CLIO.

Ross, C. S., McKechnie, L. E., & Rothbauer, P. M. (2006). *Reading matters: What the research reveals about reading, libraries, and community*. Libraries Unlimited.

Ross, C. S., McKechnie, L. E., & Rothbauer, P. M. (2018). *Reading still matters: What the research reveals about reading, libraries, and community.* ABC-CLIO.

Rothbauer, P., & Dalmer, N. (2018). Reading as a lifeline among aging readers: Findings from a qualitative interview study with older adults. *Library & Information Science Research, 40*(3–4), 165–172. https://doi.org/10.1016/j.lisr.2018.08.001

Sawchuk, D., & Ly, M. (2022). Older women using women's magazines: The construction of knowledgeable selves. *Ageing & Society, 42*(4), 765–785. https://doi.org/10.1017/S0144686X20001129

Scales, A. M., & Rhee, O. (2001). Adult reading habits and patterns. *Reading Psychology, 22*(3), 175–203. https://doi.org/10.1080/027027101753170610

Silk, M., Millington, B., Rich, E., & Bush, A. (2016). Digital leisure cultures [Special issue]. *Leisure Studies 35,* 6.

Smith, M. C. (1993). The reading abilities and practices of older adults. *Educational Gerontology, 19*(5), 417–432. https://doi.org/10.1080/0360127930190505

Smith, M. C. (1996). Differences in adults' reading practices and literacy proficiencies. *Reading Research Quarterly, 31*(2), 196–219. https://doi.org/10.1598/RRQ.31.2.5

Smith, J. (2020). Information in crisis: Analysing the future roles of public libraries during and post-COVID-19. *Journal of the Australian Library and Information Association, 69*(4), 422–429. https://doi.org/10.1080/24750158.2020.1840719

Stebbins, R. A. (2009). Leisure and its relationship to library and information science: Bridging the gap. *Library Trends, 57*(4), 618–631. https://doi.org/10.1353/lib.0.0064

Stevens, L., Maclaran, P., & Catterall, M. (2007). A space of one's own: Women's magazine consumption within family life. *Journal of Consumer Behaviour: An International Research Review, 6*(4), 236–252. https://doi.org/10.1002/cb.219

Vaportzis, E., Clausen, M. G., & Gow, A. J. (2017). Older adults perceptions of technology and barriers to interacting with tablet computers: A focus group study. *Frontiers in Psychology, 8.* https://doi.org/10.3389/fpsyg.2017.01687

Wang, T., & Lund, B. (2020). Announcement information provided by United States' public libraries during the 2020 COVID-19 pandemic. *Public Library Quarterly, 39*(4), 283–294. https://doi.org/10.1080/01616846.2020.1764325

Winship, J. (1987). *Inside women's magazines.* Pandora.

Wolf, M. (2018). *Reader, come home.* Harper Collins.

Ylänne, V. (2021). UK magazine advertising portrayals of older adults: A longitudinal, content analytic, and a social semiotic lens. *International Journal of Ageing and Later Life, 15*(1), 7–38. https://doi.org/10.3384/ijal.1652-8670.1700

Ytre-Arne, B. (2011a). Women's magazines and their readers: The relationship between textual features and practices of reading. *European Journal of Cultural Studies, 14*(2), 213–228. https://doi.org/10.1177/1367549410389928

Ytre-Arne, B. (2011b). 'I want to hold it in my hands': Readers' experiences of the phenomenological differences between women's magazines online and in print. *Media, Culture & Society, 33*(3), 467–477. https://doi.org/10.1177/0163443711398766

Armchair travel through video games: stories from elsewheres and elsewhens

Serkan Uzunogullari

ABSTRACT
COVID-19 has caused stress, negative emotions, and a reduction in physical and social activity due to the lockdown measures that were necessary for public health. During this period, many had to negotiate professional and familial responsibilities and were challenged to carve out time for leisure indoors. Using autoethnography as a method of inquiry, this research explores 'armchair travel' through video games as a leisure activity. Therefore, the article discusses memories and feelings of escaping the confines of domestic space from the perspective of self. Armchair travel via video games may provide an endless array of sights and sensations, bringing up feelings of leisure and contentment when real-world isolation and restriction are the norms.

Introduction

Lockdown, shutdown, and self-isolation were the primary responses to COVID-19 worldwide. While restrictions were aimed at protecting people's biological health, their consequential behavioural, emotional, and social impact did not go unnoticed (Brooks et al., 2020; Zhang et al., 2020). From a psychological perspective, confinement, loss of routine, and diminished social contact contributed to feelings of depression, irritation, insomnia, anger or emotional tiredness (Brooks et al., 2020). Lockdown measures have also increased time spent in-home leisure activities, which generally entail watching television in the living room (Beck & Arnold, 2009). However, recent research on the pandemic's impact on leisure highlighted other in-home activities such as gaming (Deloitte, 2021)

Some people consider video gaming a simple pastime, but for others, it is an integral part of contemporary cultural, commercial, social, and personal life (Bryce & Rutter, 2003; Mills, 2019). Even before the Covid-19, virtual, spatial and perceptual experiences were hot topics (Verhoeff, 2012). According to Kavanagh et al. (2016), virtual worlds and new technologies have altered contemporary leisure time and offered vast alternatives for leisure. Consequently, there is an increasing interest in virtual experiences in the tourism and leisure industry (tom Dieck et al., 2018). Lawrence (2003) stated that many of us are becoming 'virtual leisurists' by getting used to spending our leisure time in confined cyberspace rather than getting out and mingling with others physically. Hence, video gaming can fulfil various personal, social and emotional needs by providing enjoyment, escape, a form of social contact, or a stress relief mechanism (Barr & Copeland-Stewart, 2022; Calleja, 2010; Granic et al., 2014; Mills, 2019; Muriel & Crawford, 2018; Wardyga, 2019).

This paper aims to analyse lockdown leisure in single-player sandbox video games and how they become a tool for armchair travel, permitting a getaway from cosy but restricted domestic space. The paper will share personal reflections of the author's spatial, social, and emotional encounters as an armchair traveller during the lockdown. Therefore, the paper will discuss video gaming as lockdown leisure from the perspective of the self, which is a common method for autoethnography (Adams et al., 2015). Consequently, this study is novel, as no previous research has examined video games in relation to armchair travel, and there has been little research on video games using autoethnography (A. Rapp, 2017, A. Rapp, 2017).

Literature review

Intricacies of Armchair Travel: Narrative and Aesthetics

Armchair travel is an umbrella term explaining the mediated experience of locations and landscapes through a variety of forms of media, including literature, arts, paintings, panoramas, photographs, moving pictures, and sound (Byerly, 2012; Hornstein, 2011; Jørgensen, 2014; Stiegler, 2013; Wolf, 2018). In other words, the experience of a journey through the power of verbal or visual representations is referred to as armchair travel (Byerly, 2012). Therefore, armchair travel is integrating the two key antecedent concepts, narrative and aesthetics, into a relational meaning to explain what is experienced by a partaker.

The concept of narrative as a journey is ingrained in literary tradition (Byerly, 2012). Wolf (2018) suggests that early attempts at virtual travel began with Aristophanes' The Birds (414 B.C.) or Shakespeare's The Tempest (1611), to the more familiar Alice in Wonderland (1865). Famously, in the Theory of the Literary Chronotope. Bakthin (Bakhtin & Holquist, 1981) discusses the fundamental unity of narrative time and space in literary representations and emphasises the importance of shifting spatial and temporal awareness from physical to fictional worlds through narrative. Consequently, the experience of cognitive, emotional and perceptual captivation in a narrative is often known as 'narrative transportation (Gerrig, 1993; Green & Brock, 2002; Green et al., 2004; Greenwood, 2008).

The act of travelling is also employed as a metaphor for aesthetic engagement, which encompasses the absorption of aesthetics as an experience, temporary sensory activity (Byerly, 2012). Perspective-based or ceiling paintings of the 16th and 17th centuries (Wolf, 2018), mass printing and early photography of the 19th century (Stiegler, 2013), or visual devices of the early 20th-century including the magic lantern, phantasmagoria, panorama, and diorama facilitated 'motionless trips' (Clarke and Doel, 2005) or 'travelling without travelling' (Stiegler, 2013). Indeed, *'armchair travel'* has become a common term describing qualities of the aesthetic experience of seeing the world through the mediation of art and literature (Byerly, 2012; Stiegler, 2013).

Although aesthetic contemplation is typically emphasised in the visual arts, when the item remains still and the viewer's experience evolves over time (Atkinson & Parsayi, 2021), films may deliver a noticeably richer and more satisfying aesthetic experience by abandoning such fixed points of view (Byerly, 2012). Appraising the idea of armchair travel in films through the lenses of narrative and aesthetics invites us to consider Deleuze's (2005, 2013) reflections on the construction of perceptive worlds in cinema through movement and time. Deleuze (2005) argues that films can create images that illustrate and perform, which ultimately results in new aesthetics. Similar to Bakhtin's idea of narrative time and space in literary works, films also allow a journey into the fabric of space and time, which is independent of real-time and space (Arnheim, 1957; Clarke and Doel, 2005). Hence, Leonard (1996) charmingly proposed that films are space-and-time transports that allow spectators to travel 'elsewheres and elsewhens'. However, armchair travel can be about presence just as well as virtual transportation. Indeed, Deleuze (2013) goes further to suggest that cinema could induce an immersive state in which a spectator coexists in a fluid reality between physical and imaginary. Not surprisingly, this discussion reminds readers of Bergson's Mind-

Energy (Bergson, 1975), which also highlights the duality of an individual in narrative theory or literary experiences. Byerly (2012) has suggested a similar thesis in armchair travel and adds that aesthetic absorption allows users to interact with two places simultaneously, being both a spectator and an actual traveller. Moreover, in video games, the player is aware of and experiencing both their non-game and in-game identities at the same time (Mukherjee, 2015).

In this context, as a narrative and aesthetic experience, armchair travel has evolved with the media. In contemporary society, video games are commonly associated with escapism (Calleja, 2010; Muriel & Crawford, 2018; Newman, 2017; Wardyga, 2019). Escapism is defined as the way we temporarily get away from mundane parts of our everyday lives (Muriel & Crawford, 2018). While video games offer an escape from the mundanity and limited possibilities of reality (Muriel & Crawford, 2018), they can also be regarded as forms of art (Atkinson & Parsayi, 2021; Kim, 2023; Niedenthal, 2009; Tavinor, 2009). Due to their narrative, they are a form of minor literature (Mukherjee, 2015). Like the traditional forms of art, video games engage with themes concerning aesthetics, representation, narrative, emotional engagement, and even morality (Tavinor, 2009). Therefore, they are suitable for analysis from an aesthetic perspective, even though the historical aesthetic values and classifications developed for static art forms might not be entirely appropriate for evaluating video games due to their immersive and interactive aspects (Atkinson & Parsayi, 2021; Kim, 2023).

In traditional media, the focus is on replicability and static representations that can be thoroughly analysed and positioned in relation to their unique timeframes (Wessely, 2013). A video game, on the other hand, allows for a wide variety of gaming paths (Wessely, 2013). As a form of art, video games are not only able to illustrate imaginative worlds and narratives, but they can also depict worlds that change based on how the player interacts with them (Tavinor, 2009). While a moviegoer has no effect on the portrayed fictional world, a player has an active part in creating it (Tavinor, 2009). Therefore, a video game player is often identified as a flaneur (Dalal, 2014; Pelurson, 2019). Discussing the virtual mobility in video games, Dalal (2014) concludes that the player becomes a new kind of virtual flânerie who engages in a virtual form of mobility infused with the pleasures of exploring through the viewing and playing experience. It is thus possible to imagine a virtual travel experience in many quest-based or open world games (Byerly, 2012).

In sum, an armchair traveller is someone who explores the world from home, discovering cultures, meanings, narratives, and connections (Bayard, 2016; Jørgensen, 2014). Similarly, many modern video games can offer an opportunity for armchair travel to a new reproduced space and time, which is virtual, temporal and ephemeral. While the academic backgrounds for armchair travel are derived from different theoretical perspectives, they often complement each other to offer a fuller discourse on the phenomenon.

The Interplay of Flow and Rule-Breaking

The research in armchair travel through video games has followed other research into the forests of flow and rule-breaking. Flow refers to a state in which a person is engaged and very focused, to the point of losing any sense of self-awareness or of time as a result of immersion (Csikszentmihalyi, 1990, 2000). In video games, flow often refers to a condition of focused, engaged happiness and enjoyment (Salen Tekinbaş & Zimmerman, 2003; Schell, 2008). Moreover, flow occurs when an experience meets eight criteria: 'a challenging activity that requires skills, the merging of action and awareness clear goals and feedback, concentration on the task at hand, the paradox of control, the loss of self-consciousness, the transformation of time' (Csikszentmihalyi, 1990, p.49). It is precisely those properties of games that make them fertile ground for a flow experience (Salen Tekinbaş & Zimmerman, 2003). Therefore, flow is extensively discussed in the field of video game studies (Nah et al., 2014; Salen Tekinbaş & Zimmerman, 2003). For example, challenges and skills are an integral part of gaming. To avoid frustration or boredom, a video game cannot be too hard or too easy (Schell, 2008; Siitonen, 2014). Likewise, players receive positive feedback from successful performance in a game, enhancing their perception of competence through flow (Nah et al., 2014). Indeed, the goal of game designers is to get their players into a state of flow (Salen Tekinbaş & Zimmerman, 2003).

However, viewing armchair travel through video games from the perspective of flow, which typically considers the player's flow state as a response to proportionate challenges, may be limited, given that not pressuring the player to constantly engage with challenges and achieve objectives are more likely to encourage contemplation and attention to the aesthetics (Atkinson & Parsayi, 2021). Therefore, armchair travel through video games invites us to consider players' behaviours that contend with the game designers' anticipations, structures, rules and choices. Subsequently, this kind of gaming behaviour may be linked to violating the designed and anticipated rules of the video game. Rule-breaking means having a different connection with the games than what those games are designed to imply and endorse (Salen Tekinbaş & Zimmerman, 2003). Therefore, rule-breaking ranges from being only slightly transgressive to being completely contrary to the law, and it can include examples of easter eggs (secrets hidden in a game), cheats, gaming guides, walkthroughs, workarounds, and forms of hacking (Salen Tekinbaş & Zimmerman, 2003). Rule-breaking is not exceptional; many theories of gaming are concerned with disobeying behaviours.

The concepts of countergaming (Galloway, 2006), counterplay (Meades, 2015) or queer gaming (Pelurson, 2019, 2021) have similar approaches in their consideration of challenges for the pre-determined order, structure, and guidelines of video games. Galloway's (2006) concept of countergaming primarily focuses on modifying games to disrupt their natural flow of gameplay, their visual design, the laws of the game and even software technology. Most importantly, it emphasises aesthetics instead of interactive play. Galloway's (2006) states that countergaming is not intended to enhance the gameplay in any way but rather to impede it. On the other hand, 'counterplay' is defined as a kind of gaming in which players actively work against the rules and against each other in order to find new methods to have fun and experience new kinds of pleasures, and includes, but is not limited to, cheating, modding (the alteration of game aspects), hacking and griefing (deliberately irritating other players inside a game) (Meades, 2015). Queer game studies also challenge and examine traditional gaming culture and its identities, values, and structures by highlighting unusual video games, breaking their rules, and experiencing and playing them differently (Pelurson, 2021). Most importantly, it finely complements the previous theories of countergaming and counterplay, as well as draws attention to ideas of exploration, orientation and embodiment (Pelurson, 2021).

To sum up, the flow theory explains the holistic sensation, complete immersion in games, what a player feels when they act with total involvement and development and the distinction between flow-state and non-flow state. In contrast, theories that consider breaking the rules make room for aesthetic experiences and new kinds of pleasures, even if this is simply against the gameplay.

Embodiment and Avatar

As the digital culture grows, leisure has become more complex and intertwined with physical and virtual lives (Kavanagh et al., 2016; Lawrence, 2003; Silk et al., 2016). Consequently, the notion of technology as a separate entity has shifted to one of embodiment (Kavanagh et al., 2016). Likewise, an individual's embodiment in a virtual world is an avatar, and it is through this extension that one sees the virtual world (Behm-Morawitz, 2013).

In terms of armchair travel, the avatar is not a new concept, as many forms of art and literature use a proxy figure, a surrogate that transports audiences, readers, or spectators into a world of imagination to captivate them (Byerly, 2012). Although these approaches have their differences, the concept of an avatar links the virtual and physical body (Behm-Morawitz, 2013). Thus, a person's digital identity becomes an extension of their physical identity and self (Behm-Morawitz, 2013; Kavanagh et al., 2016) or even more (Silk et al., 2016). Moreover, avatar identification, a temporary merging of characteristics of the avatar with concepts of the self, has the potential to magnify some of the effects and consequences of gaming (Allen & Anderson, 2021). Indeed, instead of the third-person protagonist of a novel or film, players speak about their characters in a game using their own first-person pronouns, such as 'I', rather than using the third-person narrator (Bernal-Merino, 2015).

According to Salen Tekinbaş and Zimmerman (2003), a gaming avatar is both a mask to wear and a tool to view and manipulate. A player's actions will decide the course of events for the avatar, and by extension, they will affect the course of events for the virtual world (Ryan, 2006). Subsequently, players can choose their avatar's gender, race, or occupation in certain games, and this information can also have a profound impact on the virtual world (Bernal-Merino, 2015).

Playing a video game is an embodied experience (Muriel & Crawford, 2018). The only method to perceive a game's environment is via immersive perception and movement of the avatar (Kim, 2023). A game is played by seeing, feeling, hearing, smelling, and tasting it; by moving the body, feeling the unfolding of events, communicating with others and changing thought patterns (Salen Tekinbaş & Zimmerman, 2003). The players inhabit the virtual world and the bodies of their avatars and adopt the persona of the characters for as long as they choose (Bernal-Merino, 2015). Most importantly, the visual presentation of avatars might continue to influence our thoughts and actions long after we have stopped playing games (Madigan, 2016).

Methodology

Ellis (2004, p. 37) defines autoethnography as 'writing about the personal and its relationship to culture'. Autoethnography also allow a researcher to share their reflections and understandings with others (Adams et al., 2015). It requires an author to display multiple layers of consciousness (Ellis, 2004). The significance of autoethnographic research lies in giving an insight to the reader about how we perceived the situation and why we did what we did (Adams & Ellis, 2012). Indeed, autoethnography revolves around acknowledgement, confrontation and integration of subjective experiences, beliefs and values (Trussell, 2010). It is a cultural analysis through personal narrative (Ellis, 2004), which allows readers to see the world from the autoethnographer's eyes (Denzin, 2006; Trussell, 2010). Consequently, the lived experience is drawn a great deal of attention in leisure autoethnographies (Anderson and Austin, 2012).

According to Adams et al. (2015), self-examination of our own identity, experiences, relationships, and communities represent the core aspects of autoethnography. It requires authors to critically interrogate their personal relationships and take the front stage by using an active voice while disclosing their understandings (Markwell, 2019). Consequently, it is an intimate activity with significant personal risks (Adams et al., 2015). On the other hand, it also offers a unique and useful perspective on social life, one that may lead to compelling discoveries for researchers and readers (Anderson and Austin, 2012).

Considering that leisure in isolation is something unique to each person, who was vis à vis with lockdown measures and lacked access to typical leisure activities with increased social barriers, a reflexive discourse through auto-ethnography where one questions, analyses, and reveals their personal, social or cultural experiences appears to be appropriate.

Ultimately, the study comprises personal reflections and meaning-making (Miles, 2019). It is a form of storytelling based on the lived experience of one's own past (Bochner & Ellis, 2016), where the 'story is theory and theory is story' (Adams et al., 2015, p.90). Therefore, this autoethnographic study came to life as a by-product of COVID-19 lockdown and my interest in video games. It became clear to me that there were recurring themes in my experiences as I wrote down my emotions, thoughts and epiphanies and chronicled my play during the lockdown. The discovery of these patterns caused me to critically reflect on my life of confinement and the ways in which I sought solace in virtual worlds. An important caveat concerning this article is 'where my story cannot be your story, and where your story cannot be mine' (Gannon, 2013, p.21). In other words, the stories of the author and reader might only resonate or ripple with each other, but they are never quite unified nor universal (Gannon, 2013).

Research Context

I live in the North East of England, and my life revolves around my nuclear family, which consists of my wife, two children, and a hamster. Other than one or two annual short-haul trips, our family leisure time was usually spent visiting local restaurants, pubs, cinemas, or national parks. Society's biggest change in terms of family life challenges came when the entire population of the United Kingdom was sentenced to house arrest on 26 March 2020. I got caught up in my own health concerns, working from home, family chores and homeschooling. Suddenly, my life has filled with an array of intense emotions alternating between; denial, shock, fear, anxiety, loneliness, gratitude and appreciation on a daily basis. Even though we had looked at the different ways to pass the time and stay entertained, I realised that spending time as a family forms better memories than being in a lockdown together. I realised that home-based leisure activities for a transnational (British-Turkish), dual-earner family are hard. There is already evidence suggesting that indoor family leisure is scarce, fragmented, time-limited, relatively passive, and rather dissatisfying (Beck & Arnold, 2009).

As time passed, the bizarre novelty of lockdown quickly evolved into something grimmer and depressing. With each day, I became hazy, fatigued and conflicted between my duties as a lecturer, researcher, father, homeschooling teacher and husband, each interacting with or interrupting each other. Ultimately, I must wake up, feed and set the homeschooling tasks for my kids, work, research, tidy each day and begin the next day all over again. Consequently, my principles of what makes a 'good' person, employee, father or husband blurred. I felt like an actor who was cast for multiple plays and had to play them simultaneously. It was a hard, mind-boggling, conflicted experience. Due to the sheer lack of time, I got into a routine ritual of video gaming at night. It is not unusual for a parent to carve out personal leisure time when the other people in the house are not around (Beck & Arnold, 2009). Therefore, when everybody in the house was in bed, I launched video games where I could travel and explore without my wallet, passport or fear of infection.

Thus, I utilised autoethnography to analyse my own leisure and armchair travel during lockdown when I often lost myself in the virtual worlds of single-player, narrative-driven and sandbox games, including Horizon Zero Dawn (Guerrilla Games, 2017), Red Dead Redemption 2 (Studios, 2018), Hitman 2 (IO Interactive, 2018), Mafia 3 (2K Games, 2016) and Assassin's Creed Valhalla (Ubisoft Montreal, 2020). In these games, there are little to no constraints put on how a player might achieve their objectives. Therefore, with every playthrough, I decide how quickly or slowly space-time, narrative and characters unfold. This has proven to be the most gratifying, memorable, and interesting for me.

Through my experiences, I visited cities of the Early Middle Ages (Assassin's Creed Valhalla) or post-apocalyptic civilisations (Horizon Zero Dawn) and crossed majestic mountains, rivers and plateaus. I enjoyed walks by the houses with verandas in fictional New Orleans (Mafia 3), or sipping coffee in the western frontier (Red Dead Redemption 2). The journey put me in the crossover of technology, embodiment, memory and inspiration, where I became an armchair traveller. The selected fragments of my notes and epiphanies are utilised in the findings and discussion chapter. After thematic analysis, I organised my findings under the following subheadings; the precarity of armchair travel, the escapism and alternative gaming: elsewheres and elsewhens, and becoming the avatar.

Findings and Discussion

The Precarity of Armchair Travel

'It is 11:16 pm. The television in the family room is turned off. I told my wife that I would stay awake longer. She is never particularly pleased when I say that. She said: "don't stay up too late". She knows that I will be probably tired tomorrow. After I put on my pyjamas, I came back into the room and lay down on the floor

facing the television. I turned the TV and PlayStation on and flicked through the games until I found something that I wanted to play'.
(April 2020)

[Same night] I climb slowly up into the Meridian city, which is sitting on a mesa. The sun is shining from the light blue sky. The climate feels arid and hot. Orangey-red walls surround the city[...] (Game: Horizon Zero Dawn)
(April 2020)

I could hear the hamster running on her wheel from where I sit. I got up and gave the hamster a treat. She has been making too much noise. Then lied down on the floor and unpaused my game. A few minutes later, the hamster continued to run on her wheel.
(May 2020)

The aforementioned vignettes provide the impression that armchair travel has its own ritual, in addition to demonstrating the many ways in which such experiences might potentially flourish or fail. Pre-travel moments often include one's typical routine; maybe finishing off my work, having dinner, putting the kids to bed or feeding our pet. Then the armchair travel moments directly involved me in exploring the unknown or the familiar places and communities and carving my own story. As Salen Tekinbaş and Zimmerman (2003) stated, flow is a sensation of control and mastery over one's own destiny and performance.

The quiet withdrawal of single players who are in a state of flow is a common occurrence (Schell, 2008). Similarly, I was filled with happiness within a few minutes of video gaming when I settled on my sofa in the dark. After all, the optimal happiness that someone feels is something that is shared across all types of flow states (Salen Tekinbaş & Zimmerman, 2003). It is also known that there is a significant link between happiness and one's satisfaction with leisure and recreational activities (Lyubomirsky et al., 2005). Early days of the lockdown, I also noted; 'For many travellers, a station or a terminal is the starting point of their journey. For me, a two-seater sofa across my tv screen. It is leisurely and effortless'.

Early on, I pointed out in the vignettes the colour of the sky and climate in a video game session which was played and recorded in the middle of the night. Thus, armchair travel includes a wide variety of emotional and sensory experiences, many of which would not be explained merely with the flow. The relationship between players and the gameplay environment has also been explored in aesthetics. Niedenthal (2009) recognises that visual, aural and tactile pleasures can be derived from the play experience. Consequently, the development of aesthetics occurs as the result of our own physiological enjoyment of the game's mechanics (Niedenthal, 2009). In spite of Atkinson and Parsayi's (Atkinson & Parsayi, 2021) assertion that the connection between video games and their players may be incompatible with aesthetic contemplation because of the immersion, interaction, and speed of gameplay; Kim (Kim, 2023) claims that the audio-visual stimuli of video games do indeed broaden the manner in which aesthetic values are absorbed and experienced. In point of fact, a player's total immersion and engagement in a game are prerequisites for a sublime experience (Kim, 2023). Furthermore, Wolf (2013) asserts that, apart from engagement and emotional involvement, the mental experience of an imaginary world offered by an artefact is the most important aspect of experiencing an aesthetic illusion.

However, not every video gaming session can create the same mental state of armchair travel, same emotions, or the same involvement with the same intensity. Similarly, Wolf (2013) considers that aesthetic illusion is gradable and unstable. As in the early vignette, extraneous distractions such as an unexpected noise may interfere with armchair travel and disturb the journey. Furthermore, aesthetic illusion can be suspended, broken, or destroyed by various external factors, such as a lack of concentration or the emergence of a subconscious knowledge of representation (Wolf, 2013). Likewise, the flow state requires that other thoughts are removed, and distractions are ignored while focusing on the task (Csikszentmihalyi, 1990; Nah et al., 2014; Salen Tekinbaş & Zimmerman, 2003; Schell, 2008). In addition to that, solo gamers in a flow state may be reluctant to interact with others or even frustrated by external distractions (Schell, 2008). From this viewpoint, the aesthetic illusion and state of flow in video games are wrapped up with armchair travel. Simply, armchair travel is fragile and vulnerable. Whenever a change in the external environment or background events occur, they put the armchair traveller into a new dynamic, perhaps a more stranded one.

Escapism and Alternative Gaming: Elsewheres and Elsewhens

> It is perhaps one of the grandest spectacles in the world, big rivers, lakes, and marshes. I am unanchored. I am about to cross a river and some mountains wondering what was still to be found ahead of me. Deers, ducks, geese, hares or grizzly bears. (Game: Red Dead Redemption 2)
>
> [Mumbai] These alleyways feel lively and busy, jammed with people and cluttered with market stalls. Some are selling traditional Indian clothing like choli or dupatta. Others are selling food. It is vibrant [...] While the environment might be designed to look exotic to Western eyes, I feel rather familiar with the spectacle. It reminds me overwhelming streets of Istanbul [my home town], the back alleys of Grand Bazaar or Egyptian Market. Thus, I am used to places like this, a fascinating maze, full of people, goods, food, local trinkets and cheap knockoffs.
> *(Game: Hitman 2)*
>
> I like cities that are imperfect and slightly unpleasant. It just adds it to its character. I like the idea of exploring places where locals outnumber the tourists, where the streets might not be kind. Alternatively, indeed, they might be slightly belligerent. (Game: Mafia 3)
>
> Occasionally, I found myself spending quite a bit of time on the virtual campfires and sipping coffee. Brewing the coffee from coffee grounds using a percolator and drinking it black. It is strong yet oddly comforting. I like my coffee black in real life too. It is bitter and unpretentious. No milk, no froth, no fuss.
> *(Game: Red Dead Redemption 2)*

To an observer, an armchair traveller appears 'here and now' while one can be in 'elsewhere and elsewhen'. In this simultaneous event, which is a puzzling aspect of armchair travel that remains unknown to the observer, the observer is stranded in rational space and time while the traveller is experiencing different time, movements or spaces. Multiple sources seem to confirm one another and highlight this phenomenon as a kind of paradigm for aesthetic or narrative absorption (Bergson, 1975; Byerly, 2012; Deleuze, 2013).

Following Bergson (1975), I assert that armchair travel splits the player into two; one who travels, acts and experiences, and one who stays and watches. Simply, this metaphorical concept comes into existence in the subjective and selective mind of an armchair traveller who is experiencing a dream, reverie, or fantasy. Consequently, the human capacity for imagination is intrinsically linked to escapism (Calleja, 2010). Armchair travel is fuelled by one's shifting attention from the physical world to the aesthetic illusion of the virtual world or simply escaping from an undesirable place to a favourable imaginative one (Calleja, 2010). Accordingly, the autonomy provided by open-world and sandbox games (Atkinson & Parsayi, 2021) allowed me to escape from my restricted domestic space in the lockdown and be elsewhere that is more favourable, pleasant and free. My escape to virtual worlds was intensified by navigation, a process that often rewards the curious. I discovered more profound things that reconnected me with the real world, such as my home town, Istanbul, even though Hitman 2 game was based in Mumbai. Similarly, Atkinson and Parsayi (2021) state that navigation can be a precondition of aesthetic engagement.

It is not surprising that my leisurely in-game actions often prevented the video game from progressing and ending my travel experience. The games allow players to occupy the virtual environment and their avatars for as long as they like (Bernal-Merino, 2015). Thus, I continued to engage in leisurely activities. One of these experiences I enjoyed during the lockdown was listening to myths and stories from Jomsvikings (warrior oarsmen and women) in Assassin's Creed Valhalla. Similarly, in Red Dead Redemption 2, I periodically engaged with virtual stargazing, fishing, brewing and drinking coffee. These were unexpected acts, of course, that are contrary to video gaming which demands players to progress by following the established rules. This type of gaming behaviour is commonly associated with rule-breaking (Salen Tekinbaş & Zimmerman, 2003), countergaming (Galloway, 2006), counterplay (Meades, 2015) or queer gaming (Pelurson,

2019, 2021). All of these concepts pose a challenge for the predetermined order, structure, and guidelines that are typically associated with games. Rule-breaking means having a different connection with the games than what that games are designed to imply and endorse (Salen Tekinbaş & Zimmerman, 2003).

During the lockdown, I was able to return to my favourite virtual places over and over again in favour of directionless but rather fabulous experiences. Pelurson (2019, 2021) discusses this type of player as a gaming flaneur who takes their time, roams aimlessly, or postpones a primary plot for no apparent reason, even though such behaviour can be considered meaningless by ordinary players. From the countergaming perspective, my aesthetic experimentation took precedence over interactive gameplay (Galloway, 2006). This is not to deny that some games can be fundamentally more engaging due to their interactivity. Instead, my experience highlights that some games can offer players discovering their own sense of fulfilment via aimless exploration of elsewheres and elsewhens offered by game worlds.

Becoming the Avatar

The game tells a story of who I am alongside what happened to the earth. I am [Aloy is] am determined, and strong-minded. She reminds me of Lara Croft. But somehow, she feels more authentic, less sexualised[...] Leather, hide, and fur combined with robotic dinosaur parts and plates look seriously fashionable.

(Game: Horizon Zero Dawn)

I am [Lincoln is] a Vietnam veteran. He is a complex, emotional and somewhat honourable character. He is a smart talker, direct and straight to the point. You know where you stand with Lincoln. No hidden agendas or what-ifs. It is a simple [...]. A three-piece black suit with a tie is my go-to outfit. It gives me a sophisticated, sleek look with its sharp cut. It certainly makes a statement.

(Game: Mafia 3)

I am a Caucasian male, with a distinctively pale complexion, blue eyes and no hair, who is trying to blend in the streets of Mumbai. Sadly, I stick out like a sore thumb. Simply, I am an outsider and unwary traveller who is knocked every time when passing people.

(Game: Hitman 2)

[...] I chose to be the lone traveller, with an intent on finding things and wandering places. [...] I have a traditional oval-shape brim hat, ready to salute a friendly passer-by [...] My gang is mostly composed of criminals, robbers and those who want to live outside of the societal norms. They are a charming company, yet there is plenty of dust and dirt on them. Old boots or moccasins, cattleman hats, vests or jackets made from fur or pelt, worn trousers or dresses are the common looks.

(Game: Red Dead Redemption 2)

This part of the findings draws upon the idea of the avatar in the armchair travel as an agent of embodiment. Armchair travel in video games allowed my physical body to be submitted to a virtual one which is invulnerable to contamination and the Covid-19 infection from the outside world. My exemplars were included a deeply flawed, a talkative outlaw who, in the fictionalised American frontier, conducts a series of socially undesirable actions (Red Dead Redemption 2); a Viking clan leader from Norway who can alternate between male and female appearance via the game mechanic (Assassin's Creed Valhalla); a Dominican descent Vietnam veteran in 1960s (Mafia 3); an apathetic and reticent assassin for hire with a noticeably pale complexion (Hitman 2); a Caucasian female with long red hair and freckles in the year 3000s whose curiosity about the world can be infectious (Horizon Zero Dawn).

With a switch of a button, I can be anyone who is a little bit of me and a little bit of an algorithm. Consequently, the avatar serves as a virtual representation of oneself and allows one to experience a virtual landscape and participate in the events. (Byerly, 2012; Kim, 2023). As Bernal-Merino (2015) stated, rather than relying on a third-person language to describe my in-game experiences, the majority of my notes and vignettes were written in the first-person language, demonstrating my internalisation of my in-game avatars regardless of their appearances or backgrounds.

Considering many video games allow one to decide on their gender, race or simply appearance within the limits of the game mechanic (Bernal-Merino, 2015), or what I call pseudo-societal norms of the game, an armchair traveller as an avatar often fits into the virtual world. For example, in the Red Dead Redemption 2, with my avatar's oval-shape brim hat and boots, I felt like a member of the virtual world and its community. I talked to the residents, played cards or ride horses with them. Similarly, I spent significant amount of time talking and interacting with the members of different tribes in the Horizon Zero Dawn. Though my avatars, my concerns about interacting with strangers, and the anxiety of being in social settings during the lockdown have reduced. I enjoyed being in the company of virtual strangers. Playing video games might help one re-evaluate emotional experiences and deal with feelings of anxiety or stress (Granic et al., 2014).

However, video games do not renounce all troubles of being in the world, they rather replace these by new troubles of their own. Rather than being a part of the community, I experienced the struggle of being a stranger in the Hitman 2. For example, the vignette about Hitman 2 above draws readers' attention to my perception of the embodied avatar as an outsider in terms of race or ethnicity rather than the game mechanics themselves. Similarly, the Mafia 3 game offers players around twenty different outfits for Lincoln Clay, the main protagonist. Yet, I found myself using the same sharp-looking 'three-piece black suit' all the time. Perhaps, my choice of outfit reflects my emotions about the character who was not only seeking revenge but also respect within conflicted, racially segregated American society in the 60s.

Due to their pre-programmed algorithms, video games cannot replicate the complexities of real-world social encounters, neither they are designed to do so. However, the embodied avatar, its customisation, and our behaviour or feelings as a result of it as a whole could not be restricted to simple attributes of the game. The appearance of an avatar can convey valuable information about the player and their personality (Madigan, 2016). While representing the player's physical reality, the avatar also serves as something that transcends it (Wessely, 2013). It grants opportunities for experimenting with self-identity, which exceeds the physical limits and real-life appearance of one's body (Shilling, 2005). The more you play, your avatar gets stronger, healthier, known or even more social within the game.

An avatar is not a mere copy of the self, but rather it is a simulated extension of the self that may influence one's feelings about the self, views of the world, and behaviours (Behm-Morawitz, 2013). Even more crucially, the interaction between the player and the avatar has repercussions not just in the virtual environment but also in the physical world (Behm-Morawitz, 2013; Madigan, 2016). Therefore, my avatars were both 'me' and 'not-me' at the same time (Wessely, 2013).

The player's decisions actually cause the in-game events to take place (Ryan, 2006). Therefore, the immersion of an avatar in an environment adds to the illusion that one is in a setting that is more real than it actually is (Byerly, 2012). This view has considerable implications. Because, the player is represented and so physically present inside the game as an avatar, their experiences are taken to be real (Wessely, 2013). In other words, my embodied avatar's experiences, choices or its reactions to fictional worlds, their events and characters might have been slightly different than my real-life situation and feelings, but I did experience them nevertheless.

Conclusion

Long before the COVID-19 pandemic and following lockdowns, Lawrence (2003) stated that in the age of cyberspace, the idea of leisure needs to be revisited. Similarly, Jørgensen (2014) argued that armchair travel is about directing our attention to the mediated character of locations, even though the shape and content of this mediation have changed over time. Due to significantly reduced time spent outdoors and ever-changing restrictions on leisure activities and social relationships due to the Covid-19, the concept of armchair travel required attention.

In light of this, the study investigated video games within the context of armchair travel during the lockdown. When many people's lives were characterised by inexorable loneliness and containment due to lockdowns, armchair travel through video games could provide all kinds of sights and experiences, eliciting feelings of leisure and happiness. Thus, the study established a record of the leisure episodes which were carved out during the multitude of struggles, contractions and concerns. Moreover, it demonstrated that armchair travel continues to pertain to dimensions of human experiences, including cognitive, interactive, aesthetic, imaginal, social and emotional experiences.

The study analysed how video games deliver the experience of armchair travel through aesthetic and embodied experiences in that they provide not only a means of escape from a confined physical space, or reduction in anxiety but also new pleasures, emotions, and associations with one's body, environment, and time. The study exposed that through interacting with the different aspects of a video game, a player reaches the point at which one no longer needs to pay conscious attention to the mechanics or the objectives of the video game. Instead, they gradually descend into a new reality where various gaming elements such as observation, exploration, movement or action turn into meaningful aesthetic insights. In contrast, Niedenthal (2009) states that from an aesthetic design standpoint, anticipation, motivation, and creating long-term memories are all important factors to consider while creating a video game. Through this, a player's aesthetic contemplation and pleasures are seen as anticipated response patterns that emerge as a result of programmers' design choices. If aesthetic experiences are simply design-based, they must result in reasonably standard patterns of behaviour and emotions in other players. Consequently, the question, as pointed out by Atkinson and Parsayi (2021, p.524), 'whether aesthetic contemplation can be scripted into the game design, or it occurs irrespective of the gameplay', remains. Considering the autoethnographic nature of the study, regardless of the validity of competing arguments, the fact that I participated in the events or was influenced by them makes my experiences unique and meaningful.

Video games often have a set sequence, structure, and rules. However, when a game offers freedom, experimentation, and a sense of being elsewhere and elsewhen, it is easy to get sidetracked, start wandering off to find different in-game pleasures and spend many hours without paying attention to the rules, structures or primary storyline. Interestingly, all theories of rule-breaking (Salen Tekinbaş & Zimmerman, 2003), countergaming (Galloway, 2006), counterplay (Meades, 2015) or queer gaming (Pelurson, 2019, 2021) seem to have a place for players' aimless wandering. While flânerie behaviour can be explained by these theories, they also pack many other aspects of gaming into their consideration, such as cheating, modding, hacking, altering algorithms, playing against other players, or wider matters of gender and inclusion. Despite the fact that these are important theories, it appears that breaking the rules is a natural element of playing games (Salen Tekinbaş & Zimmerman, 2003).

In terms of the embodied experience of armchair travel, following the Deleuzian perspective, I suspect that the player-armchair traveller is almost always positioned in a fluid reality, oscillating between physical and imaginary. Thus, a thin and fragile threshold distinguishes; mere video gaming from armchair travel, the physical world from the virtual one, real body from the avatar. Taken together, the characteristics of flow as well as other dimensions of experience such as aesthetics, imagination and emotions, the study suggests that video gaming can be classified as armchair travel when one feels deeper about the virtual world rather than the material one. Hence, the findings provide strong support for Byerly (2012), who asserted that the ultimate goal of all virtual environments is immersiveness.

In terms of limitations, it should also be noted that autoethnography has a highly self-centred nature (Bochner & Ellis, 2016). Therefore, the study's findings may not be generalisable. In one sense, that is true. However, autoethnography has always been tested by readers as they take into account whether a story resonates with their life or the others they know (Bochner & Ellis, 2016).

In terms of research implications, video games have never been examined in relation to armchair travel, and the autoethnography of video games has been relatively understudied (A. Rapp, 2017, A. Rapp, 2017). Even though the number of studies that investigate video games and game culture as a form of leisure is growing each and every day, they are less concerned with the first-hand lived experiences and rarely, if ever, consider the experience of video games in solitude. In addition to that, the multiplayer video games, due to their popularity and copresence experience that they provide, also call for scholarly attention using auto-ethnographic or duo-ethnographic methodologies. Thus, the research into armchair travel and video games should be continued, as virtual worlds are proving to be increasingly accessible and comfortable places to enjoy leisure.

Disclosure statement

No potential conflict of interest was reported by the author(s).

ORCID

Serkan Uzunogullari http://orcid.org/0000-0003-2866-3132

References

2K Games. (2016). *Mafia 3*. 2K Games.
Adams, T. E., & Ellis, C.2012.'Trekking Through Autoethnography'. *Qualitative research: An introduction to methods and designs* In: S. D. Lapan, M. T. Quartaroli, & F. J. Riemer Eds. 1st Jossey-Bass pp. 189–215
Adams, T. E., Holman Jones, S. L., & Ellis, C. (2015). *Autoethnography*. Oxford University Press.
Allen, J. J., & Anderson, C. A. (2021). Does avatar identification make unjustified video game violence more morally consequential? *Media psychology*, 24(2), 236–258. https://doi.org/10.1080/15213269.2019.1683030
Anderson L and Austin M. (2012). Auto-ethnography in leisure studies. Leisure Studies, 31(2), 131–146. 10.1080/02614367.2011.599069
Arnheim, Rudolf 1957 Film as Art (London: University of California Press, Ltd.)0-520-24837-6
Atkinson, P., & Parsayi, F. (2021). Video Games and Aesthetic Contemplation. *Games and Culture*, 16(5), 519–537. https://doi.org/10.1177/1555412020914726
Bakhtin, M. M., & Holquist, M. (1981). Forms of time and of the chronotope in the novel: Notes toward a historical poetics. In M. Holquist, C. Emerson (Eds.), *The Dialogic Imagination: Four Essays* (pp. 84–258). University of Texas Press.
Barr, M., & Copeland-Stewart, A. (2022). Playing Video Games During the COVID-19 Pandemic and Effects on Players' Well-Being. *Games and Culture*, 17(1), 15554120211017036. https://doi.org/10.1177/15554120211017036
Bayard, P. (2016). *How to talk about places you've never been: On the importance of armchair travel*. (M. Hutchison, Ed.). Bloomsbury.
Beck, M. E., & Arnold, J. E. (2009). Gendered time use at home: An ethnographic examination of leisure time in middle-class families. *Leisure Studies*, 28(2), 121–142. https://doi.org/10.1080/02614360902773888
Behm-Morawitz, E. (2013). Mirrored selves: The influence of self-presence in a virtual world on health, appearance, and well-being. *Computers in Human Behavior*, 29(1), 119–128. https://doi.org/10.1016/j.chb.2012.07.023
Bergson, H. (1975). *Mind-energy*. (W. H. Carr, Ed.). Greenwood Press (Lectures and Essays).
Bernal-Merino, M. Á. (2015). *Translation and localisation in video games: Making entertainment software global* advances in translation studies). Routledge (Routledge.
Bochner, A. P., & Ellis, C. (2016). *Evocative autoethnography: Writing lives and telling stories*. Left Coast Press (Writing lives.
Brooks, S. K., Webster, R. K., Smith, L. E., Woodland, L., Wessely, S., Greenberg, N., & Rubin, G. J. (2020). The psychological impact of quarantine and how to reduce it: Rapid review of the evidence. *The Lancet*, 395(10227), 912–920. https://doi.org/10.1016/S0140-6736(20)30460-8
Bryce, J., & Rutter, J. (2003). Gender dynamics and the social and spatial organization of computer gaming. *Leisure Studies*, 22(1), 1–15. https://doi.org/10.1080/02614360306571
Byerly, A. (2012). *Are we there yet? virtual travel and Victorian realism*. University of Michigan Press.

Calleja, G. (2010). Digital Games and Escapism. *Games and Culture*, *5*(4), 335–353. https://doi.org/10.1177/1555412009360412

Clarke D B and Doel M A. (2005). Engineering space and time: moving pictures and motionless trips. Journal of Historical Geography, 31(1), 41–60. 10.1016/j.jhg.2003.08.022

Csikszentmihalyi, M. (1990). *Flow: The psychology of optimal experience* (1st ed.). Harper & Row.

Csikszentmihalyi, M. (2000). *Beyond boredom and anxiety: Experiencing Flow in Work and Play* (25th anniversary ed.). Jossey-Bass Publishers.

Dalal, R. (2014). Spaces of the Past: Nostalgia in the Murder on the Orient Express and the Last Express. In D. Stobbart & M. Evans (Eds.), *Engaging with Videogames: Play, Theory and Practice* (pp. 265–275). Inter-Disciplinary Press.

Deleuze, G.2005*Cinema 1: The movement-image*ReprEds.H. Tomlinson & B. Habberjam. Athlone (Cinema/Gilles Deleuze

Deleuze, G.2013*Cinema 2: The time-image*Paperback editionEds.H. Tomlinson & R. GaletaBloomsbury AcademicCinema2

Deloitte. (2021) *The Leisure Consumer 2021 - Emerging from Pandemic*. Available at: https://www2.deloitte.com/content/dam/Deloitte/uk/Documents/consumer-business/deloitte-uk-the-leisure-consumer-2021.pdf (Accessed:26 August 2021).

Denzin, N. K. (2006). Analytic Autoethnography, or Déjà Vu all Over Again. *Journal of Contemporary Ethnography*, *35*(4), 419–428. https://doi.org/10.1177/0891241606286985

Ellis, C. (2004). *The ethnographic I: A methodological novel about autoethnography* Ethnographic alternatives book series, v. 13. AltaMira Press.

Galloway, A. R. (2006). *Gaming: Essays on algorithmic culture* Electronic mediations, 18. University of Minnesota Press.

Gannon, S. (2013). Troubling Autoethnography: Critical, Creative, and Deconstructive Approaches to Writing. In S. L. Holman Jones, T. E. Adams, & C. Ellis (Eds.), *Handbook of autoethnography* (pp. 21–37). Left Coast Press, Inc.

Gerrig, R. J. (1993). *Experiencing narrative worlds: On the psychological activities of reading*. Yale University Press.

Granic, I., Lobel, A., & Engels, R. C. M. E. (2014). The benefits of playing video games. *The American Psychologist*, *69* (1), 66–78. https://doi.org/10.1037/a0034857

Green, M. C., & Brock, T. C. (2002). In the mind's eye: Transportation-imagery model of narrative persuasion. In Green, M. C., Strange, J. J., & Brock, T. C. (Eds.), *Narrative impact: Social and cognitive foundations* (pp. 315–341). Lawrence Erlbaum Associates.

Green, M. C., Brock, T. C., & Kaufman, G. F. (2004). Understanding media enjoyment: The role of transportation into narrative worlds. *Communication Theory*, *14*(4), 311–327. https://doi.org/10.1111/j.1468-2885.2004.tb00317.x

Greenwood, D. N. (2008). Television as escape from self: Psychological predictors of media involvement. *Personality and Individual Differences*, *44*(2), 414–424. https://doi.org/10.1016/j.paid.2007.09.001

Guerrilla Games. (2017). *Horizon Zero Dawn*. Sony Interactive Entertainment.

Hornstein, S. (2011). *Losing site: Architecture, memory and place*. Ashgate.

IO Interactive. (2018) . *Hitman 2*. Warner Bros. Interactive Entertainment.

Jørgensen, F. A. (2014). The armchair traveler's guide to digital environmental humanities. *Environmental Humanities*, *4*(1), 95–112. https://doi.org/10.1215/22011919-3614944

Kavanagh, E., Jones, I., & Sheppard-Marks, L. (2016). Towards typologies of virtual maltreatment: Sport, digital cultures & dark leisure. *Leisure Studies*, *35*(6), 783–796. https://doi.org/10.1080/02614367.2016.1216581

Kim, Y. (2023). "Beyond Their Actual Limits": Immersion, Interactivity, and the Virtual Sublime in Burke and Video Games. *Games and Culture*, *18*(1), 155541202210844. https://doi.org/10.1177/15554120221084454

Lawrence, L. (2003). "'These are the voyages … '": Interaction in real and virtual space environments in leisure'. *Leisure Studies*, *22*(4), 301–315. https://doi.org/10.1080/0261436032000148451

Lyubomirsky, S., King, L., & Diener, E. (2005). The Benefits of Frequent Positive Affect: Does Happiness Lead to Success? *Psychological Bulletin*, *131*(6), 803–855. https://doi.org/10.1037/0033-2909.131.6.803

Madigan, J. (2016). *Getting gamers: The psychology of video games and their impact on the people who play them*. Rowman & Littlefield.

Markwell, K. (2019). Relating to reptiles: An autoethnographic account of animal–leisure relationships. *Leisure Studies*, *38*(3), 341–352. https://doi.org/10.1080/02614367.2018.1544657

Meades, A. F. (2015). *Understanding Counterplay in Video Games*. Routledge.

Miles, S. (2019). Immersive narratives of "self-work" in an experience society: Understanding the cruise ship experience. *Leisure Studies*, *38*(4), 523–534. https://doi.org/10.1080/02614367.2019.1597148

Mills, D. J. (2019). Does dispositional mindfulness moderate how individuals engage in their passions? An investigation into video games. *Leisure Studies*, *38*(5), 651–665. https://doi.org/10.1080/02614367.2019.1633682

Mukherjee, S. (2015). *Video games and storytelling: Reading games and playing books*. Palgrave Macmillan.

Muriel, D., & Crawford, G. (2018). *Video games as culture: Considering the role and importance of video games in contemporary society* sociology, 241. Routledge (Routledge advances in.

Nah, F. F. H., Eschenbrenner, B., Zeng, Q., Telaprolu, V. R., & Sepehr, S. (2014). Flow in gaming: Literature synthesis and framework development. *International Journal of Information Systems and Management, 1*(1/2), 83. https://doi.org/10.1504/IJISAM.2014.062288

Newman, M. Z. (2017). *Atari age: The emergence of video games in America*. MIT Press.

Niedenthal, S. (2009). What we talk about when we talk about game aesthetics. In Barry, A., Helen, K., & Tanya, K. (Eds.), *Breaking new ground: Innovation in games, play, practice and theory: Proceedings of the 2009 Digital Games Research Association Conference*. Uxbridge: Brunel University.

Pelurson, G. (2019). Flânerie in the dark woods: Shattering innocence and queering time in *The Path*. *Convergence: The International Journal of Research into New Media Technologies, 25*(5–6), 918–936. https://doi.org/10.1177/1354856518772421

Pelurson, G. (2021). Cathartic corridors: Queering linearity in *Final Fantasy XIII*. *Continuum, 35*(1), 43–57. https://doi.org/10.1080/10304312.2020.1845612

Rapp, A. (2017). Designing interactive systems through a game lens: An ethnographic approach. *Computers in Human Behavior, 71*, 455–468. https://doi.org/10.1016/j.chb.2015.02.048

Rapp, A. (2017). Drawing Inspiration from World of Warcraft: Gamification Design Elements for Behavior Change Technologies. *Interacting with Computers, 29*(5), 648–678. https://doi.org/10.1093/iwc/iwx001

Ryan, M. L. (2006). *Avatars of story*. v. 17: University of Minnesota Press (Electronic mediations,

Salen Tekinbaş, K., & Zimmerman, E. (2003). *Rules of play: Game design fundamentals*. MIT Press.

Schell, J. (2008). *The art of game design: A book of lenses*. Elsevier/Morgan Kaufmann.

Shilling, C. (2005). *The body in culture, technology and society* Theory, culture & society. SAGE.

Siitonen, M. (2014). 'Conflict'. In M. J. P. Wolf & B. Perron (Eds.), *The Routledge companion to video game studies* (pp. 166–173). Routledge (Routledge companions.

Silk, M., Millington, B., Rich, E., & Bush, A. (2016). (Re-)thinking digital leisure. *Leisure Studies, 35*(6), 712–723. https://doi.org/10.1080/02614367.2016.1240223

Stiegler, B. (2013). *Traveling in place: A history of armchair travel*. The University of Chicago Press.

Studios, R. (2018). *Red Dead Redemption 2*. Rockstar Games.

Tavinor, G. (2009). *The art of videogames*. Wiley-Blackwell. https://doi.org/10.1002/9781444310177

tom Dieck, D., tom Dieck, M. C., Jung, T., & Moorhouse, N. (2018). Tourists' virtual reality adoption: An exploratory study from Lake District National Park. *Leisure Studies, 37*(4), 371–383. https://doi.org/10.1080/02614367.2018.1466905

Trussell, D. E. (2010). Gazing from the inside out during ethically heightened moments. *Leisure Studies, 29*(4), 377–395. https://doi.org/10.1080/02614367.2010.523835

Ubisoft Montreal. (2020) . *Assassin's Creed Valhalla*. Ubisoft.

Verhoeff, N. (2012). *Mobile screens: The visual regime of navigation*. Amsterdam University Press (MediaMatters).

Wardyga, B. J. (2019). *The Video Games Textbook: History - Business - Technology*. Taylor & Francis.

Wessely, C. (2013). Columns of Figures as Sources of Aesthetic Illusion: Browser-Based Multiplayer Online Games. In W. Wolf, W. Bernhart, & A. Mahler (Eds.), *Immersion and distance: Aesthetic illusion in literature and other media* (Vol. 6, pp. 339–365). Rodopi (Studies in intermediality (SIM).

Wolf, M. J. P. (Ed.). (2018). *The Routledge companion to imaginary worlds*. Routledge.

Zhang, S. X., Wang, Y., Rauch, A., & Wei, F. (2020). Unprecedented disruption of lives and work: Health, distress and life satisfaction of working adults in China one month into the COVID-19 outbreak. *Psychiatry Research, 288*, 112958. https://doi.org/10.1016/j.psychres.2020.112958

Children and young people's perspectives from UK lockdown: leisure-less experiences

Ellie Gennings, Hazel J Brown, Denise Hewlett and John Batten

ABSTRACT

If researchers are to understand the impacts of lockdown on children and young people, then the experiences of lockdown need to be explored from the perspective of the child. Young people participate in leisure for a multitude of reasons, yet, within the UK, children were largely unable to access their regular leisure activities for a six-month period during the first national lockdown. Within the context of this paper, leisure includes outdoor sports and physical activities within blue spaces. Following interviews with parents and young people (aged 11–16) focused on experiences of leisure during the Covid-19 pandemic, this qualitative study identified that children felt an intense sense of missing out on opportunities and found day-to-day life without leisure monotonous. However, there were some positive impacts of reduced leisure, such as a greater appreciation for what was once a regular activity. This research empowered the voice of children, so their distinct experiences were made visible to those who aim to support their wellbeing. Findings suggest that the promotion of leisure activities in the current climate could mitigate poor wellbeing among children associated with the Covid-19 pandemic.

Introduction

During the national lockdown in England, almost all leisure spaces, including parks, sports centres, and beaches were closed to public use (Lashua et al., 2021). Physical activity as leisure is recognised as a significant factor in childhood for personal development (Sivan et al., 2019). Within England, over half of the young people aged 7–16 years surveyed by Sport England (n= 1,164) reported being less physically active during national lockdown (Sport England, 2020). This is reflective of other countries across the globe (Moore et al., 2020; Schmidt et al., 2020; Xiang et al., 2020) and is unsurprising given increases in screen time (Pouso et al., 2021; Xiang et al., 2020). Unfortunately, however, 60% of English children also spent less time outside throughout the national lockdown (Natural England, 2020). During the first lockdown, GovUK (2020) reported that young people coped 'generally well', but YoungMinds (2020) findings showed that 75% of the children they surveyed in England said the second lockdown was harder, and 67% believed the pandemic would have a long-term negative impact on their mental health. Although there is a wealth of literature focused on the impact of lockdown on children's education Holt and Murray (2021) called for research on the specific experiences of children during lockdown in other domains such as leisure. Thus, this study sought to share children and young people's (CYP) accounts of the impact of lockdown on leisure activities from the perspectives of both parents and CYP.

Methods

This paper adopted a qualitative methodology to explore the experiences of CYP in lockdown. Data collection occurred at one Multi-Activity Centre based in the South of England. The centre is based on the coastline and offers a variety of physical activities including windsurfing, sailing, and high ropes. Authors employed a person-based approach (Yardley et al., 2015) due to the belief that CYP are the experts on their own experiences. Parents were included to provide a different perspective of their children's experience of leisure in lockdown.

Participants

The study included 19 participants, nine children and 10 parents. The characteristics of the CYP are shown in Table 1 below. Children were included in the study if they regularly participated in sport and physical activity for leisure purposes at the Multi-Activity Centre before the first lockdown occurred in England.

All CPY self-reported as White British and rated their socioeconomic status towards the middle/upper end of the MacArthur Scale of Subjective Social Status. Parents were all the same ethnicity as their children. Although not reflective of the wider city, these characteristics are reflective of those who generally attend the Multi-Activity Centre.

Protocol

Institutional ethical approval was obtained. Participants were contacted regarding the study through a Multi-Activity Centre based in the South of England. The Multi-Activity Centre emailed the parents of members aged between 11 and 16 years, inviting them and their child to participate in a semi-structured interview. Before the interview took place, children were asked to complete an online form where they reported their age, gender, ethnicity and were asked to complete the MacArthur Scale of Subjective Social Status. The aim of the interview was to understand young people's experiences of lockdown with a focus on leisure from both the perspective of the child and their parent. Interviews occurred at the Multi-Activity Centre ($n = 17$) and over the phone ($n = 2$). Participants and parents were informed that the interview would be recorded to assist in the development of a transcript and to support analysis.

Table 1. Participant characteristics.

Gender	Age	Usual leisure activities	Familial Placement in Society*	Personal Placement in Society*
Female	12	Sailing, tennis, cycling, and hiking	3	3
Female	12	Windsurfing, sailing, paddleboarding, kayaking, cricket, hockey, and netball	3	5
Female	13	Taekwondo, swimming, sailing, and cycling	5	2
Female	14	Windsurfing and football	6	5
Female	16	Windsurfing and cycling	5	3
Male	11	Football and sailing	3	2
Male	13	Sailing, cricket, and scouts	5	5
Male	13	Windsurfing, sailing, rugby and cricket	5	2
Male	15	Sailing and rugby	4	3

*Note: Using the MacArthur Scale of Subjective Social Status: score out of 10 with 1 being the highest rated in society and 10 being the lowest.

Data analysis

Thematic analysis has been described as well suited for qualitative research within the field of health and wellbeing (Braun & Clarke, 2014). As such, analysis was guided by Braun and Clarke's (2006) six-phase framework of thematic analysis, with a reflexive approach adopted. Interviews were transcribed by the researcher to help them become familiar with the data. Upon completion of transcription, each transcript was read two more times, before coding began. Data collected from parents and CYP were analysed together as a collective data set.

Codes were driven by the data and the researcher's role was to co-create, while minimising bias from their own experiences or research findings. This was due to the belief that lockdown experiences are unique to each individual. While codes represented one meaningful or unique facet within the data, they were used to help develop multifaceted themes (Braun & Clarke, 2021). This stage of the analysis was an active process where the researcher revisited codes and themes multiple times to check for accuracy and whether they were a credible reflection of the transcripts. To ensure methodological rigour, a critical friend provided feedback on the analysis.

Results and discussion

Table 2 demonstrates how codes were developed into multifaceted themes. The developed themes were 'missing out on opportunities', 'monotonous nature of life in lockdown', and 'positive impacts of lockdown'.

Missing out on opportunities

The first theme to be discussed, 'missing out on opportunities', refers to CYP's experiences of having milestone events cancelled and dealing with the emotions of returning to normal, but not actually being at their normal level of performance in their physical activity-based leisure activities.

Young people reported their limited ability to stay active during the lockdown, as well as feelings of missing out on their usual physical activities. During this time, English schools were closed, or partially open due to local lockdowns, and did not return to normal from 19th of March 2020 until the 8th of March 2021. There was also a *stay-at-home* order from the English Government, with children only being permitted to exercise in the local outdoors with one other person for an hour per day. Goals and opportunities that participants once had were no longer attainable due to these restrictions. For instance, one parent stated that:

Table 2. Development of themes.

Codes	Sub-themes	Final Themes
Goals	Opportunities	Missing Out on Opportunities
Uncertainty		
Body Image	Health	
Frustration		
Physical Fitness		
Variety	Lack of Adventure	Monotonous Nature of Life in Lockdown
Boredom		
Daily Routine		
Uncertainty		
Emotions	Disconnected Friendships	
Interaction		
Technology		
Walking		Positive Impacts of Lockdown
Appreciation		

She has missed out on her opportunity to go to the Youth Championships because that has been delayed. Her goal has always been to go and compete there and now she will never be able to do that because she will be too old. So she has just missed out (Mother of a 16-year-old female).

Lockdown impacted all areas of CYP's lives, with participants also discussing changes to examination structures, school induction days, and the ability of children to stay physically fit and healthy, as well as maintain friendships and improve their skills. One child explained:

I missed being on the water and the atmosphere ... everyone knows each other and everyone is friendly. So, it made a real difference not being here [the Multi-Activity Centre] for such a long amount of time (Male, aged 15-years-old).

Restrictions on all outdoor leisure activities were lifted in March 2021 and indoor leisure activities from April 2021. Wider national surveys have concluded that 52% of children aged 7–16 years were less physically active during lockdown (Sport England, 2020). Restrictions regarding spaces and time to be physically active, in addition to online learning and the *stay-at-home* order, encouraged excessive use of technology and an increase in children's screen time and sedentary behaviour (Mondragon et al., 2021). Screen time specifically has been shown to have significantly predicted anxiety and depression symptomatology during the Covid-19 pandemic (McArthur et al., 2021). Decreases in physical activity and increases in screen time are associated with poor physical and mental health, as well as a reduction in time spent outdoors (Mondragon et al., 2021). During interviews with parents, it was described that sometimes the impact of lockdown was not visible for CYP until they returned to their regular routines, as one parent reported:

She can see for herself now getting back into things but also how, how hard it is to start training again ... She cried, at taekwondo after her first session. One hour was fine but the second hour she was so exhausted ... she felt like she used to be able to do more and she felt she would have done much better before too (Mother of a 13-year-old female).

Monotonous nature of life in lockdown

During the lockdown, children often described being bored due to multiple different factors, including not seeing friends, going to school, or participating in their usual leisure activities. Codes within the theme 'Monotonous nature of life in lockdown' represented children's unique feelings and experiences of a boring life in lockdown. Within the sample, CYP frequently commented on missing their friends and spending time with them. Reduced opportunities for social interaction also increased feelings of loneliness amongst CYP, something that is associated with poor wellbeing and mental health (Loades et al., 2020; Mondragon et al., 2021). Thinking specifically about the Multi-Activity Centre, one young person stated:

I couldn't see the friends I have here. I couldn't see any friends in general or even just like have fun (Male, 13-years-old)

Similarly, O'Sullivan et al. (2021) found in their study of Irish youth's experience of lockdown that poor mental health was provoked by experiences of loneliness and social isolation in children as young as 5 years old. In addition, McKinlay et al. (2022) labelled quarantine as a 'significant mental health threat' and that the impacts of isolation and loneliness are likely to persist after lockdown restrictions have relaxed due to anxiety around socialising after the pandemic. Children also perceived that the impacts of lockdown on mental health will continue beyond the lifting of restrictions, with 67% of 2,438 British children believing the pandemic would have a long-term negative impact on their mental health and wellbeing (YoungMinds, 2020). Parents commented on their children's increased use of technology to connect with their friends. This was identified by one child as *'not being the same as real life'* (Female, 14-years-old) and parents expressed concerns regarding screen time and sedentary behaviours. Children within this study expressed frustration with not being able to see friends in-person. One participant stated that,

> *I missed seeing my friends here most and just chatting and socialising in real life, rather than online* (Male, 13-years-old).

Social interactions, in-person, contribute to health by enhancing a sense of belonging, which Oosterhoff et al. (2020) consider a crucial interpersonal need and Gennings et al. (2021) include as a crucial aspect of the conceptualisation of children's wellbeing.

Upon the easing of lockdown restrictions, many parents described their children as finding it difficult to deal with the emotional stress of a return to normal. Throughout lockdown, social media was used to mitigate the impact of loneliness and isolation from peers (Deolmi & Pisani, 2020). One parent expressed,

> *They're a bit more sensitive and they didn't have that interaction with friends for so long . . . maybe it is harder with the girls that age, maybe they have more problems, you know, with being face to face. They've got friends that they haven't seen that much and have just been chatting online and then they're suddenly back at school and having all those emotions* (Mother of a 13-year-old female).

Despite the negative long-term effects of social media, it was often identified by participants as their way of keeping in contact with friends and preventing boredom. Parents often expressed guilt in interviews about letting their children spend extensive time using technology/looking at a screen. Hammons et al. (2021) also reported that parents were concerned that their children were too attached to screens during the pandemic, but that screen time and use of technology was one of the limited things children and families could do. Although screen time has not been shown to impair psychological development (Ophir et al., 2021), it has been identified as a significant predictor of Covid-19 anxiety and depression (McArthur et al., 2021). The pandemic occurred while habits were being established by young children; meaning the potential (and possibly negative) long-term impact of an increase in screen time must be monitored by health care professionals to safeguard CYP's wellbeing and mental health moving forward (Hammons et al., 2021).

During the lockdown, CYP were isolated physically from friends, but not their families. Some parents reported this as a positive, as difficulties with friendship groups and lockdown brought their families together, particularly families who were forced to work from home. However, children did not have independence from their families and missed engaging in leisure activities. One participant described this: *'I just missed the freedom of going out and doing what I wanted'* (Female, aged 14-years-old) *while another added*:

> *It's just fun here [the Multi-Activity Centre], you get to see nice people and you get to sail which gets you fitter and gives you something else to do in the evening* (Male, 11-years-old).

While thinking specifically about their regular leisure at the Multi-Activity Centre, one participant explained how the variability of the environment provided them with a sense of adventure which being inside during lockdown could not provide for them,

> *There is always something new on the water. You don't get the exact same day twice and you know something is always going to be different* (Male, aged 15-years-old).

This highlights a lack of adventure and a disconnect between CYP due to the *stay-at-home* order and enforced social distancing. O'Sullivan et al. (2021) state that 'Children and young people were seen as having the worst experiences in the Covid-19 crisis because they could not be children' (p. 6). A parent stated that:

I think she certainly missed doing something that was her thing, rather than yes let's do something all four of us as a family. Which we do a lot of but it's nice for them to interact with someone else (Mother of a 12-year-old female).

Typically, in middle childhood, children's peer relationships optimise developmental health compared to parental/caregiver relationships, but quarantining and social distancing meant that these relationships could not flourish (McArthur et al., 2021). Parents described their children as *frustrated, vulnerable* and *trapped* people; particularly because CYP had no release and were not able to do what they were passionate about, which was mostly engaging in their leisure activities. One participant commented on this,

I like this [their leisure activities] because it means that I get a break from like homework and stuff. When I am on the water, I just don't really think about school at all, ever (Female, 12-years-old).

Before another added how:

Coming here gives you something else to think about so instead of focusing on exams for example, you have something to take your mind off it (Male, 15-years-old).

Having a lack of space to play in and other children to play with has been shown to exacerbate inequalities, alongside a reliance on online technologies to deliver education and connect with friends (Marston et al., 2020; Watts, 2020). During interviews, parents expressed concerns regarding the wellbeing of their children who they felt needed face-to-face social interaction with other CYP (something which leisure activities would typically provide) as online socialising was viewed as *not the same*. Findings also revealed that participants receive a sense of belonging and acceptance while at the Multi-Activity Centre. This sense of belonging was taken away from them during lockdown.

Positive impacts of lockdown

While the impacts of lockdown and quarantining are largely negative, the smaller benefits of lockdown should have recognition. Parents and children, while reflecting on their lockdown experiences, described some key positives such as developing an appreciation for what was once considered normal, spending time with family, and time away from school. Based on these meaningful facets within the data, the theme 'positive impacts of lockdown' was developed. Parents commented on some positive consequences of time away from school and an appreciation of what was once normal. Chawla et al. (2021) suggested a *'silver lining'* (p. 1) to lockdown is that some CYP were protected from issues that relate to attendance at school such as bullying, peer's disruptive behaviour, and examination pressure. Parents within this study reported that lockdown gave their children a break from social structures at school. Indeed, one parent noted how:

He enjoyed learning from home because he doesn't like the people in his class who distract the teacher (Mother of a 15-year-old male).

In addition, some children were reflective of lockdown and showed new appreciation for what was once their everyday leisure activities, such as sailing, going for walks, and spending time with family. These factors will have improved the wellbeing of some individuals (McKinlay et al., 2022). For instance, one child stated that:

There was a point where I would only really come [windsurfing] in the summer because of the cold. I have now got more into it even though it's still pretty cold, but I like coming here whereas during lockdown I couldn't, and I realised how much I missed it (Female, 13-years-old).

Parents also reflected on the implications of lockdown and how it enabled their family to bond and become closer:

Lockdown also had benefits for me not doing a commute to London. And so I was able to do stuff like go paddle boarding at six in the evening where I would usually be stuck on a train at that time (Father of a 12-year-old female).

Summary

The impact of Covid-19 on CYP is not yet fully understood, particularly from a qualitative perspective focused on CYP's leisure experiences (Holt & Murray, 2021; O'Sullivan et al., 2021). Yet, initial findings suggest that national lockdown restrictions had adverse impacts on young people's wellbeing. Children and parents discussed the impact of missing out on milestone events they had been planning for (such as examinations) or had goals aligned to (such as sporting competitions). Missing milestone events are not exclusive to this sample; O'Sullivan et al. (2021) reported that Irish adolescents mourned the cancellation of events and parents commented on the disruption that cancelled events had on children's routines.

A frequently used term by participants to describe lockdown during the interviews was *boring*. Reasons for this are likely to be multifaceted, but often included the lack of interaction with friends, not being able to participate in leisure activities, or leave their homes. Other research has commented on the lack of freedom and feeling of entrapment at home expressed by children (McKinlay et al., 2022; O'Sullivan et al., 2021). Whilst considering the experiences of CYP in lockdown, it is important to recognise that individual experiences of lockdown, and returning back to normal, will be different. In addition, there will have been both positive and negative impacts during and after lockdown on children's lives as demonstrated by the theme 'positive impacts of lockdown'. Here, children enjoyed time away from the social structures of school and developed an appreciation for what was once their usual leisure activities. The return to normal was both stressful and a relief for many.

Conclusion

This study aimed to give CYP a voice to widen the discussion of children's experiences of lockdown. The focus on leisure was to provide a narrative beyond the associations between the impacts of Covid-19 on education (Holt & Murray, 2021). Here the national lockdown had a significant impact on participants' lives, including their ability to engage in leisure activities, with supporting literature highlighting the prevalence of loneliness amongst CYP. Changes and disruptions to regular routines can also precipitate poor wellbeing and mental health for children (Drouin et al., 2020; Mantovani et al., 2021; McArthur et al., 2021). It should be noted, however, that this study is limited by a homogeneous sample of White British children who rate their socioeconomic status mid-high on the MacArthur Scale of Subjective Social Status. Thus, future research should seek to understand the experiences of those with differing ethnicities and families with a low socio-economic status. For these children, leisure-less lives may be the norm outside of lockdown. Research focusing on this issue is particularly important considering research relating to Covid-19, lockdowns and children has suggested exacerbation of existing inequalities (Chzhen, 2020). Nevertheless, the findings of this study have implications for policy, educators, and parents, whereby encouraging leisure and sporting activities post lockdown could mitigate poor wellbeing and loneliness in children (McKinlay et al., 2022).

Acknowledgments

With thanks to the children, their parents and the Multi-Activity Centre for their time and support.

Disclosure statement

No potential conflict of interest was reported by the author(s).

Funding

The authors have no funding to report.

ORCID

Ellie Gennings http://orcid.org/0000-0003-3500-1946
Hazel J Brown http://orcid.org/0000-0002-3327-3510
Denise Hewlett http://orcid.org/0000-0001-7452-6484
John Batten http://orcid.org/0000-0001-7499-7817

References

Braun, V., & Clarke, V. (2006). Using thematic analysis in psychology. *Qualitative Research in Psychology*, *3*(2), 77–101. https://doi.org/10.1191/1478088706qp063oa
Braun, V., & Clarke, V. (2014). What can "thematic analysis" offer health and wellbeing researchers? *International Journal of Qualitative Studies on Health and well-being*, *9*(1), 26152. https://doi.org/10.3402/qhw.v9.26152
Braun, V., & Clarke, V. (2021). One size fits all? What counts as quality practice in (reflexive) thematic analysis? *Qualitative Research in Psychology*, *18*(3), 328–352. https://doi.org/10.1080/14780887.2020.1769238
Chawla, N., Sharma, P., & Sagar, R. (2021). Psychological impact of COVID-19 on children and adolescents: Is there a silver lining? *The Indian Journal of Pediatrics*, *88*(1), 91. https://doi.org/10.1007/s12098-020-03472-z
Chzhen, Y. (2020). The 'lost decade' of austerity: The UK makes no progress on child wellbeing. *British Politics and Policy at LSE*. https://blogs.lse.ac.uk/politicsandpolicy/the-lost-decade-child-wellbeing/
Deolmi, M., & Pisani, F. (2020). Psychological and psychiatric impact of COVID-19 pandemic among children and adolescents. *Acta Bio Medica: Atenei Parmensis*, *91*(4), 1–5. https://doi.org/10.23750/abm.v91i4.10870
Drouin, M., McDaniel, B. T., Pater, J., & Toscos, T. (2020). How parents and their children used social media and technology at the beginning of the COVID-19 pandemic and associations with anxiety. *Cyberpsychology, Behavior, Social Networking*, *23*(11), 727–736. https://doi.org/10.1089/cyber.2020.0284
Gennings, E. K., Brown, H., & Hewlett, D. (2021). Constructing a definition: Adolescent wellbeing from the perspective of the child and expert. *International Journal of Wellbeing*, *11*(1), 69–88. https://doi.org/10.5502/ijw.v11i1.1461
GovUK. (2020). *COVID-19: Mental health and wellbeing surveillance report*. Public Health England
Hammons, A. J., Villegas, E., & Robart, R. (2021). "It's Been Negative for Us Just All the Way Across the Board": Focus Group Study Exploring Parent Perceptions of Child Screen Time During the COVID-19 Pandemic. *JMIR Pediatrics Parenting*, *4*(2), e29411. https://doi.org/10.2196/29411
Holt, L., & Murray, L. (2021). Children and Covid 19 in the UK. *Children's Geographies*, 1–8. https://doi.org/10.1080/14733285.2021.1921699
Lashua, B., Johnson, C. W., & Parry, D. C. (2021). Leisure in the time of coronavirus: A rapid response special issue. *Leisure Sciences*, *43*(1–2), 6–11. https://doi.org/10.1080/01490400.2020.1774827

Loades, M. E., Chatburn, E., Higson-Sweeney, N., Reynolds, S., Shafran, R., Brigden, A., Crawley, E., McManus, M. N., Borwick, C., & Crawley, E. (2020). Rapid systematic review: The impact of social isolation and loneliness on the mental health of children and adolescents in the context of COVID-19. *Journal of the American Academy of Child Adolescent Psychiatry*, 59(11), 1218–1239.e1213. https://doi.org/10.1016/j.jaac.2020.05.009

Mantovani, S., Bove, C., Ferri, P., Manzoni, P., Cesa Bianchi, A., & Picca, M. (2021). Children 'under lockdown': Voices, experiences, and resources during and after the COVID-19 emergency. Insights from a survey with children and families in the Lombardy region of Italy. *European Early Childhood Education Research Journal*, 29(1), 35–50. https://doi.org/10.1080/1350293X.2021.1872673

Marston, H., Wilson, G., Morgan, D. J., & Gates, J. (2020). *The reliance and impact of digital technologies on the social and emotional wellbeing of citizens during the Covid-19 pandemic.* UK Government.

McArthur, B. A., Racine, N., & McDonald, S. (2021). Child and family factors associated with child mental health and wellbeing during COVID-19. *European Child Adolescent Psychiatry*, 30(1), 1–11. https://doi.org/10.1007/s00787-020-01685-3

McKinlay, A. R., May, T., Dawes, J., Fancourt, D., & Burton, A. (2022). You're just there, alone in your room with your thoughts: A qualitative study about the impact of lockdown among young people during the COVID-19 pandemic. *BMJ Open*. https://doi.org/10.1136/bmjopen-2021-053676

Mondragon, N., Berasategi Sancho, N., Dosil Santamaria, M., & Eiguren Munitis, A. (2021). Struggling to breathe: A qualitative study of children's wellbeing during lockdown in Spain. *Psychology Health & Place*, 36(2), 179–194. https://doi.org/10.1080/08870446.2020.1804570

Moore, S. A., Faulkner, G., Rhodes, R. E., Brussoni, M., Chulak-Bozzer, T., Ferguson, L. J., & Vanderloo, L. M. (2020). Impact of the COVID-19 virus outbreak on movement and play behaviours of Canadian children and youth: A national survey. *International Journal of Behavioral Nutrition*, (17), 85. https://doi.org/10.1186/s12966-020-00987-8

Natural England. (2020). *The People and Nature Survey for England: Children's Survey.* GovUK

O'Sullivan, K., Clark, S., McGrane, A., Rock, N., Burke, L., Boyle, N., & Marshall, K. (2021). A qualitative study of child and adolescent mental health during the COVID-19 pandemic in Ireland. *International Journal of Environmental Research*, 18(3), 1062. https://doi.org/10.3390/ijerph18031062

Oosterhoff, B., Palmer, C. A., Wilson, J., & Shook, N. (2020). Adolescents' motivations to engage in social distancing during the COVID-19 pandemic: Associations with mental and social health. *Journal of Adolescent Health*, 67(2), 179–185. https://doi.org/10.1016/j.jadohealth.2020.05.004

Ophir, Y., Rosenberg, H., & Tikochinski, R. (2021). What are the psychological impacts of children's screen use? A critical review and meta-analysis of the literature underlying the World Health Organization guidelines. *Computers in Human Behavior*, 124, 106925. https://doi.org/10.1016/j.chb.2021.106925

Pouso, S., Borja, Á., Fleming, L. E., Gómez-Baggethun, E., White, M. P., & Uyarra, M. C. (2021). Contact with blue-green spaces during the COVID-19 pandemic lockdown beneficial for mental health. *Science of the Total Environment*, 756, 143984. https://doi.org/10.1016/j.scitotenv.2020.143984

Schmidt, S. C., Anedda, B., Burchartz, A., Eichsteller, A., Kolb, S., Nigg, C., Woll, A., Oriwol, D., Worth, A., & Woll, A. (2020). Physical activity and screen time of children and adolescents before and during the COVID-19 lockdown in Germany: A natural experiment. *Scientific Reports*, 10(1), 1–12. https://doi.org/10.1038/s41598-020-78438-4

Sivan, A., Tam, V., Siu, G., & Stebbins, R. (2019). Adolescents' choice and pursuit of their most important and interesting leisure activities. *Leisure Studies*, 38(1), 98–113. https://doi.org/10.1080/02614367.2018.1539867

Sport England. (2020). Children's Experience of Physical Activity in Lockdown. *Sport England Insight.* https://www.thinkactive.org/wp-content/uploads/2020/07/Sport-England-Childrens-experience-of-physical-activity.pdf

Watts G. (2020). COVID-19 and the digital divide in the UK. *The Lancet Digital Health*, 2((8), e395–e396. https://doi.org/10.1016/S2589-7500(20)30169-2

Xiang, M., Zhang, Z., & Kuwahara, K. (2020). Impact of COVID-19 pandemic on children and adolescents' lifestyle behavior larger than expected. *Progress in Cardiovascular Diseases*, 63(4), 531. https://doi.org/10.1016/j.pcad.2020.04.013

Yardley, L., Morrison, L., Bradbury, K., & Muller, I. (2015). The person-based approach to intervention development: Application to digital health-related behavior change interventions. *J Med Internet Res*, 17(1), e30. https://doi.org/10.2196/jmir.4055

YoungMinds. (2020). *Coronavirus: Impact on young people with mental health needs.* Available: https://youngminds.org.uk/about-us/reports/coronavirus-impact-on-young-people-with-mental-health-needs/(02/2021).

A ramp that leads to nothing: outdoor recreation experiences of children with physical disabilities during the COVID-19 pandemic

Annika L. Vogt, Chris A. B. Zajchowski and Eddie L. Hill

ABSTRACT
During the global COVID-19 pandemic, access to outdoor recreation is desperately needed for youth; however, children with physical disabilities who regularly experience barriers and constraints to engagement in outdoor physical activity may experience additional challenges. We examined the outdoor recreation experiences of children with physical disabilities (ages 6–10) living in Coastal Virginia during the COVID-19 pandemic by interviewing their parents using a modified Interpretive Phenomenological Analysis. Responses were coded inductively and then deductively using a typology of factors related to physical activity participation among children and adults with physical disabilities. Our findings indicate the barriers experienced by children existed before and were compounded by the pandemic. Parents struggled to find meaningful outdoor experiences for their children with disabilities and attributed most of the barriers to institutional-level factors. We share actionable steps municipalities can take to provide more inclusive access for children in outdoor and nature-based settings.

Introduction

Building a connection with nature is especially difficult for children with physical disabilities (e.g. Shields et al., 2012). In this research note, we detail our findings from an exploratory study questioning how children with physical disabilities and their families responded to the COVID-19 pandemic with regards to their nature-based outdoor recreation behaviours (hereafter, outdoor recreation). Despite the boom in outdoor recreation for adults during the pandemic (Outdoor Industry Association, 2021), it is clear not all populations benefited from this increase (e.g. Jackson et al., 2021; Moore et al., 2020). Findings prior to the pandemic (e.g. Shields et al., 2012), suggest that the physical abilities of a child may constrain their access to existing outdoor recreation experiences. In this study, we assessed how the perceived barriers and constraints children with disabilities experience when accessing outdoor recreation were impacted by the COVID-19 pandemic. By understanding children's experiences, outdoor recreation managers can better steward their environments and programmes to meet the needs of all participating youth during this dynamic time.

The benefits of nature-based experiences

A lack of access to outdoor recreation is especially problematic for youth due to the benefits they can derive from immersion in natural environments. Access to immersive experiences within nature positively influences physical, intellectual, psychological, social and emotional development for youth (e.g. Franco et al., 2017; Skår & Krogh, 2009). Outdoor recreation can help prevent obesity, while at the same time promoting physical activity in both children (Schmaltz et al., 2019) and adults (Beyer et al., 2018). In addition, nature-based experiences can contribute to youth development on both a psychological and physical level (Lovelock et al., 2016). Outdoor recreation experiences also enhance areas of intellectual development, such as concentration, creativity and problem solving (e.g. Zajchowski et al., 2021). Children who are engaged in natural environments are also more likely to respect the outdoors (i.e. reduce littering behaviour) and grow up to concerned with environmental quality (Asah et al., 2018). Instrumentally, youth also show more enthusiasm for learning and perform better exams when learning in a nature-based setting (Bølling et al., 2019). In contrast, children who spend more time indoors are more likely to be diagnosed with ADHD and depression (Bølling et al., 2019; Kuo & Faber, 2004) and less likely to be resilient in the future (Nazir & Pedretti, 2016). Physiologically, excessive time indoors causes a rise in Vitamin D deficiency in children and higher risk for a variety of health issues, such as cancer and cardiovascular diseases (Dresp-Langley, 2020).

Barriers and constraints

Given the multiple positive benefits stemming from outdoor recreation, it is crucial to understand and seek to mitigate the barriers and constraints that impact children's access. Previous research illustrates that structural barriers, such as lack of accessibility, health issues, financial or transportation factors, keep children from participating in outdoor-based leisure (e.g. Larson et al., 2011). While these structural barriers exist, interpersonal and intrapersonal constraints are also present for youth (Crawford et al., 1991), particularly for individuals experiencing physical or intellectual disabilities (Wooley, 2013). Both caregivers and children identify these barriers and constraints as what keeps them from engaging within nature (Shaw et al., 2015). Martin Ginis et al. (2016) systematically reviewed literature detailing barriers and constraints for physical activity for people with physical disabilities employing social ecological systems theory and detailed intrapersonal-, interpersonal-, institutional-, community- and policy-level barriers and constraints (Table 1). Given these complex social-ecological factors that may impact the ability of youth with physical disabilities to interact with nature, we were curious in what way the COVID-19 pandemic either exacerbated or removed these barriers for children with disabilities and their families. Did these children participate in the trend of increased outdoor recreation? Or were these youths further prevented from accessing important spaces for physical, social, and emotional growth?

Method

To answer these questions, we employed a modified Interpretative Phenomenological Analysis (IPA). The IPA methodology considers the experiences of each individual participant holistically, and treats the individual as the expert of their own lived experience (Howard et al., 2019). Using an IPA approach allows for participants to share and interpret their own experiences through reflective prompts, while the researcher simultaneously interprets the participants' representation of the lived experience. This 'dual hermeneutic' gives the participants the freedom to share their thoughts and feelings, while charging the researcher(s) to maintain high fidelity in interpreting participants' experiences (Smith, 2004). Accordingly, IPAs are often conducted with a small sample size (e.g. Smith, 2011) to prevent abstraction from the participants' experience. While previous research has leveraged the IPA approach to understand the lived experiences of individuals with intellectual (i.e. autism; Howard et al., 2019) and physical (i.e. visually impaired; Haegele et al., 2017) disabilities, prior to this study no research had previously explored the outdoor recreation experiences of children with physical disabilities during the COVID-19 pandemic.

Modification of IPA approach occurred during second round coding, when emergent themes began to align closely with a previously published systematic review of barriers and constraints experienced by children with disabilities accessing recreation (Martin Ginis et al., 2016). Accordingly, we present participants' lived experiences gleaned from the IPA using components of Martin Ginis et al.'s (2016) typology (Table 1) to both present the idiosyncratic nature of the barriers and constraints they face in outdoor recreation and situate them within the landscape of the broader literature regarding physical activity for individuals with disabilities.

Sample

Our sample included parents of participants of the 'Mighty Monarchs' wheelchair sport programme operated by Old Dominion University, a public institution of higher education in the southeastern United States (U.S.). Following the COVID-19 National Emergency declaration in the U.S. and subsequent public health regulations and guidance issued by Old Dominion University, in-person programming offered by this institution was cancelled. Parents of children with physical disabilities who participated in this programme were then left to substitute this recreational opportunity with other recreational pursuits. And, while the dominant recreational narrative in the U.S. highlighted increased participation in outdoor recreation (e.g. OIA, 2021), due to the ability to physically distance and the relatively-lesser risk in outdoor environments (Morawska et al., 2020), we were concerned that this trend would not hold true for children with physical disabilities. Thus, we contacted parents of programme participants to see how their children were experiencing the pandemic.

Recruitment through existing programmatic structures, such as Mighty Monarchs can provide a voice to programme participants, however, can also be subject to social desirability biases (i.e. positive statements about the programme through which participants were recruited). As a result, human subjects' approval was necessary for this research, as was the exclusion of any specific questions related to Mighty Monarchs programme quality. Families with children participating in the programme

Table 1. Social ecological model of themes and sub-themes related to barriers and constraints for individuals with disability engaging in physical activity.

Social ecological level	**Themes** and *sub-themes*
1. Intrapersonal	a) **Psychological factors**: *(1) negative affect and emotion, (2) attitudes/beliefs/perceived benefits/self-perceptions, (3) other (e.g. use of behaviour change strategies, travel, personalities)* b) **Body functions and structures** c) **Employment status**
2. Interpersonal	a) **Social support**: *(1) family, (2) friends, (3) acquaintances, peers, colleagues, neighbours and community members* b) **Societal attitudes** c) **Social processes**
3. Institutional	a) **Knowledge of individuals within institutions/organisations (e.g. disability-specific knowledge areas)** b) **Rehabilitation processes** c) **Design construction and building products and technology of buildings for public use** d) **Program factors**
4. Community	a) **Products and technology**: *(1) Products and technology of land development, (2) Products and technology for education (information), (3) Products and technology for culture, recreation and sport (equipment)* b) **Climate** c) **Relationships among groups and organisations**
5. Policy	a) **Health policies** b) **Transportation services, systems, and policies,** c) **Architecture and construction policies** d) **Association and organisational policies**: *(1) Costs, (2) Need for training* e) **Other (Restrictive policies and bureaucracy)**

Adapted from Martin Ginis et al. (2016).

(n = 10) were contacted in June and July of 2020 via email by the programme director. To incentivise participation, families were offered a $50 Amazon gift card. Four families consented to participate in an interview. As is common in research involving leisure experiences of minors (e.g. Shaw et al., 2015), parents' perspectives were used as a proxy for children's experiences; however, in some cases, children also participated along with their parents throughout the interviews. Family representatives included (1) a mother of a 7-year-old daughter, who has cerebral palsy and is a full-time wheelchair user; (2) a mother of a 10-year-old son with Spina Bifida, who uses crutches to walk; (3) a mother of a 10-year-old boy who has latex precaution and Spina Bifida and is a full-time wheelchair user; and (4) mother of two children with Spina Bifida: her son was 9-years-old at the time of interview and used a wheelchair full time, and her daughter was 6-years-old and used crutches to walk.

Instrument

Due to the COVID-19 pandemic, health protocols related to human subjects research, and an abundance of caution, all interviews occurred using a web-based meeting platform (i.e. Zoom). During these semi-structured interviews, parents were asked a series of questions related to their family experience with outdoor recreation during the COVID-19 pandemic. Questions were designed principally from leisure constraint and barrier theory (e.g. Crawford et al., 1991). The interviewer sought to develop rapport through her previous participation with parents in Mighty Monarchs to allow parents to speak freely and candidly while interviewed. Audio files from interviews were then transcribed for subsequent analysis.

Analysis

All three authors then engaged in a first round descriptive coding following multiple readings of transcripts and common initial coding procedures (e.g. Saldaña, 2021), in line with common IPA analysis techniques (i.e. codes labelled in the margin of each case; Jachyra et al., 2018). We then participated in iterative meetings using reflexive dialogue to compare and contrast findings from first-round coding and discuss potential categories of codes. During this process, it was apparent that multiple categories aligned with the ecological systems levels and specific barriers and constraints presented by Martin Ginis et al. (2016) categories. This alignment prompted the first author to then use a second round coding procedure, which consisted of deductive coding using these categories. This modified IPA process allowed us to highlight the congruence between the barriers and constraints present in their work and ours, while emphasising parents' and children's lived experiences, in order to retain fidelity with the initial phenomenological intent of the project. Iterative meetings between all authors following this procedure focused on thematic groups and deviant cases (cases which contrasted with other participants' shared answers) and leveraged each author's respective expertise to describe and interpret the phenomenon of outdoor recreation for children with physical disabilities during the COVID-19 pandemic.

Positionality

The lead author's passions, interests and knowledge drove the creation of this project. As a white female with no physical disabilities, at the time of data collection and final writing, she was studying Park, Recreation and Tourism Studies with a concentration in Therapeutic Recreation. She was also a live-in caretaker for an adolescent with both physical and neurological disabilities who used a wheelchair and walker with assistance. Her passion for creating an accessible and inclusive society for people with disabilities sparked her interest in this study, a passion which is shared by her co-authors. The second and third authors are white, male faculty in the programme in which the lead author was studying at the time of this research. The second author is a brother of a person with autism, and both authors have previously worked as recreation programmers and coaches with individuals with physical and cognitive disabilities.

Results

Broadly speaking, results of this inquiry indicate the majority of the institutional, community, and policy barriers and constraints parents mentioned their children experienced existed before the pandemic; however, the impact of these barriers was compounded by the risks posed by COVID-19 and fewer recreational programmatic opportunities. We list these below using intrapersonal, interpersonal, institutional, community and policy levels.

Intrapersonal level

Attitudes/beliefs/perceived benefits

While Martin Ginis et al. (2016) outlined several sub-themes at the intrapersonal level, our results indicated only one of the subfactors present in our sample. This may be, in part, because the parents of the participants were interviewed, and intrapersonal factors were presented using parents' perspectives. With regards to attitudes, when asked if their child enjoyed outdoor recreation, three out of four parents identified that their child did not. In addition to this, when asked about their child's intrinsic motivation to engage in outdoor recreation during the COVID-19 pandemic, three out of the four parents reported their child was not motivated. This may be, in part, due to a child's and parent's frustration when attempting to participate in outdoor recreation activities. As one parent stated, 'So, I wouldn't say that she really has a feeling towards it. It's more of the frustration that I have that she's unable to do and enjoy'. This lack of self- (child) and collective (family) efficacy beliefs likely informs the negative attitude towards outdoor recreation participation.

Interpersonal level

Social, including family and friends

Social barriers were identified by analysing the lack of individuals with whom the participant's child was engaging in outdoor recreation during the COVID-19 pandemic. Most children had not seen or engaged in outdoor recreation with friends since the start of the pandemic, but rather with nuclear family members. As one parent mentioned, this was true for both outdoor and indoor recreation as well:

> [He's been] less outside. It's just now getting back to normal just now, right? Because he was not doing hockey or wheelchair basketball [with his friends] for a few months, and we couldn't go to places that we normally do, like Busch Gardens. We did go out hiking and things like that. Okay, so we did change that a little bit, but we didn't get to go as much as we used to.

Participants explained that their children recreated with the same core of individuals as prior to the pandemic, but additional friends and family members who would occasionally participate in outdoor recreation with the children were prevented due to COVID-19 restrictions, leading to an overall decrease in participation.

Societal attitudes

It is important to note that parents also stated that societal attitudes play a role in the outdoor recreation opportunities available for their children with disabilities, but felt that this barrier existed prior to the pandemic. As one parent stated,

I think people just don't even realize how it's [outdoor recreation] not completely inclusive. You know, I think people would just kind of have a 'if there's a will, there's a way' [mentality], and it makes it very hard, especially as the child's getting older, to completely be involved and stuff like that. So, I think overall community awareness is incredibly important.

Institutional level

The concern about societal attitudes mirrored additional concerns voiced by parents, which were coded as institutional-level barriers, including knowledge of individuals within institutions/organisations. In addition to disability-specific knowledge, (1) the design, construction and building products and technology of buildings for public use, and (2) program factors were mentioned by parents.

Disability-specific knowledge areas

Parents expressed frustration with (1) the way programmes prior to the pandemic structured recreational opportunities for children with physical disabilities, and (2) the focus on specific disabilities (i.e. autism) over others (i.e. cerebral palsy). As one parent stated,

> The one thing that we've always complained about is – because he's not *mentally* disabled but he's *physically* disabled – a lot of their programs in the area are more geared towards mental disabilities. So, he tried baseball one summer, but because they didn't actually teach it as a team and how to play the sport, he didn't like it. Because he didn't want to just run around the bases. He wanted to learn how to play the sport.

While this quote indicates the pre-pandemic outdoor recreation barriers for children with physical disabilities, the focus on these knowledge areas by parents is demonstrative of the durable challenges their children face at the institutional level. This may imply the need for more education to create programmes for children with physical disabilities or integrated, inclusive programmes that cater to a spectrum of ability, rather than those with intellectual or other disabilities.

Design construction and building products and technology of buildings for public use

The difficulty of accessibility in public spaces was a dominant theme during all four interviews. This included access to playgrounds, parks, pools and beaches in Coastal Virginia. Playgrounds were discussed the most by the parents – not due to COVID-19 closures, but rather design and construction features,

> We haven't found a park that is [disability] friendly like that. So, the only thing that we're able to do when we do go out to a park as a family is a walk around and she's in her wheelchair. Well, I don't think that's very fun for her because she's just, you know, will be in a wheelchair the entire time.

In regards to pools and beaches, parents mentioned difficulty finding ramps and beach wheelchairs that were easy to use. While participants stated one very busy beach in Coastal Virginia has a ramp, it does not go perpendicular to the water. Thus, strolling on the beach, where COVID-19 exposure is less likely, wasn't an accessible choice for spending time outdoors. While this issue was present prior to the pandemic, the ability to physically distance at the same beach that is afforded to individuals *not* using wheelchairs (e.g. Kane et al., 2021) is absent to these parents and children, further preventing them from accessing outdoor recreation during this time. Additionally, parents shared accessible infrastructure that is built is often used by both those with and without disabilities, both before and during the pandemic: 'There's a swing and you can't get in the swing because every kid's waiting for that particular swing because they don't know it's a handicap accessible'.

Programme factors

Programme factors stated by parents included the location, advertising, and availability of programmes for children with physical disabilities in Coastal Virginia. As one parent mentioned, this was particularly important during the pandemic as school opportunities were foreclosed to children: 'Now it's very limited. In fact, we're going to meeting with a nutritionist this afternoon to figure out what we can do because overall he just has less activity than he did when he was in school. And when there's more space to move around, even just having that gives him more, you know, activity. But, you know, being in a small house ... overall, he just has less activity'. Additionally, specific to the pandemic, parents expressed their children were often at higher risk and avoided programmed opportunities: '... because of the pandemic [...] we're not going to send [our kids] in a group of people because they're already get that underlying vulnerability'. Furthermore, all parents interviewed had children who had participated in the Mighty Monarchs programme that had temporarily suspended programming due to the pandemic.

Independent of the pandemic, participants also expressed that they were aware of programmes outside of Coastal Virginia that they would like to have in their area, as well as discrepancies between offerings within municipalities in the region. 'He can't do as many of the activities as they offer in bigger cities. So, I would say the biggest thing for us would be that if more was available, we would make them do more', explained a parent. Parents also expressed frustrations, pre-pandemic, a wealth of programmes were offered to children with intellectual disabilities (i.e. autism), but not physical disabilities; other than Mighty Monarchs they shared a lack of programmes available for children with physical disabilities. Overall, the need for programmes more suitable for children with physical disabilities in Coastal Virginia, within the pandemic and beyond, was expressed by every participant.

Community level

Under the community level, parents addressed issues with the development and availability of spaces that are designed to provide outdoor recreation experiences for children with disabilities. Importantly, these design issues were mentioned broadly, as opposed to specific to institutions or agencies, placing them in the community level of Martin Ginis et al.'s (2016) framework.

Products and technology for culture, recreation and sport equipment

Parents discussed the difficulty finding playground equipment with which their child could engage. As mentioned in previous sections, parents explained that the equipment may have some ADA compliant features, such as a ramp, but that ramp may not lead to anything that is meaningful to the child's experience. As one parent mentioned, '[There's a need for] diverse equipment. It's not just a swing, but it's things that they can kind of manipulate with their hands, other types of manipulatives. So, I would say design is a big part'. When asking how children engage with outdoor recreation, only one family mentioned having an adaptive bicycle; we attribute this to cost – this family needed to apply for a grant to obtain it. The lack of equipment available for these children in Coastal Virginia was expressed by all of the parents. This also came up in our discussion when parents expressed wanting to take their kids to the beach and not having an easy to use or access beach wheelchair.

Policy level

Parents' main concerns at the policy level were not focused on state or national policies related to the COVID-19 virus, but rather were in regard to the difference in environments being ADA compliant rather than truly accessible. Under this theme parents, again, highlighted that training needs to occur to create programmes and spaces inclusive for their children to enjoy and that complying with ADA may still hinder *de facto* accessibility.

Architecture and construction policies
Specifically, parents discussed the difficulty of substrates in playgrounds. One mother expressed, 'There's so much lack of awareness. I mean, you know, woodchips in a park are actually ADA compliant, which is very, very frustrating because they are not accessible at all'. Another explained how the flooring of a playground would ideally be cushioned for safety reasons, but that this isn't required by ADA and very few parks in the Coastal Virginia area have these features.

Association and organisational policies
While no association and organisational policies were directly mentioned, the participants expressed their concern with regards to the disbursement of programmes available within cities of Coastal Virginia. For example, a parent felt that the City of Portsmouth received better programmes for people with disabilities than their city of residence. This speaks less to the policies that drive specific therapeutic recreation centres, but more broadly to the policies and practices that dictate resource allocation within proximate municipalities.

Need for training
As mentioned previously, the parents found programming geared to children with physical disabilities lacking or unsatisfying. This, in addition to the construction and policies with regards to open spaces for outdoor recreation, shows there is a need for additional and resources to provide diverse programming, infrastructure, and opportunities across abilities

Discussion

Nearly all youth experienced a decrease of outdoor physical activity during the COVID-19 pandemic (e.g. Jackson et al., 2021). Research also suggests, even prior to COVID-19, that youth with disabilities experience less outdoor recreation access than their non-disabled peers (Shaw et al., 2015). Thus, the purpose of this research note was to explore and evidence the perceived barriers and constraints children with physical disabilities experienced when accessing outdoor recreation during the COVID-19 pandemic. Using Martin Ginis et al.'s (2016) social ecological model, parents identified a variety of themes preventing their children from outdoor recreation participation; however, many themes pre-dated the pandemic. Themes and sub-themes, such as design and construction (e.g. playground sets), disability-specific knowledge, and architecture and construction policies featured prominently as enduring barriers preceding the pandemic. Conversely, programme and interpersonal factors, stemming from a reduction in outdoor recreation and overall activity at the family or institutional levels, were attributed to risk mitigation related to the pandemic. These data can be used to inform policy makers, recreation professionals, and others who help to reduce barriers of children with disabilities.

One particularly salient finding from these data involved the differentiation parents made between the constraints of children with physical and intellectual/development disabilities. Parents' voiced concern over the perceived disproportionate programmatic attention paid to intellectual disabilities (i.e. autism), as opposed to differences in physical ability. And, like many constraints voice by parents, these concerns appeared to predate the pandemic. Accordingly, it was clear that while important scholarship documented the impact of the pandemic on the experiences of individuals with intellectual and developmental disabilities (e.g. Lake et al., 2021), this research can not necessarily serve as proxy for the experience of those with physical abilities in our sample, further justifying this effort. Accordingly, we now focus our discussion primarily on the implications stemming from this exploratory research.

Implications for practitioners

Since children benefit on a holistic level from spending time outdoors (e.g. Skår & Krogh, 2009), practitioners should ensure that these experiences are truly accessible, irrespective of COVID-19. Our research indicates institutions should reconsider the programmes they create and the inclusivity they offer. Staff training should specify the difference between abilities of a wheelchair user and a child with an intellectual disability. Since therapeutic recreation specialists receive the education on inclusive programming, they can provide these trainings for other recreation professionals. Therapeutic recreation professionals can be pioneers and advocates when encouraging improvements of these structures, programmes and institutions.

Structurally, it is abundantly clear that additional design and technology features are necessary to create accessible outdoor recreation spaces. Put differently, the creation of playgrounds should involve more than just an accessible swing. Playgrounds should offer inclusivity from the substrate to the play structure to offering ramps that lead to accessible slides. Families voiced their need for these features, as their experiences outlined accessibility barriers. Further, the design of structures is often made with compliance to the Americans with Disabilities Act standards, but the participants of this study voiced that these features were not seen as accessible. For example, instead of having wood chips on a playground, the substrate could be made out of recycled rubber mats to provide ease in navigating a wheelchair. Providing structures that children can manipulate with their hands independently on different levels of the playground also allows for exploration. Rather than meeting minimum requirements, institutions should strive for creating an accessible environment, in order for children of all ability levels the opportunity to reap the benefits.

Limitations

Our project studied a unique group of children in a globally unprecedented time. That said, our study features a small sample size from a limited geographical range in the southeastern United States. While this maintained fidelity with the IPA approach, additional research using alternative methodologies could expand the scale and allow for potential generalisability. In addition, in this study, the focus was on the parental perspective of chidlren's experiences. While various obstacles to collecting first-person data from youth exist, it may be suitable to solely provide the child's perspective of the phenomenon in future studies.

Conclusion

Barriers and constraints were and continue to be present for children with disabilities attempting to access outdoor recreation before and during the pandemic. These barriers and constraints largely prevent children with disabilities from experiencing the benefits that outdoor recreation offers. The research completed suggests there are improvements that can be made for the well-being of children with physical disabilities in Coastal Virginia. Children with disabilities deserve meaningful time spent outdoors, but are still awaiting access to inclusive experiences and structures to join the ongoing increase of outdoor recreation participation.

Acknowledgments

Thanks are due to Mrs Betsy Kennedy and Dr Justin Haegele for their support of this research.

Disclosure statement

No potential conflict of interest was reported by the author(s).

Funding

This work was supported by the Perry Honors College at Old Dominion University.

ORCID

Chris A. B. Zajchowski http://orcid.org/0000-0002-9909-2624

References

Asah, S. T., Bengston, D. N., Westphal, L. M., & Gowan, H. (2018). Mechanisms of children's exposure to nature: Predicting adulthood environmental citizenship and commitment to nature-based activities. *Environment and Behavior*, *50*(7), 807–836. https://doi.org/10.1177/0013916517718021

Beyer, K. M., Szabo, A., Hoormann, K., & Stolley, M. (2018). Time spent outdoors, activity levels, and chronic disease among American adults. *Journal of Behavioral Medicine*, *41*(4), 494–503. https://doi.org/10.1007/s10865-018-9911-1

Bølling, M., Niclasen, J., Bentsen, P., & Nielsen, G. (2019). Association of education outside the classroom and pupils' psychosocial well-being: Results from a school year implementation. *The Journal of School Health*, *89*(3), 210–218. https://doi.org/10.1111/josh.12730

Crawford, D., Jackson, E., & Godbey, G. (1991). A hierarchical model of leisure constraints. *Leisure Sciences*, *13*(4), 309–320. https://doi.org/10.1080/01490409109513147

Dresp-Langley, B. (2020). Children's health in the digital age. *International Journal of Environmental Research and Public Health*, *17*(9), 3240. https://doi.org/10.3390/ijerph17093240

Franco, L. S., Shanahan, D. F., & Fuller, R. A. (2017). A review of the benefits of nature experiences: More than meets the eye. *International Journal of Environmental Research and Public Health*, *14*(8), 864. https://doi.org/10.3390/ijerph14080864

Haegele, J. A., Sato, T., Zhu, X., & Avery, T. (2017). Physical education experiences at residential schools for the blind: A phenomenological inquiry. *Journal of Visual Impairment & Blindness*, *112*(2), 135–146. https://doi.org/10.1177/0145482X1711100205

Howard, K., Katsos, N., & Gibson, J. (2019). Using interpretive phenomenological analysis in autism research. *Autism*, *23*(7), 1871–1876. https://doi.org/10.1177/1362361318823902

Jachyra, P., Anagnostou, E., Knibbe, T. J., Petta, C., Cosgrove, S., Chen, L., Capano, L., Moltisanti, L., & McPherson, A. C. (2018). Weighty conversations: Caregivers', children's, and clinicians' perspectives and experiences of discussing weight-related topics in healthcare consultations. *Autism Research*, *11*(11), 1500–1510. https://doi.org/10.1002/aur.2017

Jackson, S. B., Stevenson, K. T., Larson, L. R., Peterson, M. N., & Seekamp, E. (2021). Outdoor activity participation improves adolescents' mental health and well-being during the COVID-19 pandemic. *International Journal of Environmental Research and Public Health*, *18*(5), 2506. https://doi.org/10.3390/ijerph18052506

Kane, B., Zajchowski, C. A. B., Allen, T. R., McLeod, G., & Allen, N. H. (2021). Is it safer at the beach?: Spatial and temporal analyses of beachgoer behaviors during the COVID-19 pandemic. *Ocean & Coastal Management*, *205*, 105533. https://doi.org/10.1016/j.ocecoaman.2021.105533

Kuo, F. E., & Faber, T. A. (2004). A potential natural treatment for attention deficit disorder/ hyperactivity disorder: Evidence from a national study. *American Journal of Public Health*, *94*, 1580–1586. https://doi.org/10.2105/AJPH.94.9.1580

Lake, J. K., Jachyra, P., Volpe, T., Lunsky, Y., Magnacca, C., Marcinkiewicz, A., & Hamdani, Y. (2021). The wellbeing and mental health care experiences of adults with intellectual and developmental disabilities during COVID-19. *Journal of Mental Health Research in Intellectual Disabilities*, *14*(3), 285–300. https://doi.org/10.1080/19315864.2021.1892890

Larson, L. R., Green, G. T., & Cordell, H. K. (2011). Children's time outdoors: Results and implications of the National Kids Survey. *Journal of Park and Recreation Administration, 29*(2), 1–20. https://www.srs.fs.usda.gov/pubs/ja/2011/ja_2011_larson_001.pdf

Lovelock, B., Walters, T., Jellum, C., & Thompson-Carr, A. (2016). The participation of children, adolescents, and young adults in nature-based recreation. *Leisure Sciences, 38*(5), 441–460. https://doi.org/10.1080/01490400.2016.1151388

Martin Ginis, K. A., Ma, J. K., Latimer-Cheung, A. E., & Rimmer, J. H. (2016). A systematic review of review articles addressing factors related to physical activity participation among children and adults with physical disabilities. *Health Psychology Review, 10*(4), 478–494. https://doi.org/10.1080/17437199.2016.1198240

Moore, S. A., Faulkner, G., Rhodes, R. E., Brussoni, M., Chulak-Bozzer, T., Ferguson, L. J., Mitra, R., O'Reilly, N., Spence, J. C., Vanderloo, L. M., & Tremblay, M. S. (2020). Impact of the COVID-19 virus outbreak on movement and play behaviours of Canadian children and youth: A national survey. *International Journal of Behavioral Nutrition and Physical Activity, 17*(85). https://doi.org/10.1186/s12966-020-00987-8

Morawska, L., Tang, J.W., Bahnfleth, W., Bluyssen, P.M., Boerstra, A., ..., Yao, M. (2020). How can airborne transmission of COVID-19 indoors be minimized? *Environment International, 142*, 105832. https://doi.org/10.1016/j.envint.2020.105832

Nazir, J., & Pedretti, E. (2016). Educators' perceptions of bringing students to environmental consciousness through engaging outdoor experiences. *Environmental Education Research, 22*(2), 288–304. https://doi.org/10.1080/13504622.2014.996208

Outdoor Industry Association. (2021, March 31). *2021 special report: The new outdoor participant (COVID and beyond)*. https://outdoorindustry.org/resource/2021-special-report-new-outdoor-participant-covid-beyond/

Saldaña, J. (2021). *The coding manual for qualitative researchers*. SAGE.

Schmaltz, D. L., Griffin, S. F., Blomquist, K. K., Reeves, C., & Sease, K. K. (2019). New impact: A community-based approach to childhood obesity treatment. *Recreation, Parks, and Tourism in Public Health, 3*, 47–65. https://doi.org/10.2979/rptph.3.1.05

Shaw, K., Anderson, D. M., & Barcelona, B. (2015). Parental perceptions of constraints to family participation in nature-based, outdoor experiences. *Journal of Outdoor Recreation, Education, and Leadership, 7*(1), 3–19. https://doi.org/10.7768/1948-5123.1241

Shields, N., Synnot, A., & Barr, M. (2012). Perceived barriers and facilitators to physical activity for children with disability: A systematic review. *British Journal of Sports Medicine, 46*(14), 989–997. https://doi.org/10.1136/bjsports-2011-090236

Skår, M., & Krogh, E. (2009). Changes in children's nature-based experiences near home: From spontaneous play to adult-controlled, planned and organised activities. *Children's Geographies, 7*(3), 339–354. https://doi.org/10.1080/14733280903024506

Smith, J. A. (2004). Reflecting on the development of interpretative phenomenological analysis and its contribution to qualitative research in psychology. *Qualitative Research in Psychology, 1*(1), 39–54. https://doi.org/10.1191/1478088704qp004oa

Smith, J. A. (2011). Evaluating the contribution of interpretative phenomenological analysis. *Health Psychology Review, 5*(1), 9–27. https://doi.org/10.1080/17437199.2010.510659

Wooley, H. (2013). Now being social: The barrier of designing outdoor play spaces for disabled children. *Children & Society, 27*(6), 448–458. https://doi-org.proxy.lib.odu.edu/10.1111/j.1099-0860.2012.00464.x

Zajchowski, C. A. B., Dustin, D. L., & Hill, E. L. (2021). The freedom to make mistakes': Youth, nature, and the Anthropocene. *Journal of Outdoor and Environmental Education, 24*(1), 87–103. https://doi.org/10.1007/s42322-021-00076-9

Index

Page numbers in **bold** refer to tables and those in *italic* refer to figures.

access and use of technology: challenges with 33; online physical activity beyond pandemic 34
Activity Alliance (2021) 10
Adams, T. E. 151
The *Admit* organization: community sport programming 11; cultural products 12; digital packages 13; disability sport charity 10–11; human resources 12; human rights movement 11; interview schedules 14; lockdown periods 13; mainstreaming 11; material resources 12; moral resources 12; national and international movements 11; participant pseudonyms and nature of work 14, **14**; primary and secondary cycles of analysis 15; RMT scholars 12; social-organisational resources 12; *see also* resource mobilisation theory (RMT)
affordance theory 116
aggregation of resources 13
Alexander, A. C. 70
Allen, G. 4
alternative gaming 154–5
American Library Association 143
Americans with Disabilities Act 178
anthropocene and post-anthropause 87–8
Antó, J. M. 87
architecture and construction policies 177
armchair travel: defined 148; 'elsewheres and elsewhens' 148, 154–5; escapism 149; literary tradition 148; narrative transportation 148; perspective-based/ceiling paintings 148; precarity of 152–4; video games 149; virtual, temporal and ephemeral 149
Assassin's Creed Valhalla 152
association and organisational policies 177
Atkinson, P. 153, 154, 157
Audience Agency COVID-19 Cultural Participation Monitor survey 42
autoethnography 151

Ball, S. J. 24
Barnes, R. 28
Beck, U. 95
Bergson, H. 148–9, 154

Bernal-Merino, M. Á. 155
Binnie, J. 121, 126
The Birds (414 B.C.) 148
Bourdieu, P. 39
Bournemouth, Christchurch, Poole (BCP) urban conurbation 118
Bratland-Sanda, S. 3
Braun, V. 136, 163
Breedveld, K. 106
Brighton to Shoreham urban conurbation 118
Brinkmann, S. 75
The British Broadcasting Corporation (BBC) 57, 86
Buckley, R. 91
Business-to-Business (B2B) companies' operations 8
Bustad, J. J. 4
Byerly, A. 149, 157
Byrne, R. 25

Canadian Federation of Library Associations 143
canonical correlation 107, *108*
Carter, A. 70
Carter, S. J. 100–1
Cavanagh, M. F. 142
changing leisure practices 3
Chawla, N. 166
children and young people (CYP): data analysis 163; missing out on opportunities **163**, 163–4; monotonous nature of life, lockdown 164–6; participants 162, **162**; protocol 162
children use technology 25–6
Clarke, V. 136, 163
collective effervescence 73
Collins, R. 70, 72–4, 76, 78–81
commercialised sporting activities 24
Connell, R. 2
Constandt, B. 108
Cooney, C. 10
co-optation 13
Coronavirus Job Retention Scheme 26
Cortez, R. M. 8, 9, 20
Cosmic Kids, yoga programme 30
countergaming 150

counterplay 150
COVID-19 measures 101
COVID-19 passport 71
CrossFit: complement/replace physical communities 70; emotional energy 79–80; interviewees 74, **75**; during lockdown in Denmark 71, *71*; loss of emotional energy and one's identity 77–8; outsiders and insiders 75–6; participants' intense exercise regimes 70; socio-cultural research 71–2; *see also* Interaction Ritual Chains
CrossFit boxes 71
CrossFitters 4
Cuadrado-García, M. 41
Cuberos, Chacón 109
cultural consumption: algorithmic recommendations, digital platforms 41; analysis 43–4; Bourdieusian theories 40; continued sociological research 40; data 42–3; differentiation and stratification of 39; digital, impact of 40–2; lifestyles 42; musical genres 40; nonparticipants/non-consumers 40; shared patterns of 40

Dalal, R. 149
Dalmer, N. K. 5, 133
Davies, B. 25
DCMS Taking Part Web Panel COVID-19 survey 42
De Haan, J. 106
Deleuze, G. 148
Department for Digital, Culture, Media and Sports (DCMS) 41
De', R. 33
Dickinson, J. 4–5
digital and/or online exclusion 26
digital turn 3
disability-specific knowledge areas 175
disability sport charities (DSCs) 9
Dobson, J. 115
Durkheim, É. 73

early care and education providers (ECE) 25
early years and technology use: online physical activity 30–1; parenting, digital technology and screen time 28, **29**, 30; specialist and social spaces 32–3
economic austerity policies 10
Edwards, B. 12, 13, 16
Edwards, R. 12, 13
Ehrlén, V. 109
Elkington, S. 101, 103, 109
Ellis, C. 151
embodiment and avatar 150–1, 155–6
environmental affordances 116
Environmental Protection Agency (EPA) 92
escapism 149, 154–5
European Non-Governmental Sports Organization, 2022 9
European Structural and Investment Funds 10
European Union (EU) 10
Evans, A. B. 103
Evans, J. 25

Factor Analysis or Hierarchical Cluster Analysis 43
family representatives 173
Feder, T. 4
Ferrell-Schweppenstedde, D. 10
financial-based crises 8
Finnessey, L. 89
fitness centres 102
Flanders: club-organised sports 106; competent authority for sports 104; dependent and independent variables 104, **105**; logistic regressions 104; online questionnaires 104; OVERALS method 106
Fletcher, R. 95
flow and rule-breaking interplay: countergaming 150; counterplay 150; defined 149–50; queer gaming 150; *see also* armchair travel
'frontline' social service provision 10

Galloway, A. R. 150
Gennings, E. K. 5, 165
Germann Molz, J. 120
Gershuny, J. 58
Gibson, H. J. 133
Gibson, J. J. 116
Gillham, P. 12, 13
Glover, T. D. 121
Glynn, L. G. 109
Goffman, E. 73
'good' parenting and concerted cultivation 24
Green, K. 24
growth of early years commercialised sport and leisure spaces 24–5
Guest Editors 5

Hammons, A. J. 165
Han, B.-C. 88, 93–5
Harlow, M. 35
Harris, T. 58
Hastings, A. 20
Helsen, K. 110
Hempel, M. 91
Heyd, T. 87
Hill, I. 10
Hitman 2, 152
Holden, E. 92
Hollenhorst, S. J. S. 115
Holt, L. 161–2
home schooling 27
Horizon Zero Dawn 152
Ho, S. A. 133
Huppatz, K. 2

individual 'light-organized' sports participants 103
Interaction Ritual Chains 70; barriers to outsiders 73; bodily co-presence 73; collective effervescence 73; collective symbols 73; before COVID-19 pandemic 76–7; description 74; emotional energy 73; feelings of morality 73; group solidarity 73; micro-sociological theory 73; mutual focus of attention 73; rhythmic entrainment 73; theory of religious rituals 73

Interpretative Phenomenological Analysis (IPA): definition 171; second round coding 172
Ito, M. 26

Jensen, O. B. 5
Jisc's Online Survey platform 27
Johnston, W. 8, 9, 20
Jørgensen, F. A. 156
Joseph, E. D. 25

Kaplan, R. 124, 127
Kaplan, S. 124, 127
Kaufmann, K. 118
Kaur, H. 70
Kavanagh, E. 147
Kim, Y. 153
King, K. 4–5
Kitchin, P. J. 13, 20
Kvale, S. 75
Kyle, G. 116

Lareau, A. 24, 35
latent class analysis (LCA) 43–4
Lawrence, H. 72
Lawrence, L. 147, 156
leisure: defined 101; and urban green spaces 115–16
leisure evidence, time use research: actions 62–4, **63**; experiences 65; qualitative 62
leisure/leisure activities concept 2
leisure-time physical activity (LTPA): Danish adult population 69; gym goers 70; participation rates 70; social distancing and assembly bans 69; *see also* CrossFit
Lenneis, V. 4
Lepoša, N. 117
Library and Information Science 137
light-organised sports participation 103
light sports participation settings 110
livestreamed gigs 38
locavism 115
lockdown light 102
lockdown measures: anthropause 85–6; BBC report 86; description 85; *see also* post-anthropause
longer-term patronage 16
Lupton, D. 109
Luyt, B. 133
Ly, M. 133

Mafia 3, 152
Manning, R. E. 89–90
Martin Ginis, K. A. 171–4, 176, 177
mass sports participation events 101
Matthewman, S. 2
Maxwell, C. 30
Mayan, M. J. 136
McCarthy, J. D. 12, 15
McCullogh, N. 3
McCullough, B. P. 94
McKechnie, L. E. 133
McKinlay, A. R. 164

Menheere, D. 109
'Mighty Monarchs' wheelchair sport programme 172
Mihelj, S. 41, 42, 51
Millward, P. 12, 20
mobile instant messaging (MIM) diaries 117
mobile methods 117
monotonous nature of life in lockdown 164–6
Montoro-Pons, J. D. 41
Monz, C. 90
Moran, Joe 2
Multi-Activity Centre 162, 166
multinomial regression 44, **48**, **50**
Murray, L. 161–2

narrative transportation 148
National Council of Voluntary Organisations, 2020 10
National Parks Service 89
'National Theatre at Home' Thursday night broadcasts 39
nature-based experiences 170–1
nature connectivity 114–16
'new normal' temporal period 1
Niedenthal, S. 153, 157
Nimrod, G. 142
Nisbet, E. K. 116
non-essential services and business 9
nonparticipants/non-consumers 40
non-profit organisations 9
Nordh, H. 116–17

O'Callaghan-Gordo, C. 87
Office for National Statistics 59, 60, 65, 114
online activities *vs.* live classes: children's engagement and interest 31–2; specialist and social spaces, early years children 32–3
online technology 25
Ontario Library Association 134
Oosterhoff, B. 165
Organisation for Economic Co-operation and Development (OECD) 93
Ornella, A. D. 72
Østby, K. 116–17
O'Sullivan, K. 164, 165, 167
outdoor-based leisures 171
Outdoor Industry Association 170
outdoor recreation: barriers and constraints 171, **172**; community level 176; definition 171; institutional level: design construction, building products and technology of buildings 175; disability-specific knowledge areas 175; programme factors 176; interpersonal level: social, including family and friends 174; societal attitudes 174–5; intrapersonal level: attitudes/beliefs/perceived benefits 174; policy level 176–7; outdoor recreation and post-anthropause 92–4; *see also* Interpretative Phenomenological Analysis (IPA)

Paired Peers project 30
parenting perceptions: data analysis 28; digital technology and screen time 25–6, 28, 30; and ECE providers 25, 27; online physical activity, early

years children 30–1; procedures 27–8; UK Covid-19 26–7; *see also* access and use of technology; online activities *vs.* live classes
Parsayi, F. 153, 154, 157
participant demographic data 28, **29**
partner endorsement 16
Peil, C. 118
Pelurson, G. 155
Perkins, S. E. 92
physical activity leisure 161
place ballet 116
poLCA R package 43
positionality 173–4
positive impacts of lockdown 166–7
post-anthropause: anthropocene and 87–8; consumer-oriented forms 86; description 86; 'nature-society' dimensions, leisure 86; outdoor recreation and 92–4; physical culture 86; and protected areas 89–92; research design 88–9
Potter, A. 28
professional sport events 3
project-based leisure 103
protected areas and post-anthropause: anthropotrumpism 91–2; landscapes 89; Maryland Department of Natural Resources 91; National Parks 90–1; National Parks Service 89; outdoor recreational pursuits 90; service visitors 90; US federal agencies 92
proximity tourism 95
public libraries and leisure reading: ageing/older adults 133; catalyst for adaptation, COVID-19 140–1; closures 133; materials and methods **135**, 135–6; Ontario public libraries' COVID-19 lockdown 134–5; patrons' leisure needs 132; social institutions 132; time of loss, COVID-19 138–40; transforming experiences, COVID-19 137–8

Quan-Haase, A. 140, 142
queer gaming 150

Reckwitz, A. 116
re-conceptualisation 2–3
reconfigured leisure spaces 3, 4
Red Dead Redemption 2, 152
re-definition 2–3
re-negotiation 2–3
resource mobilisation theory (RMT) 9, 12; legitimate selection 17–18; mutual benefits 15–16; quality pays dividends 16–17; upshots of online provision 18–19
rhythmic entrainment 73
Richardson, M. 116
Robbins, W. 142
Roberts, K. 1–2, 4, 5, 9, 51
Robinson, J. D. 133, 141
Ross, C. S. 133
Rothbauer, P. M. 133
Ryan, R. M. 109

Saarinen, J. 88
Salen Tekinbas, K. 151, 153

Sawchuk, D. 133
Scheerder, J. 110
sector's deep-rooted inequalities 39
serious leisure perspective (SLP) 101
service providers 19
sharing magazines 141
Sharon Shen, X. 103
Shove, E. 116
Singleton, J. F. 133
Smith, M. C. 133
Smyth, C. 35
social institutions 132
social movement organisations (SMOs) 12; aggregation of resources 13; co-optation 13; patronage 13
social practices theory 116
societal attitudes 174–5
sociodemographic variables 104
soft-play centres 26–7
Soper, K. 94
Spenceley, A. 90
Sport England's (2021) 9
sport mega-events 2
sports participation: behaviour pre- *vs.* post-COVID-19 restrictions **107**; COVID-19-related restrictive measures 102–3; Flanders (*see* Flanders)
sports-specific clusters 103–4
sports-specific independent variables **106**
staff training 178
'stay-at-home challenge' 3
Stebbins, R. 101, 103, 109
Stirrup, J. 25
Summers-Effler, E. 74
swapping magazines 141

Taff, B. D. 91
Taking Part Web Panel COVID-19 survey (TPCOVID) 42, 44–6, *45*, **48**, 48–9
technology devices 25
The Tempest (1611) 148
theatre productions delivered online 38
The audience agency (TAAW2) data 46–8, *47*, 49–50, **50**
third sector organisations (TSOs) 10
third sector sport organisations (TSSOs) 10
time use research: communist authorities 57; comparative studies 58–9; heavy television viewing 57; technical difficulties 57; UK time use surveys 57–8; between the World Wars 56; *see also* leisure evidence, time use research; UK (2015–2022), time use
#ToiletRollChallenge 3
Tracy, S. J. 75

UK Government's 25 year Environment Plan 115
UK (2015–2022), time use: before, during, between and following 2020 and 2021 lockdowns **59**, 60–2; pandemic surveys 59–60, **60**; surveys 57–8
urban green spaces 4–5; action possibilities 127; affordance theory 116; coding lists 118–19; consistency and repetition 122;

creative projects 122–3; description 114; discourses of nature 119–20, *120*; environmental affordances 116; grass verges, dog rolling *125*; 'hidden patches of green' *126*; left messages *124*; leisure and 115–16; lockdown restrictions 119; mental and physical health 114; merging and reframing 119; MIM diaries 117; nature connectivity 114; navigating and negotiating 120–2; participants 118; place ballet 116; research ethics approval 118; rock finding project *123*; socially distant methods and digital domain 117; social practices theory 116; 'The Hill' *125*; UK Government's 25 year Environment Plan 115; urban park use 116; visual data 118
Uzunogullari, S. 5

Vansteenkiste, M. 109
Veal, A. J. 58
Velija, P. 4
Vincent, C. 24, 30, 35
virtual leisurists 147

virtual museum tours 38
visualisation method 117

Weingartner, S. 41
Wheeler, S. 24
Wicks, Joe 30
Wolf, M. J. P. 148, 153
Woolf, J. 72
'Workout of the Day' (WOD) 76
World Health Organisation 114

Xie, H. 109

Yarnal, C. 103
younger respondents 49
YoungMinds (2020) 161

Zald, M. N. 12, 15
Zelenski, J. M. 116
Zhu, Q. 101
Zimmerman, E. 151, 153
Zoom, web-based meeting platform 173

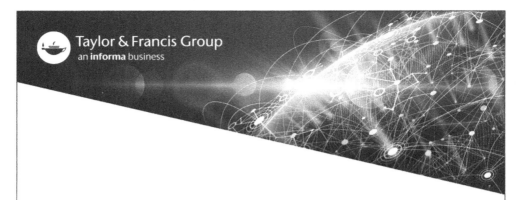